FRANCIS THOMPSON
Poems and Essays

THREE VOLUMES IN ONE
VOLUME ONE: *Poems*

Francis Thompson
From a drawing by the Hon. Neville Lytton
October 1907

FRANCIS THOMPSON

POEMS AND ESSAYS
Edited by
WILFRED MEYNELL

THREE VOLUMES IN ONE
VOLUME ONE
Poems

Essay Index Reprint Series

BOOKS FOR LIBRARIES PRESS
FREEPORT, NEW YORK

Copyright, 1947 The Newman Bookshop

Reprinted 1969 by arrangement with
Paulist Newman Press

STANDARD BOOK NUMBER:
8369-0032-4

LIBRARY OF CONGRESS CATALOG CARD NUMBER:
73-76917

PRINTED IN THE UNITED STATES OF AMERICA

A NOTE by Francis Thompson's Literary Executor

IN making this Collection I have been governed by Francis Thompson's express instructions, or guided by a knowledge of his feelings and preferences acquired during an unbroken intimacy of nineteen years. His own list of new inclusions and his own suggested reconsiderations of his formerly published text have been followed in this definitive edition of his Poetical Works.

May 1913.   *W. M.*

THE CONTENTS

Dedication of 'Poems'	page xiii
Poems on Children:	
Daisy	3
The Poppy	6
To Monica thought Dying	10
The Making of Viola	13
To my Godchild	17
To Olivia	20
Little Jesus	21
Sister Songs:	
The Proem	25
Part the First	27
Part the Second	40
Inscription	67
Love in Dian's Lap:	
Proemion	71
Before her Portrait in Youth	77
To a Poet Breaking Silence	79
'Manus Animam Pinxit'	82
A Carrier Song	85
Scala Jacobi Portaque Eburnea	89
Gilded Gold	90
Her Portrait	92
Epilogue to the Poet's Sitter	98
Domus Tua	100
In her Paths	101
After her Going	102
Beneath a Photograph	104

CONTENTS

The Hound of Heaven	107
Ode to the Setting Sun:	
Prelude	117
Ode	118
After-Strain	126
To the Dead Cardinal of Westminster	131
A Corymbus for Autumn	141
Ecclesiastical Ballads:	
The Veteran of Heaven	149
Lilium Regis	151
Translations:	
A Sunset	155
Heard on the Mountain	158
An Echo of Victor Hugo	163
Miscellaneous Poems:	
Dream-Tryst	167
Arab Love-Song	168
Buona Notte	169
The Passion of Mary	171
Messages	173
At Lord's	174
Love and the Child	175
Daphne	176
Absence	178
To W. M.	180
A Fallen Yew	181
A Judgement in Heaven	185
Epilogue	190

CONTENTS

The Sere of the Leaf	192
To Stars	198
For a Drawing of Our Lady of the Night	200
Orison-Tryst	201
'Whereto art Thou Come?'	203
Song of the Hours	204
Pastoral	211
Past Thinking of Solomon	213
A Dead Astronomer	215
Cheated Elsie	216
The Fair Inconstant	220
Threatened Tears	221
The House of Sorrows	222
Insentience	225
Envoy	226

DEDICATION OF POEMS
(1893)

To Wilfrid and Alice Meynell

IF the rose in meek duty
  May dedicate humbly
  To her grower the beauty
    Wherewith she is comely;
If the mine to the miner
    The jewels that pined in it,
Earth to diviner
    The springs he divined in it;
To the grapes the wine-pitcher
    Their juice that was crushed in it,
Viol to its witcher
    The music lay hushed in it;
If the lips may pay Gladness
    In laughters she wakened,
And the heart to its sadness
    Weeping unslakened,
If the hid and sealed coffer,
    Whose having not his is,
To the loosers may proffer
    Their finding—here this is;
Their lives if all livers
    To the Life of all living,—
To you, O dear givers!
    I give your own giving.

POEMS ON CHILDREN

DAISY

WHERE the thistle lifts a purple crown
    Six foot out of the turf,
      And the harebell shakes on the windy hill—
O the breath of the distant surf!—

The hills look over on the South,
    And southward dreams the sea;
And with the sea-breeze hand in hand
    Came innocence and she.

Where 'mid the gorse the raspberry
    Red for the gatherer springs,
Two children did we stray and talk
    Wise, idle, childish things.

She listened with big-lipped surprise,
    Breast-deep mid flower and spine:
Her skin was like a grape, whose veins
    Run snow instead of wine.

She knew not those sweet words she spake,
    Nor knew her own sweet way;
But there's never a bird, so sweet a song
    Thronged in whose throat that day.

Oh, there were flowers in Storrington
    On the turf and on the spray;
But the sweetest flower on Sussex hills
    Was the Daisy-flower that day!

POEMS ON CHILDREN

Her beauty smoothed earth's furrowed face
    She gave me tokens three :—
A look, a word of her winsome mouth,
    And a wild raspberry.

A berry red, a guileless look,
    A still word,—strings of sand !
And yet they made my wild, wild heart
    Fly down to her little hand.

For standing artless as the air,
    And candid as the skies,
She took the berries with her hand,
    And the love with her sweet eyes.

The fairest things have fleetest end,
    Their scent survives their close :
But the rose's scent is bitterness
    To him that loved the rose.

She looked a little wistfully,
    Then went her sunshine way :—
The sea's eye had a mist on it,
    And the leaves fell from the day.

She went her unremembering way,
    She went and left in me
The pang of all the partings gone,
    And partings yet to be.

She left me marvelling why my soul
    Was sad that she was glad ;
At all the sadness in the sweet,
    The sweetness in the sad.

DAISY

Still, still I seemed to see her, still
    Look up with soft replies,
And take the berries with her hand,
    And the love with her lovely eyes.

Nothing begins, and nothing ends,
    That is not paid with moan ;
For we are born in other's pain,
    And perish in our own.

THE POPPY
To Monica

SUMMER set lip to earth's bosom bare,
  And left the flushed print in a poppy there :
  Like a yawn of fire from the grass it came,
And the fanning wind puffed it to flapping flame.

With burnt mouth, red like a lion's, it drank
The blood of the sun as he slaughtered sank,
And dipped its cup in the purpurate shine
When the eastern conduits ran with wine.

Till it grew lethargied with fierce bliss,
And hot as a swinked gipsy is,
And drowsed in sleepy savageries,
With mouth wide a-pout for a sultry kiss.

A child and man paced side by side,
Treading the skirts of eventide ;
But between the clasp of his hand and hers
Lay, felt not, twenty withered years.

She turned, with the rout of her dusk South hair,
And saw the sleeping gipsy there ;
And snatched and snapped it in swift child's whim,
With—" Keep it, long as you live ! "—to him.

THE POPPY

And his smile, as nymphs from their laving meres,
Trembled up from a bath of tears;
And joy, like a mew sea-rocked apart,
Tossed on the waves of his troubled heart.

For *he* saw what she did not see,
That—as kindled by its own fervency—
The verge shrivelled inward smoulderingly:
And suddenly 'twixt his hand and hers
He knew the twenty withered years—
No flower, but twenty shrivelled years.

" Was never such thing until this hour,"
Low to his heart he said; " the flower
Of sleep brings wakening to me,
And of oblivion, memory."

" Was never this thing to me," he said,
" Though with bruisèd poppies my feet are red!"
And again to his own heart very low:
" O child! I love, for I love and know;

" But you, who love nor know at all
The diverse chambers in Love's guest-hall,
Where some rise early, few sit long:
In how differing accents hear the throng
His great Pentecostal tongue;

" Who know not love from amity,
Nor my reported self from me;
A fair fit gift is this, meseems,
You give—this withering flower of dreams.

POEMS ON CHILDREN

" O frankly fickle, and fickly true,
Do you know what the days will do to you ?
To your love and you what the days will do,
O frankly fickle, and fickly true ?

" You have loved me, Fair, three lives—or days :
'Twill pass with the passing of my face.
But where *I* go, your face goes too,
To watch lest I play false to you.

" I am but, my sweet, your foster-lover,
Knowing well when certain years are over
You vanish from me to another ;
Yet I know, and love, like the foster-mother.

" So, frankly fickle, and fickly true !
For my brief life-while I take from you
This token, fair and fit, meseems,
For me—this withering flower of dreams."

The sleep-flower sways in the wheat its head,
Heavy with dreams, as that with bread :
The goodly grain and the sun-flushed sleeper
The reaper reaps, and Time the reaper.

I hang 'mid men my needless head,
And my fruit is dreams, as theirs is bread :
The goodly men and the sun-hazed sleeper
Time shall reap, but after the reaper
The world shall glean of me, me the sleeper.

THE POPPY

Love, love! your flower of withered dream
In leavèd rhyme lies safe, I deem,
Sheltered and shut in a nook of rhyme,
From the reaper man, and his reaper Time.

Love! *I* fall into the claws of Time:
But lasts within a leavèd rhyme
All that the world of me esteems—
My withered dreams, my withered dreams.

TO MONICA THOUGHT DYING

YOU, O the piteous you !
    Who all the long night through
    Anticipatedly
Disclose yourself to me
Already in the ways
Beyond our human comfortable days ;
    How can you deem what Death
    Impitiably saith
    To me, who listening wake
    For your poor sake ?
    When a grown woman dies
You know we think unceasingly
What things she said, how sweet, how wise ;
And these do make our misery.
    But you were (you to me
The dead anticipatedly !)
You—eleven years, was't not, or so ?—
    Were just a child, you know ;
    And so you never said
Things sweet immeditatably and wise
To interdict from closure my wet eyes :
    But foolish things, my dead, my dead !
    Little and laughable,
    Your age that fitted well.
And was it such things all unmemorable,
    Was it such things could make
Me sob all night for your implacable sake ?

TO MONICA THOUGHT DYING

      Yet, as you said to me,
  In pretty make-believe of revelry,
      So the night long said Death
        With his magniloquent breath;
(And that remembered laughter,
Which in our daily uses followed after,
Was all untuned to pity and to awe:)
    "*A cup of chocolate,*
    One farthing is the rate,
    You drink it through a straw."

    How could I know, how know
Those laughing words when drenched with sobbing so?
Another voice than yours, than yours, he hath.
    My dear, was't worth his breath,
His mighty utterance?—yet he saith, and saith!
This dreadful Death to his own dreadfulness
    Doth dreadful wrong,
This dreadful childish babble on his tongue.
That iron tongue made to speak sentences,
And wisdom insupportably complete,
Why should it only say the long night through,
    In mimicry of you,—
    "*A cup of chocolate,*
    One farthing is the rate,
You drink it through a straw, a straw, a straw"

    Oh, of all sentences,
    Piercingly incomplete!
Why did you teach that fatal mouth to draw,
    Child, impermissible awe,

POEMS ON CHILDREN

    From your old trivialness?
    Why have you done me this
    Most unsustainable wrong,
    And into Death's control
Betrayed the secret places of my soul?—
    Teaching him that his lips,
Uttering their native earthquake and eclipse,
    Could never so avail
To rend from hem to hem the ultimate veil
    Of this most desolate
  Spirit, and leave it stripped and desecrate,—
      Nay, never so have wrung
  From eyes and speech weakness unmanned, unmeet,
  As when his terrible dotage to repeat
  Its little lesson learneth at your feet;
      As when he sits among
      His sepulchres, to play
With broken toys your hand has cast away,
With derelict trinkets of the darling young.
Why have you taught—that he might so complete
      His awful panoply
    From your cast playthings—why,
This dreadful childish babble to his tongue,
    Dreadful and sweet?

THE MAKING OF VIOLA

I

The Father of Heaven.
    SPIN, daughter Mary, spin,
    Twirl your wheel with silver din;
    Spin, daughter Mary, spin,
      Spin a tress for Viola.

Angels.
    Spin, Queen Mary, a
    Brown tress for Viola!

II

The Father of Heaven.
    Weave, hands angelical,
    Weave a woof of flesh to pall—
    Weave, hands angelical—
      Flesh to pall our Viola.

Angels.
    Weave, singing brothers, a
    Velvet flesh for Viola!

III

The Father of Heaven.
    Scoop, young Jesus, for her eyes,
    Wood-browned pools of Paradise—
    Young Jesus, for the eyes,
      For the eyes of Viola.

POEMS ON CHILDREN

Angels.
   Tint, Prince Jesus, a
   Duskèd eye for Viola !

IV

The Father of Heaven.
   Cast a star therein to drown,
   Like a torch in cavern brown,
   Sink a burning star to drown
     Whelmed in eyes of Viola.

Angels.
   Lave, Prince Jesus, a
   Star in eyes of Viola !

V

The Father of Heaven.
   Breathe, Lord Paraclete,
   To a bubbled crystal meet—
   Breathe, Lord Paraclete—
     Crystal soul for Viola.

Angels.
   Breathe, Regal Spirit, a
   Flashing soul for Viola !

VI

The Father of Heaven.
   Child-angels, from your wings
   Fall the roseal hoverings,
   Child-angels, from your wings,
     On the cheeks of Viola.

THE MAKING OF VIOLA

Angels.
  Linger, rosy reflex, a
  Quenchless stain, on Viola!

VII
All things being accomplished, saith the Father of Heaven:
  Bear her down, and bearing, sing,
  Bear her down on spyless wing,
  Bear her down, and bearing, sing,
    With a sound of viola.
Angels.
  Music as her name is, a
  Sweet sound of Viola!

VIII
  Wheeling angels, past espial,
  Danced her down with sound of viol;
  Wheeling angels, past espial,
    Descanting on "Viola."
Angels.
  Sing, in our footing, a
  Lovely lilt of " Viola ! "

IX
  Baby smiled, mother wailed,
  Earthward while the sweetling sailed;
  Mother smiled, baby wailed,
    When to earth came Viola.
And her elders shall say:
  So soon have we taught you a
  Way to weep, poor Viola!

POEMS ON CHILDREN

x

Smile, sweet baby, smile,
For you will have weeping-while;
Native in your Heaven is smile,—
    But your weeping, Viola ?

Whence your smiles we know, but ah !
Whence your weeping, Viola ?—
Our first gift to you is a
Gift of tears, my Viola !

TO MY GODCHILD
Francis M. W. M.

THIS labouring, vast, Tellurian galleon,
   Riding at anchor off the orient sun,
   Had broken its cable, and stood out to space
Down some frore Arctic of the aërial ways :
And now, back warping from the inclement main,
Its vaporous shroudage drenched with icy rain,
It swung into its azure roads again ;
When, floated on the prosperous sun-gale, you
Lit, a white halcyon auspice, 'mid our frozen crew.

To the Sun, stranger, surely you belong,
Giver of golden days and golden song ;
Nor is it by an all-unhappy plan
You bear the name of me, his constant Magian.
Yet ah ! from any other that it came,
Lest fated to my fate you be, as to my name.
When at the first those tidings did they bring,
My heart turned troubled at the ominous thing :
Though well may such a title him endower,
For whom a poet's prayer implores a poet's power.
The Assisian, who kept plighted faith to three,
To Song, to Sanctitude, and Poverty,
(In two alone of whom most singers prove
A fatal faithfulness of during love !) ;
He the sweet Sales, of whom we scarcely ken
How God he could love more, he so loved men ;
The crown and crowned of Laura and Italy ;
And Fletcher's fellow—from these, and not from me,
Take you your name, and take your legacy !

POEMS ON CHILDREN

Or, if a right successive you declare
When worms, for ivies, intertwine my hair,
Take but this Poesy that now followeth
My clayey hest with sullen servile breath,
Made then your happy freedman by testating death.
My song I do but hold for you in trust,
I ask you but to blossom from my dust.
When you have compassed all weak I began,
Diviner poet, and ah! diviner man;
The man at feud with the perduring child
In you before Song's altar nobly reconciled;
From the wise heavens I half shall smile to see
How little a world, which owned you, needed me.
If, while you keep the vigils of the night,
For your wild tears make darkness all too bright,
Some lone orb through your lonely window peeps,
As it played lover over your sweet sleeps;
Think it a golden crevice in the sky,
Which I have pierced but to behold you by!

And when, immortal mortal, droops your head,
And you, the child of deathless song, are dead;
Then, as you search with unaccustomed glance
The ranks of Paradise for my countenance,
Turn not your tread along the Uranian sod
Among the bearded counsellors of God;
For if in Eden as on earth are we,
I sure shall keep a younger company:
Pass where beneath their rangèd gonfalons
The starry cohorts shake their shielded suns,
The dreadful mass of their enridgèd spears;

TO MY GODCHILD

Pass where majestical the eternal peers,
The stately choice of the great Saintdom, meet—
A silvern segregation, globed complete
In sandalled shadow of the Triune feet;
Pass by where wait, young poet-wayfarer,
Your cousined clusters, emulous to share
With you the roseal lightnings burning 'mid their hair;
Pass the crystalline sea, the Lampads seven :—
Look for me in the nurseries of Heaven.

TO OLIVIA

I FEAR to love thee, Sweet, because
Love's the ambassador of loss;
White flake of childhood, clinging so
To my soiled raiment, thy shy snow
At tenderest touch will shrink and go.
Love me not, delightful child.
My heart, by many snares beguiled,
Has grown timorous and wild.
It would fear thee not at all,
Wert thou not so harmless-small.
Because thy arrows, not yet dire,
Are still unbarbed with destined fire,
I fear thee more than hadst thou stood
Full-panoplied in womanhood.

LITTLE JESUS

*Ex ore infantium Deus et lactentium
perfecisti laudem*

LITTLE Jesus, wast Thou shy
   Once, and just so small as I ?
   And what did it feel like to be
Out of Heaven, and just like me ?
Didst Thou sometimes think of *there*,
And ask where all the angels were ?
I should think that I would cry
For my house all made of sky ;
I would look about the air,
And wonder where my angels were ;
And at waking 'twould distress me—
Not an angel there to dress me !
Hadst Thou ever any toys,
Like us little girls and boys ?
And didst Thou play in Heaven with all
The angels that were not too tall,
With stars for marbles ? Did the things
Play *Can you see me ?* through their wings ?
And did Thy Mother let Thee spoil
Thy robes, with playing on *our* soil ?
How nice to have them always new
In Heaven, because 'twas quite clean blue !

Didst Thou kneel at night to pray,
And didst Thou join Thy hands, this way ?
And did they tire sometimes, being young,
And make the prayer seem very long ?

POEMS ON CHILDREN

And dost Thou like it best, that we
Should join our hands to pray to Thee?
I used to think, before I knew,
The prayer not said unless we do.
And did Thy Mother at the night
Kiss Thee, and fold the clothes in right?
And didst Thou feel quite good in bed,
Kissed, and sweet, and thy prayers said?

Thou canst not have forgotten all
That it feels like to be small:
And Thou know'st I cannot pray
To Thee in my father's way—
When Thou wast so little, say,
Couldst Thou talk Thy Father's way?—

So, a little Child, come down
And hear a child's tongue like Thy own;
Take me by the hand and walk,
And listen to my baby-talk.
To Thy Father show my prayer
(He will look, Thou art so fair),
And say: " O Father, I, Thy Son,
Bring the prayer of a little one."

And He will smile, that children's tongue
Has not changed since Thou wast young!

SISTER SONGS
AN OFFERING TO TWO SISTERS
MONICA & MADELINE (SYLVIA)

SISTER SONGS
AN OFFERING TO TWO SISTERS

THE PROEM

SHREWD winds and shrill—were these the
    speech of May ?
    A ragged, slag-grey sky—invested so,
  Mary's spoilt nursling ! wert thou wont to go ?
    Or *thou*, Sun-god and song-god, say
Could singer pipe one tiniest linnet-lay,
    While Song did turn away his face from song ?
        Or who could be
In spirit or in body hale for long,—
    Old Æsculap's best Master !—lacking thee ?
      At length, then, thou art here !
      On the earth's lethèd ear
  Thy voice of light rings out exultant, strong ;
Through dreams she stirs and murmurs at that
    summons dear :
  From its red leash my heart strains tamelessly,
For Spring leaps in the womb of the young year !
    Nay, was it not brought forth before,
      And we waited, to behold it,
      Till the sun's hand should unfold it,
    What the year's young bosom bore ?
Even so ; it came, nor knew we that it came,
    In the sun's eclipse.
    Yet the birds have plighted vows,
And from the branches pipe each other's name ;

SISTER SONGS

    Yet the season all the boughs
    Has kindled to the finger-tips,—
Mark yonder, how the long laburnum drips
Its jocund spilth of fire, its honey of wild flame !
Yea, and myself put on swift quickening,
And answer to the presence of a sudden Spring.

From cloud-zoned pinnacles of the secret spirit
    Song falls precipitant in dizzying streams ;
And, like a mountain-hold when war-shouts stir it,
The mind's recessèd fastness casts to light
Its gleaming multitudes, that from every height
    Unfurl the flaming of a thousand dreams.
Now therefore, thou who bring'st the year to birth,
    Who guid'st the bare and dabbled feet of May ;
Sweet stem to that rose Christ, who from the earth
Suck'st our poor prayers, conveying them to Him ;
    Be aidant, tender Lady, to my lay !
Of thy two maidens somewhat must I say,
Ere shadowy twilight lashes, drooping, dim
      Day's dreamy eyes from us ;
      Ere eve has struck and furled
The beamy-textured tent transpicuous,
    Of webbèd cœrule wrought and woven calms,
      Whence has paced forth the lambent-footed sun.
And Thou disclose my flower of song upcurled,
    Who from Thy fair irradiant palms
      Scatterest all love and loveliness as alms ;
      Yea, Holy One,
Who coin'st Thyself to beauty for the world !

SISTER SONGS

Then, Spring's little children, your lauds do ye upraise
To Sylvia, O Sylvia, her sweet, feat ways!
Your lovesome labours lay away,
And trick you out in holiday,
    For syllabling to Sylvia;
And all you birds on branches, lave your mouths with May,
To bear with me this burthen,
    For singing to Sylvia.

PART THE FIRST

THE leaves dance, the leaves sing,
    The leaves dance in the breath of the Spring.
    I bid them dance,
    I bid them sing,
    For the limpid glance
    Of my ladyling;
For the gift to the Spring of a dewier spring,
For God's good grace of this ladyling!
I know in the lane, by the hedgerow track,
    The long, broad grasses underneath
Are warted with rain like a toad's knobbed back;
    But here May weareth a rainless wreath.
In the new-sucked milk of the sun's bosom
Is dabbled the mouth of the daisy-blossom;
    The smouldering rosebud chars through its sheath;
The lily stirs her snowy limbs,
    Ere she swims
Naked up through her cloven green,
Like the wave-born Lady of Love Hellene;

SISTER SONGS

And the scattered snowdrop exquisite
    Twinkles and gleams,
  As if the showers of the sunny beams
Were splashed from the earth in drops of light.
    Everything
    That is child of Spring
  Casts its bud or blossoming
Upon the stream of my delight.

Their voices, that scents are, now let them upraise
To Sylvia, O Sylvia, her sweet, feat ways;
    Their lovely mother them array,
    And prank them out in holiday,
      For syllabling to Sylvia;
And all the birds on branches lave their mouths with May,
    To bear with me this burthen,
      For singing to Sylvia.

    While thus I stood in mazes bound
      Of vernal sorcery,
    I heard a dainty dubious sound,
      As of goodly melody;
    Which first was faint as if in swound,
      Then burst so suddenly
    In warring concord all around,
    That, whence this thing might be,
        To see
    The very marrow longed in me!
      It seemed of air, it seemed of ground,
        And never any witchery
      Drawn from pipe, or reed, or string,
      Made such dulcet ravishing.

SISTER SONGS

'Twas like no earthly instrument,
  Yet had something of them all
  In its rise, and in its fall;
As if in one sweet consort there were blent
  Those archetypes celestial
Which our endeavouring instruments recall.
So heavenly flutes made murmurous plain
To heavenly viols, that again
  —Aching with music—wailed back pain;
Regals release their notes, which rise
Welling, like tears from heart to eyes;
And the harp thrills with thronging sighs.
Horns in mellow flattering
Parley with the cithern-string :—
Hark!—the floating, long-drawn note
Woos the throbbing cithern-string!

Their pretty, pretty prating those citherns sure upraise
For homage unto Sylvia, her sweet, feat ways:
Those flutes do flute their vowelled lay,
Their lovely languid language say,
  For lisping to Sylvia;
Those viols' lissom bowings break the heart of May,
  And harps harp their burthen,
    For singing to Sylvia.

  Now at that music and that mirth
  Rose, as 'twere, veils from earth;
    And I spied
    How beside
  Bud, bell, bloom, an elf

SISTER SONGS

Stood, or was the flower itself;
    'Mid radiant air
    All the fair
Frequence swayed in irised wavers.
Some against the gleaming rims
    Their bosoms prest
Of the kingcups, to the brims
Filled with sun, and their white limbs
Bathèd in those golden lavers;
Some on the brown, glowing breast
Of that Indian maid, the pansy
(Through its tenuous veils confest
Of swathing light), in a quaint fancy
Tied her knot of yellow favours;
Others dared open draw
Snapdragon's dreadful jaw:
Some, just sprung from out the soil,
Sleeked and shook their rumpled fans
    Dropt with sheen
    Of moony green;
Others, not yet extricate,
On their hands leaned their weight,
And writhed them free with mickle toil,
Still folded in their veiny vans:
And all with an unsought accord
Sang together from the sward;
Whence had come, and from sprites
Yet unseen, those delights,
As of tempered musics blent,
Which had given me such content.
For haply our best instrument,

SISTER SONGS

    Pipe or cithern, stopped or strung,
    Mimics but some spirit tongue.

Their amiable voices, I bid them upraise
To Sylvia, O Sylvia, her sweet, feat ways ;
  Their lovesome labours laid away,
  To linger out this holiday
    In syllabling to Sylvia ;
While all the birds on branches lave their mouths with May,
  To bear with me this burthen,
    For singing to Sylvia.

    Next I saw, wonder-whist,
    How from the atmosphere a mist,
    So it seemed, slow uprist ;
    And, looking from those elfin swarms,
        I was 'ware
        How the air
    Was all populous with forms
    Of the Hours, floating down,
    Like Nereids through a watery town.
    Some, with languors of waved arms,
    Fluctuous oared their flexile way ;
    Some were borne half resupine
    On the aërial hyaline,
    Their fluid limbs and rare array
    Flickering on the wind, as quivers
    Trailing weed in running rivers ;
    And others, in far prospect seen,
    Newly loosed on this terrene,
    Shot in piercing swiftness came,

SISTER SONGS

    With hair a-stream like pale and goblin flame.
    As crystálline ice in water,
    Lay in air each faint daughter;
    Inseparate (or but separate dim)
    Circumfused wind from wind-like vest,
    Wind-like vest from wind-like limb.
    But outward from each lucid breast,
    When some passion left its haunt,
    Radiate surge of colour came,
    Diffusing blush-wise, palpitant,
    Dying all the filmy frame.
    With some sweet tenderness they would
Turn to an amber-clear and glossy gold;
    Or a fine sorrow, lovely to behold,
Would sweep them as the sun and wind's joined flood
    Sweeps a greening-sapphire sea;
    Or they would glow enamouredly
Illustrious sanguine, like a grape of blood;
    Or with mantling poetry
Curd to the tincture which the opal hath,
Like rainbows thawing in a moonbeam bath.
So paled they, flushed they, swam they, sang melodiously.

Their chanting, soon fading, let them too, upraise
For homage unto Sylvia, her sweet, feat ways;
  Weave with suave float their wavèd way,
  And colours take of holiday,
    For syllabling to Sylvia;
And all the birds on branches lave their mouths with May,
  To bear with me this burthen,
    For singing to Sylvia.

SISTER SONGS

Then, through those translucencies,
As grew my senses clearer clear,
Did I see, and did I hear,
How under an elm's canopy
Wheeled a flight of Dryades
Murmuring measured melody.
Gyre in gyre their treading was,
Wheeling with an adverse flight,
In twi-circle o'er the grass,
These to left, and those to right;
    All the band
Linkèd by each other's hand;
Decked in raiment stainèd as
The blue-helmèd aconite.
And they advance with flutter, with grace,
    To the dance,
Moving on with a dainty pace,
As blossoms mince it on river swells.
Over their heads their cymbals shine,
Round each ankle gleams a twine
    Of twinkling bells—
Tune twirled golden from their cells.
Every step was a tinkling sound,
As they glanced in their dancing-ground.
Clouds in cluster with such a sailing
Float o'er the light of the wasting moon,
As the cloud of their gliding veiling
Swung in the sway of the dancing-tune.
There was the clash of their cymbals clanging,
Ringing of swinging bells clinging their feet;
And the clang on wing it seemed a-hanging,

Hovering round their dancing so fleet.—
I stirred, I rustled more than meet;
Whereat they broke to the left and right,
With eddying robes like aconite
    Blue of helm;
And I beheld to the foot o' the elm.

They have not tripped those dances, betrayed to my gaze,
To glad the heart of Sylvia, beholding of their maze;
  Through barky walls have slid away,
  And tricked them in their holiday,
    For other than for Sylvia;
While all the birds on branches lave their mouths with May,
  And bear with me this burthen,
    For singing to Sylvia.

Where its umbrage was enrooted,
    Sat, white-suited,
Sat, green-amiced and bare-footed,
    Spring, amid her minstrelsy;
There she sat amid her ladies,
    Where the shade is
Sheen as Enna mead ere Hades'
    Gloom fell 'thwart Persephone.
Dewy buds were interstrown
Through her tresses hanging down,
    And her feet
    Were most sweet,
Tinged like sea-stars, rosied brown.
A throng of children like to flowers were sown
About the grass beside, or clomb her knee:
I looked who were that favoured company.

SISTER SONGS

    And one there stood
    Against the beamy flood
Of sinking day, which, pouring its abundance,
Sublimed the illuminous and volute redundance
Of locks that, half dissolving, floated round her face;
    As see I might
Far off a lily-cluster poised in sun
    Dispread its gracile curls of light.
I knew what chosen child was there in place!
I knew there might no brows be, save of one,
  With such Hesperian fulgence compassèd,
Which in her moving seemed to wheel about her head.

O Spring's little children, more loud your lauds upraise,
For this is even Sylvia, with her sweet, feat ways!
  Your lovesome labours lay away,
  And prank you out in holiday,
    For syllabling to Sylvia;
And all you birds on branches, lave your mouths with May,
  To bear with me this burthen,
    For singing to Sylvia!

  Spring, goddess, is it thou, desirèd long?
  And art thou girded round with this young train?—
  If ever I did do thee ease in song,
  Now of thy grace let me one meed obtain,
    And list thou to one plain.
    Oh, keep still in thy train,
  After the years when others therefrom fade,
    This tiny, well-belovèd maid!
  To whom the gate of my heart's fortalice,

SISTER SONGS

   With all which in it is,
  And the shy self who doth therein immew him
  'Gainst what loud leaguerers battailously woo him,
   I, bribèd traitor to him,
   Set open for one kiss.

Then suffer, Spring, thy children, that lauds they should upraise
To Sylvia, this Sylvia, her sweet, feat ways ;
 Their lovely labours lay away,
 And trick them out in holiday,
  For syllabling to Sylvia ;
And that all birds on branches lave their mouths with May,
 To bear with me this burthen,
  For singing to Sylvia.

   A kiss ? for a child's kiss ?
   Aye, goddess, even for this.
  Once, bright Sylviola, in days not far,
 Once—in that nightmare-time which still doth haunt
 My dreams, a grim, unbidden visitant—
   Forlorn, and faint, and stark,
  I had endured through watches of the dark
  The abashless inquisition of each star,
 Yea, was the outcast mark
   Of all those heavenly passers' scrutiny ;
   Stood bound and helplessly
 For Time to shoot his barbèd minutes at me ;
 Suffered the trampling hoof of every hour
   In night's slow-wheelèd car ;
  Until the tardy dawn dragged me at length
  From under those dread wheels ; and, bled of strength,

SISTER SONGS

    I waited the inevitable last.
        Then there came past
A child ; like thee, a spring-flower ; but a flower
Fallen from the budded coronal of Spring,
And through the city-streets blown withering.
She passed,—O brave, sad, lovingest, tender thing !
And of her own scant pittance did she give,
        That I might eat and live :
Then fled, a swift and trackless fugitive.
        Therefore I kissed in thee
The heart of Childhood, so divine for me ;
        And her, through what sore ways,
        And what unchildish days,
Borne from me now, as then, a trackless fugitive.
        Therefore I kissed in thee
        Her, child ! and innocency,
And spring, and all things that have gone from me,
        And that shall never be ;
All vanished hopes, and all most hopeless bliss,
        Came with thee to my kiss.
And ah ! so long myself had strayed afar
From child, and woman, and the boon earth's green,
And all wherewith life's face is fair beseen ;
        Journeying its journey bare
Five suns, except of the all-kissing sun
            Unkissed of one ;
            Almost I had forgot
            The healing harms,
And whitest witchery, a-lurk in that
Authentic cestus of two girdling arms :
        And I remembered not

SISTER SONGS

  The subtle sanctities which dart
From childish lips' unvalued precious brush,
Nor how it makes the sudden lilies push
  Between the loosening fibres of the heart.
    Then, that thy little kiss
    Should be to me all this,
Let workaday wisdom blink sage lids thereat;
Which towers a flight three hedgerows high, poor bat!
  And straightway charts me out the empyreal air.
Its chart I wing not by, its canon of worth
Scorn not, nor reck though mine should breed it mirth:
And howso thou and I may be disjoint,
Yet still my falcon spirit makes her point
    Over the covert where
Thou, sweetest quarry, hast put in from her!

*(Soul, hush these sad numbers, too sad to upraise
In hymning bright Sylvia, unlearn'd in such ways!
  Our mournful moods lay we away,
  And prank our thoughts in holiday,
    For syllabling to Sylvia;
When all the birds on branches lave their mouths with May,
  To bear with us this burthen,
    For singing to Sylvia!)*

Then thus Spring, bounteous lady, made reply:
'O lover of me and all my progeny,
    For grace to you
I take her ever to my retinue.
Over thy form, dear child, alas! my art
Cannot prevail; but mine immortalizing

SISTER SONGS

  Touch I lay upon thy heart.
  Thy soul's fair shape
In my unfading mantle's green I drape,
And thy white mind shall rest by my devising
 A Gideon-fleece amid life's dusty drouth.
If Even burst yon globèd yellow grape
(Which is the sun to mortal's sealèd sight)
  Against her stainèd mouth;
  Or if white-handed light
Draw thee yet dripping from the quiet pools,
  Still lucencies and cools,
Of sleep, which all night mirror constellate dreams;
Like to the sign which led the Israelite,
  Thy soul, through day or dark,
A visible brightness on the chosen ark
  Of thy sweet body and pure,
  Shall it assure,
With auspice large and tutelary gleams,
Appointed solemn courts, and covenanted streams.'

Cease, Spring's little children, now cease your lauds to raise;
That dream is past, and Sylvia, with her sweet, feat ways.
 Our lovèd labour, laid away,
 Is smoothly ended; said our say,
  Our syllabling to Sylvia.
Make sweet, you birds on branches! make sweet your mouths
 with May!
  But borne is this burthen,
  Sung unto Sylvia.

SISTER SONGS

PART THE SECOND

And now, thou elder nursling of the nest;
    Ere all the intertangled west
      Be one magnificence
Of multitudinous blossoms that o'errun
The flaming brazen bowl o' the burnished sun
      Which they do flower from,
How shall I 'stablish *thy* memorial?
Nay, how or with what countenance shall I come
      To plead in my defence
      For loving thee at all?
I who can scarcely speak my fellows' speech,
Love their love, or mine own love to them teach;
A bastard barred from their inheritance,
    Who seem, in this dim shape's uneasy nook,
Some sun-flower's spirit which by luckless chance
    Has mournfully its tenement mistook;
When it were better in its right abode,
Heartless and happy lackeying its god.
How com'st thou, little tender thing of white,
Whose very touch full scantly me beseems,
How com'st thou resting on my vaporous dreams,
    Kindling a wraith there of earth's vernal green?
      Even so as I have seen,
   In night's aërial sea with no wind blust'rous,
A ribbèd tract of cloudy malachite
      Curve a shored crescent wide;
And on its slope marge shelving to the night
    The stranded moon lay quivering like a lustrous
      Medusa newly washed up from the tide,
Lay in an oozy pool of its own deliquious light.

SISTER SONGS

Yet hear how my excuses may prevail,
    Nor, tender white orb, be thou opposite!
  Life and life's beauty only hold their revels
In the abysmal ocean's luminous levels.
There, like the phantasms of a poet pale,
    The exquisite marvels sail :
Clarified silver ; greens and azures frail
As if the colours sighed themselves away,
And blent in supersubtile interplay
  As if they swooned into each other's arms ;
    Repured vermilion,
    Like ear-tips 'gainst the sun ;
And beings that, under night's swart pinion,
Make every wave upon the harbour-bars
    A beaten yolk of stars.
But where day's glance turns baffled from the deeps,
    Die out those lovely swarms ;
And in the immense profound no creature glides or creep

Love and love's beauty only hold their revels
In life's familiar, penetrable levels :
    What of its ocean-floor ?
    I dwell there evermore.
    From almost earliest youth
    I raised the lids o' the truth,
And forced her bend on me her shrinking sight ;
Ever I knew me Beauty's eremite,
  In antre of this lowly body set,
    Girt with a thirsty solitude of soul.
    Natheless I not forget
How I have, even as the anchorite,

SISTER SONGS

I too, imperishing essences that console.
Under my ruined passions, fallen and sere,
   The wild dreams stir, like little radiant girls
Whom in the moulted plumage of the year
   Their comrades sweet have buried to the curls.
Yet, though their dedicated amorist,
How often do I bid my visions hist,
   Deaf to them, pleading all their piteous fills;
Who weep, as weep the maidens of the mist
   Clinging the necks of the unheeding hills:
And their tears wash them lovelier than before,
That from grief's self our sad delight grows more.
Fair are the soul's uncrispèd calms, indeed,
   Endiapered with many a spiritual form
      Of blosmy-tinctured weed;
But scarce itself is conscious of the store
   Suckled by it, and only after storm
Casts up its loosened thoughts upon the shore.
     To this end my deeps are stirred;
     And I deem well why life unshared
     Was ordainèd me of yore.
     In pairing-time, we know, the bird
     Kindles to its deepmost splendour,
       And the tender
      Voice is tenderest in its throat:
     Were its love, for ever nigh it,
       Never by it,
      It might keep a vernal note,
     The crocean and amethystine
       In their pristine
      Lustre linger on its coat.

SISTER SONGS

Therefore must my song-bower lone be,
    That my tone be
  Fresh with dewy pain alway;
She, who scorns my dearest care ta'en,
    An uncertain
  Shadow of the sprite of May.
  And is my song sweet, as they say?
'Tis sweet for one whose voice has no reply,
    Save silence's sad cry:
And are its plumes a burning bright array?
They burn for an unincarnated eye.
A bubble, charioteered by the inward breath
  Which, ardorous for its own invisible lure,
Urges me glittering to aërial death,
  I am rapt towards that bodiless paramour;
Blindly the uncomprehended tyranny
    Obeying of my heart's impetuous might.
    The earth and all its planetary kin,
Starry buds tangled in the whirling hair
That flames round the Phœbean wassailer,
  Speed no more ignorant, more predestined flight,
    Than I, *her* viewless tresses netted in.
As some most beautiful one, with lovely taunting,
Her eyes of guileless guile o'ercanopies,
    Does her hid visage bow,
And miserly your covetous gaze allow,
    By inchmeal, coy degrees,
    Saying—'Can you see me now?'
Yet from the mouth's reflex you guess the wanting
    Smile of the coming eyes
In all their upturned grievous witcheries,

SISTER SONGS

  Before that sunbreak rise;
And each still hidden feature view within
Your mind, as eager scrutinies detail
The moon's young rondure through the shamefast veil
   Drawn to her gleaming chin:
   After this wise,
From the enticing smile of earth and skies
I dream my unknown Fair's refusèd gaze;
And guessingly her love's close traits devise,
  Which she with subtile coquetries
Through little human glimpses slow displays,
   Cozening my mateless days
   By sick, intolerable delays.
And so I keep mine uncompanioned ways;
And so my touch, to golden poesies
Turning love's bread, is bought at hunger's price.
So,—in the inextinguishable wars
Which roll song's Orient on the sullen night
Whose ragged banners in their own despite
Take on the tinges of the hated light,—
So Sultan Phœbus has his Janizars.
But if mine unappeasèd cicatrices
   Might get them lawful ease;
Were any gentle passion hallowed me,
  Who must none other breath of passion feel
  Save such as winnows to the fledgèd heel
   The tremulous Paradisal plumages;
    The conscious sacramental trees
     Which ever be
     Shaken celestially,
Consentient with enamoured wings, might know my
  love for thee.

SISTER SONGS

Yet is there more, whereat none guesseth, love!
   Upon the ending of my deadly night
(Whereof thou hast not the surmise, and slight
Is all that any mortal knows thereof),
   Thou wert to me that earnest of day's light,
When, like the back of a gold-mailèd saurian
   Heaving its slow length from Nilotic slime,
The first long gleaming fissure runs Aurorian
   Athwart the yet dun firmament of prime.
Stretched on the margin of the cruel sea
     Whence they had rescued me,
   With faint and painful pulses was I lying;
     Not yet discerning well
If I had 'scaped, or were an icicle,
     Whose thawing is its dying.
Like one who sweats before a despot's gate,
Summoned by some presaging scroll of fate,
And knows not whether kiss or dagger wait;
And all so sickened is his countenance,
The courtiers buzz, ' Lo, doomed ! ' and look at
   him askance :—
     At Fate's dread portal then
     Even so stood I, I ken,
Even so stood I, between a joy and tear,
And said to mine own heart, ' Now if the end
     be here ! '

     They say, Earth's beauty seems completest
       To them that on their death-beds rest;
     Gentle lady ! she smiles sweetest
       Just ere she clasps us to her breast.

SISTER SONGS

And I,—now *my* Earth's countenance grew bright,
Did she but smile me towards that nuptial-night?
But, whileas on such dubious bed I lay,
      One unforgotten day,
   As a sick child waking sees
      Wide-eyed daisies
  Gazing on it from its hand,
  Slipped there for its dear amazes;
  So between thy father's knees
     I saw *thee* stand,
    And through my hazes
Of pain and fear thine eyes' young wonder shone.
Then, as flies scatter from a carrion,
  Or rooks in spreading gyres like broken smoke
  Wheel, when some sound their quietude has broke,
Fled, at thy countenance, all that doubting spawn:
  The heart which I had questioned spoke,
A cry impetuous from its depth was drawn,—
' I take the omen of this face of dawn!'
And with the omen to my heart cam'st thou.
    Even with a spray of tears
That one light draft was fixed there for the years.

      And now?—
The hours I tread ooze memories of thee, Sweet,
    Beneath my casual feet.
    With rainfall as the lea,
   The day is drenched with thee;
  In little exquisite surprises
Bubbling deliciousness of thee arises
    From sudden places,

SISTER SONGS

Under the common traces
Of my most lethargied and customed paces.

As an Arab journeyeth
Through a sand of Ayaman,
Lean Thirst, lolling its cracked tongue,
Lagging by his side along;
And a rusty-wingèd Death
Grating its low flight before,
Casting ribbèd shadows o'er
The blank desert, blank and tan:
He lifts by hap toward where the morning's roots are
His weary stare,—
Sees, although they plashless mutes are,
Set in a silver air
Fountains of gelid shoots are,
Making the daylight fairest fair;
Sees the palm and tamarind
Tangle the tresses of a phantom wind;—
A sight like innocence when one has sinned!
A green and maiden freshness smiling there,
While with unblinking glare
The tawny-hided desert crouches watching her.

'Tis a vision:
Yet the greeneries Elysian
He has known in tracts afar;
Thus the enamouring fountains flow,
Those the very palms that grow,
By rare-gummed Sava, or Herbalimar.—
Such a watered dream has tarried

SISTER SONGS

    Trembling on my desert arid;
        Even so
      Its lovely gleamings
       Seemings show
     Of things not seemings;
       And I gaze,
  Knowing that, beyond my ways,
        Verily
  All these *are*, for these are She.

Eve no gentlier lays her cooling cheek
On the burning brow of the sick earth,
  Sick with death, and sick with birth,
Aeon to aeon, in secular fever twirled,
   Than thy shadow soothes this weak
   And distempered being of mine.
In all I work, my hand includeth thine;
  Thou rushest down in every stream
Whose passion frets my spirit's deepening gorge;
Unhood'st mine eyas-heart, and fliest my dream;
  Thou swing'st the hammers of my forge;
As the innocent moon, that nothing does but shine,
Moves all the labouring surges of the world.
  Pierce where thou wilt the springing thought in me,
And there thy pictured countenance lies enfurled,
  As in the cut fern lies the imaged tree.
    This poor song that sings of thee,
   This fragile song, is but a curled
    Shell outgathered from thy sea,
  And murmurous still of its nativity.
      Princess of Smiles,

SISTER SONGS

Sorceress of most unlawful-lawful wiles,
    Cunning pit for gazers' senses,
    Overstrewn with innocences!
    Purities gleam white like statues
    In the fair lakes of thine eyes,
    And I watch the sparkles that use
        There to rise,
        Knowing these
    Are bubbles from the calyces
    Of the lovely thoughts that breathe
Paving, like water-flowers, thy spirit's floor beneath.

        O thou most dear!
Who art thy sex's complex harmony
        God-set more facilely;
        To thee may love draw near
        Without one blame or fear,
Unchidden save by his humility:
Thou Perseus' Shield wherein I view secure
The mirrored Woman's fateful-fair allure!
Whom Heaven still leaves a twofold dignity,
As girlhood gentle, and as boyhood free;
With whom no most diaphanous webs enwind
The barèd limbs of the rebukeless mind.
Wild Dryad, all unconscious of thy tree,
        With which indissolubly
The tyrannous time shall one day make thee whole;
Whose frank arms pass unfretted through its bole:
        Who wear'st thy femineity
Light as entrailèd blossoms, that shalt find
It erelong silver shackles unto thee.

SISTER SONGS

Thou whose young sex is yet but in thy soul;—
    As hoarded in the vine
Hang the gold skins of undelirious wine,
As air sleeps, till it toss its limbs in breeze :—
    In whom the mystery which lures and sunders,
        Grapples and thrusts apart, endears, estranges,
—The dragon to its own Hesperides—
Is gated under slow-revolving changes,
Manifold doors of heavy-hingèd years.
    So once, ere Heaven's eyes were filled with wonders
        To see Laughter rise from Tears,
        Lay in beauty not yet mighty,
            Conchèd in translucencies,
        The antenatal Aphrodite,
Caved magically under magic seas;
Caved dreamlessly beneath the dreamful seas.

        'Whose sex is in thy soul!'
        What think we of thy soul?
    Which has no parts, and cannot grow,
        Unfurled not from an embryo;
Born of full stature, lineal to control;
    And yet a pigmy's yoke must undergo:
Yet must keep pace and tarry, patient, kind,
With its unwilling scholar, the dull, tardy mind;
Must be obsequious to the body's powers,
Whose low hands mete its paths, set ope and close its
    ways;
        Must do obeisance to the days,
And wait the little pleasure of the hours;
        Yea, ripe for kingship, yet must be

SISTER SONGS

Captive in statuted minority!
So is all power fulfilled, as soul in thee.
So still the ruler by the ruled takes rule,
And wisdom weaves itself i' the loom o' the fool.
The splendent sun no splendour can display
Till on gross things he dash his broken ray,
From cloud and tree and flower re-tossed in prismy
    spray.
Did not obstruction's vessel hem it in,
Force were not force, would spill itself in vain;
We know the Titan by his champèd chain.
Stay is heat's cradle, it is rocked therein,
And by check's hand is burnished into light;
If hate were none, would love burn lowlier bright?
God's Fair were guessed scarce but for opposite sin;
Yea, and His Mercy, I do think it well,
Is flashed back from the brazen gates of Hell.
      The heavens decree
All power fulfil itself as soul in thee.
For supreme Spirit subject was to clay,
  And Law from its own servants learned a law,
And Light besought a lamp unto its way,
      And Awe was reined in awe,
    At one small house of Nazareth;
      And Golgotha
Saw Breath to breathlessness resign its breath,
And Life do homage for its crown to death.

So is all power, as soul in thee, increased!
  But, knowing this, in knowledge's despite
  I fret against the law severe that stains

SISTER SONGS

        Thy spirit with eclipse;
When—as a nymph's carven head sweet water drips,
  For others oozing so the cool delight
  Which cannot steep her stiffened mouth of stone—
Thy nescient lips repeat maternal strains.
        Memnonian lips!
Smitten with singing from thy mother's east,
  And murmurous with music not their own:
  Nay, the lips flexile, while the mind alone
      A passionless statue stands.
      Oh, pardon, innocent one!
    Pardon at thine unconscious hands!
' Murmurous with music not their own,' I say?
And in that saying how do I missay,
     When from the common sands
Of poorest common speech of common day
Thine accents sift the golden musics out!
    And ah, we poets, I misdoubt,
      Are little more than thou!
We speak a lesson taught we know not how,
  And what it is that from us flows
The hearer better than the utterer knows.

     Thou canst foreshape thy word;
      The poet is not lord
    Of the next syllable may come
    With the returning pendulum;
    And what he plans to-day in song,
To-morrow sings it in another tongue.
    Where the last leaf fell from his bough,
    He knows not if a leaf shall grow;

SISTER SONGS

    Where he sows he doth not reap,
    He reapeth where he did not sow;
    He sleeps, and dreams forsake his sleep
    To meet him on his waking way.
Vision will mate him not by law and vow:
    Disguised in life's most hodden-grey,
By the most beaten road of everyday
She waits him, unsuspected and unknown.
    The hardest pang whereon
He lays his mutinous head may be a Jacob's stone.
In the most iron crag his foot can tread
    A Dream may strew her bed,
    And suddenly his limbs entwine,
And draw him down through rock as sea-nymphs might
    through brine.
But, unlike those feigned temptress-ladies who
In guerdon of a night the lover slew,
When the embrace has failed, the rapture fled,
Not he, not he, the wild sweet witch is dead!
    And though he cherisheth
The babe most strangely born from out her death,
Some tender trick of her it hath, maybe,—
    It is not she!

Yet, even as the air is rumorous of fray
    Before the first shafts of the sun's onslaught
      From gloom's black harness splinter,
      And Summer move on Winter
With the trumpet of the March, and the pennon of the
    May;
    As gesture outstrips thought;

SISTER SONGS

So haply, toyer with ethereal strings,
Are thy blind repetitions of high things
The murmurous gnats whose aimless hoverings
    Reveal song's summer in the air;
The outstretched hand, which cannot thought declare,
    Yet is thought's harbinger.
These strains the way for thine own strains prepare;
We feel the music moist upon this breeze,
And hope the congregating poesies.
    Sundered yet by thee from us
    Wait, with wild eyes luminous,
All thy winged things that are to be;
They flit against thee, Gate of Ivory!
They clamour on the portress Destiny,—
' Set her wide, so we may issue through,
Our vans are quick for that they have to do!'
    Suffer still your young desire;
Your plumes but bicker at the tips with fire;
Tarry their kindling—they will beat the higher.
And thou, bright girl, not long shalt thou repeat
Idly the music from thy mother caught;
    Not vainly has she wrought,
Not vainly from the cloudward-jetting turret
Of her aërial mind for thy weak feet
Let down the silken ladder of her thought.
    She bare thee with a double pain,
      Of the body and the spirit;
    Thou thy fleshly weeds hast ta'en,
      Thy diviner weeds inherit!
The precious streams which through thy young lips roll
Shall leave their lovely delta in thy soul:

SISTER SONGS

 Where sprites of so essential kind
  Set their paces,
Surely they shall leave behind
  The green traces
Of their sportance in the mind;
And thou shalt, ere we well may know it,
 Turn that daintiness, a poet,—
  Elfin-ring
 Where sweet fancies foot and sing.
 So it may be, so it *shall* be,—
 Oh, take the prophecy from me!
What if the old fastidious sculptor, Time,
 This crescent marvel of his hands
 Carveth all too painfully,
And I who prophesy shall never see?
What if the niche of its predestined rhyme,
 Its aching niche, too long expectant stands?
  Yet shall he after sore delays
  On some exultant day of days
  The white enshrouding childhood raise
From thy fair spirit, finished for our gaze;
 While we (but 'mongst that happy ' we '
  The prophet cannot be!)—
While we behold with no astonishments,
 With that serene fulfilment of delight
  Wherewith we view the sight
  When the stars pitch the golden tents
Of their high campment on the plains of night.
Why should amazement be our satellite?
  What wonder in such things?
If angels have hereditary wings,

SISTER SONGS

    If not by Salic law is handed down
        The poet's crown,
  To thee, born in the purple of the throne,
        The laurel must belong:
        Thou, in thy mother's right
Descendant of Castalian-chrismèd kings—
    O Princess of the Blood of Song!

Peace! Too impetuously have I been winging
    Toward vaporous heights which beckon and beguile.
     I sink back, saddened to my inmost mind;
Even as I list a-dream that mother singing
    The poesy of sweet tone, and sadden while
       Her voice is cast in troubled wake behind
       The keel of her keen spirit. Thou art enshrined
In a too primal innocence for this eye—
Intent on such untempered radiancy—
Not to be pained; my clay can scarce endure
Ungrieved the effluence near of essences so pure.
       Therefore, little tender maiden,
       Never be thou overshaden
       With a mind whose canopy
       Would shut out the sky from thee;
Whose tangled branches intercept Heaven's light:
    I will not feed my unpastured heart
    On thee, green pleasaunce as thou art,
To lessen by one flower thy happy daisies white.
The water-rat is earth-hued like the runlet
    Whereon he swims; and how in me should lurk
Thoughts apt to neighbour thine, thou creature sunlit?
       If through long fret and irk

SISTER SONGS

Thine eyes within their browed recesses were
Worn caves where thought lay couchant in its lair;
Wert thou a spark among dank leaves, ah ruth!
With age in all thy veins, while all thy heart was youth;
    Our contact might run smooth.
But life's Eoan dews still moist thy ringèd hair;
    Dian's chill finger-tips
Thaw if at night they happen on thy lips;
The flying fringes of the sun's cloak frush
The fragile leaves which on those warm lips blush;
    And joy only lurks retirèd
    In the dim gloaming of thine irid.
Then since my love drags this poor shadow, me,
And one without the other may not be,
    From both I guard thee free.
    It still is much, yes, it is much,
Only—my dream!—to love my love of thee;
    And it is much, yes, it is much,
In hands which thou hast touched to feel thy touch;
In voices which have mingled with thine own
    To hear a double tone.
As anguish, for supreme expression prest,
    Borrows its saddest tongue from jest,
    Thou hast of absence so create
    A presence more importunate;
    And thy voice pleads its sweetest suit
    When it is mute.
    I thank the once accursèd star
    Which did me teach
To make of Silence my familiar,
Who hath the rich reversion of thy speech,

SISTER SONGS

Since the most charming sounds thy thought can wear,
Cast off, fall to that pale attendant's share;
  And thank the gift which made my mind
A shadow-world, wherethrough the shadows wind
Of all the loved and lovely of my kind.

  Like a maiden Saxon, folden,
   As she flits, in moon-drenched mist;
  Whose curls streaming flaxen-golden,
   By the misted moonbeams kist,
  Dispread their filmy floating silk
   Like honey steeped in milk:
  So, vague goldenness remote,
   Through my thoughts I watch thee float.
When the snake summer casts her blazoned skin
We find it at the turn of autumn's path,
And think it summer that rewinded hath,
   Joying therein;
And this enamouring slough of thee, mine elf,
   I take it for thyself;
Content. Content? Yea, title it content.
The very loves that belt thee must prevent
My love, I know, with their legitimacy:
As the metallic vapours, that are swept
Athwart the sun, in his light intercept
   The very hues
Which their conflagrant elements effuse.
  But, my love, my heart, my fair,
   That only I should see thee rare,
Or tent to the hid core thy rarity,—
  This were a mournfulness more piercing far

SISTER SONGS

Than that those other loves my own must bar,
Or thine for others leave thee none for me.

  But on a day whereof I think,
  One shall dip his hand to drink
  In that still water of thy soul,
  And its imaged tremors race
  Over thy joy-troubled face,
  As the intervolved reflections roll
  From a shaken fountain's brink,
  With swift light wrinkling its alcove.
  From the hovering wing of Love
The warm stain shall flit roseal on thy cheek.
  Then, sweet blushet ! whenas he,
The destined paramount of thy universe,
  Who has no worlds to sigh for, ruling thee,
  Ascends his vermeil throne of empery,
    One grace alone I seek.
Oh ! may this treasure-galleon of my verse,
Fraught with its golden passion, oared with cadent
  rhyme,
Set with a towering press of fantasies,
  Drop safely down the time,
Leaving mine isled self behind it far
Soon to be sunken in the abysm of seas
(As down the years the splendour voyages
  From some long ruined and night-submergèd star),
And in thy subject sovereign's havening heart
Anchor the freightage of its virgin ore ;
  Adding its wasteful more
To his own overflowing treasury.

SISTER SONGS

So through his river mine shall reach thy sea,
        Bearing its confluent part;
        In his pulse mine shall thrill;
And the quick heart shall quicken from the heart that's
    still.

Ah, help, my Dæmon that hast served me well!
    Not at this last, oh, do not me disgrace!
    I faint, I sicken, darkens all my sight,
    As, poised upon this unprevisioned height,
        I lift into its place
The utmost aery traceried pinnacle.
So; it is builded, the high tenement,
        —God grant!—to mine intent:
Most like a palace of the Occident,
        Up-thrusting, toppling maze on maze,
            Its mounded blaze,
And washèd by the sunset's rosy waves,
Whose sea drinks rarer hue from those rare walls it
    laves.
        Yet wail, my spirits, wail!
So few therein to enter shall prevail.
Scarce fewer could win way, if their desire
A dragon baulked, with involuted spire,
And writhen snout spattered with yeasty fire.
For at the elfin portal hangs a horn
        Which none can wind aright
        Save the appointed knight
Whose lids the fay-wings brushed when he was born.
        All others stray forlorn,
Or glimpsing, through the blazoned windows scrolled,

SISTER SONGS

Receding labyrinths lessening tortuously
    In half obscurity ;
With mystic images, inhuman, cold,
    That flameless torches hold.
    But who can wind that horn of might
(The horn of dead Heliades) aright,—
        Straight
Open for him shall roll the conscious gate ;
And light leap up from all the torches there,
And life leap up in every torchbearer,
And the stone faces kindle in the glow,
And into the blank eyes the irids grow,
And through the dawning irids ambushed meanings
    show.
        Illumined this wise on,
He threads securely the far intricacies,
    With brede from Heaven's wrought vesture
        overstrewn ;
Swift Tellus' purfled tunic, girt upon
With the blown chlamys of her fluttering seas ;
    And the freaked kirtle of the pearlèd moon :
Until he gain the structure's core, where stands—
    A toil of magic hands—
The unbodied spirit of the sorcerer,
        Most strangely rare,
    As is a vision remembered in the noon ;
Unbodied, yet to mortal seeing clear,
Like sighs exhaled in eager atmosphere.
From human haps and mutabilities
It rests exempt, beneath the edifice
        To which itself gave rise ;

SISTER SONGS

Sustaining centre to the bubble of stone
Which, breathed from it, exists by it alone.
Yea, ere Saturnian earth her child consumes,
    And I lie down with outworn ossuaries,
Ere death's grim tongue anticipates the tomb's
    Siste viator, in this storied urn
      My living heart is laid to throb and burn,
    Till end be ended, and till ceasing cease.

And thou by whom this strain hath parentage;
    Wantoner between the yet untreacherous claws
    Of newly-whelped existence! ere he pause,
What gift to thee can yield the archimage?
      For coming seasons' frets
      What aids, what amulets,
      What softenings, or what brightenings?
As Thunder writhes the lash of his long lightnings
    About the growling heads of the brute main
    Foaming at mouth, until it wallow again
    In the scooped oozes of its bed of pain;
So all the gnashing jaws, the leaping heads
Of hungry menaces, and of ravening dreads,
      Of pangs
Twitch-lipped, with quivering nostrils and immitigate
    fangs,
I scourge beneath the torment of my charms
That their repentless nature fear to work thee harms.
And as yon Apollonian harp-player,
    Yon wandering psalterist of the sky,
With flickering strings which scatter melody,
The silver-stolèd damsels of the sea,

SISTER SONGS

      Or lake, or fount, or stream,
   Enchants from their ancestral heaven of waters
To Naiad it through the unfrothing air;
   My song enchants so out of undulous dream
    The glimmering shapes of its dim-tressèd
       daughters,
And missions each to be thy minister,
      Saying: 'O ye,
The organ-stops of being's harmony;
The blushes on existence's pale face,
    Lending it sudden grace;
Without whom we should but guess Heaven's worth
By blank negations of this sordid earth
    (So haply to the blind may light
Be but gloom's undetermined opposite);
Ye who are thus as the refracting air
Whereby we see Heaven's sun before it rise
Above the dull line of our mortal skies;
As breathing on the strainèd ear that sighs
From comrades viewless unto strainèd eyes,
Soothing our terrors in the lampless night;
Ye who can make this world, where all is deeming,
What world ye list, being arbiters of seeming;
Attend upon her ways, benignant powers!
Unroll ye life a carpet for her feet,
And cast ye down before them blossomy hours,
Until her going shall be clogged with sweet!
All dear emotions whose new-bathèd hair,
Still streaming from the soul, in love's warm air
Smokes with a mist of tender fantasies;
       All these,

SISTER SONGS

And all the heart's wild growths which, swiftly bright,
Spring up the crimson agarics of a night,
No pain in withering, yet a joy arisen;
And all thin shapes more exquisitely rare,
    More subtly fair,
Than these weak ministering words have spell to prison
Within the magic circle of this rhyme;
And all the fays who in our creedless clime
    Have sadly ceased,
Bearing to other children childhood's proper feast;
Whose robes are fluent crystal, crocus-hued,
    Whose wings are wind a-fire, whose mantles
      wrought
    From spray that falling rainbows shake to air;
    These, ye familiars to my wizard thought,
    Make things of journal custom unto her;
      With lucent feet imbrued,
    If young Day tread, a glorious vintager,
The wine-press of the purple-foamèd east;
Or round the nodding sun, flush-faced and sunken,
    His wild Bacchantes drunken
Reel, with rent woofs a-flaunt, their westering rout.'

—But lo! at length the day is lingered out,
At length my Ariel lays his viol by;
We sing no more to thee, child, he and I;
    The day is lingered out:
    In slow wreaths folden
    Around yon censer, spherèd, golden,
    Vague Vesper's fumes aspire;
    And, glimmering to eclipse,

SISTER SONGS

      The long laburnum drips
Its honey of wild flame, its jocund spilth of fire.

    Now pass your ways, fair bird, and pass your ways,
        If you will ;
      I have you through the days !
      And flit or hold you still,
      And perch you where you list
        On what wrist,—
    You are mine through the times !
I have caught you fast for ever in a tangle of sweet rhymes.
    And in your young maiden morn
        You may scorn
      But you must be
    Bound and sociate to me ;
*With this thread from out the tomb my dead hand shall
    tether thee !*

Go, Sister-songs, to that sweet Sister-pair
For whom I have your frail limbs fashionèd,
    And framèd feateously ;—
For whom I have your frail limbs fashionèd
With how great shamefastness and how great dread,
Knowing you frail, but not if you be fair,
    Though framèd feateously ;
    Go unto them from me.
Go from my shadow to their sunshine sight,
    Made for all sights' delight ;
Go like twin swans that oar the surgy storms
To bate with pennoned snows in candent air :

SISTER SONGS

   Nigh with abasèd head,
Yourselves linked sisterly, that Sister-pair,
   And go in presence there;
Saying—' Your young eyes cannot see our forms,
Nor read the yearning of our looks aright;
But Time shall trail the veilings from our hair,
And cleanse your seeing with his euphrasy
(Yea, even your bright seeing make more bright,
   Which is all sights' delight),
And ye shall know us for what things we be.

' Whilom, within a poet's calyxed heart,
A dewy love we trembled all apart;
   Whence it took rise
   Beneath your radiant eyes,
Which misted it to music. We must long,
A floating haze of silver subtile song,
   Await love-laden
   Above each maiden
The appointed hour that o'er the hearts of you—
   As vapours into dew
   Unweave, whence they were wove,—
Shall turn our loosening musics back to love.'

SISTER SONGS

INSCRIPTION

WHEN the last stir of bubbling melodies
    Broke, as my chants sank underneath the wave
    Of dulcitude, but sank again to rise
Where man's embaying mind those waters lave
(For music hath its Oceanides
Flexuously floating through their parent seas,
    And such are these),
I saw a vision—or may it be
The effluence of a dear desired reality?
    I saw two spirits high,—
Two spirits, dim within the silver smoke
    Which is for ever woke
By snowing lights of fountained Poesy.
Two shapes they were, familiar as love;
    They were those souls, whereof
One twines from finest gracious daily things,
Strong, constant, noticeless, as are heart-strings,
The golden cage wherein this song-bird sings;
And the other's sun gives hue to all my flowers,
Which else pale flowers of Tartarus would grow,
Where ghosts watch ghosts of blooms in ghostly bowers;—
    For we do know
The hidden player by his harmonies,
And by my thoughts I know what still hands thrill the keys.

And to these twain—as from the mind's abysses
All thoughts draw toward the awakening heart's sweet
    kisses,
With proffer of their wreathen fantasies,—
    Even so to these

SISTER SONGS

I saw how many brought their garlands fair,
Whether of song, or simple love, they were,—
Of simple love, that makes best garlands fair.
But one I marked who lingered still behind,
As for such souls no seemly gift had he:
    He was not of their strain,
Nor worthy of so bright beings to entertain,
Nor fit compeer for such high company.
Yet was he, surely, born to them in mind,
Their youngest nursling of the spirit's kind.
    Last stole this one,
With timid glance, of watching eyes adread,
And dropped his frightened flower when all were gone;
And where the frail flower fell, it witherèd.
But yet methought those high souls smiled thereon;
As when a child, upstraining at your knees
Some fond and fancied nothings, says, ' I give you
      these!'

LOVE IN DIAN'S LAP

PROEMION

HEAR, my Muses, I demand
    A little labour at your hand,
    Ere quite is loosed our amity :
A little husband out the sand
    That times the gasps of Poesy !

O belovèd, O ye Two,
When the Years last met, to you
    I sent a gift exultingly.
My song's sands, like the Year's, are few ;
    But take this last weak gift from me.

One year ago (one year, one year !)
I had no prescience, no, nor fear ;
    I said to Oblivion : ' Dread thou me ! '
What cared I for the mortal year ?
    I was not of its company.

Before mine own Elect stood I,
And said to Death, ' Not these shall die ! '
    I issued mandate royally.
I bade Decay : ' Avoid and fly,
    For I am fatal unto thee.'

LOVE IN DIAN'S LAP

I sprinkled a few drops of verse,
And said to Ruin, ' Quit thy hearse : '
  To my Loved, ' Pale not, come with me ;
I will escort thee down the years,
  With me thou walk'st immortally.'

Rhyme did I as a charmed cup give,
That who I would might drink and live.
  ' Enter,' I cried, ' song's ark with me ! '
And knew not that a witch's sieve
  Were built somewhat more seamanly.

I said unto my heart : ' Be light !
Thy grain will soon for long delight
  Oppress the future's granary : '
Poor fool ! and did not hear—' This night
  They shall demand thy song of thee.'

Of God and you I pardon crave ;
Who would save others, nor can save
  My own self from mortality :
I throw my whole songs in the grave—
  They will not fill that pit for me.

But thou, to whom I sing this last—
The bitterest bitterness I taste
  Is that thy children have from me
The best I had where all is waste,
  And but the crumbs were cast to thee.

PROEMION

It may be I did little wrong;
Since no notes of thy lyre belong
   To them; thou leftest them for me;
And what didst *thou* want of my song,—
   Thou, thine own immortality?

Ah, I would that I had yet
Given thy head one coronet
   With thine ivies to agree!
Ere thou restest where are set
   Wreaths but on the breast of thee.

Though what avails?—The ivies twined
By thine own hand thou must unbind,
   When there thy temples laid shall be:
'Tis haply Death's prevision kind
   That ungirt brows lie easily.

' *Of all thy trees thou lovest so,*
None with thee to grave shall go,
   Save the abhorrèd cypress tree.'*
The abhorrèd?—Ah, I know, I know,
   Thy dearest follower it would be!

Thou would'st sweetly lie in death
The dark southerner beneath:
   We should interpret, knowing thee,—
' Here I rest ' (her symbol saith),
   ' And above me, Italy.'

* The words of Horace.

LOVE IN DIAN'S LAP

But above thy English grave
Who knows if a tree shall wave ?
   Save—when the far certainty
Of thy fame fulfilled is—save
   The laurel that shall spring from thee.

Very little carest thou
If the world no laurel-bough
   Set in thy dead hand, ah me !
But *my* heart to grieve allow
   For the fame thou shalt not see !

Yet my heart to grieve allow,
With the grief that grieves it now,
   Looking to futurity,
With too sure presaging how
   Fools will blind blind eyes from thee :—

Bitterly presaging how
Sightless death must them endow
   With sight, who gladder blind would be.
' Though our eyes be blind enow,
   Let us hide them, lest we see ! '

I would their hearts but hardened were
In the way that I aver
   All men shall find this heart of me :
Which is so hard, thy name cut there
   Never worn or blurred can be.

PROEMION

If my song as much might say!
But in all too late a day
   I use thy name for melody;
And with the sweet theme assay
   To hide my descant's poverty.

When that last song gave I you,
Ye and I, beloved Two,
   Were each to each half mystery!
Now the tender veil is through;
   Unafraid the whole we see.

Small for you the danger was!
Statued deity but thaws
   In you to warm divinity;
Some fair defect completion flaws
   With a completing grace to me.

But when I my veiling raised—
The Milonian ess were crazed
   To talk with men incarnately:
The poor goddess but appraised
   By her lacking arms would be.

Though Pan may have delicious throat,
'Tis hard to tolerate the goat.
   What if Pan were suddenly
To lose his singing, every note?—
   Then pity have of Pan, and me!

LOVE IN DIAN'S LAP

Love and Song together sing;
Song is weak and fain to cling
  About Love's shoulder wearily.
Let her voice, poor fainting thing,
  In his strong voice drownèd be!

In my soul's Temple seems a sound
Of unfolding wings around
  The vacant shrine of poesy:
Voices of parting songs resound:—
  ' Let us go hence!' *A space let be!*

A space, my Muses, I demand
This last of labours at your hand,
  Ere quite is loosed our amity:
A little stay the cruel sand
  That times the gasps of Poesy!

I

BEFORE HER PORTRAIT IN YOUTH

AS lovers, banished from their lady's face,
    And hopeless of her grace,
Fashion a ghostly sweetness in its place,
    Fondly adore
Some stealth-won cast attire she wore,
    A kerchief, or a glove:
    And at the lover's beck
Into the glove there fleets the hand,
    Or at impetuous command
Up from the kerchief floats the virgin neck:
So I, in very lowlihead of love,—
    Too shyly reverencing
    To let one thought's light footfall smooth
Tread near the living, consecrated thing,—
    Treasure me thy cast youth.
This outworn vesture, tenantless of thee,
    Hath yet my knee,
For that, with show and semblance fair
    Of the past Her
Who once the beautiful, discarded raiment bare,
    It cheateth me.
    As gale to gale drifts breath
    Of blossoms' death,
So, dropping down the years from hour to hour,
    This dead youth's scent is wafted me to-day:
I sit, and from the fragrance dream the flower.

LOVE IN DIAN'S LAP

      So, then, she looked (I say);
      And so her front sank down
Heavy beneath the poet's iron crown:
        On her mouth museful sweet
        (Even as the twin lips meet)
        Did thought and sadness greet:
          Sighs
      In those mournful eyes
    So put on visibilities;
As viewless ether turns, in deep on deep, to dyes.
        Thus, long ago,
She kept her meditative paces slow
Through maiden meads, with wavèd shadow and gleam
Of locks half-lifted on the winds of dream,
Till Love up-caught her to his chariot's glow.
Yet, voluntary, happier Proserpine!
      This drooping flower of youth thou lettest fall
      I, faring in the cockshut-light, astray,
        Find on my 'lated way,
    And stoop, and gather for memorial,
And lay it on my bosom, and make it mine.
To this, the all of love the stars allow me,
        I dedicate and vow me.
        I reach back through the days
A trothed hand to the dead the last trump shall not raise.
        The water-wraith that cries
From those eternal sorrows of thy pictured eyes
Entwines and draws me down their soundless intricacies.

II

TO A POET BREAKING SILENCE

TOO wearily had we and song
Been left to look and left to long,
Yea, song and we to long and look,
Since thine acquainted feet forsook
The mountain where the Muses hymn
For Sinai and the Seraphim.
Now in both the mountains' shine
Dress thy countenance, twice divine!
From Moses and the Muses draw
The Tables of thy double Law!
His rod-born fount and Castaly
Let the one rock bring forth for thee,
Renewing so from either spring
The songs which both thy countries sing:
Or we shall fear lest, heavened thus long,
Thou should'st forget thy native song,
And mar thy mortal melodies
With broken stammer of the skies.

Ah! let the sweet birds of the Lord
With earth's waters make accord;
Teach how the crucifix may be
Carven from the laurel-tree,
Fruit of the Hesperides
Burnish take on Eden-trees,
The Muses' sacred grove be wet
With the red dew of Olivet,

LOVE IN DIAN'S LAP

And Sappho lay her burning brows
In white Cecilia's lap of snows!

   Thy childhood must have felt the stings
Of too divine o'ershadowings;
Its odorous heart have been a blossom
That in darkness did unbosom,
Those fire-flies of God to invite,
Burning spirits, which by night
Bear upon their laden wing
To such hearts impregnating.
For flowers that night-wings fertilize
Mock down the stars' unsteady eyes,
And with a happy, sleepless glance
Gaze the moon out of countenance.
I think thy girlhood's watchers must
Have took thy folded songs on trust,
And felt them, as one feels the stir
Of still lightnings in the hair,
When conscious hush expects the cloud
To speak the golden secret loud
Which tacit air is privy to;
Flasked in the grape the wine they knew,
Ere thy poet-mouth was able
For its first young starry babble.
Keep'st thou not yet that subtle grace?
Yea, in this silent interspace,
God sets His poems in thy face!

   The loom which mortal verse affords,
Out of weak and mortal words,

TO A POET BREAKING SILENCE

Wovest thou thy singing-weed in,
To a rune of thy far Eden.
Vain are all disguises ! Ah,
Heavenly *incognita !*
Thy mien bewrayeth through that wrong
The great Uranian House of Song !
As the vintages of earth
Taste of the sun that riped their birth,
We know what never-cadent Sun
Thy lampèd clusters throbbed upon,
What plumed feet the winepress trod ;
Thy wine is flavorous of God.
Whatever singing-robe thou wear
Has the Paradisal air ;
And some gold feather it has kept
Shows what Floor it lately swept !

III

"MANUS ANIMAM PINXIT"

LADY who hold'st on me dominion!
    Within your spirit's arms I stay me fast
        Against the fell
Immitigate ravening of the gates of hell;
And claim my right in you, most hardly won,
Of chaste fidelity upon the chaste:
Hold me and hold by me, lest both should fall
(O in high escalade high companion!)
Even in the breach of Heaven's assaulted wall.
Like to a wind-sown sapling grow I from
The clift, Sweet, of your skyward-jetting soul,—
Shook by all gusts that sweep it, overcome
By all its clouds incumbent: O be true
To your soul, dearest, as my life to you!
For if that soil grow sterile, then the whole
Of me must shrivel, from the topmost shoot
Of climbing poesy, and my life, killed through,
Dry down and perish to the foodless root.

Sweet Summer! unto you this swallow drew,
    By secret instincts inappeasable,
        That did direct him well,
Lured from his gelid North which wrought him
    wrong,
        Wintered of sunning song;—
    By happy instincts inappeasable,
        Ah yes! that led him well,
Lured to the untried regions and the new

"MANUS ANIMAM PINXIT"

    Climes of auspicious you;
To twitter there, and in his singing dwell.
    But ah! if you, my Summer, should grow waste,
    With grieving skies o'ercast,
For such migration my poor wing was strong
But once; it has no power to fare again
    Forth o'er the heads of men,
Nor other Summers for its Sanctuary:
    But from your mind's chilled sky
It needs must drop, and lie with stiffened wings
    Among your soul's forlornest things;
A speck upon your memory, alack!
A dead fly in a dusty window-crack.

    O therefore you who are
    What words, being to such mysteries
    As raiment to the body is,
    Should rather hide than tell;
    Chaste and intelligential love:
    Whose form is as a grove
Hushed with the cooing of an unseen dove;
Whose spirit to my touch thrills purer far
Than is the tingling of a silver bell;
Whose body other ladies well might bear
As soul,—yea, which it profanation were
For all but you to take as fleshly woof,
    Being spirit truest proof;
Whose spirit sure is lineal to that
    Which sang *Magnificat*:
      Chastest, since such you are,
      Take this curbed spirit of mine,

LOVE IN DIAN'S LAP

Which your own eyes invest with light divine,
For lofty love and high auxiliar
    In daily exalt emprise
      Which outsoars mortal eyes;
   This soul which on your soul is laid,
  As maid's breast against breast of maid;
Beholding how your own I have engraved
On it, and with what purging thoughts have laved
This love of mine from all mortality.
Indeed the copy is a painful one,
      And with long labour done!
O if you doubt the thing you are, lady,
      Come then, and look in me;
Your beauty, Dian, dress and contemplate
Within a pool to Dian consecrate!
Unveil this spirit, lady, when you will,
For unto all but you 'tis veilèd still:
Unveil, and fearless gaze there, you alone,
And if you love the image—'tis your own!

IV
A CARRIER SONG

I

SINCE you have waned from us,
    Fairest of women!
I am a darkened cage
    Song cannot hymn in.
My songs have followed you,
    Like birds the summer;
Ah! bring them back to me,
    Swiftly, dear comer!
        Seraphim,
        Her to hymn,
        Might leave their portals;
        And at my feet learn
        The harping of mortals!

II

Where wings to rustle use,
    But this poor tarrier—
Searching my spirit's eaves—
    Find I for carrier.
Ah! bring them back to me
    Swiftly, sweet comer—
Swift, swift, and bring with you
    Song's Indian summer!
        Seraphim,
        Her to hymn,
        Might leave their portals;
        And at my feet learn
        The harping of mortals!

LOVE IN DIAN'S LAP

III

Whereso your angel is.
  My angel goeth;
I am left guardianless,
  Paradise knoweth!
I have no Heaven left
  To weep my wrongs to;
Heaven, when you went from us,
  Went with my songs too.
     Seraphim,
     Her to hymn,
     Might leave their portals;
     And at my feet learn
     The harping of mortals!

IV

I have no angels left
  Now, Sweet, to pray to:
Where you have made your shrine
  They are away to.
They have struck Heaven's tent,
  And gone to cover you:
Whereso you keep your state
  Heaven is pitched over you!
     Seraphim,
     Her to hymn,
     Might leave their portals;
     And at my feet learn
     The harping of mortals!

A CARRIER SONG

V

She that is Heaven's Queen
   Her title borrows,
For that she, pitiful,
   Beareth our sorrows.
So thou, *Regina mî*,
   Spes infirmorum;
With all our grieving crowned
   Mater dolorum!
     Seraphim,
     Her to hymn,
     Might leave their portals;
     And at my feet learn
     The harping of mortals!

VI

Yet, envious coveter
   Of other's grieving!
This lonely longing yet
   'Scapeth your reaving.
Cruel, to take from a
   Sinner his Heaven!
Think you with contrite smiles
   To be forgiven?
     Seraphim,
     Her to hymn,
     Might leave their portals;
     And at my feet learn
     The harping of mortals!

LOVE IN DIAN'S LAP

VII

Penitent ! give me back
　　Angels, and Heaven ;
Render your stolen self,
　　And be forgiven !
How frontier Heaven from you ?
　　For my soul prays, Sweet,
Still to your face in Heaven,
　　Heaven in your face, Sweet !
　　　　Seraphim,
　　　　Her to hymn,
　　　Might leave their portals ;
　　　And at my feet learn
　　　The harping of mortals !

V
SCALA JACOBI PORTAQUE EBURNEA

HER soul from earth to Heaven lies,
    Like the ladder of the vision,
        Whereon go
        To and fro,
In ascension and demission,
Star-flecked feet of Paradise.

Now she is drawn up from me,
All my angels, wet-eyed, tristful,
        Gaze from great
        Heaven's gate
Like pent children, very wistful,
That below a playmate see.

Dream-dispensing face of hers!
Ivory port which loosed upon me
        Wings, I wist,
        Whose amethyst
Trepidations have forgone me,—
Hesper's filmy traffickers!

VI

GILDED GOLD

THOU dost to rich attire a grace,
    To let it deck itself with thee,
    And teachest pomp strange cunning ways
To be thought simplicity.
But lilies, stolen from grassy mold,
No more curlèd state unfold
Translated to a vase of gold;
In burning throne though they keep still
Serenities unthawed and chill.
Therefore, albeit thou'rt stately so,
In statelier state thou us'dst to go.

Though jewels should phosphoric burn
Through those night-waters of thine hair,
A flower from its translucid urn
Poured silver flame more lunar-fair.
These futile trappings but recall
Degenerate worshippers who fall
In purfled kirtle and brocade
To 'parel the white Mother-Maid.
For, as her image stood arrayed
In vests of its self-substance wrought
To measure of the sculptor's thought—
Slurred by those added braveries;
So for thy spirit did devise
Its Maker seemly garniture,
Of its own essence parcel pure,—
From grave simplicities a dress,

GILDED GOLD

And reticent demurenesses,
And love encinctured with reserve;
Which the woven vesture should subserve.
For outward robes in their ostents
Should show the soul's habiliments.
Therefore I say,—Thou'rt fair even so,
But better Fair I use to know.

The violet would thy dusk hair deck
With graces like thine own unsought.
Ah! but such place would daze and wreck
Its simple, lowly, rustic thought;
For so advancèd, dear, to thee,
It would unlearn humility!
Yet do not, with an altered look,
In these weak numbers read rebuke;
Which are but jealous lest too much
God's master-piece thou shouldst retouch.
Where a sweetness is complete,
Add not sweets unto the sweet!
Or, as thou wilt, for others so
In unfamiliar richness go;
But keep for mine acquainted eyes
The fashions of thy Paradise.

VII
HER PORTRAIT

OH, but the heavenly grammar did I hold
　　Of that high speech which angels'tongues turn gold!
　　So should her deathless beauty take no wrong,
Praised in her own great kindred's fit and cognate tongue :
Or if that language yet with us abode
Which Adam in the garden talked with God !
But our untempered speech descends—poor heirs !
Grimy and rough-cast still from Babel's bricklayers :
Curse on the brutish jargon we inherit,
Strong but to damn, not memorize, a spirit !
A cheek, a lip, a limb, a bosom, they
Move with light ease in speech of working-day ;
And women we do use to praise even so.
But here the gates we burst, and to the temple go.
Their praise were her dispraise : who dare, who dare,
Adulate the seraphim for their burning hair ?
How, if with them I dared, here should I dare it ?
How praise the woman, who but know the spirit ?
How praise the colour of her eyes, uncaught
While they were coloured with her varying thought ?
How her mouth's shape, who only use to know
What tender shape her speech will fit it to ?
Or her lips redness, when their joinèd veil
Song's fervid hand has parted till it wore them pale ?

If I would praise her soul (temerarious if !),
All must be mystery and hieroglyph.

HER PORTRAIT

Heaven, which not oft is prodigal of its more
To singers, in their song too great before
(By which the hierarch of large poesy is
Restrained to his one sacred benefice)
Only for her the salutary awe
Relaxes and stern canon of its law;
To her alone concedes pluralities,
In her alone to reconcile agrees
The Muse, the Graces, and the Charities;
To her, who can the trust so well conduct,
To her it gives the use, to us the usufruct.

What of the dear administress then may
I utter, though I spoke her own carved perfect way?
What of her daily gracious converse known,
Whose heavenly despotism must needs dethrone
And subjugate all sweetness but its own?
Deep in my heart subsides the infrequent word,
And there dies slowly throbbing like a wounded bird.
What of her silence, that outsweetens speech?
What of her thoughts, high marks for mine own
      thoughts to reach?
Yet, (Chaucer's antique sentence so to turn)
Most gladly will she teach, and gladly learn;
And teaching her, by her enchanting art,
The master threefold learns for all he can impart.
Now all is said, and all being said,—aye me!
There yet remains unsaid the very She.
Nay, to conclude (so to conclude I dare),
If of her virtues you evade the snare,
Then for her faults you'll fall in love with her.

LOVE IN DIAN'S LAP

Alas, and I have spoken of her Muse—
Her Muse, that died with her auroral dews!
Learn, the wise cherubim from harps of gold
Seduce a trepidating music manifold;
But the superior seraphim do know
None other music but to flame and glow.
So she first lighted on our frosty earth,
A sad musician, of cherubic birth,
Playing to alien ears—which did not prize
The uncomprehended music of the skies—
The exiled airs of her far Paradise.
But soon, from her own harpings taking fire,
In love and light her melodies expire.
Now Heaven affords her, for her silenced hymn,
A double portion of the seraphim.

At the rich odours from her heart that rise,
My soul remembers its lost Paradise,
And antenatal gales blow from Heaven's shores of spice;
I grow essential all, uncloaking me
From this encumbering virility,
And feel the primal sex of heaven and poetry:
And, parting from her, in me linger on
Vague snatches of Uranian antiphon.

How to the petty prison could she shrink
Of femineity?—Nay, but I think
In a dear courtesy her spirit would
Woman assume, for grace to womanhood.
Or, votaress to the virgin Sanctitude
Of reticent withdrawal's sweet, courted pale,

HER PORTRAIT

She took the cloistral flesh, the sexual veil,
Of her sad, aboriginal sisterhood;
The habit of cloistral flesh which founding Eve indued.

Thus do I know her. But for what men call
Beauty—the loveliness corporeal,
Its most just praise a thing unproper were
To singer or to listener, me or her.
She wears that body but as one indues
A robe, half careless, for it is the use;
Although her soul and it so fair agree,
We sure may, unattaint of heresy,
Conceit it might the soul's begetter be.
The immortal could we cease to contemplate,
The mortal part suggests its every trait.
God laid His fingers on the ivories
Of her pure members as on smoothèd keys,
And there out-breathed her spirit's harmonies.
I'll speak a little proudly :—I disdain
To count the beauty worth my wish or gain,
Which the dull daily fool can covet or obtain.
I do confess the fairness of the spoil,
But from such rivalry it takes a soil.
For her I'll proudlier speak :—how could it be
That I should praise the gilding on the psaltery?
'Tis not for her to hold that prize a prize,
Or praise much praise, though proudest in its wise,
To which even hopes of merely women rise.
Such strife would to the vanquished laurels yield,
Against *her* suffered to have lost a field.
Herself must with herself be sole compeer,

LOVE IN DIAN'S LAP

Unless the people of her distant sphere
Some gold migration send to melodize the year.
But first our hearts must burn in larger guise,
To reformate the uncharitable skies,
And so the deathless plumage to acclimatize:
Since this, their sole congener in our clime,
Droops her sad, ruffled thoughts for half the shivering time.

Yet I have felt what terrors may consort
In women's cheeks, the Graces' soft resort;
My hand hath shook at gentle hands' access,
And trembled at the waving of a tress;
My blood known panic fear, and fled dismayed,
Where ladies' eyes have set their ambuscade;
The rustle of a robe hath been to me
The very rattle of love's musketry;
Although my heart hath beat the loud advance,
I have recoiled before a challenging glance,
Proved gay alarms where warlike ribbons dance.
And from it all, this knowledge have I got,—
The whole that others have, is less than they have not;
All which makes other women noted fair,
Unnoted would remain and overshone in her.

How should I gauge what beauty is her dole,
Who cannot see her countenance for her soul,
As birds see not the casement for the sky?
And, as 'tis check they prove its presence by,
I know not of her body till I find
My flight debarred the heaven of her mind.
Hers is the face whence all should copied be,

HER PORTRAIT

Did God make replicas of such as she;
Its presence felt by what it does abate,
Because the soul shines through tempered and mitigate:
Where—as a figure labouring at night
Beside the body of a splendid light—
Dark Time works hidden by its luminousness;
And every line he labours to impress
Turns added beauty, like the veins that run
Athwart a leaf which hangs against the sun.

There regent Melancholy wide controls;
There Earth- and Heaven-Love play for aureoles;
There Sweetness out of Sadness breaks at fits,
Like bubbles on dark water, or as flits
A sudden silver fin through its deep infinites;
There amorous Thought has sucked pale Fancy's breath,
And Tenderness sits looking toward the lands of Death:
There Feeling stills her breathing with her hand,
And Dream from Melancholy part wrests the wand;
And on this lady's heart, looked you so deep,
Poor Poetry has rocked himself to sleep:
Upon the heavy blossom of her lips
Hangs the bee Musing; nigh her lids eclipse
Each half-occulted star beneath that lies;
And, in the contemplation of those eyes,
Passionless passion, wild tranquillities.

EPILOGUE TO THE POET S SITTER

herein he excuseth himself for the manner of the Portrait.

ALAS! now wilt thou chide, and say (I deem)
My figured descant hides the simple theme:
Or, in another wise reproving, say
I ill observe thine own high reticent way.
Oh, pardon, that I testify of thee
What thou couldst never speak, nor others be!

Yet (for the book is not more innocent
Of what the gazer's eyes makes so intent),
She will but smile, perhaps, that I find my fair
Sufficing scope in such strait theme as her.
' Bird of the sun! the stars' wild honey-bee!
Is your gold browsing done so thoroughly?
Or sinks a singèd wing to narrow nest in me?'
(Thus she might say: for not this lowly vein
Out-deprecates her deprecating strain.)
Oh, you mistake, dear lady, quite; nor know
Ether was strict as you, its loftiness as low!

The heavens do not advance their majesty
Over their marge; beyond his empery
The ensigns of the wind are not unfurled,
His reign is hooped in by the pale o' the world.
'Tis not the continent, but the contained,
That pleasaunce makes or prison, loose o: chained.
Too much alike or little captives me,
For all oppression is captivity.

EPILOGUE TO THE POET'S SITTER

What groweth to its height demands no higher;
The limit limits not, but the desire.
Our minds make their own Termini, nor call
The issuing circumscriptions great or small;
So high constructing Nature lessons to us all:
Who optics gives accommodate to see
Your countenance large as looks the sun to be,
And distant greatness less than near humanity.

We, therefore, with a sure instinctive mind,
An equal spaciousness of bondage find
In confines far or near, of air or our own kind.
Our looks and longings, which affront the stars,
Most richly bruised against their golden bars,
Delighted captives of their flaming spears,
Find a restraint restrainless which appears
As that is, and so simply natural,
In you;—the fair detention freedom call,
And overscroll with fancies the loved prison-wall.

Such sweet captivity, and only such,
In you, as in those golden bars, we touch!
Our gazes for sufficing limits know
The firmament above, your face below;
Our longings are contented with the skies,
Contented with the heaven, and your eyes.
My restless wings, that beat the whole world through,
Flag on the confines of the sun and you;
And find the human pale remoter of the two.

VIII.

DOMUS TUA

A PERFECT woman—Thine be laud!
Her body is a Temple of God.
At Doom-bar dare I make avows:
I have loved the beauty of Thy house.

IX
IN HER PATHS

AND she has trod before me in these ways!
    I think that she has left here heavenlier days;
    And I do guess her passage, as the skies
        Of holy Paradise
        Turn deeply holier,
And, looking up with sudden new delight,
One knows a seraph-wing has passed in flight.

The air is purer for her breathing, sure!
        And all the fields do wear
        The beauty fallen from her;
The winds do brush me with her robe's allure.
'Tis she has taught the heavens to look sweet,
        And they do but repeat
The heaven, heaven, heaven of her face!
The clouds have studied going from her grace!
The pools whose marges had forgot the tread
Of Naiad, disenchanted, fled,
        A second time must mourn,
        Bereaven and forlorn.

    *   *   *   *   *   *

Ah, foolish pools and meads! You did not see
Essence of old, essential pure as she.
For this was even that Lady, and none other,
The man in me calls 'Love,' the child calls 'Mother.'

X
AFTER HER GOING

THE after-even! Ah, did I walk,
    Indeed, in her or even?
    For nothing of me or around
But absent She did leaven,
Felt in my body as its soul,
    And in my soul its heaven.

'Ah me! my very flesh turns soul,
    Essenced,' I sighed, 'with bliss!'
And the blackbird held his lutany,
    All fragrant-through with bliss;
And all things stilled were as a maid
    Sweet with a single kiss.

For grief of perfect fairness, eve
    Could nothing do but smile;
The time was far too perfect fair,
    Being but for a while;
And ah, in me, too happy grief
    Blinded herself with smile!

The sunset at its radiant heart
    Had somewhat unconfest:
The bird was loath of speech, its song
    Half-refluent on its breast,
And made melodious toyings with
    A note or two at best.

AFTER HER GOING

And she was gone, my sole, my Fair,
  Ah, sole my Fair, was gone!
Methinks, throughout the world 'twere right
  I had been sad alone;
And yet, such sweet in all things' heart,
  And such sweet in my own!

XI
BENEATH A PHOTOGRAPH

PHŒBUS, who taught me art divine,
   Here tried his hand where I did mine;
   And his white fingers in this face
Set my Fair's sigh-suggesting grace.
O sweetness past profaning guess,
Grievous with its own exquisiteness!
Vesper-like face, its shadows bright
With meanings of sequestered light;
Drooped with shamefast sanctities
She purely fears eyes cannot miss,
Yet would blush to know she *is*.
Ah, who can view with passionless glance
This tear-compelling countenance?
He has cozened it to tell
Almost its own miracle.
Yet I, all-viewing though he be,
Methinks saw further here than he;
And, Master gay, I swear I drew
Something the better of the two!

THE HOUND OF HEAVEN

THE HOUND OF HEAVEN

I FLED Him, down the nights and down the days;
I fled Him, down the arches of the years;
I fled Him, down the labyrinthine ways
  Of my own mind; and in the mist of tears
I hid from Him, and under running laughter.
      Up vistaed hopes I sped;
      And shot, precipitated,
Adown Titanic glooms of chasmèd fears,
  From those strong Feet that followed, followed after.
      But with unhurrying chase,
      And unperturbèd pace,
  Deliberate speed, majestic instancy,
      They beat—and a Voice beat
      More instant than the Feet—
'All things betray thee, who betrayest Me.'

      I pleaded, outlaw-wise,
By many a hearted casement, curtained red,
  Trellised with intertwining charities;
(For, though I knew His love Who followèd,
      Yet was I sore adread
Lest, having Him, I must have naught beside).
But, if one little casement parted wide,
  The gust of His approach would clash it to.
  Fear wist not to evade, as Love wist to pursue.
Across the margent of the world I fled,
  And troubled the gold gateways of the stars,
  Smiting for shelter on their clangèd bars;

THE HOUND OF HEAVEN

  Fretted to dulcet jars
And silvern chatter the pale ports o' the moon.
I said to Dawn : Be sudden—to Eve : Be soon ;
  With thy young skiey blossoms heap me over
   From this tremendous Lover—
Float thy vague veil about me, lest He see !
I tempted all His servitors, but to find
My own betrayal in their constancy,
In faith to Him their fickleness to me,
  Their traitorous trueness, and their loyal deceit.
To all swift things for swiftness did I sue ;
  Clung to the whistling mane of every wind.
   But whether they swept, smoothly fleet,
    The long savannahs of the blue ;
    Or whether, Thunder-driven,
   They clanged his chariot 'thwart a heaven,
Plashy with flying lightnings round the spurn o' their
  feet :—
Fear wist not to evade as Love wist to pursue.
   Still with unhurrying chase,
   And unperturbèd pace,
  Deliberate speed, majestic instancy,
   Came on the following Feet,
   And a Voice above their beat—
' Naught shelters thee, who wilt not shelter Me.'

I sought no more that after which I strayed
   In face of man or maid ;
But still within the little children's eyes
  Seems something, something that replies,
They at least are for me, surely for me !

THE HOUND OF HEAVEN

I turned me to them very wistfully;
But just as their young eyes grew sudden fair
   With dawning answers there,
Their angel plucked them from me by the hair.
' Come then, ye other children, Nature's—share
With me ' (said I) ' your delicate fellowship;
   Let me greet you lip to lip,
   Let me twine with you caresses,
     Wantoning
   With our Lady-Mother's vagrant tresses,
     Banqueting
   With her in her wind-walled palace,
   Underneath her azured daïs,
   Quaffing, as your taintless way is,
     From a chalice
Lucent-weeping out of the dayspring.'
     So it was done:
I in their delicate fellowship was one—
Drew the bolt of Nature's secrecies.
   I knew all the swift importings
   On the wilful face of skies;
   I knew how the clouds arise
   Spumèd of the wild sea-snortings;
     All that's born or dies
   Rose and drooped with; made them shapers
Of mine own moods, or wailful or divine;
   With them joyed and was bereaven.
   I was heavy with the even,
   When she lit her glimmering tapers
   Round the day's dead sanctities.
   I laughed in the morning's eyes.

THE HOUND OF HEAVEN

I triumphed and I saddened with all weather,
    Heaven and I wept together,
And its sweet tears were salt with mortal mine;
Against the red throb of its sunset-heart
    I laid my own to beat,
    And share commingling heat;
But not by that, by that, was eased my human smart.
In vain my tears were wet on Heaven's grey cheek.
For ah! we know not what each other says,
    These things and I; in sound *I* speak—
Their sound is but their stir, they speak by silences.
Nature, poor stepdame, cannot slake my drouth;
    Let her, if she would owe me,
Drop yon blue bosom-veil of sky, and show me
    The breasts o' her tenderness:
Never did any milk of hers once bless
    My thirsting mouth.
    Nigh and nigh draws the chase,
    With unperturbèd pace,
    Deliberate speed, majestic instancy;
    And past those noisèd Feet
    A voice comes yet more fleet—
' Lo! naught contents thee, who content'st
    not Me.'

Naked I wait Thy love's uplifted stroke!
My harness piece by piece Thou hast hewn from me,
    And smitten me to my knee;
    I am defenceless utterly.
    I slept, methinks, and woke,
And, slowly gazing, find me stripped in sleep.

THE HOUND OF HEAVEN

In the rash lustihead of my young powers,
    I shook the pillaring hours
And pulled my life upon me; grimed with smears,
I stand amid the dust o' the moulded years—
My mangled youth lies dead beneath the heap.
My days have crackled and gone up in smoke,
Have puffed and burst as sun-starts on a stream.
    Yea, faileth now even dream
The dreamer, and the lute the lutanist;
Even the linked fantasies, in whose blossomy twist
I swung the earth a trinket at my wrist,
Are yielding; cords of all too weak account
For earth with heavy griefs so overplussed.
    Ah! is Thy love indeed
A weed, albeit an amaranthine weed,
Suffering no flowers except its own to mount?
    Ah! must—
      Designer infinite!—
Ah! must Thou char the wood ere Thou canst limn
    with it?
My freshness spent its wavering shower i' the dust;
And now my heart is as a broken fount,
Wherein tear-drippings stagnate, spilt down ever
    From the dank thoughts that shiver
Upon the sighful branches of my mind.
    Such is; what is to be?
The pulp so bitter, how shall taste the rind?
I dimly guess what Time in mists confounds;
Yet ever and anon a trumpet sounds
From the hid battlements of Eternity;
Those shaken mists a space unsettle, then

THE HOUND OF HEAVEN

Round the half-glimpsèd turrets slowly wash again.
    But not ere him who summoneth
    I first have seen, enwound
With glooming robes purpureal, cypress-crowned;
His name I know, and what his trumpet saith.
Whether man's heart or life it be which yields
    Thee harvest, must Thy harvest-fields
    Be dunged with rotten death?

        Now of that long pursuit
        Comes on at hand the bruit;
    That Voice is round me like a bursting sea:
        ' And is thy earth so marred,
        Shattered in shard on shard?
    Lo, all things fly thee, for thou fliest Me!
    Strange, piteous, futile thing!
Wherefore should any set thee love apart?
Seeing none but I makes much of naught' (He said),
' And human love needs human meriting:
    How hast thou merited—
Of all man's clotted clay the dingiest clot?
    Alack, thou knowest not
How little worthy of any love thou art!
Whom wilt thou find to love ignoble thee,
    Save Me, save only Me?
All which I took from thee I did but take,
    Not for thy harms,
But just that thou might'st seek it in My arms.
    All which thy child's mistake
Fancies as lost, I have stored for thee at home:
    Rise, clasp My hand, and come!'

THE HOUND OF HEAVEN

    Halts by me that footfall :
    Is my gloom, after all,
Shade of His hand, outstretched caressingly ?
    ' Ah, fondest, blindest, weakest,
    I am He Whom thou seekest !
Thou dravest love from thee, who dravest Me.'

ODE TO THE SETTING SUN

ODE TO THE SETTING SUN
PRELUDE

THE wailful sweetness of the violin
    Floats down the hushèd waters of the wind,
    The heart-strings of the throbbing harp begin
To long in aching music. Spirit-pined,

In wafts that poignant sweetness drifts, until
    The wounded soul ooze sadness. The red sun,
A bubble of fire, drops slowly toward the hill,
    While one bird prattles that the day is done.

O setting Sun, that as in reverent days
    Sinkest in music to thy smoothèd sleep,
Discrowned of homage, though yet crowned with rays,
    Hymned not at harvest more, though reapers reap:

For thee this music wakes not. O deceived,
    If thou hear in these thoughtless harmonies
A pious phantom of adorings reaved,
    And echo of fair ancient flatteries!

Yet, in this field where the Cross planted reigns,
    I know not what strange passion bows my head
To thee, whose great command upon my veins
    Proves thee a god for me not dead, not dead!

ODE TO THE SETTING SUN

For worship it is too incredulous,
 For doubt—oh, too believing-passionate!
What wild divinity makes my heart thus
 A fount of most baptismal tears?—Thy straight

Long beam lies steady on the Cross. Ah me!
 What secret would thy radiant finger show?
Of thy bright mastership is this the key?
 Is *this* thy secret, then? And is it woe?

Fling from thine ear the burning curls, and hark
 A song thou hast not heard in Northern day;
For Rome too daring, and for Greece too dark,
 Sweet with wild wings that pass, that pass away!

ODE

ALPHA and Omega, sadness and mirth,
 The springing music, and its wasting breath—
 The fairest things in life are Death and Birth,
And of these two the fairer thing is Death.
Mystical twins of Time inseparable,
 The younger hath the holier array,
 And hath the awfuller sway:
 It is the falling star that trails the light,
 It is the breaking wave that hath the might,
The passing shower that rainbows maniple.
 Is it not so, O thou down-stricken Day,
That draw'st thy splendours round thee in thy fall?
High was thine Eastern pomp inaugural;

ODE TO THE SETTING SUN

But thou dost set in statelier pageantry,
   Lauded with tumults of a firmament:
Thy visible music-blasts make deaf the sky,
   Thy cymbals clang to fire the Occident,
Thou dost thy dying so triumphally:
I *see* the crimson blaring of thy shawms!
       Why do those lucent palms
Strew thy feet's failing thicklier than their might,
Who dost but hood thy glorious eyes with night,
And vex the heels of all the yesterdays?
       Lo! this loud, lackeying praise
Will stay behind to greet the usurping moon,
   When they have cloud-barred over thee the West.
Oh, shake the bright dust from thy parting shoon!
   The earth not pæans thee, nor serves thy hest;
Be godded not by Heaven! avert thy face,
       And leave to blank disgrace
The oblivious world! unsceptre thee of state and place!

Ha! but bethink thee what thou gazedst on,
   Ere yet the snake Decay had venomed tooth;
The name thou bar'st in those vast seasons gone—
       Candid Hyperion,
   Clad in the light of thine immortal youth!
       Ere Dionysus bled thy vines,
Or Artemis drave her clamours through the wood,
      Thou saw'st how once against Olympus' height
        The brawny Titans stood,
And shook the gods' world 'bout their ears, and how
Enceladus (whom Etna cumbers now)
   Shouldered me Pelion with its swinging pines,

ODE TO THE SETTING SUN

The river unrecked, that did its broken flood
Spurt on his back : before the mountainous shock
    The rankèd gods dislock,
Scared to their skies ; wide o'er rout-trampled night
Flew spurned the pebbled stars : those splendours then
   Had tempested on earth, star upon star
   Mounded in ruin, if a longer war
Had quaked Olympus and cold-fearing men.
        Then did the ample marge
        And circuit of thy targe
     Sullenly redden all the vaward fight,
       Above the blusterous clash
       Wheeled thy swung falchion's flash,
     And hewed their forces into splintered flight.

Yet ere Olympus thou wast, and a god !
    Though we deny thy nod,
We cannot spoil thee of thy divinity.
    What know we elder than thee ?
When thou didst, bursting from the great void's husk,
Leap like a lion on the throat o' the dusk ;
    When the angels rose-chapleted
      Sang each to other,
     The vaulted blaze overhead
     Of their vast pinions spread,
      Hailing thee brother ;
How chaos rolled back from the wonder,
And the First Morn knelt down to thy visage of
    thunder !
    Thou didst draw to thy side
    Thy young Auroral bride,

ODE TO THE SETTING SUN

    And lift her veil of night and mystery;
        Tellus with baby hands
        Shook off her swaddling-bands,
    And from the unswathèd vapours laughed to thee.

Thou twi-form deity, nurse at once and sire!
    Thou genitor that all things nourishest!
    The earth was suckled at thy shining breast,
And in her veins is quick thy milky fire.
Who scarfed her with the morning? and who set
Upon her brow the day-fall's carcanet?
    Who queened her front with the enrondured moon?
    Who dug night's jewels from their vaulty mine
        To dower her, past an eastern wizard's dreams,
    When, hovering on him through his haschish-swoon,
    All the rained gems of the old Tartarian line
Shiver in lustrous throbbings of tinged flame?
        Whereof a moiety in the Paolis' seams
        Statelily builded their Venetian name.
        Thou hast enwoofèd her
        An empress of the air,
And all her births are propertied by thee:
        Her teeming centuries
        Drew being from thine eyes:
Thou fatt'st the marrow of all quality.

Who lit the furnace of the mammoth's heart?
    Who shagged him like Pilatus' ribbèd flanks?
        Who raised the columned ranks
Of that old pre-diluvian forestry,
Which like a continent torn oppressed the sea,

ODE TO THE SETTING SUN

When the ancient heavens did in rains depart,
   While the high-truncèd whirls
Of the tossed scud made hiss thy drenchèd curls?
   Thou rear'dst the enormous brood;
   Who hast with life imbued
   The lion maned in tawny majesty,
      The tiger velvet-barred,
      The stealthy-stepping pard,
And the lithe panther's flexuous symmetry.

How came the entombèd tree a light-bearer,
      Though sunk in lightless lair?
      Friend of the forgers of earth,
   Mate of the earthquake and thunders volcanic,
   Clasped in the arms of the forces Titanic
      Which rock like a cradle the girth
         Of the ether-hung world;
      Swart son of the swarthy mine,
   When flame on the breath of his nostrils feeds
      How is his countenance half-divine,
      Like thee in thy sanguine weeds?
      Thou gavest him his light,
      Though sepultured in night
Beneath the dead bones of a perished world;
      Over his prostrate form
      Though cold, and heat, and storm,
The mountainous wrack of a creation hurled.

   Who made the splendid rose
   Saturate with purple glows;
Cupped to the marge with beauty; a perfume-press

122

ODE TO THE SETTING SUN

    Whence the wind vintages
Gushes of warmèd fragrance richer far
  Than all the flavorous ooze of Cyprus' vats?
Lo, in yon gale which waves her green cymar,
    With dusky cheeks burnt red
    She sways her heavy head,
Drunk with the must of her own odorousness;
  While in a moted trouble the vexed gnats
  Maze, and vibrate, and tease the noontide hush.
  Who girt dissolvèd lightnings in the grape?
  Summered the opal with an Irised flush?
    Is it not thou that dost the tulip drape,
      And huest the daffodilly,
      Yet who hast snowed the lily,
And her frail sister, whom the waters name,
  Dost vestal-vesture 'mid the blaze of June,
  Cold as the new-sprung girlhood of the moon
Ere Autumn's kiss sultry her cheek with flame?
    Thou sway'st thy sceptred beam
    O'er all delight and dream,
Beauty is beautiful but in thy glance:
    And like a jocund maid
    In garland-flowers arrayed,
Before thy ark Earth keeps her sacred dance.

And now, O shaken from thine antique throne,
  And sunken from thy cœrule empery,
Now that the red glare of thy fall is blown
  In smoke and flame about the windy sky,
Where are the wailing voices that should meet
  From hill, stream, grove, and all of mortal shape

ODE TO THE SETTING SUN

Who tread thy gifts, in vineyards as stray feet
  Pulp the globed weight of juiced Iberia's grape?
    Where is the threne o' the sea?
    And why not dirges thee
The wind, that sings to himself as he makes stride
  Lonely and terrible on the Andéan height?
    Where is the Naiad 'mid her sworded sedge?
    The Nymph wan-glimmering by her wan fount's
      verge?
The Dryad at timid gaze by the wood-side?
    The Oread jutting light
  On one up-strainèd sole from the rock-ledge?
    The Nereid tip-toe on the scud o' the surge,
With whistling tresses dank athwart her face,
And all her figure poised in lithe Circean grace?
    Why withers their lament?
    Their tresses tear-besprent,
  Have they sighed hence with trailing garment-hem?
    O sweet, O sad, O fair,
    I catch your flying hair,
Draw your eyes down to me, and dream on them!

A space, and they fleet from me. Must ye fade—
O old, essential candours, ye who made
    The earth a living and a radiant thing—
      And leave her corpse in our strained, cheated arms?
      Lo ever thus, when Song with chorded charms
Draws from dull death his lost Eurydice,
  Lo ever thus, even at consummating,
  Even in the swooning minute that claims her his,
  Even as he trembles to the impassioned kiss

ODE TO THE SETTING SUN

    Of reincarnate Beauty, his control
    Clasps the cold body, and forgoes the soul !
      Whatso looks lovelily
Is but the rainbow on life's weeping rain.
Why have we longings of immortal pain,
And all we long for mortal ? Woe is me,
And all our chants but chaplet some decay,
As mine this vanishing—nay, vanished Day.
The low sky-line dusks to a leaden hue,
    No rift disturbs the heavy shade and chill,
Save one, where the charred firmament lets through
    The scorching dazzle of Heaven ; 'gainst which
        the hill,
      Out-flattened sombrely,
Stands black as life against eternity.
      Against eternity ?
      A rifting light in me
Burns through the leaden broodings of the mind :
    O blessèd Sun, thy state
    Uprisen or derogate
Dafts me no more with doubt ; I seek and find.

    If with exultant tread
      Thou foot the Eastern sea,
      Or like a golden bee
    Sting the West to angry red,
Thou dost image, thou dost follow
    That King-Maker of Creation,
    Who, ere Hellas hailed Apollo,
      Gave thee, angel-god, thy station ;
Thou art of Him a type memorial.

ODE TO THE SETTING SUN

Like Him thou hang'st in dreadful pomp of blood
    Upon thy Western rood;
And His stained brow did vail like thine to night,
    Yet lift once more Its light,
And, risen, again departed from our ball,
But when It set on earth arose in Heaven.
Thus hath He unto death His beauty given:
And so of all which form inheriteth
    The fall doth pass the rise in worth;
For birth hath in itself the germ of death,
    But death hath in itself the germ of birth.
It is the falling acorn buds the tree,
The falling rain that bears the greenery,
    The fern-plants moulder when the ferns arise.
    For there is nothing lives but something dies,
And there is nothing dies but something lives.
    Till skies be fugitives,
Till Time, the hidden root of change, updries,
Are Birth and Death inseparable on earth;
For they are twain yet one, and Death is Birth.

AFTER-STRAIN

NOW with wan ray that other sun of Song
    Sets in the bleakening waters of my soul:
One step, and lo! the Cross stands gaunt and long
    'Twixt me and yet bright skies, a presaged dole.

Even so, O Cross! thine is the victory.
    Thy roots are fast within our fairest fields;

ODE TO THE SETTING SUN

Brightness may emanate in Heaven from thee,
Here thy dread symbol only shadow yields.

Of reapèd joys thou art the heavy sheaf
  Which must be lifted, though the reaper groan;
Yea, we may cry till Heaven's great ear be deaf,
  But we must bear thee, and must bear alone.

Vain were a Simon; of the Antipodes
  Our night not borrows the superfluous day.
Yet woe to him that from his burden flees,
  Crushed in the fall of what he cast away.

Therefore, O tender Lady, Queen Mary,
  Thou gentleness that dost enmoss and drape
The Cross's rigorous austerity,
  Wipe thou the blood from wounds that needs must gape.

' Lo, though suns rise and set, but crosses stay,
  I leave thee ever,' saith she, ' light of cheer.'
'Tis so : yon sky still thinks upon the Day,
  And showers aërial blossoms on his bier.

Yon cloud with wrinkled fire is edgèd sharp;
  And once more welling through the air, ah me!
How the sweet viol plains him to the harp,
  Whose pangèd sobbings throng tumultuously.

Oh, this Medusa-pleasure with her stings!
This essence of all suffering, which is joy!

ODE TO THE SETTING SUN

I am not thankless for the spell it brings,
    Though tears must be told down for the charmed toy.

No; while soul, sky, and music bleed together,
    Let me give thanks even for those griefs in me,
The restless windward stirrings of whose feather
    Prove them the brood of immortality.

My soul is quitted of death-neighbouring swoon,
    Who shall not slake her immitigable scars
Until she hear ' My sister! ' from the moon,
    And take the kindred kisses of the stars.

TO THE DEAD CARDINAL OF WESTMINSTER
(Henry Edward Manning : Died January 1892)

TO THE DEAD CARDINAL
OF WESTMINSTER

I WILL not perturbate
Thy Paradisal state
 With praise
Of thy dead days;

To the new-heavened say,
' Spirit, thou wert fine clay ':
 This do,
Thy praise who knew.

Therefore my spirit clings
Heaven's porter by the wings,
 And holds
Its gated golds

Apart, with thee to press
A private business ;—
 Whence,
Deign me audience.

Anchorite, who didst dwell
With all the world for cell,
 My soul
Round me doth roll

A sequestration bare.
Too far alike we were,
 Too far
Dissimilar.

TO THE DEAD CARDINAL OF WESTMINSTER

For its burning fruitage I
Do climb the tree o' the sky;
　　Do prize
　Some human eyes.

You smelt the Heaven-blossoms,
And all the sweet embosoms
　　The dear
　Uranian year.

Those Eyes my weak gaze shuns,
Which to the suns are Suns,
　　Did
　Not affray your lid.

The carpet was let down
(With golden moultings strown)
　　For you
　Of the angels' blue.

But I, ex-Paradised,
The shoulder of your Christ
　　Find high
　To lean thereby.

So flaps my helpless sail,
Bellying with neither gale,
　　Of Heaven
　Nor Orcus even.

TO THE DEAD CARDINAL OF WESTMINSTER

Life is a coquetry
Of Death, which wearies me,
    Too sure
    Of the amour;

A tiring-room where I
Death's divers garments try,
    Till fit
    Some fashion sit.

It seemeth me too much
I do rehearse for such
    A mean
    And single scene.

The sandy glass hence bear—
Antique remembrancer:
    My veins
    Do spare its pains.

With secret sympathy
My thoughts repeat in me
    Infirm
    The turn o' the worm

Beneath my appointed sod;
The grave is in my blood;
    I shake
    To winds that take

TO THE DEAD CARDINAL OF WESTMINSTER

Its grasses by the top;
The rains thereon that drop
    Perturb
  With drip acerb

My subtly answering soul;
The feet across its knoll
    Do jar
  Me from afar.

As sap foretastes the spring;
As Earth ere blossoming
    Thrills
  With far daffodils,

And feels her breast turn sweet
With the unconceivèd wheat;
    So doth
  My flesh foreloathe

The abhorrèd spring of Dis,
With seething presciences
    Affirm
  The preparate worm.

I have no thought that I,
When at the last I die,
    Shall reach
  To gain your speech.

TO THE DEAD CARDINAL OF WESTMINSTER

But you, should that be so,
May very well, I know,
  May well
  To me in hell

With recognizing eyes
Look from your Paradise—
  ' God bless
  Thy hopelessness ! '

Call, holy soul, O call
The hosts angelical,
  And say,—
  ' See, far away

' Lies one I saw on earth ;
One stricken from his birth
  With curse
  Of destinate verse.

' What place doth He ye serve
For such sad spirit reserve,—
  Given,
  In dark lieu of Heaven,

' The impitiable Dæmon,
Beauty, to adore and dream on,
  To be
  Perpetually

TO THE DEAD CARDINAL OF WESTMINSTER

' Hers, but she never his ?
He reapeth miseries ;
    Foreknows
    His wages woes ;

' He lives detachèd days ;
He serveth not for praise ;
    For gold
    He is not sold ;

' Deaf is he to world's tongue ;
He scorneth for his song
    The loud
    Shouts of the crowd ;

' He asketh not world's eyes ;
Not to world's ears he cries ;
    Saith,—" These
    Shut, if ye please ! "

' He measureth world's pleasure,
World's ease, as Saints might measure ;
    For hire
    Just love entire

' He asks, not grudging pain ;
And knows his asking vain,
    And cries—
    " Love ! Love ! " and dies

TO THE DEAD CARDINAL OF WESTMINSTER

' In guerdon of long duty,
Unowned by Love or Beauty;
  And goes—
 Tell, tell, who knows!

' Aliens from Heaven's worth,
Fine beasts who nose i' the earth,
  Do there
 Reward prepare.

' But are *his* great desires
Food but for nether fires?
  Ah me,
 A mystery!

' Can it be his alone,
To find when all is known,
  That what
 He solely sought

' Is lost, and thereto lost
All that its seeking cost?
  That he
 Must finally,

' Through sacrificial tears,
And anchoretic years,
  Tryst
 With the sensualist?'

TO THE DEAD CARDINAL OF WESTMINSTER

    So ask; and if they tell
    The secret terrible,
        Good friend,
    I pray thee send

    Some high gold embassage
    To teach my unripe age.
        Tell!
    Lest my feet walk hell.

A CORYMBUS FOR AUTUMN

A CORYMBUS FOR AUTUMN

HEARKEN my chant, 'tis
    As a Bacchante's,
    A grape-spurt, a vine-splash, a tossed
tress, flown vaunt 'tis!
    Suffer my singing,
Gipsy of Seasons, ere thou go winging;
    Ere Winter throws
    His slaking snows
In thy feasting-flagon's impurpurate glows!
The sopped sun—toper as ever drank hard—
    Stares foolish, hazed,
    Rubicund, dazed,
Totty with thine October tankard.
Tanned maiden! with cheeks like apples russet,
    And breast a brown agaric faint-flushing at tip
And a mouth too red for the moon to buss it
    But her cheek unvow its vestalship;
    Thy mists enclip
Her steel-clear circuit illuminous,
    Until it crust
    Rubiginous
With the glorious gules of a glowing rust.

Far other saw we, other indeed,
    The crescent moon, in the May-days dead,
    Fly up with its slender white wings spread
Out of its nest in the sea's waved mead.

A CORYMBUS FOR AUTUMN

How are the veins of thee, Autumn, laden ?
    Umbered juices,
    And pulpèd oozes
Pappy out of the cherry-bruises,
Froth the veins of thee, wild, wild maiden !
    With hair that musters
    In globèd clusters,
In tumbling clusters, like swarthy grapes,
Round thy brow and thine ears o'ershaden ;
With the burning darkness of eyes like pansies,
    Like velvet pansies
    Wherethrough escapes
The splendid might of thy conflagrate fancies ;
    With robe gold-tawny not hiding the shapes
        Of the feet whereunto it falleth down,
    Thy naked feet unsandallèd ;
With robe gold-tawny that does not veil
    Feet where the red
    Is meshed in the brown,
Like a rubied sun in a Venice-sail.

The wassailous heart of the Year is thine !
His Bacchic fingers disentwine
    His coronal
    At thy festival ;
His revelling fingers disentwine
    Leaf, flower, and all,
    And let them fall
Blossom and all in thy wavering wine.
The Summer looks out from her brazen tower,
    Through the flashing bars of July,

A CORYMBUS FOR AUTUMN

Waiting thy ripened golden shower;
   Whereof there cometh, with sandals fleet,
     The North-west flying viewlessly,
   With a sword to sheer, and untameable feet,
     And the gorgon-head of the Winter shown
     To stiffen the gazing earth as stone.

   In crystal Heaven's magic sphere
     Poised in the palm of thy fervid hand,
   Thou seest the enchanted shows appear
   That stain Favonian firmament;
   Richer than ever the Occident
     Gave up to bygone Summer's wand.
Day's dying dragon lies drooping his crest,
Panting red pants into the West.
Or the butterfly sunset claps its wings
   With flitter alit on the swinging blossom,
The gusty blossom, that tosses and swings,
   Of the sea with its blown and ruffled bosom;
Its ruffled bosom wherethrough the wind sings
Till the crispèd petals are loosened and strown
     Overblown, on the sand;
     Shed, curling as dead
Rose-leaves curl, on the fleckèd strand.

Or higher, holier, saintlier when, as now,
All Nature sacerdotal seems, and thou.
   The calm hour strikes on yon golden gong,
     In tones of floating and mellow light
   A spreading summons to even-song:

A CORYMBUS FOR AUTUMN

      See how there
      The cowlèd Night
  Kneels on the Eastern sanctuary-stair.
What is this feel of incense everywhere?
  Clings it round folds of the blanch-amiced clouds,
Upwafted by the solemn thurifer,
      The mighty Spirit unknown,
That swingeth the slow earth before the embannered
      Throne?
Or is't the Season under all these shrouds
Of light, and sense, and silence, makes her known
      A presence everywhere,
      An inarticulate prayer,
A hand on the soothed tresses of the air?
      But there is one hour scant
Of this Titanian, primal liturgy;
    As there is but one hour for me and thee,
  Autumn, for thee and thine hierophant,
      Of this grave-ending chant.
      Round the earth still and stark
Heaven's death-lights kindle, yellow spark by spark,
Beneath the dreadful catafalque of the dark.

      And I had ended there:
But a great wind blew all the stars to flare,
And cried, 'I sweep the path before the moon!
Tarry ye now the coming of the moon,
      For she is coming soon';
Then died before the coming of the moon.
And she came forth upon the trepidant air,
      In vesture unimagined-fair,

A CORYMBUS FOR AUTUMN

    Woven as woof of flag-lilies;
    And curdled as of flag-lilies
    The vapour at the feet of her,
And a haze about her tinged in fainter wise;
    As if she had trodden the stars in press,
    Till the gold wine spurted over her dress,
    Till the gold wine gushed out round her feet;
    Spouted over her stainèd wear,
    And bubbled in golden froth at her feet,
    And hung like a whirlpool's mist round her.

    Still, mighty Season, do I see't,
    Thy sway is still majestical!
    Thou hold'st of God, by title sure,
Thine indefeasible investiture,
    And that right round thy locks are native to;
The heavens upon thy brow imperial,
    This huge terrene thy ball,
And o'er thy shoulders thrown wide air's depending pall.
    What if thine earth be blear and bleak of hue?
    Still, still the skies are sweet!
    Still, Season, still thou hast thy triumphs there!
    How have I, unaware,
Forgetful of my strain inaugural,
    Cleft the great rondure of thy reign complete,
Yielding thee half, who hast indeed the all?
    I will not think thy sovereignty begun
        But with the shepherd Sun
    That washes in the sea the stars' gold fleeces;
        Or that with Day it ceases,

A CORYMBUS FOR AUTUMN

Who sets his burning lips to the salt brine,
    And purples it to wine;
While I behold how ermined Artemis
    Ordainèd weed must wear,
    And toil thy business;
Who witness am of her,
Her too in autumn turned a vintager;
And, laden with its lampèd clusters bright,
The fiery-fruited vineyard of this night.

ECCLESIASTICAL BALLADS

[Of this series only two Ballads were completed: 'The Veteran of Heaven'—in some sense a divine parody of Macaulay's 'On the Battle of Naseby'; and a prophetic apostrophe of the Church under the title of 'The Lily of the King.']

I

THE VETERAN OF HEAVEN

O CAPTAIN of the wars, whence won Ye so great scars?
    In what fight did Ye smite, and what manner was the foe?
Was it on a day of rout they compassed Thee about,
    Or gat Ye these adornings when Ye wrought their overthrow?

' 'Twas on a day of rout they girded Me about,
    They wounded all My brow, and they smote Me through the side:
My hand held no sword when I met their armèd horde,
    And the conqueror fell down, and the Conquered bruised his pride.'

What is this, unheard before, that the Unarmed make war,
    And the Slain hath the gain, and the Victor hath the rout?
What wars, then, are these, and what the enemies,
    Strange Chief, with the scars of Thy conquest trenched about?

ECCLESIASTICAL BALLADS

' The Prince I drave forth held the Mount of the North,
   Girt with the guards of flame that roll round the pole.
I drave him with My wars from all his fortress-stars,
   And the sea of death divided that My march might strike its goal.

' In the keep of Northern Guard, many a great dæmonian sword
   Burns as it turns round the Mount occult, apart:
There is given him power and place still for some certain days,
   And his name would turn the Sun's blood back upon its heart.'

What is *Thy* Name? Oh, show!—' My Name ye may not know;
   'Tis a going forth with banners, and a baring of much swords:
But My tit'es that are high, are they not upon My thigh?
   " King of Kings!" are the words, " Lord of Lords!";
It is written " King of Kings, Lord of Lords." '

II
LILIUM REGIS

O LILY of the King! low lies thy silver wing,
 And long has been the hour of thine unqueening;
 And thy scent of Paradise on the night-wind
  spills its sighs,
 Nor any take the secrets of its meaning.
O Lily of the King! I speak a heavy thing,
 O patience, most sorrowful of daughters!
Lo, the hour is at hand for the troubling of the land,
 And red shall be the breaking of the waters.

Sit fast upon thy stalk, when the blast shall with thee talk,
 With the mercies of the King for thine awning;
And the just understand that thine hour is at hand,
 Thine hour at hand with power in the dawning.
When the nations lie in blood, and their kings a broken
  brood,
 Look up, O most sorrowful of daughters!
Lift up thy head and hark what sounds are in the dark,
 For His feet are coming to thee on the waters!

O Lily of the King! I shall not see, that sing,
 I shall not see the hour of thy queening!
But my Song shall see, and wake like a flower that dawn-
  winds shake,
 And sigh with joy the odours of its meaning.
O Lily of the King, remember then the thing
 That this dead mouth sang; and thy daughters,
As they dance before His way, sing there on the Day
 What I sang when the Night was on the waters!

TRANSLATIONS

A SUNSET

FROM HUGO'S 'FEUILLES D'AUTOMNE'

I LOVE the evenings, passionless and fair, I love the evens,
Whether old manor-fronts their ray with golden fulgence leavens,
    In numerous leafage bosomed close;
Whether the mist in reefs of fire extend its reaches sheer,
Or a hundred sunbeams splinter in an azure atmosphere
    On cloudy archipelagos.

Oh gaze ye on the firmament! a hundred clouds in motion,
Up-piled in the immense sublime beneath the winds' commotion,
    Their unimagined shapes accord:
Under their waves at intervals flames a pale levin through,
As if some giant of the air amid the vapours drew
    A sudden elemental sword.

The sun at bay with splendid thrusts still keeps the sullen fold;
And momently at distance sets, as a cupola of gold,
    The thatched roof of a cot a-glance;
Or on the blurred horizons joins his battle with the haze;
Or pools the glooming fields about with inter-isolate blaze,
    Great moveless meres of radiance.

TRANSLATIONS

Then mark you how there hangs athwart the firmament's swept track,
Yonder, a mighty crocodile with vast irradiant back,
    A triple row of pointed teeth ?
Under its burnished belly slips a ray of eventide,
The flickerings of a hundred glowing clouds its tenebrous side
    With scales of golden mail ensheathe.

Then mounts a palace, then the air vibrates—the vision flees.
Confounded to its base, the fearful cloudy edifice
    Ruins immense in mounded wrack :
Afar the fragments strew the sky, and each envermeiled cone
Hangeth, peak downward, overhead, like mountains overthrown
    When the earthquake heaves its hugy back.

These vapours, with their leaden, golden, iron, bronzèd glows,
Where the hurricane, the waterspout, thunder, and hell repose,
    Muttering hoarse dreams of destined harms,—
'Tis God who hangs their multitude amid the skiey deep,
As a warrior that suspendeth from the roof-tree of his keep
    His dreadful and resounding arms !

A SUNSET

All vanishes! The sun, from topmost heaven precipitated,
Like to a globe of iron which is tossed back fiery red
    Into the furnace stirred to fume,
Shocking the cloudy surges, plashed from its impetuous
    ire,
Even to the zenith spattereth in a flecking scud of fire
    The vaporous and inflamèd spume.

O contemplate the heavens! Whenas the vein-drawn
    day dies pale,
In every season, every place, gaze through their every
    veil,
    With love that has not speech for need!
Beneath their solemn beauty is a mystery infinite:
If winter hue them like a pall, or if the summer night
    Fantasy them with starry brede.

HEARD ON THE MOUNTAIN
FROM HUGO'S 'FEUILLES D'AUTOMNE'

HAVE you sometimes, calm, silent, let your tread aspirant rise
Up to the mountain's summit, in the presence of the skies?
Was't on the borders of the South? or on the Bretagne coast?
And at the basis of the mount had you the Ocean tossed?
And there, leaned o'er the wave and o'er the immeasurableness,
Calm, silent, have you hearkened what it says? Lo, what it says!
One day at least, whereon my thought, enlicensèd to muse,
Had drooped its wing above the beachèd margent of the ooze,
And, plunging from the mountain height into the immensity,
Beheld upon one side the land, on the other side the sea.
I hearkened, comprehended,—never, as from those abysses,
No, never issued from a mouth, nor moved an ear such voice as this is!

A sound it was, at outset, immeasurable, confused,
Vaguer than is the wind among the tufted trees effused,
Full of magnificent accords, suave murmurs, sweet as is
The evensong, and mighty as the shock of panoplies

HEARD ON THE MOUNTAIN

When the hoarse *mêlée* in its arms the closing squadrons grips,
And pants, in furious breathings, from the clarions' brazen lips.
Unutterable the harmony, unsearchable its deep,
Whose fluid undulations round the world a girdle keep,
And through the vasty heavens, which by its surges are washed young,
Its infinite volutions roll, enlarging as they throng,
Even to the profound arcane, whose ultimate chasms sombre
Its shattered flood englut with time, with space and form and number.
Like to another atmosphere, with thin o'erflowing robe,
The hymn eternal covers all the inundated globe :
And the world, swathed about with this investuring symphony,
Even as it trepidates in the air, so trepidates in the harmony.

And pensive, I attended the ethereal lutany,
Lost within the containing voice as if within the sea.

Soon I distinguished, yet as tone which veils confuse and smother,
Amid this voice two voices, one commingled with the other,
Which did from off the land and seas even to the heavens aspire ;
Chanting the universal chant in simultaneous quire.

TRANSLATIONS

And I distinguished them amid that deep and rumorous sound,
As who beholds two currents thwart amid the fluctuous profound.

The one was of the waters; a be-radiant hymnal speech!
That was the voice o' the surges, as they parleyed each with each.
The other, which arose from our abode terranean,
Was sorrowful; and that, alack! the murmur was of man;
And in this mighty quire, whose chantings day and night resound,
Every wave had its utterance, and every man his sound.

Now, the magnificent Ocean, as I said, unbannering
A voice of joy, a voice of peace, did never stint to sing,
Most like in Sion's temples to a psaltery psaltering,
And to creation's beauty reared the great lauds of his song.
Upon the gale, upon the squall, his clamour borne along
Unpausingly arose to God in more triumphal swell;
And every one among his waves, that God alone can quell,
When the other of its song made end, into the singing pressed.
Like that majestic lion whereof Daniel was the guest,
At intervals the Ocean his tremendous murmur awed;
And, toward where the sunset fires fell shaggily and broad,
Under his golden mane, methought that I saw pass the hand of God.

HEARD ON THE MOUNTAIN

Meanwhile, and side by side with that august fanfaronnade
The other voice, like the sudden scream of a destrier
    affrayed,
Like an infernal door that grates ajar its rusty throat,
Like to a bow of iron that gnarls upon an iron rote,
Grinded ; and tears, and shriekings, the anathema, the
    lewd taunt,
Refusal of viaticum, refusal of the font,
And clamour, and malediction, and dread blasphemy,
    among
That hurtling crowd of rumour from the diverse human
    tongue,
Went by as who beholdeth, when the valleys thick
    t'ward night,
The long drifts of the birds of dusk pass, blackening
    flight on flight.
What was this sound whose thousand echoes vibrated
    unsleeping ?
Alas ! the sound was earth's and man's, for earth and
    man were weeping.

Brothers ! of these two voices strange, most unimagin-
    ably,
Unceasingly regenerated, dying unceasingly,
Hearkenèd of the Eternal throughout His Eternity,
The one voice uttereth NATURE, and the other voice
    HUMANITY.

Then I alit in reverie ; for my ministering sprite,
Alack ! had never yet deployed a pinion of an ampler
    flight,

TRANSLATIONS

Nor ever had my shadow endured so large a day to burn:
And long I rested dreaming, contemplating turn by turn
Now that abyss obscure which lurked beneath the water's roll,
And now that other untemptable abyss which opened in my soul.
And I made question of me, to what issues are we here,
Whither should tend the thwarting threads of all this ravelled gear;
What doth the soul; to be or live if better worth it is;
And why the Lord, Who, only, reads within that book of His,
In fatal hymeneals hath eternally entwined
The vintage-chant of nature with the dirging cry of humankind?

The metre of the second of these two translations is an experiment. The splendid fourteen syllable metre of Chapman I have treated after the manner of Drydenian rhyming heroics, with the occasional triplet, and even the occasional Alexandrine, a treatment which can well extend, I believe, the majestic resources of the metre.

AN ECHO OF VICTOR HUGO

LIFE'S a veil the real has :
    All the shadows of our scene
  Are but shows of things that pass
    On the other side the screen.

Time his glass sits nodding by ;
    'Twixt its turn and turn a spawn
Of universes buzz and die
    Like the ephemeris of the dawn.

Turn again the wasted glass !
    Kingly crown and warrior's crest
Are not worth the blade of grass
    God fashions for the swallow's nest.

Kings must lay gold circlets down
    In God's sepulchral ante-rooms,
The wear of Heaven's the thorny crown :
    He paves His temples with their tombs.

O our towered altitudes !
    O the lustres of our thrones !
What ! old Time shall have his moods
    Like Cæsars and Napoleons ;

Have his towers and conquerors forth,
    Till he, weary of the toys,
Put back Rameses in the earth
    And break his Ninevehs and Troys.

The first two stanzas and the last are my own : the thoughts of the others are Victor Hugo's. The metre of the original is departed from.

MISCELLANEOUS POEMS

DREAM-TRYST

THE breaths of kissing night and day
　　Were mingled in the eastern Heaven
　　Throbbing with unheard melody
Shook Lyra all its star-chord seven:
　　When dusk shrunk cold, and light trod shy,
　　　And dawn's grey eyes were troubled grey;
　　And souls went palely up the sky,
　　　And mine to Lucidé.

There was no change in her sweet eyes
　　Since last I saw those sweet eyes shine;
There was no change in her deep heart
　　Since last that deep heart knocked at mine.
　　　Her eyes were clear, her eyes were Hope's,
　　　　Wherein did ever come and go
　　　The sparkle of the fountain-drops
　　　　From her sweet soul below.

The chambers in the house of dreams
　　Are fed with so divine an air,
That Time's hoar wings grow young therein,
　　And they who walk there are most fair.
　　　I joyed for me, I joyed for her,
　　　　Who with the Past meet girt about:
　　　Where our last kiss still warms the air,
　　　　Nor can her eyes go out.

ARAB LOVE-SONG

THE hunchèd camels of the night*
    Trouble the bright
    And silver waters of the moon.
The Maiden of the Morn will soon
Through Heaven stray and sing,
Star gathering.

Now while the dark about our loves is strewn,
Light of my dark, blood of my heart, O come!
And night will catch her breath up, and be dumb.

Leave thy father, leave thy mother
And thy brother;
Leave the black tents of thy tribe apart!
Am I not thy father and thy brother,
And thy mother?
And thou—what needest with thy tribe's black tents
Who hast the red pavilion of my heart?

    * Cloud-shapes observed by travellers in the East.

BUONA NOTTE

*Jane Williams, in her last letter to Shelley, wrote:
'Why do you talk of never enjoying moments like the past?
Are you going to join your friend Plato, or do you expect I
shall do so soon? Buona Notte.' This letter was dated
July 6th, and Shelley was drowned on the 8th. The verses
are supposed to be addressed to Jane by the poet's spirit
while his body is tossing on the waters of Spezzia.*

ARIEL to Miranda :—Hear
    This good-night the sea-winds bear ;
    And let thine unacquainted ear
Take grief for their interpreter.

Good-night! I have risen so high
Into slumber's rarity,
Not a dream can beat its feather
Through the unsustaining ether.
Let the sea-winds make avouch
How thunder summoned me to couch,
Tempest curtained me about
And turned the sun with his own hand out :
And though I toss upon my bed
My dream is not disquieted ;
Nay, deep I sleep upon the deep,
And my eyes are wet, but I do not weep ;
And I fell to sleep so suddenly
That my lips are moist yet—could'st thou see—
With the good-night draught I have drunk to thee.
Thou canst not wipe them ; for it was Death
Damped my lips that has dried my breath.

MISCELLANEOUS POEMS

A little while—it is not long—
The salt shall dry on them like the song.
Now know'st thou that voice desolate,—
Mourning ruined joy's estate,—
Reached thee through a closing gate.
'Go'st thou to Plato?' Ah, girl, no!
It is to Pluto that I go.

THE PASSION OF MARY
VERSES IN PASSION-TIDE

O LADY Mary, thy bright crown
   Is no mere crown of majesty;
   For with the reflex of His own
Resplendent thorns Christ circled thee.

The red rose of this Passion-tide
   Doth take a deeper hue from thee,
In the five wounds of Jesus dyed,
   And in thy bleeding thoughts, Mary!

The soldier struck a triple stroke,
   That smote thy Jesus on the tree:
He broke the Heart of Hearts, and broke
   The Saint's and Mother's hearts in thee.

Thy Son went up the angels' ways,
   His passion ended; but, ah me!
Thou found'st the road of further days
   A longer way of Calvary:

On the hard cross of hope deferred
   Thou hung'st in loving agony,
Until the mortal-dreaded word
   Which chills *our* mirth, spake mirth to thee.

The angel Death from this cold tomb
   Of life did roll the stone away;
And He thou barest in thy womb
   Caught thee at last into the day,
Before the living throne of Whom
   The Lights of Heaven burning pray.

MISCELLANEOUS POEMS
L'ENVOY

O thou who dwellest in the day!
   Behold, I pace amidst the gloom:
Darkness is ever round my way
   With little space for sunbeam-room.

Yet Christian sadness is divine
   Even as *thy* patient sadness was:
The salt tears in our life's dark wine
   Fell in it from the saving cross.

Bitter the bread of our repast;
   Yet doth a sweet the bitter leaven:
Our sorrow is the shadow cast
   Around it by the light of Heaven.

O light in Light, shine down from Heaven!

MESSAGES

WHAT shall I your true-love tell,
  Earth-forsaking maid?
What shall I your true-love tell,
When life's spectre's laid?

' Tell him that, our side the grave,
  Maid may not conceive
Life should be so sad to have,
  That's so sad to leave!'

What shall I your true-love tell,
  When I come to him?
What shall I your true-love tell—
  Eyes growing dim!

' Tell him this, when you shall part
  From a maiden pined;
That I see him with my heart,
  Now my eyes are blind.'

What shall I your true-love tell?
  Speaking-while is scant.
What shall I your true-love tell,
  Death's white postulant?

' Tell him—love, with speech at strife,
  For last utterance saith:
I, who loved with all my life,
  Love with all my death.'

AT LORD'S

IT is little I repair to the matches of the Southron folk,
   Though my own red roses there may blow;
It is little I repair to the matches of the Southron folk,
   Though the red roses crest the caps, I know.
For the field is full of shades as I near the shadowy coast,
And a ghostly batsman plays to the bowling of a ghost,
And I look through my tears on a soundless-clapping host
   As the run-stealers flicker to and fro,
      To and fro:—
O my Hornby and my Barlow long ago!

LOVE AND THE CHILD

'WHY do you so clasp me,
    And draw me to your knee?
    Forsooth, you do but chafe me,
I pray you let me be:
I will but be loved now and then
    When it liketh me!'

So I heard a young child,
    A thwart child, a young child
Rebellious against love's arms,
    Make its peevish cry.

To the tender God I turn:—
    'Pardon, Love most High!
For I think those arms were even Thine,
    And that child even I.'

DAPHNE

THE river-god's daughter,—the sun-god sought her
   Sleeping with never a zephyr by her.
   Under the noon he made his prey sure,
Woofed in weeds of a woven azure,
   As down he shot in a whistle of fire.

Slid off, fair daughter! her vesturing water;
   Like a cloud from the scourge of the winds fled she:
With the breath in her hair of the keen Apollo,
And feet less fleet than the feet that follow,
   She throes in his arms to a laurel-tree.

Risen out of birth's waters the soul distraught errs,
   Nor whom nor whither she flieth knows she:
With the breath in her hair of the keen Apollo,
And fleet the beat of the feet that follow,
   She throes in his arms to a poet, woe's me!

You plucked the boughed verse the poet bears—
   It shudders and bleeds as it snaps from the tree.
A love-banning love, did the god but know it,
Which barks the man about with the poet,
   And muffles his heart of mortality!

Yet I translate—ward of song's gate!—
   Perchance all ill this mystery.
We both are struck with the self-same quarrel;
We grasp the maiden, and clasp the laurel—
   Do we weep or we laugh more, *Phœbe mi?*

DAPHNE

'His own green lays, unwithering bays,
   Gird Keats' unwithering brow,' say ye?
O fools, that is only the empty crown!
The sacred head has laid it down
   With Hob, Dick, Marian, and Margery.

ABSENCE

WHEN music's fading 's faded,
    And the rose's death is dead,
    And my heart is fain of tears, because
Mine eyes have none to shed;
      I said,
Whence shall faith be fed?

Canst thou be what thou hast been?
    No, no more what thou hast!
Lo, all last things that I have known,
    And all that shall be last,
      Went past
With the thing thou wast!

If the petal of this Spring be
    As of the Spring that 's flown,
If the thought that now is sweet is
    As the sweet thought overblown;
      Alone
Canst thou be thy self gone.

To yester-rose a richer
    The rose-spray may bear;
Thrice thousand fairer you may be,—
    But tears for the fair
      You were
When you first were fair!

Know you where they have laid her,
    Maiden May that died?

ABSENCE

With the loves that lived not
   Strowing her soft side ?
      I cried ;
Where Has-been may hide ?

To him that waiteth, all things !
   Even death, if thou wait !
And they that part too early
   May meet again too late :—
      Ah, fate !
If meeting be too late !

And when the year new-launchèd
   Shall from its wake extend
The blossomy foam of Summer,
   What shall I attend,
      My friend !
Flower of thee, my friend ?

Sweet shall have its sorrow,
   The rainbow its rain,
Loving have its leaving,
   And bliss is of pain
      So fain,
Ah, is she bliss or pain ?

TO W. M.

O TREE of many branches! One thou hast
Thou barest not, but grafted'st on thee. Now,
Should all men's thunders break on thee, and leave
Thee reft of bough and blossom, that one branch
Shall cling to thee, my Father, Brother, Friend,
Shall cling to thee, until the end of end.

A FALLEN YEW

IT seemed corrival of the world's great prime,
  Made to un-edge the scythe of Time,
    And last with stateliest rhyme.

No tender Dryad ever did indue
  That rigid chiton of rough yew,
    To fret her white flesh through:

But some god like to those grim Asgard lords,
  Who walk the fables of the hordes
    From Scandinavian fjords,

Upheaved its stubborn girth, and raised unriven,
  Against the whirl-blast and the levin,
    Defiant arms to Heaven.

When doom puffed out the stars, we might have said,
  It would decline its heavy head,
    And see the world to bed.

For this firm yew did from the vassal leas,
  And rain and air, its tributaries,
    Its revenues increase,

And levy impost on the golden sun,
  Take the blind years as they might run,
    And no fate seek or shun.

But now our yew is strook, is fallen—yea,
  Hacked like dull wood of every day
    To this and that, men say.

MISCELLANEOUS POEMS

Never!—To Hades' shadowy shipyards gone,
  Dim barge of Dis, down Acheron
    It drops, or Lethe wan.

Stirred by its fall—poor destined bark of Dis!—
  Along my soul a bruit there is
    Of echoing images,

Reverberations of mortality:
  Spelt backward from its death, to me
    Its life reads saddenedly.

Its breast was hollowed as the tooth of eld;
  And boys, there creeping unbeheld,
    A laughing moment dwelled.

Yet they, within its very heart so crept,
  Reached not the heart that courage kept
    With winds and years beswept.

And in its boughs did close and kindly nest
  The birds, as they within its breast,
    By all its leaves caressed.

But bird nor child might touch by any art
  Each other's or the tree's hid heart,
    A whole God's breadth apart;

The breadth of God, the breadth of death and life!
  Even so, even so, in undreamed strife
    With pulseless Law, the wife,—

A FALLEN YEW

The sweetest wife on sweetest marriage-day,—
  Their souls at grapple in mid-way,
    Sweet to her sweet may say:

'I take you to my inmost heart, my true!'
  Ah, fool! but there is one heart you
    Shall never take him to!

The hold that falls not when the town is got,
  The heart's heart, whose immurèd plot
    Hath keys yourself keep not!

Its ports you cannot burst—you are withstood—
  For him that to your listening blood
    Sends precepts as he would.

Its gates are deaf to Love, high summoner;
  Yea, Love's great warrant runs not there:
    You are your prisoner.

Yourself are with yourself the sole consortress
  In that unleaguerable fortress;
    It knows you not for portress.

Its keys are at the cincture hung of God;
  Its gates are trepidant to His nod;
    By Him its floors are trod.

And if His feet shall rock those floors in wrath,
  Or blest aspersion sleek His path,
    Is only choice it hath

MISCELLANEOUS POEMS

Yea, in that ultimate heart's occult abode
To lie as in an oubliette of God,
   Or in a bower untrod,

Built by a secret Lover for His Spouse;—
Sole choice is this your life allows,
   Sad tree, whose perishing boughs
   So few birds house!

A JUDGEMENT IN HEAVEN

ATHWART the sod which is treading for God * the Poet paced with his splendid eyes ;
Paradise-verdure he stately passes * to win to the Father of Paradise,
Through the conscious and palpitant grasses * of intertangled relucent dyes.

The angels a-play on its fields of Summer * (their wild wings rustled his guides' cymars)
Looked up from disport at the passing comer, * as they pelted each other with handfuls of stars ;
And the warden-spirits with startled feet rose,* hand on sword, by their tethered cars.

With plumes night-tinctured englobed and cinctured * of Saints, his guided steps held on
To where on the far crystálline pale * of that transtellar Heaven there shone
The immutable crocean dawn * effusing from the Father's Throne.

Through the reverberant Eden-ways * the bruit of his great advent driven,
Back from the fulgent justle and press * with mighty echoing so was given,
As when the surly thunder smites * upon the clangèd gates of Heaven.

I have throughout this poem used an asterisk to indicate the caesura in the middle of the line, after the manner of the old Saxon section-point.

MISCELLANEOUS POEMS

Over the bickering gonfalons, * far-ranged as for Tartarean wars,
Went a waver of ribbèd fire * —as night-seas on phosphoric bars
Like a flame-plumed fan shake slowly out * their ridgy reach of crumbling stars.

At length to where on His fretted Throne * sat in the heart of His aged dominions
The great Triune, and Mary nigh, * lit round with spears of their hauberked minions,
The Poet drew, in the thunderous blue * involvèd dread of those mounted pinions.

As in a secret and tenebrous cloud * the watcher from the disquiet earth
At momentary intervals * beholds from its raggèd rifts break forth
The flash of a golden perturbation, * the travelling threat of a witchèd birth;

Till heavily parts a sinister chasm, * a grisly jaw, whose verges soon,
Slowly and ominously filled * by the on-coming plenilune,
Supportlessly congest with fire, * and suddenly spit forth the moon :—

With beauty, not terror, through tangled error * of night-dipt plumes so burned their charge;

A JUDGEMENT IN HEAVEN

Swayed and parted the globing clusters * so,—— disclosed from their kindling marge,
Roseal-chapleted, splendent-vestured, * the Poet there where God's light lay large.

Hu, hu! a wonder! a wonder! see, * clasping the Poet's glories clings
A dingy creature, even to laughter * cloaked and clad in patchwork things,
Shrinking close from the unused glows * of the seraphs' versicoloured wings.

A Rhymer, rhyming a futile rhyme, * he had crept for convoy through Eden-ways
Into the shade of the Poet's glory, * darkened under his prevalent rays,
Fearfully hoping a distant welcome * as a poor kinsman of his lays.

The angels laughed with a lovely scorning: * — ' Who has done this sorry deed in
The garden of our Father, God? * 'mid his blossoms to sow this weed in?
Never our fingers knew this stuff: * not so fashion the looms of Eden!'

The Poet bowed his brow majestic,* searching that patchwork through and through,
Feeling God's lucent gazes traverse * his singing-stoling and spirit too:

MISCELLANEOUS POEMS

The hallowed harpers were fain to frown * on the strange thing come 'mid their sacred crew.
Only the Poet that was earth * his fellow-earth and his own self knew.

Then the Poet rent off robe and wreath, * so as a sloughing serpent doth,
Laid them at the Rhymer's feet, * shed down wreath and raiment both,
Stood in a dim and shamèd stole, * like the tattered wing of a musty moth.

(*The Poet addresses his Maker*)
' Thou gav'st the weed and wreath of song, * the weed and wreath are solely Thine,
And this dishonest vesture * is the only vesture that is mine ;
The life *I* textured, Thou the song : * —— *my* handicraft is not divine ! '

(*The Poet addresses the Rhymer*)
He wrested o'er the Rhymer's head * that garmenting which wrought him wrong ;
A flickering tissue argentine * down dripped its shivering silvers long :—
' Better thou wov'st thy woof of life * than thou didst weave thy woof of song ! '

Never a chief in Saintdom was, * but turned him from the Poet then ;

A JUDGEMENT IN HEAVEN

Never an eye looked mild on him * 'mid all the angel myriads ten,
Save sinless Mary, and sinful Mary * —the Mary titled Magdalen.

' Turn yon robe,' spake Magdalen, * ' of torn bright song, and see and feel.'
They turned the raiment, saw and felt * what their turning did reveal—
All the inner surface piled * with bloodied hairs, like hairs of steel.

' Take, I pray, yon chaplet up, * thrown down ruddied from his head.'
They took the roseal chaplet up,* and they stood astonishèd:
Every leaf between their fingers,* as they bruised it, burst and bled.

' See his torn flesh through those rents;* see the punctures round his hair,
As if the chaplet-flowers had driven * deep roots in to nourish there—
Lord, who gav'st him robe and wreath,* *what* was this Thou gav'st for wear ? '

' Fetch forth the Paradisal garb! ' * spake the Father, sweet and low;
Drew them both by the frightened hand * where Mary's throne made irised bow—
' Take, Princess Mary, of thy good grace,* two spirits greater than they know.'

EPILOGUE TO
'A JUDGEMENT IN HEAVEN'

VIRTUE may unlock hell, or even
   A sin turn in the wards of Heaven,
   (As ethics of the text-book go,)
So little men their own deeds know,
Or through the intricate *mêlée*
Guess witherward draws the battle-sway;
So little, if they know the deed,
Discern what therefrom shall succeed.
To wisest moralists 'tis but given
To work rough border-law of Heaven,
Within this narrow life of ours,
These marches 'twixt delimitless Powers.
Is it, if Heaven the future showed,
Is it the all-severest mode
To see ourselves with the eyes of God?
God rather grant, at His assize,
He see us not with our own eyes!

Heaven, which man's generations draws,
Nor deviates into replicas,
Must of as deep diversity
In judgement as creation be.
There is no expeditious road
To pack and label men for God,
And save them by the barrel-load.
Some may perchance, with strange surprise,
Have blundered into Paradise.
In vasty dusk of life abroad,

EPILOGUE

They fondly thought to err from God,
Nor knew the circle that they trod;
And, wandering all the night about,
Found them at morn where they set out.
Death dawned; Heaven lay in prospect wide:—
Lo! they were standing by His side!

The Rhymer a life uncomplex,
With just such cares as mortals vex,
So simply felt as all men feel,
Lived purely out to his soul's weal.
A double life the Poet lived,
And with a double burthen grieved;
The life of flesh and life of song,
The pangs to both lives that belong;
Immortal knew and mortal pain,
Who in two worlds could lose and gain,
And found immortal fruits must be
Mortal through his mortality.
The life of flesh and life of song!
If one life worked the other wrong,
What expiating agony
May for him, damned to poesy,
Shut in that little sentence be—
What deep austerities of strife—
'He lived his life.' He lived *his* life!

THE SERE OF THE LEAF

WINTER wore a flapping wind, and his beard,
disentwined,
Blew cloudy in the face of the Fall,
When a poet-soul flew South, with a singing in her
mouth,
O'er the azure Irish parting-wall. *
There stood one beneath a tree whose matted greenery
Was fruited with the songs of birds;
By the melancholy water drooped the slender sedge, its
daughter,
Whose silence was a sadness passing words:
He held him very still,
And he heard the running rill,
And the soul-voice singing blither than the birds.

All Summer the sunbeams drew the curtains from the
dreams
Of the rose-fay, while the sweet South wind
Lapped the silken swathing close round her virginal
repose
When night swathed folding slumbers round her mind.
Now the elf of the flower had sickened in her bower,
And fainted in a thrill of scent;
But her lover of the South, with a moan upon his
mouth,
Caught her spirit to his arms as it went:
Then the storms of West and North
Sent a gusty vaward forth,
Sent a skirring desolation, and he went.

* Miss Katharine Tynan's visit to London, 1889.

THE SERE OF THE LEAF

And a troop of roving gales rent the lily's silver veils,
    And tore her from her trembling leaves;
And the Autumn's smitten face flushed to a red disgrace,
    And she grieved as a captive grieves.
Once the gold-barred cage of skies with the sunset's moulted dyes
    Was splendorously littered at the even;
Beauty-fraught o'er shining sea, once the sun's argosy
    To rich wreck on the Western reefs was driven;
      Now the sun, in Indian pall,
      Treads the russet-amber fall
From the ruined trees of Heaven.

Too soon fails the light, and the swart boar, night,
    Gores to death the bleeding day;
And the dusk has no more a calm at its core,
    But is turbid with obscene array.
For the cloud, a thing of ill dilating baleful o'er the hill,
    Spreads a bulk like a huge Afreet
Drifting in gigantic sloth, or a murky behemoth,
    For the moon to set her silver feet;
      For the moon's white paces,
      And its nostril for her traces,
As she urges it with wild witch feet.

And the stars, forlornly fair, shiver keenly through the air,
    All an-aching till their watch be ceased;
And the hours like maimed flies lag on, ere night hatch
    her golden dragon

MISCELLANEOUS POEMS

    In the mold of the upheaved East.
  As the cadent languor lingers after Music droops her
      fingers,
    Beauty still falls dying, dying through the days;
But ah!' said he who stood in that Autumn solitude,
    ' Singing-soul, thou art 'lated with thy lays!
      All things that on this globe err
      Fleet into dark October,
When day and night encounter, the nights war down
      the days.

' For the song in thy mouth is all of the South,
    Though Winter wax in strength more and more,
And at eve with breath of malice the stained windows
      of day's palace
  Pile in shatters on the Western floor.'
But the song sank down his soul like a Naiad through
    her pool,
  He could not bid the visitant depart;
For he felt the melody make tune like a bee
    In the red rose of his heart:
      Like a Naiad in her pool
      It lay within his soul,
Like a bee in the red rose of his heart.

She sang of the shrill East fled and bitterness sur-
    ceased:—
  ' O the blue South wind is musical!
And the garden's drenched with scent, and my soul
    hath its content,
    This eve or any eve at all.'

THE SERE OF THE LEAF

On his form the blushing shames of her ruby-plumaged
 flames
 Flickered hotly, like a quivering crimson snow:
'And hast thou thy content? Were some rain of it
 besprent
 On the soil where I am drifted to and fro,
 My soul, blown o'er the ways
 Of these arid latter days,
Would blossom like a rose of Jericho.

' I know not equipoise, only purgatorial joys,
 Grief's singing to the soul's instrument,
And forgetfulness which yet knoweth that it doth forget;
 But content—what is content?
For a harp of singeing wire, and a goblet dripping fire,
 And desires that hunt down Beauty through the
 Heaven
With unslackenable bounds, as the deep-mouthed
 thunder-hounds
 Bay at heel the fleeing levin,—
 The chaliced lucencies
 From pure holy-wells of eyes,
And the bliss unbarbed with pain I have given.

' Is—O framed to suffer joys!—*thine* the sweet without
 alloys
 Of the many, who art numbered with the few?
And thy flashing breath of song, does it do *thy* lips no
 wrong,
 Nor sear them as the heats spill through?
When the welling musics rise, like tears from heart to
 eyes,

MISCELLANEOUS POEMS

    Is there not a pang dissolved in them for thee?
Does not Song, like the Queen of radiant Love,
      Hellene,
    Float up dripping from a bitter sea?
      No tunèd metal known
      Unless stricken yields a tone,
Be it silver, or sad iron like to me.

' Yet the rhymes still roll from the bell-tower of thy
      soul,
    Though no tongued griefs give them vent;
If they ring to me no gladness, if *my* joy be sceptred
      sadness,
    I am glad, yet, for *thy* content.
Not always does the lost, 'twixt the fires of heat and
      frost,
    Envy those whom the healing lustres bless;
But may sometimes, in the pain of a yearning past
      attain,
    Thank the angels for their happiness;
      'Twixt the fire and fiery ice,
      Looking up to Paradise
Thank the angels for their happiness.

'The heart, a censered fire whence fuming chants aspire,
    Is fed with oozèd gums of precious pain;
And unrest swings denser, denser, the fragrance from
      that censer,
    With the heart-strings for its quivering chain.
Yet 'tis vain to scale the turret of the cloud-uplifted
      spirit,
    And bar the immortal in, the mortal out;

THE SERE OF THE LEAF

For sometime unaware comes a footfall up the stair,
   And a soft knock under which no bolts are stout,
     And lo, there pleadeth sore
     The heart's voice at the door,
"I am your child, you may not shut me out!"

'The breath of poetry in the mind's autumnal tree
   Shakes down the saddened thoughts in singing
     showers,
But fallen from their stem, what part have we in them?
   "Nay," pine the trees, "they were, but are not ours."
Not for the mind's delight these serèd leaves alight,
   But, loosened by the breezes, fall they must.
What ill if they decay? yet some a little way
   May flit before deserted by the gust,
     May touch some spirit's hair,
     May cling one moment there,—
   She turns; they tremble down. Drift o'er them,
     dust!'

TO STARS

YOU, my unrest, and Night's tranquillity,
Bringers of peace to it, and pang to me :
You that on heaven and on my heart cast fire,
To heaven a purging light, my heart unpurged desire;
Bright juts for foothold to the climbing sight
Which else must slip from the steep infinite;
Reared standards which the sequent centuries
Snatch, each from his forerunner's grasp who dies,
To lead our forlorn hope upon the skies;
Bells that from night's great bell-tower hang in gold,
Whereon God rings His changes manifold;
Meek guides and daughters to the blinded heaven
In Œdipean, remitless wandering driven;
The burning rhetoric, quenchless oratory,
Of the magniloquent and all-suasive sky;
I see and feel you—but to feel and see
How two child-eyes have dulled a firmament for me.

Once did I bring her, hurt upon her bed,
Flowers we had loved together ; brought, and said :—
' I plucked them ; yester-morn you liked them wild.'
And then she laid them on my eyes, and smiled.
And now, poor Stars, your fairness is not fair,
Because I cannot gather it for her ;
I cannot sheave you in my arms, and say :—
' See, sweet, you liked these yester-eve ; like them for
    me to-day ! '

She has no care, my Stars, of you or me ;
She has no care, we tire her speedily ;

TO STARS

She has no care, because she cannot see—
She cannot see, who sees not past her sight.
We are set too high, we tire her with our height :
Her years are small, and ill to strain above.
She may not love us : wherefore keep we love
To her who may not love us—you and I ?
And yet you thrill down towards her, even as I,
With all your golden eloquence held in mute.
We may not plead, we may not plead our suit ;
Our wingèd love must beat against its bars :
For should she enter once within those guarding bars,
Our love would do her hurt—oh, think of that, my Stars !

LINES FOR A DRAWING OF OUR LADY OF THE NIGHT

THIS, could I paint my inward sight,
This were Our Lady of the Night:

She bears on her front's lucency
The starlight of her purity:

For as the white rays of that star
The union of all colours are,

She sums all virtues that may be
In her sweet light of purity.

The mantle which she holds on high
Is the great mantle of the sky.

Think, O sick toiler, when the night
Comes on thee, sad and infinite,

Think, sometimes, 'tis our own Lady
Spreads her blue mantle over thee,

And folds the earth, a wearied thing,
Beneath its gentle shadowing;

Then rest a little; and in sleep
Forget to weep, forget to weep!

ORISON-TRYST

SHE told me, in the morning her white thought
   Did beat to Godward, like a carrier-dove,
   My name beneath its wing. And I—how long!—
That, like a bubble from a water-flower
Released as it withdraws itself up-curled
Into the nightly lake, her sighèd name
So loosened from my sleepward-sinking heart;
And in the morning did like Phosphor set it
To lead the vanward of my orient soul
When it storms Heaven; and did all alone,
Methought, upon the live coals of my love
Those distillations of rich memory cast
To feed the fumes of prayer:—oh! I was then
Like one who, dreaming solitude, awakes
In sobbing from his dream; and, straining arms
That ache for their own void, with sudden shock
Takes a dear form beside him.
                Now, when light
Pricks at my lids, I never rouse but think—
' Is 't orison-time with her?'—And then my hand
Presses thy letters in my pulses shook;
Where, neighboured on my heart with those pure lines
In amity of kindred pureness, lies
Image of Her conceived Immaculate;
And on the purple inward, thine,—ah! thine
O' the purple-linèd side.
                And I do set
Tryst with thy soul in its own Paradise;
As lovers of an earthly rate that use,
In severance, for their sweet messages
Some concave of a tree, and do their hearts

MISCELLANEOUS POEMS

Enharbour in its continent heart—I drop
My message in the hollow breast of God.
Thy name is known in Heaven; yea, Heaven is weary
With the reverberation of thy name;
I fill with it the gap between two sleeps,
The inter-pause of dream: hell's gates have learned
To shake in it; and their fierce forayers
Before the iterate echoing recoil,
In armèd watches when my preparate soul
(A war-cry in the alarums of the Night)
Conjoins thy name with Hers, Auxiliatrix.

'WHERETO ART THOU COME?'

'FRIEND, whereto art thou come?' Thus Verity;
Of each that to the world's sad Olivet
Comes with no multitude, but alone by night,
Lit with the one torch of his lifted soul,
Seeking her that he may lay hands on her;
Thus: and waits answer from the mouth of deed.
Truth is a maid, whom men woo diversely;
This, as a spouse; that, as a light-o'-love,
To know, and having known, to make his brag.
But woe to him that takes the immortal kiss,
And not estates her in his housing life,
Mother of all his seed! So he betrays,
Not Truth, the unbetrayable, but himself:
And with his kiss's rated traitor-craft
The Haceldama of a plot of days
He buys, to consummate his Judasry
Therein with Judas' guerdon of despair.

SONG OF THE HOURS

SCENE : Before the Palace of the Sun, into which a god has just passed as the guest of Hyperion. TIME : *Dawn. The Hours of Night and Day advance on each other as the gates close.*

MORNING HOURS

IN curbed expanses our wheeling dances
Meet from the left and right;
Under this vaporous awning
   Tarrying awhile in our flight,
Waiting the day's advances,
   We, the children of light,
Clasp you on verge of the dawning,
   Sisters of Even and Night!

CHORUS

We who lash from the way of the sun
   With the whip of the winds the thronging clouds
Who puff out the lights of the stars, or run
   To scare dreams back to their shrouds,
Or tiar the temples of Heaven
   With a crystalline gleam of showers;

EVENING HOURS

While to flit with the soft moth, Even,
   Round the lamp of the day is ours;

NIGHT HOURS

And ours with her crescent argentine,
   To make Night's forehead fair,
To wheel up her throne of the earth, and twine
   The daffodils in her hair;

SONG OF THE HOURS

ALL
We, moulted as plumes are,
From the wings whereon Time is borne;

MORNING HOURS
We, buds who in blossoming foretell
The date when our leaves shall be torn;

NIGHT HOURS
We, knowing our dooms are to plunge with the gloom's car
Down the steep ruin of morn;

ALL
We hail thee, Immortal!
We robes of Life, mouldering while worn.

NIGHT HOURS
Sea-birds, winging o'er sea calm-strewn
To the lure of the beacon-stars, are we,
O'er the foamy wake of the white-sailed moon,
Which to men is the Galaxy.

MORNING HOURS
Our eyes, through our pinions folden,
By the filtered flame are teased
As we bow when the sun makes golden
Earthquake in the East.

MISCELLANEOUS POEMS

EVENING HOURS
And *we* shake on the sky a dusted fire
　From the ripened sunset's anther,
While the flecked main, drowsing in gorged desire,
　Purrs like an outstretched panther.

MORNING HOURS
O'er the dead moon-maid
　We draw softly the day's white pall;
And our children the Moments we see as
　In drops of the dew they fall,
Or on light plumes laid they shoot the cascade
　Of colours some Heaven's bow call;

ALL
And we sing, Guest, to thee, as
Thou pacest the crystal-paved hall!

We, while the sun with his hid chain swings
　Like a censer around him the blossom-sweet earth,
Who dare the lark with our passionate wings,
　And its mirth with our masterless mirth;
　Or—when that flying laughter
　　Has sunk and died away
　Which beat against Heaven's rafter—
　　Who vex the clear eyes of day,
Who weave for the sky in the loom of the cloud
　A mantle of waving rain,
We, whose hair is jewelled with joys, or bowed
　Under veilings of misty pain;

SONG OF THE HOURS

We hymn thee at leaving
Who strew thy feet's coming, O Guest!
We, the linked cincture which girdles
Mortality's feverous breast,
Who heave in its heaving, who grieve in its grieving,
Are restless in its unrest;
Our beings unstirred else
Were it not for the bosom they pressed.

We see the wind, like a light swift leopard
Leap on the flocks of the cloud that flee,
As we follow the feet of the radiant shepherd
Whose bright sheep drink of the sea.
When that drunken Titan the Thunder
Stumbles through staggered Heaven,
And spills on the scorched earth under
The fiery wine of the levin,
With our mystic measure of rhythmic motion
We charm him in snorting sleep,
While round him the sun enchants from ocean
The walls of a cloudy keep.
Beneath the deep umbers
Of night as we watch and hark,
The dim-wingèd dreams which feed on
The blossoms of day we mark,
As in murmurous numbers they swarm to the slumbers
That cell the hive of the dark;
And life shakes, a reed on
Our tide, in the death-wind stark.

MISCELLANEOUS POEMS

Time, Eternity's fountain, whose waters
    Fall back thither from whence they rose,
Deweth with us, its showery daughters,
    The Life that is green in its flows.
But whether in grief or mirth we shower,
    We make not the thing we breed,
For what may come of the passing Hour
    Is what was hid in the seed.
        And now as wakes,
           Like love in its first blind guesses,
        Or a snake just stirring its coils,
        Sweet tune into half-caresses,
    Before the sun shakes the clinging flakes
        Of gloom from his spouting tresses,
    Let winds have toils
        To catch at our fluttering dresses!
Winter, that numbeth the throstle and stilled wren,
    Has keen frost-edges our plumes to pare,
Till we break, with the Summer's laughing children,
    Over the fields of air.
        While the winds in their tricksome courses
           The snowy steeds vault upon
        That are foaled of the white sea-horses
        And washed in the streams of the sun.
Thaw, O thaw the enchanted throbbings
    Curdled at Music's heart;
Tread she her grapes till from their englobings
    The melodies spurt and smart!
        We fleet as a rain,
           Nor yearn for the being men own,

SONG OF THE HOURS

    With whom is naught beginneth
      Or endeth without some moan;
    We soar to our zenith
      And are panglessly overblown.

Yet, if the roots of the truth were bare,
    Our transience is only a mortal seeming;
Fond men, we are fixed as a still despair,
    And we fleet but in your dreaming.
      We are columns in Time's hall, mortals,
        Wherethrough Life hurrieth;
      You pass in at birth's wide portals,
        And out at the postern of death.
As you chase down the vista your dream or your love
    The swift pillars race you by,
And you think it is we who move, who move,—
    It is you who die, who die!
      O firmament, even
        You pass, by whose fixture man voweth;
      God breathes you forth as a bubble
        And shall suck you back into His mouth!
    Through earth, sea, and Heaven a doom shall be driven,
      And, sown in the furrows it plougheth,
    As fire bursts from stubble
      Shall spring the new wonders none troweth.

The bowed East lifteth the dripping sun,
    A golden cup, to the lips of Night,
Over whose cheek in flushes run
    The heats of the liquid light.

MISCELLANEOUS POEMS

MORNING HOURS

To our very pinions' ridge
    We tremble expectantly;—
Is it ready, the burnished bridge
    We must cast for our King o'er the sea?
And who will kneel with sunbeam-slips
    To dry the flowers' sweet eyes?
Who touch with fire her finger-tips
    For the lamp of the grape, as she flies?

ALL

List, list to the prances, his chariot advances,
    It comes in a dust of light!
From under our brightening awning
    We wheel in a diverse flight:
Yet the hands we unclasp, as our dances
    Sweep off to the left and the right,
Are but loosed on the verge of the dawning
    To join on the verge of the night.

PASTORAL

PAN-imbued
    Tempe wood,
      Pretty player's sporting-place;
Tempe wood's
    Solitude's
Everywhere a courting-place.
    Kiss me, sweet
    Gipsy feet,
Though a kissed maid hath her red;
    Kisses grow—
    Trust me so—
Faster than they're gatherèd!
    I will flute a tune
      On the pipes of ivory;
    All long noon
      Piping of a melody;
    A merry, merry, merry, merry,
      Merry, merry melody.
Dance, ho! foot it so! Feat fleets the melody!

    Let the wise
    Say, youth dies;—
'Tis for pleasure's mending, Sweet!
    Kisses are
    Costlier far,
That they have an ending, Sweet!
    Half a kiss's
    Dainty bliss is
From the day of kiss-no-more;

MISCELLANEOUS POEMS

    When we shall,
    Roseal
Lass, do this and this no more!
And we pipe a tune
    On the pipes of ivory;
All long noon
    Fluting of a melody:—
A merry, merry, merry, merry,
    Merry, merry melody.
Dance, ho! trip it so! Feat fleets the melody!

    My love must
    Be to trust,
While you safely fold me close:
    Yours will smile
    A kissing-while,
For the hours I hold you close.
    Maiden gold!
    Clipping bold
Here the truest mintage is:
    Lips will bear
    But, I swear,
In the press their vintages!
I will flute a tune
    On the pipes of ivory;
All long noon
    Piping of a melody:—
A merry, merry, merry, merry,
    Merry, merry melody.
Dance, ho! foot it so! Feat fleets the melody!

PAST THINKING OF SOLOMON

Remember thy Creator in the days of thy youth, before the years draw nigh of which thou shalt say : They please me not : Before the sun, and the light, and the moon, and the stars be darkened, and the clouds return after the rain.
ECCLESIASTES.

WISE-UNTO-HELL Ecclesiast,
Who siev'dst life to the gritted last !
This thy sting, thy darkness, Mage—
Cloud upon sun, upon youth age ?

Now is come a darker thing,
And is come a colder sting,

Unto us, who find the womb
Opes on the courtyard of the tomb ;

Now in this fuliginous
City of flesh our sires for us

Darkly built, the sun at prime
Is hidden, and betwixt the time

Of day and night is variance none,
Who know not altern moon and sun ;

MISCELLANEOUS POEMS

Whose deposed heaven through dungeon-bars
Looks down blinded of its stars.

Yea, in the days of youth, God wot,
Now we say : They please me not.

A DEAD ASTRONOMER

STEPHEN PERRY, S.J.

STARRY amorist, starward gone,
   Thou art—what thou didst gaze upon !
   Passed through thy golden garden's bars,
Thou seest the Gardener of the Stars.

She, about whose moonèd brows
Seven stars make seven glows,
Seven lights for seven woes ;
She, like thine own Galaxy,
All lustres in one purity :—
What said'st thou, Astronomer,
When thou did'st discover *her* ?
When thy hand its tube let fall,
Thou found'st the fairest Star of all !

CHEATED ELSIE

ELSIE was a maiden fair
    As the sun
    Shone upon :
Born to teach her swains despair
By smiling on them every one ;
Born to win all hearts to her
Just because herself had none ;
All the day she had no care,
For she was a maiden fair
    As the sun
    Shone upon,
Heartless as the brooks that run.

All the maids, with envy tart,
Sneering said, ' She has no heart.'
All the youths, with bitter smart
Sighing said, ' She has no heart ! '
    Could she care
For their sneers or their despair
When she was a maiden fair
    As the sun
    Shone upon,
Heartless as the brooks that run ?

But one day whenas she stood
    In a wood
Haunted by the fairy brood,
Did she view, or dream she viewed
    In a vision's
    Wild misprisions,

CHEATED ELSIE

How a pedlar, dry and rude
As a crook'd branch taking flesh,
Caught the spirit in a mesh,
Singing of—' What is't ye lack ? '
    Wizard-pack
    On twisted back,
Still he sang, ' What is't ye lack ?

' Lack ye land or lack ye gold,
What I give, I give unsold ;
Lack ye wisdom, lack ye beauty,
    To your suit he
Gives unpaid, the pedlar old ! '

Fairies.

Beware, beware ! the gifts he gives
One pays for, sweetheart, while one lives !

Elsie.

What is it the maidens say
That I lack ?

Pedlar.

By this bright day
Can so fair a maiden lack ?
    Maid so sweet
    Should be complete.

Elsie.

Yet a thing they say I lack.
    In thy pack,—
    Pedlar, tell—
Hast thou ever a heart to sell ?

MISCELLANEOUS POEMS

Pedlar.
      Yea, a heart I have, as tender
        As the mood of evening air.

Elsie.
      Name thy price!

Pedlar.
      The price, by Sorrow!
      Only is, the heart to wear.

Elsie.
      Not great the price, as was my fear.

Fairies.
      So cheap a price was ne'er so dear.
        Beware, beware,
        O rash and fair!
        The gifts he gives,
      Sweetheart, one pays for while one lives!

      Scarce the present did she take,
      When the heart began to ache.

Elsie.
      Ah, what is this? Take back thy gift!
        I had not, and I knew no lack;
      Now I have, I lack for ever!

Fairies.
      The gifts he gives, he takes not back.

CHEATED ELSIE

Elsie.
    Ah! why the present did I take,
    And knew not that a heart would ache?

Fairies.
    Ache! and is that all thy sorrow?—
    Beware, beware—a heart will break!

THE FAIR INCONSTANT

Dost thou still hope thou shalt be fair,
    When no more fair to me?
    Or those that by thee taken were
Hold their captivity?
Is this thy confidence? No, no;
Trust it not; it can not be so.

But thou too late, too late shalt find
    'Twas I that made thee fair;
Thy beauties never from thy mind
    But from my loving were;
And those delights that did thee stole
Confessed the vicinage of my soul.

The rosy reflex of my heart
    Did thy pale cheek attire;
And what I was, not what thou art,
    Did gazers-on admire.
Go, and too late thou shalt confess
I looked thee into loveliness!

THREATENED TEARS

DO not loose those rains thy wet
    Eyes, my Fair, unsurely threat;
    Do not, Sweet, do not so!
Thou canst not have a single woe,
But this sad and doubtful weather
Overcasts us both together.
In the aspèct of those known eyes
My soul's a captain weatherwise.
Ah me! what presages it sees
In those watery Hyades.

THE HOUSE OF SORROWS*

I

OF the white purity
  They wrought my wedding-dress,
  Inwoven silverly—
 For tears, as I do guess.
Oh, why did they with tears inweave my marriage-dress?

  A girl, I did espouse
   Destiny, grief, and fears;
  The love of Austria's house
   And its ancestral years
I learned; and my salt eyes grew erudite in tears.

  Devote our tragic line—
   One to his rebel's aim,
  One to his ignorant brine,
   One to the eyeless flame:
Who should be skilled to weep but I, O Christ's dear Dame?

[*In the opening stanzas the Empress Elizabeth of Austria addresses first Our Lady, then the 'Dark Fool' Death, and finally the Son of Sorrows, in allusion to the griefs of her own and her husband's line: the shooting of Maximilian of Mexico, her sister's burning at the Paris Bazar de la Charité, the drowning of the Archduke John and of the mad King of Bavaria, and the tragedy of the Crown Prince Rudolph. Her own assassination was the immediate occasion of these verses; and the traditional offering of her wedding-wreath to a Madonna-shrine and the making of her wedding-gown into priestly vestments elucidate other references in the text.]

THE HOUSE OF SORROWS

Give one more to the fire,
  One more for water keep:
O Death, wilt thou not tire?
  Still Austria must thou reap?
Can I have plummetless tears, that still thou bidd'st
  'Weep, weep!'?

No—thou at length with me
  Too far, Dark Fool, hast gone!
One costly cruelty
  Voids thy dominion:
I am drained to the uttermost tear: O Rudolph, O my
  son!

Take this woof of sorrows,
  Son of all Women's Tears!
I am not for the morrows,
  I am dead with the dead years.
Lo, I vest Thee, Christ, with my woven tears!

My bridal wreath take thou,
  Mary! Take Thou, O Christ,
My bridal garment! Now
  Is all my fate sufficed,
And, robed and garlanded, the victim sacrificed.

II

The Son of Weeping heard,
  The gift benignly saw;
The Women's Pitier heard.

MISCELLANEOUS POEMS

      Together, by hid law,
The life-gashed heart, the assassin's healing poniard,
   draw.

      Too long that consummation
        The obdurate seasons thwart;
      Too long were the sharp consolation
        And her breast apart;—
The remedy of steel has gone home to her sick heart.

      Her breast, dishabited,
        Revealed, her heart above,
      A little blot of red,—
        Death's reverent sign to approve
He had sealed up that royal tomb of martyred love.

      Now, Death, if thou wouldst show
        Some ruth still left in store,
      Guide thou the armèd blow
        To strike one bosom more,
Where any blow were pity, to this it struck before!

INSENTIENCE

O SWEET is Love, and sweet is Lack!
But is there any charm
When Lack from round the neck of Love
Drops her languid arm?

Weary, I no longer love,
　Weary, no more lack;
O for a pang, that listless Loss
Might wake, and, with a playmate's voice,
　Call the tired Love back!

ENVOY

GO, songs, for ended is our brief, sweet play;
   Go, children of swift joy and tardy sorrow:
   And some are sung, and that was yesterday,
And some unsung, and that may be to-morrow.

Go forth; and if it be o'er stony way,
   Old joy can lend what newer grief must borrow:
And it was sweet, and that was yesterday,
   And sweet is sweet, though purchasèd with sorrow.

Go, songs, and come not back from your far way:
   And if men ask you why ye smile and sorrow,
Tell them ye grieve, for your hearts know To-day,
   Tell them ye smile, for your eyes know To-morrow.

NOTE

'*SISTER SONGS.*' This was first called 'Amphicypellon: Wrought and upbrimmed for Two Sisters, with an Inscription,' as may be seen in the Facsimile, which shows also the Cross with which the Poet was accustomed to crest his Manuscript.

✛

Amphicypellon
Wrought and upbrimmed for Two Sisters.
With an Inscription.

The original edition contained the following Preface:

' This poem, though new in the sense of being now (1895) for the first time printed, was written some four years ago, about the same date as the *Hound of Heaven*. . . .

' One image in the *Proem* was an unconscious plagiarism from the beautiful image in Mr Patmore's *St Valentine's Day* :

    O baby Spring,
That flutter'st sudden 'neath the breast of Earth,
A month before the birth !

Finding I could not disengage it without injury to the passage in which it is embedded, I have preferred to leave it, with this acknowledgement to a Poet rich enough to lend to the poor.—FRANCIS THOMPSON.

FRANCIS THOMPSON
Poems and Essays

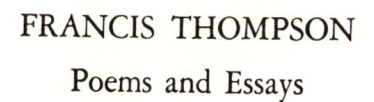

THREE VOLUMES IN ONE
VOLUME TWO: *Poems, Indices*

THE CONTENTS

Dedication of New Poems	page vii
Sight and Insight:	
The Mistress of Vision	3
Contemplation	12
'By Reason of Thy Law'	15
The Dread of Height	17
Orient Ode	21
New Year's Chimes	29
From the Night of Forebeing	32
Any Saint	45
Assumpta Maria	52
Carmen Genesis	56
Ad Castitatem	60
The After Woman	64
Grace of the Way	67
Retrospect	70
A Narrow Vessel:	
A Girl's Sin—In Her Eyes	75
A Girl's Sin—In His Eyes	80
Love Declared	82
The Way of a Maid	84
Beginning of End	85
Penelope	86
The End of It	88
Epilogue	89
Ultima:	
Love's Almsman Plaineth His Fare	93
A Holocaust	95
My Lady the Tyranness	96

CONTENTS

Unto This Last	99
Ultimum	101
An Anthem of Earth	105
Miscellaneous Odes:	
Laus Amara Doloris	121
A Captain of Song	127
Against Urania	129
To the English Martyrs	131
Ode for the Diamond Jubilee of Queen Victoria, 1897	137
The Nineteenth Century	146
Peace	153
Cecil Rhodes	157
Of Nature: Laud and Plaint	162
Sonnets:	
Ad Amicam	171
To a Child	176
Hermes	177
House of Bondage	178
The Heart	180
Desiderium Indesideratum	182
Love's Varlets	183
Non Pax—Expectatio	184
Not Even in Dream	185
Miscellaneous Poems:	
A Hollow Wood	189
To Daisies	191
To the Sinking Sun	194
A May Burden	196
July Fugitive	198

CONTENTS

Field-Flower	201
To a Snowflake	203
A Question	204
The Cloud's Swan-Song	206
Of My Friend	211
To Monica : After Nine Years	212
A Double Need	214
Grief's Harmonics	215
Memorat Memoria	216
Nocturn	218
Heaven and Hell	219
'Chose Vue'	220
St Monica	221
Marriage in Two Moods	222
All Flesh	224
The Kingdom of God	226
The Singer Saith of His Song	228
Bibliography	230
Index of Titles	237
Index of First Lines	240

DEDICATION OF *NEW POEMS*
(1897)

To Coventry Patmore

LO, my book thinks to look Time's leaguer down,
   Under the banner of your spread renown !
   Or if these levies of impuissant rhyme
Fall to the overthrow of assaulting Time,
Yet this one page shall fend oblivious shame,
Armed with your crested and prevailing Name.

This dedication was written while the dear friend and great Poet to whom it was addressed yet lived. It is left as he saw it—the last verses of mine that were to pass under his eyes.

SIGHT AND INSIGHT

Wisdom is easily seen by them that love her, and is found by them that seek her.
To think therefore upon her is perfect understanding.
WISDOM, vi.

THE MISTRESS OF VISION

I

SECRET was the garden;
  Set i' the pathless awe
  Where no star its breath can draw.
Life, that is its warden,
Sits behind the fosse of death. Mine eyes saw not, and I saw.

II

It was a mazeful wonder;
Thrice three times it was enwalled
With an emerald—
Sealèd so asunder.
All its birds in middle air hung a-dream, their music thralled.

III

The Lady of fair weeping,
At the garden's core,
Sang a song of sweet and sore
And the after-sleeping;
In the land of Luthany, and the tracts of Elenore.

IV

With sweet-pangèd singing,
Sang she through a dream-night's day;
That the bowers might stay,
Birds bate their winging,
Nor the wall of emerald float in wreathèd haze away.

SIGHT AND INSIGHT

V

The lily kept its gleaming,
In her tears (divine conservers!)
Washèd with sad art;
And the flowers of dreaming
Palèd not their fervours,
For her blood flowed through their nervures;
And the roses were most red, for she dipt them in her heart.

VI

There was never moon,
Save the white sufficing woman:
Light most heavenly-human—
Like the unseen form of sound,
Sensed invisibly in tune,—
With a sun-derivèd stole
Did inaureole
All her lovely body round;
Lovelily her lucid body with that light was interstrewn.

VII

The sun which lit that garden wholly,
Low and vibrant visible,
Tempered glory woke;
And it seemèd solely
Like a silver thurible
Solemnly swung, slowly,
Fuming clouds of golden fire, for a cloud of incense-smoke.

THE MISTRESS OF VISION

VIII

But woe 's me, and woe 's me,
For the secrets of her eyes!
In my visions fearfully
They are ever shown to be
As fringèd pools, whereof each lies
Pallid-dark beneath the skies
Of a night that is
But one blear necropolis.
And her eyes a little tremble, in the wind of her own
    sighs.

IX

Many changes rise on
Their phantasmal mysteries.
They grow to an horizon
Where earth and heaven meet;
And like a wing that dies on
The vague twilight-verges,
Many a sinking dream doth fleet
Lessening down their secrecies.
And, as dusk with day converges,
Their orbs are troublously
Over-gloomed and over-glowed with hope and fear
    of things to be.

X

There is a peak on Himalay,
And on the peak undeluged snow,
And on the snow not eagles stray;
There if your strong feet could go,—
Looking over tow'rd Cathay

SIGHT AND INSIGHT

From the never-deluged snow—
Farthest ken might not survey
Where the peoples underground dwell whom antique
fables know.

XI

East, ah, east of Himalay,
Dwell the nations underground;
Hiding from the shock of Day,
For the sun's uprising-sound:
Dare not issue from the ground
At the tumults of the Day,
So fearfully the sun doth sound
Clanging up beyond Cathay;
For the great earthquaking sunrise rolling up beyond
Cathay.

XII

Lend me, O lend me
The terrors of that sound,
That its music may attend me,
Wrap my chant in thunders round;
While I tell the ancient secrets in that Lady's singing
found.

XIII

On Ararat there grew a vine;
When Asia from her bathing rose,
Our first sailor made a twine
Thereof for his prefiguring brows.
Canst divine
Where, upon our dusty earth, of that vine a cluster
grows?

THE MISTRESS OF VISION

XIV

On Golgotha there grew a thorn
Round the long-prefigured Brows.
Mourn, O mourn!
For the vine have we the spine? Is this all the Heaven
allows?

XV

On Calvary was shook a spear;
Press the point into thy heart—
Joy and fear!
All the spines upon the thorn into curling tendrils start.

XVI

O dismay!
I, a wingless mortal, sporting
With the tresses of the sun?
I, that dare my hand to lay
On the thunder in its snorting?
Ere begun,
Falls my singed song down the sky, even the old Icarian
way.

XVII

From the fall precipitant
These dim snatches of her chant
Only have remainèd mine;—
That from spear and thorn alone
May be grown
For the front of saint or singer any divinizing twine.

SIGHT AND INSIGHT

XVIII

Her song said that no springing
Paradise but evermore
Hangeth on a singing
That has chords of weeping,
And that sings the after-sleeping
To souls which wake too sore.
'But woe the singer, woe!' she said ; 'beyond the dead
his singing-lore,
All its art of sweet and sore,
He learns, in Elenore!'

XIX

Where is the land of Luthany,
Where is the tract of Elenore ?
I am bound therefor.

XX

'Pierce thy heart to find the key ;
With thee take
Only what none else would keep ;
Learn to dream when thou dost wake,
Learn to wake when thou dost sleep.
Learn to water joy with tears,
Learn from fears to vanquish fears ;
To hope, for thou dar'st not despair,
Exult, for that thou dar'st not grieve ;
Plough thou the rock until it bear ;
Know, for thou else couldst not believe ;
Lose, that the lost thou may'st receive ;
Die, for none other way canst live.

THE MISTRESS OF VISION

When earth and heaven lay down their veil,
And that apocalypse turns thee pale;
When thy seeing blindeth thee
To what thy fellow-mortals see;
When their sight to thee is sightless;
Their living, death; their light, most lightless;
Search no more—
Pass the gates of Luthany, tread the region Elenore.'

XXI

Where is the land of Luthany,
And where the region Elenore?
I do faint therefor.

XXII

' When to the new eyes of thee
All things by immortal power,
Near or far,
Hiddenly
To each other linkèd are,
That thou canst not stir a flower
Without troubling of a star;
When thy song is shield and mirror
To the fair snake-curlèd Pain,
Where thou dar'st affront her terror
That on her thou may'st attain
Perséan conquest; seek no more,
O seek no more!
Pass the gates of Luthany, tread the region Elenore.'

SIGHT AND INSIGHT

XXIII

So sang she, so wept she,
Through a dream-night's day;
And with her magic singing kept she—
Mystical in music—
That garden of enchanting
In visionary May;
Swayless for my spirit's haunting,
Thrice-threefold walled with emerald from our mortal mornings grey.

XXIV

And as a necromancer
Raises from the rose-ash
The ghost of the rose;
My heart so made answer
To her voice's silver plash,—
Stirred in reddening flash,
And from out its mortal ruins the purpureal phantom blows.

XXV

Her tears made dulcet fretting,
Her voice had no word,
More than thunder or the bird.
Yet, unforgetting,
The ravished soul her meanings knew. Mine ears heard not, and I heard.

THE MISTRESS OF VISION

XXVI

When she shall unwind
All those wiles she wound about me,
Tears shall break from out me,
That I cannot find
Music in the holy poets to my wistful want, I doubt me!

CONTEMPLATION

THIS morning saw I, fled the shower,
 The earth reclining in a lull of power:
  The heavens, pursuing not their path,
Lay stretched out naked after bath,
Or so it seemed ; field, water, tree, were still,
Nor was there any purpose on the calm-browed hill.

The hill, which sometimes visibly is
Wrought with unresting energies,
Looked idly ; from the musing wood,
And every rock, a life renewed
Exhaled like an unconscious thought
When poets, dreaming unperplexed,
Dream that they dream of nought.
Nature one hour appears a thing unsexed,
Or to such serene balance brought
That her twin natures cease their sweet alarms,
And sleep in one another's arms.
The sun with resting pulses seems to brood,
And slacken its command upon my unurged blood.

The river has not any care
Its passionless water to the sea to bear ;
The leaves have brown content ;
The wall to me has freshness like a scent,
And takes half animate the air,
Making one life with its green moss and stain ;
And life with all things seems too perfect blent
For anything of life to be aware.
The very shades on hill, and tree, and plain,

CONTEMPLATION

Where they have fallen doze, and where they
    doze remain.

No hill can idler be than I ;
No stone its inter-particled vibration
Investeth with a stiller lie ;
No heaven with a more urgent rest betrays
The eyes that on it gaze.
We are too near akin that thou shouldst cheat
Me, Nature, with thy fair deceit.
In poets floating like a water-flower
Upon the bosom of the glassy hour,
In skies that no man sees to move,
Lurk untumultuous vortices of power,
For joy too native, and for agitation
Too instant, too entire for sense thereof,
Motion like gnats when autumn suns are low,
Perpetual as the prisoned feet of love
On the heart's floors with painèd pace that go.
From stones and poets you may know,
Nothing so active is, as that which least seems so.

For he, that conduit running wine of song,
Then to himself does most belong
When he his mortal house unbars
To the importunate and thronging feet
That round our corporal walls unheeded beat ;
Till, all containing, he exalt
His stature to the stars, or stars
Narrow their heaven to his fleshly vault :
When, like a city under ocean,

SIGHT AND INSIGHT

To human things he grows a desolation,
And is made a habitation
For the fluctuous universe
To lave with unimpeded motion.
He scarcely frets the atmosphere
With breathing, and his body shares
The immobility of rocks ;
His heart's a drop-well of tranquillity ;
His mind more still is than the limbs of fear,
And yet its unperturbed velocity
The spirit of the simoom mocks.
He round the solemn centre of his soul
Wheels like a dervish, while his being is
Streamed with the set of the world's harmonies,
In the long draft of whatsoever sphere
He lists the sweet and clear
Clangour of his high orbit on to roll,
So gracious is his heavenly grace ;
And the bold stars does hear,
Every one in his airy soar,
For evermore
Shout to each other from the peaks of space,
As 'thwart ravines of azure shouts the mountaineer.

'BY REASON OF THY LAW'

HERE I make oath—
   Although the heart that knows its
     bitterness
Hear loath,
And credit less—
That he who kens to meet Pain's kisses fierce
Which hiss against his tears,
Dread, loss, nor love frustrate,
Nor all iniquity of the froward years
Shall his inurèd wing make idly bate,
Nor of the appointed quarry his staunch sight
To lose observance quite ;
Seal from half-sad and all-elate
Sagacious eyes
Ultimate Paradise ;
Nor shake his certitude of haughty fate.

Pacing the burning shares of many dooms,
I with stern tread do the clear-witting stars
To judgement cite,
If I have borne aright
The proving of their pure-willed ordeal.
From food of all delight
The heavenly Falconer my heart debars,
And tames with fearful glooms
The haggard to His call ;
Yet sometimes comes a hand, sometimes a
   voice withal,
And she sits meek now, and expects the light.

SIGHT AND INSIGHT

In this Avernian sky,
This sultry and incumbent canopy
Of dull and doomed regret ;
Where on the unseen verges yet, O yet,
At intervals,
Trembles, and falls,
Faint lightning of remembered transient
    sweet—
Ah, far too sweet
But to be sweet a little, a little sweet, and
    fleet ;
Leaving this pallid trace,
This loitering and most fitful light, a space,
Still some sad space,
For Grief to see her own poor face :—
Here where I keep my stand
With all o'er-anguished feet,
And no live comfort near on any hand ;
Lo, I proclaim the unavoided term,
When this morass of tears, then drained
    and firm,
Shall be a land—
Unshaken I affirm—
Where seven-quired psalterings meet ;
And all the gods move with calm hand in
    hand,
And eyes that know not trouble and the
    worm.

THE DREAD OF HEIGHT

*If ye were blind, ye should have no sin : but now ye say :
We see : your sin remaineth.   JOHN ix. 41.*

NOT the Circean wine
    Most perilous is for pain :
    Grapes of the heavens' star-loaden vine,
Whereto the lofty-placed
Thoughts of fair souls attain,
Tempt with a more retributive delight,
And do disrelish all life's sober taste.
'Tis to have drunk too well
The drink that is divine,
Maketh the kind earth waste,
And breath intolerable.

Ah me !
How shall my mouth content it with mortality ?
Lo, secret music, sweetest music,
From distances of distance drifting its lone
    flight,
Down the arcane where Night would perish
    in night,
Like a god's loosened locks slips undulously :
Music that is too grievous of the height
For safe and low delight,
Too infinite
For bounded hearts which yet would girth the
    sea !

SIGHT AND INSIGHT

So let it be,
Though sweet be great, and though my heart
    be small :
So let it be,
O music, music, though you wake in me
No joy, no joy at all ;
Although you only wake
Uttermost sadness, measure of delight,
Which else I could not credit to the height
Did I not know,
That ill is statured to its opposite ;
Did I not know,
And even of sadness so,
Of utter sadness, make
Of extreme sad a rod to mete
The incredible excess of unsensed sweet,
And mystic wall of strange felicity.
So let it be,
Though sweet be great, and though my heart
    be small,
And bitter meat
The food of gods for men to eat ;
Yea, John ate daintier, and did tread
Less ways of heat,
Than whom to their wind-carpeted
High banquet-hall,
And golden love-feasts, the fair stars entreat.

But ah ! withal,
Some hold, some stay,
O difficult Joy, I pray,

THE DREAD OF HEIGHT

Some arms of thine,
Not only, only arms of mine !
Lest like a weary girl I fall
From clasping love so high,
And lacking thus thine arms, then may
Most hapless I
Turn utterly to love of basest rate ;
For low they fall whose fall is from the sky.
Yea, who me shall secure
But I, of height grown desperate,
Surcease my wing, and my lost fate
Be dashed from pure
To broken writhings in the shameful slime :
Lower than man, for I dreamed higher,
Thrust down, by how much I aspire,
And damned with drink of immortality ?
For such things be,
Yea, and the lowest reach of reeky Hell
Is but made possible
By foreta'en breath of Heaven's austerest clime.

These tidings from the vast to bring
Needeth not doctor nor divine,
Too well, too well
My flesh doth know the heart-perturbing thing ;
That dread theology alone
Is mine,
Most native and my own ;
And ever with victorious toil
When I have made
Of the deific peaks dim escalade,

SIGHT AND INSIGHT

My soul with anguish and recoil
Doth like a city in an earthquake rock,
As at my feet the abyss is cloven then,
With deeper menace than for other men,
Of my potential cousinship with mire;
That all my conquered skies do grow a hollow mock,
My fearful powers retire,
No longer strong,
Reversing the shook banners of their song.

Ah, for a heart less native to high Heaven,
A hooded eye, for jesses and restraint,
Or for a will accipitrine to pursue!—
The veil of tutelar flesh to simple livers given,
Or those brave-fledging fervours of the Saint,
Whose heavenly falcon-craft doth never taint,
Nor they in sickest time their ample virtue mew.

ORIENT ODE

LO, in the sanctuaried East,
    Day, a dedicated priest
    In all his robes pontifical exprest,
Lifteth slowly, lifteth sweetly,
From out its Orient tabernacle drawn,
Yon orbèd sacrament confest
Which sprinkles benediction through the dawn;
And when the grave procession's ceased,
The earth with due illustrious rite
Blessed,—ere the frail fingers featly
Of twilight, violet-cassocked acolyte,
His sacerdotal stoles unvest—
Sets, for high close of the mysterious feast,
The sun in august exposition meetly
Within the flaming monstrance of the West.

O salutaris hostia,
Quæ cœli pandis ostium!
Through breachèd darkness' rampart, a
Divine assaulter, art thou come!
God whom none may live and mark!
Borne within thy radiant ark,
While the Earth, a joyous David,
Dances before thee from the dawn to dark.
The moon, O leave, pale ruined Eve;
Behold her fair and greater daughter*
Offers to thee her fruitful water,
Which at thy first white *Ave* shall conceive!

    * The earth.

SIGHT AND INSIGHT

Thy gazes do on simple her
Desirable allures confer;
What happy comelinesses rise
Beneath thy beautifying eyes!
Who was, indeed, at first a maid
Such as, with sighs, misgives she is not fair,
And secret views herself afraid,
Till flatteries sweet provoke the charms they swear:
Yea, thy gazes, blissful lover,
Make the beauties they discover!
What dainty guiles and treacheries caught
From artful prompting of love's artless
    thought
Her lowly loveliness teach her to adorn,
When thy plumes shiver against the conscious
    gates of morn!

And so the love which is thy dower,
Earth, though her first-frightened breast
Against the exigent boon protest
(For she, poor maid, of her own power
Has nothing in herself, not even love,
But an unwitting void thereof),
Gives back to thee in sanctities of flower;
And holy odours do her bosom invest,
That sweeter grows for being prest:
Though dear recoil, the tremorous nurse of joy,
From thine embrace still startles coy,
Till Phosphor lead, at thy returning hour,
The laughing captive from the wishing West.

ORIENT ODE

Nor the majestic heavens less
Thy formidable sweets approve,
Thy dreads and thy delights confess,
That do draw, and that remove.
Thou as a lion roar'st, O Sun,
Upon thy satellites' vexèd heels;
Before thy terrible hunt thy planets run;
Each in his frighted orbit wheels,
Each flies through inassuageable chase,
Since the hunt o' the world begun,
The puissant approaches of thy face,
And yet thy radiant leash he feels.
Since the hunt o' the world begun,
Lashed with terror, leashed with longing,
The mighty course is ever run;
Pricked with terror, leashed with longing,
Thy rein they love, and thy rebuke they shun.
Since the hunt o' the world began,
With love that trembleth, fear that loveth,
Thou join'st the woman to the man;
And Life with Death
In obscure nuptials moveth,
Commingling alien yet affinèd breath.

Thou art the incarnated Light
Whose Sire is aboriginal, and beyond
Death and resurgence of our day and night;
From him is thy vicegerent wand
With double potence of the black and white.
Giver of Love, and Beauty, and Desire,
The terror, and the loveliness, and purging,

SIGHT AND INSIGHT

The deathfulness and lifefulness of fire!
Samson's riddling meanings merging
In thy twofold sceptre meet:
Out of thy minatory might,
Burning Lion, burning Lion,
Comes the honey of all sweet,
And out of thee, the eater, comes forth meat.
And though, by thine alternate breath,
Every kiss thou dost inspire
Echoeth
Back from the windy vaultages of death;
Yet thy clear warranty above
Augurs the wings of death too must
Occult reverberations stir of love
Crescent, and life incredible;
That even the kisses of the just
Go down not unresurgent to the dust.
Yea, not a kiss which I have given,
But shall triumph upon my lips in heaven,
Or cling a shameful fungus there in hell.

Know'st thou me not, O Sun? Yea, well
Thou know'st the ancient miracle,
The children know'st of Zeus and May;
And still thou teachest them, O splendent
    Brother,
To incarnate, the antique way,
The truth which is their heritage from their Sire
In sweet disguise of flesh from their sweet
    Mother.
My fingers thou hast taught to con

ORIENT ODE

Thy flame-chorded psalterion,
Till I can translate into mortal wire—
Till I can translate passing well—
The heavenly harping harmony,
Melodious, sealed, inaudible,
Which makes the dulcet psalter of the world's desire.
Thou whisperest in the Moon's white ear,
And she does whisper into mine,—
By night together, I and she—
With her virgin voice divine,
The things I cannot half so sweetly tell
As she can sweetly speak, I sweetly hear.

By her, the Woman, does Earth live, O Lord,
Yet she for Earth, and both in Thee.
Light out of Light!
Resplendent and prevailing Word
Of the Unheard!
Not unto thee, great Image, not to thee
Did the wise heathen bend an idle knee;
And in an age of faith grown frore
If I too shall adore,
Be it accounted unto me
A bright sciential idolatry!
God has given thee visible thunders
To utter thine apocalypse of wonders;
And what want I of prophecy,
That at the sounding from thy station
Of thy flagrant trumpet, see
The seals that melt, the open revelation?

SIGHT AND INSIGHT

Or who a God-persuading angel needs,
That only heeds
The rhetoric of thy burning deeds?
Which but to sing, if it may be,
In worship-warranting moiety,
So I would win
In such a song as hath within
A smouldering core of mystery,
Brimmèd with nimbler meanings up
Than hasty Gideons in their hands may sup;—
Lo, my suit pleads
That thou, Isaian coal of fire,
Touch from yon altar my poor mouth's desire,
And the relucent song take for thy sacred meeds.

To thine own shape
Thou round'st the chrysolite of the grape,
Bind'st thy gold lightnings in his veins;
Thou storest the white garners of the rains.
Destroyer and preserver, thou
Who medicinest sickness, and to health
Art the unthankèd marrow of its wealth;
To those apparent sovereignties we bow
And bright appurtenances of thy brow!
Thy proper blood dost thou not give,
That Earth, the gusty Mænad, drink and dance?
Art thou not life of them that live?
Yea, in glad twinkling advent, thou dost dwell
Within our body as a tabernacle!
Thou bittest with thine ordinance
The jaws of Time, and thou dost mete

ORIENT ODE

The unsustainable treading of his feet.
Thou to thy spousal universe
Art Husband, she thy Wife and Church;
Who in most dusk and vidual curch,
Her Lord being hence,
Keeps her cold sorrows by thy hearse.
The heavens renew their innocence
And morning state
But by thy sacrament communicate;
Their weeping night the symbol of our prayers,
Our darkened search,
And sinful vigil desolate.
Yea, biune in imploring dumb,
Essential Heavens and corporal Earth await;
The Spirit and the Bride say : Come!
Lo, of thy Magians I the least
Haste with my gold, my incenses and myrrhs,
To thy desired epiphany, from the spiced
Regions and odorous of Song's traded East.
Thou, for the life of all that live
The victim daily born and sacrificed;
To whom the pinion of this longing verse
Beats but with fire which first thyself did give,
To thee, O Sun—or is't perchance, to Christ?

Ay, if men say that on all high heaven's face
The saintly signs I trace
Which round my stolèd altars hold their solemn
    place,
Amen, amen! For oh, how could it be,—
When I with wingèd feet had run

SIGHT AND INSIGHT

Through all the windy earth about,
Quested its secret of the sun,
And heard what thing the stars together shout,—
I should not heed thereout
Consenting counsel won :—
' By this, O Singer, know we if thou see.
When men shall say to thee : Lo ! Christ is here,
When men shall say to thee : Lo ! Christ is there,
Believe them : yea, and this—then art thou seer,
When all thy crying clear
Is but : Lo here ! lo there !—ah me, lo everywhere ! '

NEW YEAR'S CHIMES

WHAT is the song the stars sing?
   (*And a million songs are as song of one*)
This is the song the stars sing:
(*Sweeter song's none*)

One to set, and many to sing,
   (*And a million songs are as song of one*)
One to stand, and many to cling,
The many things, and the one Thing,
   The one that runs not, the many that run.

The ever new weaveth the ever old,
   (*And a million songs are as song of one*)
Ever telling the never told;
The silver saith, and the said is gold,
   And done ever the never done.

The chase that's chased is the Lord o' the chase,
   (*And a million songs are as song of one*)
And the pursued cries on the race;
   And the hounds in leash are the hounds that run.

Hidden stars by the shown stars' sheen;
   (*And a million suns are but as one*)
Colours unseen by the colours seen,
And sounds unheard heard sounds between,
   And a night is in the light of the sun.

SIGHT AND INSIGHT

An ambuscade of light in night,
 (*And a million secrets are but as one*)
And a night is dark in the sun's light,
 And a world in the world man looks upon.

Hidden stars by the shown stars' wings,
 (*And a million cycles are but as one*)
And a world with unapparent strings
Knits the simulant world of things;
 Behold, and vision thereof is none.

The world above in the world below,
 (*And a million worlds are but as one*)
And the One in all; as the sun's strength so
Strives in all strength, glows in all glow
 Of the earth that wits not, and man thereon.

Braced in its own fourfold embrace
 (*And a million strengths are as strength of one*)
And round it all God's arms of grace,
The world, so as the Vision says,
 Doth with great lightning-tramples run.

And thunder bruiteth into thunder,
 (*And a million sounds are as sound of one*)
From stellate peak to peak is tossed a voice of wonder,
And the height stoops down to the depths thereunder,
 And sun leans forth to his brother-sun.

NEW YEAR'S CHIMES

And the more ample years unfold
   (*With a million songs as song of one*)
A little new of the ever old,
A little told of the never told,
   Added act of the never done.

Loud the descant, and low the theme,
   (*A million songs are as song of one*)
And the dream of the world is dream in dream,
But the one Is is, or nought could seem;
   And the song runs round to the song begun.

This is the song the stars sing,
   (*Tonèd all in time*)
Tintinnabulous, tuned to ring
A multitudinous-single thing
   (*Rung all in rhyme*).

FROM THE NIGHT OF FOREBEING
AN ODE AFTER EASTER

In the chaos of preordination, and night of our forebeings.
SIR THOMAS BROWNE.

Et lux in tenebris erat, et tenebræ eam non comprehenderunt.
ST. JOHN.

CAST wide the folding doorways of the East,
   For now is light increased!
   And the wind-besomed chambers of the air,
See they be garnished fair;
And look the ways exhale some precious odours,
And set ye all about wild-breathing spice,
   Most fit for Paradise!
Now is no time for sober gravity,
Season enough has Nature to be wise;
But now discinct, with raiment glittering free,
Shake she the ringing rafters of the skies
With festal footing and bold joyance sweet,
And let the earth be drunken and carouse!
For lo, into her house
Spring is come home with her world-wandering feet,
And all things are made young with young desires;
   And all for her is light increased
   In yellow stars and yellow daffodils,
   And East to West, and West to East,
   Fling answering welcome-fires,
By dawn and day-fall, on the jocund hills.
And ye, winged minstrels of her fair meinie,

FROM THE NIGHT OF FOREBEING

Being newly coated in glad livery,
Upon her steps attend,
And round her treading dance, and without end
Reel your shrill lutany.
What popular breath her coming does out-tell
The garrulous leaves among!
What little noises stir and pass
From blade to blade along the voluble grass!
O Nature, never-done
Ungaped-at Pentecostal miracle,
We hear thee, each man in his proper tongue!
Break, elemental children, break ye loose
From the strict frosty rule
Of grey-beard Winter's school.
Vault, O young winds, vault in your tricksome courses
Upon the snowy steeds that reinless use
In cœrule pampas of the heaven to run;
Foaled of the white sea-horses,
Washed in the lambent waters of the sun.
Let even the slug-abed snail upon the thorn
Put forth a conscious horn!
Mine elemental co-mates, joy each one;
And ah, my foster-brethren, seem not sad—
No, seem not sad,
That my strange heart and I should be so little glad.
Suffer me at your leafy feast
To sit apart, a somewhat alien guest,
And watch your mirth,
Unsharing in the liberal laugh of earth;
Yet with a sympathy
Begot of wholly sad and half-sweet memory—

SIGHT AND INSIGHT

The little sweetness making grief complete;
Faint wind of wings from hours that distant beat,
When I, I too,
Was once, O wild companions, as are you,—
Ran with such wilful feet;
Wraith of a recent day and dead,
Risen wanly overhead,
Frail, strengthless as a noon-belated moon,
Or as the glazing eyes of watery heaven,
When the sick night sinks into deathly swoon.

A higher and a solemn voice
I heard through your gay-hearted noise;
A solemn meaning and a stiller voice
Sounds to me from far days when I too shall rejoice,
Nor more be with your jollity at strife.
O prophecy
Of things that are, and are not, and shall be!
The great-vanned Angel March
Hath trumpeted
His clangorous ' Sleep no more ' to all the dead—
Beat his strong vans o'er earth, and air, and sea.
And they have heard;
Hark to the *Jubilate* of the bird
For them that found the dying way to life!
And they have heard,
And quicken to the great precursive word;
Green spray showers lightly down the cascade of
    the larch;
The graves are riven,

FROM THE NIGHT OF FOREBEING

And the Sun comes with power amid the clouds
 of heaven!
Before his way
Went forth the trumpet of the March;
Before his way, before his way
Dances the pennon of the May!
O Earth, unchilded, widowed Earth, so long
Lifting in patient pine and ivy-tree
Mournful belief and steadfast prophecy,
Behold how all things are made true!
Behold your bridegroom cometh in to you,
Exceeding glad and strong.
Raise up your eyes, O raise your eyes abroad!
No more shall you sit sole and vidual,
Searching, in servile pall,
Upon the hieratic night the star-sealed sense of all:
Rejoice, O barren, and look forth abroad!
Your children gathered back to your embrace
See with a mother's face.
Look up, O mortals, and the portent heed;
In very deed,
Washed with new fire to their irradiant birth,
Reintegrated are the heavens and earth!
From sky to sod,
The world's unfolded blossom smells of God.

O imagery
Of that which was the first, and is the last!
For, as the dark profound nativity,
God saw the end should be,
When the world's infant horoscope He cast.

SIGHT AND INSIGHT

Unshackled from the bright Phœbean awe,
In leaf, flower, mold, and tree,
Resolved into dividual liberty,
Most strengthless, unparticipant, inane,
Or suffered the ill peace of lethargy,
Lo, the Earth eased of rule:
Unsummered, granted to her own worst smart
The dear wish of the fool—
Disintegration, merely which man's heart
For freedom understands,
Amid the frog-like errors from the damp
And quaking swamp
Of the low popular levels spawned in all the lands.
But thou, O Earth, dost much disdain
The bondage of thy waste and futile reign,
And sweetly to the great compulsion draw
Of God's alone true-manumitting law,
And Freedom, only which the wise intend,
To work thine innate end.
Over thy vacant counterfeit of death
Broods with soft urgent breath
Love, that is child of Beauty and of Awe:
To intercleavage of sharp warring pain,
As of contending chaos come again,
Thou wak'st, O Earth,
And work'st from change to change and birth to birth
Creation old as hope, and new as sight;
For meed of toil not vain,
Hearing once more the primal fiat toll:
'Let there be light!'

FROM THE NIGHT OF FOREBEING

And there is light!
Light flagrant, manifest;
Light to the zenith, light from pole to pole;
Light from the East that waxeth to the West,
And with its puissant goings-forth
Encroaches on the South and on the North;
And with its great approaches does prevail
Upon the sullen fastness of the height,
And summoning its levied power
Crescent and confident through the crescent hour,
Goes down with laughters on the subject vale.
Light flagrant, manifest;
Light to the sentient closeness of the breast,
Light to the secret chambers of the brain!
And thou up-floatest, warm, and newly-bathed,
Earth, through delicious air,
And with thine own apparent beauties swathed,
Wringing the waters from thine arborous hair;
That all men's hearts, which do behold and see,
Grow weak with their exceeding much desire,
And turn to thee on fire,
Enamoured with their utter wish of thee,
Anadyomene!
What vine-outquickening life all creatures sup,
Feel, for the air within its sapphire cup
How it does leap, and twinkle headily!
Feel, for Earth's bosom pants, and heaves her scarfing sea;
And round and round in bacchanal rout reel the swift spheres intemperably!

SIGHT AND INSIGHT

My little-worlded self! the shadows pass
In this thy sister-world, as in a glass,
Of all processions that revolve in thee:
Not only of cyclic Man
Thou here discern'st the plan,
Not only of cyclic Man, but of the cyclic Me.
Not solely of Mortality's great years
The reflex just appears,
But thine own bosom's year, still circling round
In ample and in ampler gyre
Toward the far completion, wherewith crowned,
Love unconsumed shall chant in his own furnace-fire.
How many trampled and deciduous joys
Enrich thy soul for joys deciduous still,
Before the distance shall fulfil
Cyclic unrest with solemn equipoise!
Happiness is the shadow of things past,
Which fools still take for that which is to be!
And not all foolishly:
For all the past, read true, is prophecy,
And all the firsts are hauntings of some Last,
And all the springs are flash-lights of one Spring.
Then leaf, and flower, and fall-less fruit
Shall hang together on the unyellowing bough;
And silence shall be Music mute
For her surchargèd heart. Hush thou!
These things are far too sure that thou should'st dream
Thereof, lest they appear as things that seem.

Shade within shade! for deeper in the glass
Now other imaged meanings pass;

FROM THE NIGHT OF FOREBEING

And as the man, the poet there is read.
Winter with me, alack!
Winter on every hand I find:
Soul, brain, and pulses dead,
The mind no further by the warm sense fed,
The soul weak-stirring in the arid mind,
More tearless-weak to flash itself abroad
Than the earth's life beneath the frost-scorched sod.
My lips have drought, and crack,
By laving music long unvisited.
Beneath the austere and macerating rime
Draws back constricted in its icy urns
The genial flame of Earth, and there
With torment and with tension does prepare
The lush disclosures of the vernal time.
All joys draw inward to their icy urns,
Tormented by constraining rime,
And there
With undelight and throe prepare
The bounteous efflux of the vernal time.
Nor less beneath compulsive Law
Rebukèd draw
The numbèd musics back upon my heart;
Whose yet-triumphant course I know
And prevalent pulses forth shall start,
Like cataracts that with thunderous hoof charge the disbanding snow.
All power is bound
In quickening refusal so;
And silence is the lair of sound;
In act its impulse to deliver,

SIGHT AND INSIGHT

With fluctuance and quiver
The endeavouring thew grows rigid. Strong
From its retracted coil strikes the resilient song.

Giver of spring,
And song, and every young new thing!
Thou only seest in me, so stripped and bare,
The lyric secret waiting to be born,
The patient term allowed
Before it stretch and flutteringly unfold
Its rumpled webs of amethyst-freaked, diaphanous gold
And what hard task abstracts me from delight,
Filling with hopeless hope and dear despair
The still-born day and parchèd fields of night,
That my old way of song, no longer fair,
For lack of serene care,
Is grown a stony and a weed-choked plot,
Thou only know'st aright,
Thou only know'st, for I know not.
How many songs must die that this may live!
And shall this most rash hope and fugitive,
Fulfilled with beauty and with might
In days whose feet are rumorous on the air,
Make me forget to grieve
For songs which might have been, nor ever were?
Stern the denial, the travail slow,
The struggling wall will scantly grow:
And though with that dread rite of sacrifice
Ordained for during edifice,
How long, how long ago!
Into that wall which will not thrive

FROM THE NIGHT OF FOREBEING

I build myself alive,
Ah, who shall tell me will the wall uprise?
Thou wilt not tell me, who dost only know!
Yet still in mind I keep,
He that observes the wind shall hardly sow,
He that regards the clouds shall hardly reap.
Thine ancient way! I give,
Nor wit if I receive;
Risk all, who all would gain : and blindly. Be it so.

' And blindly,' said I ?—No!
That saying I unsay: the wings
Hear I not in prævenient winnowings
Of coming songs, that lift my hair and stir it?
What winds with music wet do the sweet storm
      foreshow!
Utter stagnation
Is the solstitial slumber of the spirit,
The blear and blank negation of all life :
But these sharp questionings mean strife, and strife
Is the negation of negation.
The thing from which I turn my troubled look,
Fearing the gods' rebuke;
That perturbation putting glory on,
As is the golden vortex in the West
Over the foundered sun;
That—but low breathe it, lest the Nemesis
Unchild me, vaunting this—
Is bliss, the hid, hugged, swaddled bliss!
O youngling Joy carest!
That on my now first-mothered breast

SIGHT AND INSIGHT

Pliest the strange wonder of thine infant lip,
What this aghast surprise of keenest panging,
Wherefrom I blench, and cry thy soft mouth rest ?
Ah hold, withhold, and let the sweet mouth slip !
So, with such pain, recoils the woolly dam,
Unused, affrighted, from her yeanling lamb :
I, one with her in cruel fellowship,
Marvel what unmaternal thing I am.

Nature, enough ! Within thy glass
Too many and too stern the shadows pass.
In this delighted season, flaming
For thy resurrection-feast,
Ah, more I think the long ensepulture cold,
Than stony winter rolled
From the unsealed mouth of the holy East ;
The snowdrop's saintly stoles less heed
Than the snow-cloistered penance of the seed.
'Tis the weak flesh reclaiming
Against the ordinance
Which yet for just the accepting spirit scans.
Earth waits, and patient heaven,
Self-bonded God doth wait
Thrice-promulgated bans
Of His fair nuptial-date.
And power is man's,
With that great word of ' Wait,'
To still the sea of tears,
And shake the iron heart of Fate.
In that one word is strong
An else, alas, much-mortal song ;

FROM THE NIGHT OF FOREBEING

With sight to pass the frontier of all spheres,
And voice which does my sight such wrong.

Not without fortitude I wait
The dark majestical ensuit
Of destiny, nor peevish rate
Calm-knowledged Fate.
I, that no part have in the time's bragged way,
And its loud bruit;
I, in this house so rifted, marred,
So ill to live in, hard to leave;
I, so star-weary, over-warred,
That have no joy in this your day—
Rather foul fume englutting, that of day
Confounds all ray—
But only stand aside and grieve;
I yet have sight beyond the smoke,
And kiss the gods' feet, though they wreak
Upon me stroke and again stroke;
And this my seeing is not weak.
The Woman I behold, whose vision seek
All eyes and know not; t'ward whom climb
The steps o' the world, and beats all wing of rhyme,
And knows not; 'twixt the sun and moon
Her inexpressible front enstarred
Tempers the wrangling spheres to tune;
Their divergent harmonies
Concluded in the concord of her eyes,
And vestal dances of her glad regard.
I see, which fretteth with surmise
Much heads grown unsagacious-grey,

SIGHT AND INSIGHT

The slow aim of wise-hearted Time,
Which folded cycles within cycles cloak :
We pass, we pass, we pass ; this does not pass away,
But holds the furrowing earth still harnessed to its yoke.
The stars still write their golden purposes
On heaven's high palimpsest, and no man sees,
Nor any therein Daniel ; I do hear
From the revolving year
A voice which cries :
' All dies ;
Lo, how all dies ! O seer,
And all things too arise :
All dies, and all is born ;
But each resurgent morn, behold, more near the Perfect Morn.'

Firm is the man, and set beyond the cast
Of Fortune's game, and the iniquitous hour,
Whose falcon soul sits fast,
And not intends her high sagacious tour
Or ere the quarry sighted ; who looks past
To slow much sweet from little instant sour,
And in the first does always see the last.

ANY SAINT

HIS shoulder did I hold
   Too high that I, o'erbold
      Weak one,
Should lean thereon.

But He a little hath
Declined His stately path
      And my
   Feet set more high;

That the slack arm may reach
His shoulder, and faint speech
      Stir
   His unwithering hair.

And bolder now and bolder
I lean upon that shoulder,
      So dear
   He is and near:

And with His aureole
The tresses of my soul
      Are blent
   In wished content.

Yea, this too gentle Lover
Hath flattering words to move her
      To pride
   By His sweet side.

SIGHT AND INSIGHT

Ah, Love! somewhat let be—-
Lest my humility
    Grow weak
   When Thou dost speak.

Rebate Thy tender suit,
Lest to herself impute
    Some worth
   Thy bride of earth!

A maid too easily
Conceits herself to be
    Those things
   Her lover sings;

And being straitly wooed,
Believes herself the Good
    And Fair
   He seeks in her.

Turn something of Thy look,
And fear me with rebuke,
    That I
   May timorously

Take tremors in Thy arms,
And with contrivèd charms
    Allure
   A love unsure.

Not to me, not to me,
Builded so flawfully,
    O God,
   Thy humbling laud!

ANY SAINT

Not to this man, but Man,—
Universe in a span;
    Point
      Of the spheres conjoint;

In whom eternally
Thou, Light, dost focus Thee!—
    Didst pave
      The way o' the wave;

Rivet with stars the Heaven,
For causeways to Thy driven
    Car
      In its coming far

Unto him, only him;
In Thy deific whim
    Didst bound
      Thy works' great round

In this small ring of flesh;
The sky's gold-knotted mesh
    Thy wrist
      Did only twist

To take him in that net.—
Man! swinging-wicket set
    Between
      The Unseen and Seen;

Lo, God's two worlds immense,
Of spirit and of sense,
    Wed
      In this narrow bed;

SIGHT AND INSIGHT

Yea, and the midge's hymn
Answers the seraphim
    Athwart
      Thy body's court!

Great arm-fellow of God!
To the ancestral clod
    Kin,
      And to cherubin;

Bread predilectedly
O' the worm and Deity!
    Hark,
      O God's clay-sealed Ark,

To praise that fits thee, clear
To the ear within the ear,
    But dense
      To clay-sealed sense.

All the Omnific made
When, in a word he said,
    (Mystery!)
      He uttered *thee;*

Thee His great utterance bore,
O secret metaphor
    Of what
      Thou dream'st no jot!

Cosmic metonymy;
Weak world-unshuttering key;
    One
      Seal of Solomon!

ANY SAINT

Trope that itself not scans
Its huge significance,
    Which tries
   Cherubic eyes.

Primer where the angels all
God's grammar spell in small,
    Nor spell
  The highest too well.

Point for the great descants
Of starry disputants;
   Equation
  Of creation.

Thou meaning, couldst thou see,
Of all which dafteth thee;
   So plain,
  It mocks thy pain.

Stone of the Law indeed,
Thine own self couldst thou read;
   Thy bliss
  Within thee is.

Compost of Heaven and mire,
Slow foot and swift desire!
   Lo,
  To have Yes, choose No;

Gird, and thou shalt unbind;
Seek not, and thou shalt find;
   To eat,
  Deny thy meat;

SIGHT AND INSIGHT

And thou shalt be fulfilled
With all sweet things unwilled :
    So best
    God loves to jest

With children small—a freak
Of heavenly hide-and-seek
    Fit
    For thy wayward wit,

Who art thyself a thing
Of whim and wavering ;
    Free
    When His wings pen thee ;

Sole fully blest, to feel
God whistle thee at heel ;
    Drunk up
    As a dew-drop,

When He bends down, sun-wise,
Intemperable eyes ;
    Most proud,
    When utterly bowed,

To feel thyself and be
His dear nonentity—
    Caught
    Beyond human thought

In the thunder-spout of Him,
Until thy being dim,
    And be
    Dead deathlessly.

ANY SAINT

Stoop, stoop ; for thou dost fear
The nettle's wrathful spear,
    So slight
  Art thou of might !

Rise ; for Heaven hath no frown
When thou to thee pluck'st down,
    Strong clod !
  The neck of God.

ASSUMPTA MARIA

Thou needst not make new songs, but say the old.—COWLEY.

'MORTALS, that behold a Woman
  Rising 'twixt the Moon and Sun;
  Who am I the heavens assume? an
All am I, and I am one.

' Multitudinous ascend I,
  Dreadful as a battle arrayed,
For I bear you whither tend I;
  Ye are I : be undismayed!
I, the Ark that for the graven
  Tables of the Law was made;
Man's own heart was one; one, Heaven;
  Both within my womb were laid.
    For there Anteros with Eros,
      Heaven with man, conjonèd was,--
    Twin-stone of the Law, *Ischyros*,
      Agios Athanatos.

' I, the flesh-girt Paradises
  Gardenered by the Adam new,
Daintied o'er with dear devices
  Which He loveth, for He grew.
I, the boundless strict savannah
  Which God's leaping feet go through;
I, the heaven whence the Manna,
  Weary Israel, slid on you!

ASSUMPTA MARIA

    He the Anteros and Eros,
      I the body, He the Cross;
    He upbeareth me, *Ischyros,*
      Agios Athanatos!

' I am Daniel's mystic Mountain,
    Whence the mighty stone was rolled;
I am the four Rivers' fountain,
    Watering Paradise of old;
Cloud down-raining the Just One am,
    Danae of the Shower of Gold;
I the Hostel of the Sun am;
    He the Lamb, and I the Fold.
    He the Anteros and Eros,
      I the body, He the Cross;
    He is fast to me, *Ischyros,*
      Agios Athanatos!

' I, the presence-hall where Angels
    Do enwheel their placèd King—
Even my thoughts which, without change else,
    Cyclic burn and cyclic sing.
To the hollow of Heaven transplanted,
    I a breathing Eden spring,
Where with venom all outpanted
    Lies the slimed Curse shrivelling.
    For the brazen Serpent clear on
      That old fangèd knowledge shone;
    I to Wisdom rise, *Ischyron,*
      Agion Athanaton!

SIGHT AND INSIGHT

' Then commanded and spake to me
    He who framed all things that be ;
And my Maker entered through me,
    In my tent His rest took He.
Lo ! He standeth, Spouse and Brother,
    I to Him, and He to me,
Who upraised me where my mother
    Fell, beneath the apple-tree.
    Risen 'twixt Anteros and Eros,
        Blood and Water, Moon and Sun,
    He upbears me, He *Ischyros*,
        I bear Him, the *Athanaton !* '

Where is laid the Lord arisen ?
    In the light we walk in gloom ;
Though the sun has burst his prison,
    We know not his biding-room.
Tell us where the Lord sojourneth,
    For we find an empty tomb.
' Whence He sprung, there he returneth,
    Mystic Sun,—the Virgin's Womb.'
    Hidden Sun, His beams so near us,
        Cloud enpillared as He was
    From of old, there He, *Ischyros*,
        Waits our search, *Athanatos*.

Who is She, in candid vesture,
    Rushing up from out the brine ?
Treading with resilient gesture
    Air, and with that Cup divine ?

ASSUMPTA MARIA

She in us and we in her are,
    Beating Godward : all that pine,
Lo, a wonder and a terror—
    The Sun hath blushed the Sea to Wine !
        He the Anteros and Eros,
            She the Bride and Spirit ; for
        Now the days of promise near us,
            And the Sea shall be no more.

Open wide thy gates, O Virgin,
    That the King may enter thee !
At all gates the clangours gurge in,
    God's paludament lightens, see !
Camp of Angels ! Well we even
    Of this thing may doubtful be,—
If thou art assumed to Heaven,
    Or is Heaven assumed to thee !
        Consummatum. Christ the promised,
            Thy maiden realm, is won, O Strong !
        Since to such sweet Kingdom comest,
            Remember me, poor Thief of Song !

Cadent fails the stars along :—
    Mortals, that behold a woman
        Rising 'txixt the Moon and Sun ;
    Who am I the heavens assume ? an
    All am I, and I am one.

CARMEN GENESIS

I

SING how the uncreated Light
   Moved first upon the deep and night,
   And, at Its *fiat lux*,
Created light unfurled, to be
God's pinions—stirred perpetually
   In flux and in reflux.

From light create, and the vexed ooze,
God shaped to potency and thews
   All things we see, and all
Which lessen, beyond human mark,
Into the spaces Man calls dark
   Because his day is small.

Far-storied, lanterned with the skies,
All Nature, magic-palace-wise,
   Did from the waters come:
The angelic singing-masons knew
How many centuried centuries through
   The awful courses clomb.

The regent light his strong decree
Then laid upon the snarling sea;
   Shook all its wallowing girth
The shaggy brute, and did (for wrath
Low bellowing in its chafèd path)
   Sullen disglut the Earth.

CARMEN GENESIS

Meanwhile the universal light
Broke itself into bounds; and Night
　And Day were two, yet one:
Dividual splendour did begin
Its procreant task, and, globing, spin
　In moon, and stars, and sun.

With interspheral counterdance
Consenting contraries advance,
　And plan is hid for plan:
In roaring harmonies would burst
The thunder's throat; the heavens, uncurst,
　Restlessly steady ran.

All day Earth waded in the sun,
Free-bosomed; and, when Night begun,
　Spelt in the secret stars.
Day unto Day did utter speech,
Night unto Night the knowledge teach
　Barred in its golden bars.

And, last, Man's self, the little world
Where was Creation's semblance furled,
　Rose at the linking nod:
For the first world, the moon and sun
Swung orbed. That human second one
　Was dark, and waited God.

His locks He spread upon the breeze,
His feet He lifted on the seas,
　Into His worlds He came:

SIGHT AND INSIGHT

Man made confession : ' There is Light ! '
And named, while Nature to its height
　　Quailed, the enormous Name.

II

Poet ! still, still thou dost rehearse,
In the great *fiat* of thy Verse,
　　Creation's primal plot ;
And what thy Maker in the whole
Worked, little maker, in thy soul
　　Thou work'st, and men know not.

Thine intellect, a luminous voice,
Compulsive moved above the noise
　　Of thy still-fluctuous sense ;
And Song, a water-child like Earth,
Stands with feet sea-washed, a wild birth
　　Amid their subsidence.

Bold copyist ! who dost relimn
The traits, in man's gross mind grown dim,
　　Of the first Masterpiece—
Re-marking all in thy one Day :—
God give thee Sabbath to repay
　　Thy sad work with full peace !

Still Nature, to the clang of doom,
Thy Verse rebeareth in her womb ;
　　Thou makest all things new,
Elias, when thou comest ! yea,
Mak'st straight the intelligential way
　　For God to pace into.

CARMEN GENESIS

His locks perturb man's eddying thought,
His feet man's surgy breast have sought,
   To man, His World, He came;
Man makes confession: 'There is Light!'
And names, while Being to its height
   Rocks, the desirèd Name.

III

God! if not yet the royal siege
Of Thee, my terrible sweet Liege,
   Hath shook my soul to fall;
If, 'gainst Thy great investment, still
Some broken bands of rebel Will
   Do man the desperate wall;

Yet, yet, Thy graciousness! I tread,
All quick, through tribes of moving dead—
   Whose life's a sepulchre
Sealed with the dull stone of a heart
No angel can roll round. I start,
   Thy secrets lie so bare!

With beautiful importunacy
All things plead, 'We are fair!' To me
   Thy world's a morning haunt,
A bride whose zone no man hath slipt
But I, with baptism still bedript
   Of the prime water's font.

AD CASTITATEM

THROUGH thee, Virginity, endure
The stars, most integral and pure,
And ever contemplate
Themselves inviolate

In waters, and do love unknown
Beauty they dream not is their own !
Through thee the waters bare
Their bosoms to the air,

And with confession never done
Admit the sacerdotal sun,
Absolved eternally
By his asperging eye.

To tread the floor of lofty souls,
With thee Love mingles aureoles;
Who walk his mountain-peak
Thy sister-hand must seek.

A hymen all unguessed of men
In dreams thou givest to my ken ;
For lacking of like mate,
Eternally frustrate :

Where, that the soul of either spouse
Securelier clasp in either's house,
They never breach at all
Their walls corporeal.

AD CASTITATEM

This was the secret of the great
And primal Paradisal state,
    Which Adam and which Eve
    Might not again retrieve.

Yet hast thou toward my vision taught
A way to draw in vernal thought,
    Not all too far from that
    Great Paradisal state,

Which for that earthy men might wrong,
Were 't uttered in this earthless song,
    Thou layest cold finger-tips
    Upon my histed lips.

But thou, who knowest the hidden thing
Thou hast instructed me to sing,
    Teach Love the way to be
    A new Virginity!

Do thou with thy protecting hand
Shelter the flame thy breath has fanned;
    Let my heart's reddest glow
    Be but as sun-flushed snow.

And if they say that snow is cold,
O Chastity, must they be told
    The hand that's chafed with snow
    Takes a redoubled glow?—

SIGHT AND INSIGHT

That extreme cold like heat doth sear ?
O to this heart of love draw near,
    And feel how scorching rise
    Its white-cold purities!

Life, ancient and o'er-childed nurse,
To turn my thirsting mouth averse,
    Her breast embittereth
    With wry foretaste of death:

But thou, sweet Lady Chastity,
Thou, and thy brother Love with thee,
    Upon her lap may'st still
    Sustain me, if thou will.

Out of the terrors of the tomb,
And unclean shapes that haunt sleep's gloom,
    Yet, yet I call on thee,—
    ' Abandon thou not me!'

Now sung is all the singing of this chant.
Lord, Lord, be nigh unto me in my want!
For to the idols of the Gentiles I
Will never make me an hierophant :—
Their false-fair gods of gold and ivory,
Which have a mouth, nor any speech thereby,
Save such as soundeth from the throat of hell
The aboriginal lie;
And eyes, nor any seeing in the light,—
Gods of the obscene night,
To whom the darkness is for diadem.

AD CASTITATEM

Let them that serve them be made like to them,
Yea, like to him who fell
Shattered in Gaza, as the Hebrews tell,
Before the simple presence of the Ark.

My singing is gone out upon the dark.

THE AFTER WOMAN

DAUGHTER of the ancient Eve,
We know the gifts ye gave—and give.
Who knows the gifts which *you* shall give,
Daughter of the newer Eve?
You, if my soul be augur, you
Shall—O what shall you not, Sweet, do?
The celestial traitress play,
And all mankind to bliss betray;
With sacrosanct cajoleries
And starry treachery of your eyes,
Tempt us back to Paradise!
Make heavenly trespass;—ay, press in
Where faint the fledge-foot seraphin,
Blest fool! Be ensign of our wars,
And shame us all to warriors!
Unbanner your bright locks,—advance,
Girl, their gilded puissance,
I' the mystic vaward, and draw on
After the lovely gonfalon
Us to out-folly the excess
Of your sweet foolhardiness;
To adventure like intense
Assault against Omnipotence!

Give me song, as She is, new,
Earth should turn in time thereto!
New, and new, and thrice so new,
All old sweets, New Sweet, meant you!
Fair, I had a dream of thee,

THE AFTER WOMAN

When my young heart beat prophecy,
And in apparition elate
Thy little breasts knew waxèd great,
Sister of the Canticle,
And thee for God grown marriageable.

How my desire desired your day,
That, wheeled in rumour on its way,
Shook me thus with presentience! Then
Eden's lopped tree shall shoot again :
For who Christ's eyes shall miss, with those
Eyes for evident nuncios ?
Or who be tardy to His call
In your accents augural ?
Who shall not feel the Heavens hid
Impend, at tremble of your lid,
And divine advent shine avowed
Under that dim and lucid cloud ;
Yea, 'fore the silver apocalypse,
Fail, at the unsealing of your lips ?
When to love *you* is (O Christ's Spouse !)
To love the beauty of His house ;
Then come the Isaian days ; the old
Shall dream ; and our young men behold
Vision—yea, the vision of Thabor-mount,
Which none to other shall recount,
Because in all men's hearts shall be
The seeing and the prophecy.
For ended is the Mystery Play,
When Christ is life, and you the way ;
When Egypt's spoils are Israel's right,

SIGHT AND INSIGHT

And Day fulfils the married arms of Night.
But here my lips are still.
Until
You and the hour shall be revealed,
This song is sung and sung not, and its words
    are sealed.

GRACE OF THE WAY

'MY brother!' spake she to the sun;
    The kindred kisses of the stars
    Were hers; her feet were set upon
The moon. If slumber solved the bars

Of sense, or sense transpicuous grown
    Fulfillèd seeing unto sight,
I know not; nor if 'twas my own
    Ingathered self that made her night.

The windy trammel of her dress,
    Her blown locks, took my soul in mesh;
God's breath they spake, with visibleness
    That stirred the raiment of her flesh:

And sensible, as her blown locks were,
    Beyond the precincts of her form
I felt the woman flow from her—
    A calm of intempestuous storm.

I failed against the affluent tide;
    Out of this abject earth of me
I was translated and enskied
    Into the heavenly-regioned She.

Now of that vision I bereaven
    This knowledge keep, that may not dim:—
Short arm needs man to reach to Heaven,
    So ready is Heaven to stoop to him;

SIGHT AND INSIGHT

Which sets, to measure of man's feet,
    No alien Tree for trysting-place;
And who can read, may read the sweet
    Direction in his Lady's face.

And pass and pass the daily crowd,
    Unwares, occulted Paradise;
Love the lost plot cries silver-loud,
    Nor any know the tongue he cries.

The light is in the darkness, and
    The darkness doth not comprehend:
God hath no haste; and God's sons stand
    Yet a day, tarrying for the end.

Dishonoured Rahab still hath hid,
    Yea still, within her house of shame,
The messengers by Jesus bid
    Forerun the coming of His Name.

The Word was flesh, and crucified,
    From the beginning, and blasphemed:
Its profaned raiment men divide,
    Damned by what, reverenced, had redeemed.

Thy Lady, was thy heart not blind,
    One hour gave to thy witless trust
The key thou go'st about to find;
    And thou hast dropped it in the dust.

GRACE OF THE WAY

Of her, the Way's one mortal grace,
    Own, save thy seeing be all forgot,
That, truly, God was in this place,
    And thou, unblessèd, knew'st it not.

But some have eyes, and will not see;
    And some would see, and have not eyes;
And fail the tryst, yet find the Tree,
    And take the lesson for the prize.

RETROSPECT

ALAS, and I have sung
    Much song of matters vain,
    And a heaven-sweetened tongue
Turned to unprofiting strain
Of vacant things, which though
Even so they be, and throughly so,
It is no boot at all for thee to know,
-But babble and false pain.

What profit if the sun
Put forth his radiant thews,
And on his circuit run,
Even after my device, to this and to that use;
And the true Orient, Christ,
Make not His cloud of thee?
I have sung vanity,
And nothing well devised.

And though the cry of stars
Give tongue before His way
Goldenly, as I say,
And each from wide Saturnus to hot Mars
He calleth by its name,
Lest that its bright feet stray;
And thou have lore of all,
But to thine own Sun's call
Thy path disorbed hast never wit to tame;
It profits not withal,
And my rede is but lame.

RETROSPECT

Only that, 'mid vain vaunt
Of wisdom ignorant,
A little kiss upon the feet of Love
My hasty verse has stayed
Sometimes a space to plant;
It has not wholly strayed,
Not wholly missed near sweet, fanning proud
    plumes above.

Therefore I do repent
That with religion vain,
And misconceivèd pain,
I have my music bent
To waste on bootless things its skiey-gendered
    rain:
Yet shall a wiser day
Fulfil more heavenly way
And with approvèd music clear this slip,
I trust in God most sweet.
Meantime the silent lip,
Meantime the climbing feet.

A NARROW VESSEL

BEING A LITTLE DRAMATIC SEQUENCE ON THE ASPECT OF PRIMITIVE GIRL-NATURE TOWARDS A LOVE BEYOND ITS CAPACITIES

A GIRL'S SIN

I.—IN HER EYES

CROSS child! red, and frowning so?
    'I, the day just over,
    Gave a lock of hair to—no!
How *dare* you say, my lover?'

He asked you?—Let me understand;
    Come, child, let me sound it!
'Of course, he *would* have asked it, and—
    And so—somehow—he—found it.

'He told it out with great loud eyes—
    Men have such little wit!
His sin I ever will chastise
    Because I gave him it.

'Shameless in me the gift, alas!
    In him his open bliss:
But for the privilege he has
    A thousand he shall miss!

'His eyes, where once I dreadless laughed,
    Call up a burning blot:
I hate him, for his shameful craft
    That asked by asking not!'

A NARROW VESSEL

Luckless boy! and all for hair
   He never asked, you said?
'Not just—but then he gazed—I swear
   He gazed it from my head!

'His silence on my cheek like breath
   I felt in subtle way;
More sweet than aught another saith
   Was what he did not say.

'He'll think me vanquished, for this lapse,
   Who should be above him;
Perhaps he'll think me light; perhaps—
   Perhaps he'll think I—love him!

'Are his eyes conscious and elate,
   I hate him that I blush;
Or are they innocent, still I hate—
   They mean a thing's to hush.

'Before he naught amiss could do,
   Now all things show amiss;
'Twas all my fault, I know that true,
   But all my fault was his.

'I hate him for his mute distress,
   'Tis insult he should care!
Because my heart's all humbleness,
   All pride is in my air.

A GIRL'S SIN

' With him, each favour that I do
    Is bold suit's hallowing text ;
Each gift a bastion levelled to
    The next one and the next.

' Each wish whose grant may him befall
    Is clogged by those withstood ;
He trembles, hoping one means all,
    And I, lest perhaps it should.

' Behind me piecemeal gifts I cast,
    My fleeing self to save ;
And that's the thing must go at last,
    For that's the thing he'd have.

' My lock the enforcèd steel did grate
    To cut ; its root-thrills came
Down to my bosom. It might sate
    His lust for my poor shame !

' His sifted dainty this should be
    For a score ambrosial years !
But his too much humility
    Alarums me with fears.

' My gracious grace a breach he counts
    For graceless escalade ;
And, though he's silent ere he mounts,
    My watch is not betrayed.

A NARROW VESSEL

' My heart hides from my soul he 's sweet :
    Ah dread, if he divine !
One touch, I might fall at his feet,
    And he might rise from mine.

' To hear him praise my eyes' brown gleams
    Was native, safe delight ;
But now it usurpation seems,
    Because I've given him right.

' Before, I'd have him not remove ;
    Now, would not have him near ;
With sacrifice I called on Love,
    And the apparition's Fear.'

Foolish to give it !—' 'Twas my whim,
    When he might parted be,
To think that I should stay by him
    In a little piece of me.

' He always said my hair was soft—
    What touches he will steal !
Each touch and look (and he 'll look oft)
    I almost thought I'd feel.

' And then, when first he saw the hair,
    To think his dear amazement !
As if he wished from skies a star,
    And found it in his casement.

A GIRL'S SIN

'He'd kiss the lock—and I had toyed
  With dreamed delight of this:
But ah, in proof, delight was void—
  I could not *see* his kiss!'

So, fond one, half this agony
  Were spared, which my hand hushes,
Could you have played, Sweet, the sweet spy,
  And blushed not for your blushes!

A GIRL'S SIN
II.—IN HIS EYES

CAN I forget her cruelty
   Who, brown miracle, gave you me ?
   Or with unmoisted eyes think on
The proud surrender overgone
(Lowlihead in haughty dress)
Of the tender tyranness ?
And ere thou for my joy wast given,
How rough the road to that blest heaven !
With what pangs I fore-expiated
Thy cold outlawry from her head ;
How was I trampled and brought low,
Because her virgin neck was so ;
How thralled beneath the jealous state
She stood at point to abdicate ;
How sacrificed, before to me
She sacrificed her pride and thee ;
How did she, struggling to abase
Herself to do me strange, sweet grace,
Enforce unwitting me to share
Her throes and abjectness with her ;
Thence heightening that hour when her lover
Her grace, with trembling, should discover,
And in adoring trouble be
Humbled at her humility !
And with what pitilessness was I
After slain, to pacify
The uneasy *manes* of her shame,

A GIRL'S SIN

Her haunting blushes!—Mine the blame:
What fair injustice did I rue
For what I—did not tempt her to!
Nor aught the judging maid might win
Me to assoil from *her* sweet sin.
But naught were extreme punishment
For that beyond-divine content,
When my with-thee-first-giddied eyes
Stooped ere their due on Paradise!
O hour of consternating bliss
When I heavened me in thy kiss;
Thy softness (daring overmuch!)
Profanèd with my licensed touch;
Worshipped, with tears, on happy knee,
Her doubt, her trust, her shyness free,
Her timorous audacity!

LOVE DECLARED

I LOOKED, she drooped, and neither spake, and cold
We stood, how unlike all forecasted thought
Of that desirèd minute! Then I leaned
Doubting; whereat she lifted—oh, brave eyes
Unfrighted :—forward like a wind-blown flame
Came bosom and mouth to mine!
       That falling kiss
Touching long-laid expectance, all went up
Suddenly into passion; yea, the night
Caught, blazed, and wrapt us round in vibrant fire.

Time's beating wing subsided, and the winds
Caught up their breathing, and the world's great pulse
Stayed in mid-throb, and the wild train of life
Reeled by, and left us stranded on a hush.
This moment is a statue unto Love
Carved from a fair white silence.
       Lo, he stands
Within us—are we not one now, one, one roof,
His roof, and the partition of weak flesh
Gone down before him, and no more for ever?—
Stands like a bird new-lit, and as he lit,
Poised in our quiet being; only, only
Within our shaken hearts the air of passion,
Cleft by his sudden coming, eddies still
And whirs round his enchanted movelessness.

LOVE DECLARED

A film of trance between two stirrings ! Lo,
It bursts ; yet dream's snapped links cling round the
 limbs
Of waking : like a running evening stream
Which no man hears, or sees, or knows to run,
(Glazed with dim quiet,) save that there the moon
Is shattered to a creamy flicker of flame,
Our eyes' sweet trouble were hid, save that the love
Trembles a little on their impassioned calms.

THE WAY OF A MAID

THE lover whose soul shaken is
In some decuman billow of bliss,
Who feels his gradual-wading feet
Sink in some sudden hollow of sweet,
And 'mid love's usèd converse comes
Sharp on a mood which all joy sums,
An instant's fine compendium of
The liberal-leavèd writ of love—
His abashed pulses beating thick
At the exigent joy and quick,
Is dumbed, by aiming utterance great
Up to the miracle of his fate.

The wise girl, such Icarian fall
Saved by her confidence that she's small,—
As what no kindred word will fit
Is uttered best by opposite,
Love in the tongue of hate exprest,
And deepest anguish in a jest,—
Feeling the infinite must be
Best said by triviality,
Speaks, where expression bates its wings,
Just happy, alien, little things;
What of all words is in excess
Implies in a sweet nothingness;
With dailiest babble shows her sense
That full speech were full impotence;
And, while she feels the heavens lie bare,
She only talks about her hair.

BEGINNING OF END

SHE was aweary of the hovering
   Of Love's incessant and tumultuous wing;
   Her lover's tokens she would answer not—
'Twere well she should be strange with him
    somewhat:
A pretty babe, this Love,—but fie on it,
That would not suffer her lay it down a whit!
Appointed tryst defiantly she balked,
And with her lightest comrade lightly walked,
Who scared the chidden Love to hide apart,
And peep from some unnoticed corner of her
    heart.
She thought not of her lover, deem it not
(There yonder, in the hollow, that's *his* cot),
But she forgot not that he was forgot.
She saw him at his gate, yet stilled her tongue—
So weak she felt her, that she would feel strong,
And she must punish him for doing him wrong:
Passed, unoblivious of oblivion still;
And, if she turned upon the brow o' the hill,
It was so openly, so lightly done,
You saw she thought he was not thought upon.
He through the gate went back in bitterness;
She that night woke and stirred, with no distress,
Glad of her doing,—sedulous to be glad,
Lest perhaps her foolish heart suspect that it
    was sad.

PENELOPE

LOVE, like a wind, shook wide your blossomy eyes,
   You trembled, and your breath came sobbing-
      wise
  For that you loved me.

You were so kind, so sweet, none could withhold
To adore, but that you were so strange, so cold,
  For that you loved me.

Like to a box of spikenard did you break
Your heart about my feet. What words you spake!
  For that you loved me.

Life fell to dust without me; so you tried
All carefullest ways to drive me from your side,
  For that you loved me.

You gave yourself as children give, that weep
And snatch back, with—' I meant you not to keep!'
  For that you loved me.

I am no woman, girl, nor ever knew
That love could teach all ways that hate could do
  To her that loved me.

Have less of love, or less of woman in
Your love, or loss may even from this begin—
  That you so love me.

PENELOPE

For, wild Penelope, the web you wove
You still unweave, unloving all your love.
    Is this to love me,

Or what rights have I that scorn could deny?
Even of your love, alas, poor Love must die,
    If so you love me!

THE END OF IT

SHE did not love to love, but hated him
   For making her to love ; and so her whim
   From passion taught misprision to begin.
And all this sin
Was because love to cast out had no skill
Self, which was regent still.
Her own self-will made void her own self's will.

EPILOGUE

IF I have studied here in part
A tale as old as maiden's heart,
   'Tis that I do see herein
   Shadow of more piteous sin.

She, that but giving part, not whole,
Took even the part back, is the Soul:
   And that so disdainèd Lover—
   Best unthought, since Love is over.

To give the pledge, and yet be pined
That a pledge should have force to bind,
   This, O Soul, too often still
   Is the recreance of thy will!

Out of Love's arms to make fond chain,
And, because struggle bringeth pain,
   Hate Love for Love's sweet constraint,
   Is the way of Souls that faint.

Such a Soul, for saddest end,
Finds Love the foe in Love the friend;
   And—ah, grief incredible!—
   Treads the way of Heaven, to Hell.

ULTIMA

LOVE'S ALMSMAN PLAINETH HIS FARE

YOU, Love's mendicancy who never tried,
    How little of your almsman me you know!
    Your little languid hand in mine you slide,
    Like to a child says—' Kiss me and let me go! '
And night for this is fretted with my tears,
    While I :—' How soon this heavenly neck doth tire,
Bending to me from its transtellar spheres! '
Ah, heart all kneaded out of honey and fire!
Who bound thee to a body nothing worth,
    And shamed thee much with an unlovely soul,
That the most strainedest charity of earth
    Distasteth soon to render back the whole
Of thine inflamèd sweets and gentilesse?
    Whereat, like an unpastured Titan, thou
Gnaw'st on thyself for famine's bitterness,
    And leap'st against thy chain. Sweet Lady, how
Little a linking of the hand to you!
    Though I should touch yours careless for a year,
Not one blue vein would lie divinelier blue
    Upon your fragile temple, to unsphere
The seraphim for kisses! Not one curve
    Of your sad mouth would droop more sad and sweet.
But little food Love's beggars needs must serve,
    That eye your plenteous graces from the street.

LOVE'S ALMSMAN PLAINETH HIS FARE

A hand-clasp I must feed on for a night,
   A noon, although the untasted feast you lay,
To mock me, of your beauty. That you might
   Be lover for one space, and make essay
What 'tis to pass unsuppered to your couch,
   Keep fast from love all day ; and so be taught
The famine which these craving lines avouch !
   Ah ! miser of good things that cost thee naught,
How know'st thou poor men's hunger ?—Misery,
When I go doleless and unfed by thee !

A HOLOCAUST

'No man ever attained supreme knowledge, unless his heart had been torn up by the roots.'

WHEN I presage the time shall come—yea, now
    Perchance is come, when you shall fail from me,
    Because the mighty spirit, to whom you vow
Faith of kin genius unrebukably,
Scourges my sloth ; and from your side dismissed
    Henceforth this sad and most, most lonely soul
Must, marching fatally through pain and mist,
    The God-bid levy of its powers enrol ;
When I presage that none shall hear the voice
    From the great Mount that clangs my ordained
        advance,
That sullen envy bade the churlish choice
    Yourself shall say, and turn your altered glance ;—
O God ! Thou knowest if this heart of flesh
    Quivers like broken entrails, when the wheel
Rolleth some dog in middle street, or fresh
    Fruit when ye tear it bleeding from the peel ;
If my soul cries the uncomprehended cry
    When the red agony oozed on Olivet.
Yet not for this, a caitiff, falter I,
    Beloved whom I must lose, nor thence regret
The doubly-vouched and twin allegiance owed
    To you in Heaven, and Heaven in you, Lady.
How could you hope, loose dealer with my God,
    That I should keep for you my fealty ?
For still 'tis thus :—because I am so true,
My Fair, to Heaven, I am so true to you !

MY LADY THE TYRANNESS

ME since your fair ambition bows
Feodary to those gracious brows,
Is nothing mine will not confess
Your sovran sweet rapaciousness?
Though use to the white yoke inures,
Half-petulant is
Your loving rebel for somewhat his,
Not yours, my love, not yours!

Behold my skies, which make with me
One passionate tranquillity!
Wrap thyself in them as a robe,
She shares them not; their azures probe,
No countering wings thy flight endures.
Nay, they do stole
Me like an aura of her soul.
I yield them, love, for yours!

But mine these hills and fields, which put
Not on the sanctity of her foot.
Far off, my dear, far off the sweet
Grave *pianissimo* of your feet!
My earth, perchance, your sway abjures?—
Your absence broods
O'er all, a subtler presence. Woods,
Fields, hills, all yours, all yours!

Nay then, I said, I have my thought,
Which never woman's reaching raught;

MY LADY THE TYRANNESS

Being strong beyond a woman's might,
And high beyond a woman's height,
Shaped to my shape in all contours.—
I looked, and knew
No thought but you were garden to.
All yours, my love, all yours!

Meseemeth still, I have my life;
All-clement Her its resolute strife
Evades; contained, relinquishing
Her mitigating eyes; a thing
Which the whole girth of God secures.
Ah, fool, pause! pause!
I had no life, until it was
All yours, my love, all yours!

Yet, stern possession! I have my death,
Sole yielding up of my sole breath,
Which all within myself I die,
All in myself must cry the cry
Which the deaf body's wall immures.—
Thought fashioneth
My death without her.—Ah, even death
All yours, my love, all yours!

Death, then, be hers. I have my heaven,
For which no arm of hers has striven;
Which solitary I must choose,
And solitary win or lose.—
Ah, but not heaven my own endures!
I must perforce

ULTIMA

Taste you, my stream, in God your source,—
So steep my heaven in yours!

At last I said—I have my God,
Who doth desire me, though a clod,
And from His liberal Heaven shall He
Bar in mine arms His privacy.
Himself for mine Himself assures.—
None shall deny
God to be mine, but He and I
All yours, my love, all yours!

I have no fear at all lest I
Without her draw felicity.
God for His Heaven will not forgo
Her whom I found such heaven below,
And she will train Him to her lures.
Naught, lady, I love
In you but more is loved above;
What made me, makes Him, yours.

' I, thy sought own, am I forgot ? '
Ha, thou ?—thou liest, I seek thee not.
Why what, thou painted parrot, Fame,
What have I taught thee but her name ?
Hear, thou slave Fame, while Time endures,
I give her thee;
Page her triumphal name!—Lady,
Take her, the thrall is yours.

UNTO THIS LAST

A BOY'S young fancy taketh love
Most simply, with the rind thereof;
A boy's young fancy tasteth more
The rind, than the deific core.
Ah, Sweet! to cast away the slips
Of unessential rind, and lips
Fix on the immortal core, is well;
But heard'st thou ever any tell
Of such a fool would take for food
Aspect and scent, however good,
Of sweetest core Love's orchards grow?
Should such a phantast please him so,
Love where Love's reverent self denies
Love to feed, but with his eyes,
All the savour, all the touch,
Another's—was there ever such?
Such were fool, if fool there be;
Such fool was I, and was for thee!
But if the touch and savour too
Of this fruit—say, Sweet, of you—
You unto another give
For sacrosanct prerogative,
Yea, even scent and aspect were
Some elected Second's share;
And one, gone mad, should rest content
With memory of show and scent;
Would not thyself vow, if there sigh
Such a fool—say, Sweet, as I—
Treble frenzy it must be
Still to love, and to love thee?

ULTIMA

Yet had I torn (man knoweth not,
Nor scarce the unweeping angels wot
Of such dread task the lightest part)
Her fingers from about my heart.
Heart, did we not think that she
Had surceased her tyranny?
Heart, we bounded, and were free!
O sacrilegious freedom!—Till
She came, and taught my apostate will
The winnowed sweet mirth cannot guess
And tear-fined peace of hopelessness;
Looked, spake, simply touched, and went.
Now old pain is fresh content,
Proved content is unproved pain.
Pangs fore-tempted, which in vain
I, faithless, have denied, now bud
To untempted fragrance and the mood
Of contrite heavenliness; all days
Joy affrights me in my ways;
Extremities of old delight
Afflict me with new exquisite
Virgin piercings of surprise,—
Stung by those wild brown bees, her eyes!

ULTIMUM

NOW in these last spent drops, slow, slower shed,
    Love dies, Love dies, Love dies—ah, Love is
    dead!
Sad Love in life, sore Love in agony,
Pale Love in death; while all his offspring songs,
Like children, versed not in death's chilly wrongs,
About him flit, frighted to see him lie
So still, who did not know that Love could die.
One lifts his wing, where dulls the vermeil all
Like clotting blood, and shrinks to find it cold,
And when she sees its lapse and nerveless fall
Clasps her fans, while her sobs ooze through the
    webbèd gold.
Thereat all weep together, and their tears
Make lights like shivered moonlight on long waters.
Have peace, O piteous daughters!
He shall not wake more through the mortal years,
Nor comfort come to my soul widowèd,
Nor breath to your wild wings; for Love is dead!
I slew, that moan for him; he lifted me
Above myself, and that I might not be
Less than myself, need was that he should die;
Since Love that first did wing, now clogged me from
    the sky.
Yet lofty Love being dead thus passeth base—
There is a soul of nobleness which stays,
The spectre of the rose: be comforted,
Songs, for the dust that dims his sacred head!
The days draw on too dark for Song or Love;
O peace, my songs, nor stir ye any wing!

ULTIMA

For lo, the thunder hushing all the grove,
And did Love live, not even Love could sing.

And, Lady, thus I dare to say,
Not all with you is passed away!
Beyond your star, still, still the stars are bright;
Beyond your highness, still I follow height;
Sole I go forth, yet still to my sad view,
Beyond your trueness, Lady, Truth stands true.
This wisdom sings my song with last firm breath,
Caught from the twisted lore of Love and Death,
The strange inwoven harmony that wakes
From Pallas' straying locks twined with her ægis-
    snakes :
' On him the unpetitioned heavens descend,
Who heaven on earth proposes not for end;
The perilous and celestial excess
Taking with peace, lacking with thankfulness.
Bliss in extreme befits thee not, until
Thou 'rt not extreme in bliss; be equal still :
Sweets to be granted think thyself unmeet
Till thou have learned to hold sweet not too sweet.'
This thing not far is he from wise in art
Who teacheth ; nor who doth, from wise in heart.

AN ANTHEM OF EARTH

AN ANTHEM OF EARTH
PROEMION

IMMEASURABLE Earth!
Through the loud vast and populacy of Heaven,
Tempested with gold schools of ponderous orbs,
That cleav'st with deep-revolving harmonies
Passage perpetual, and behind thee draw'st
A furrow sweet, a cometary wake
Of trailing music! What large effluence,
Not sole the cloudy sighing of thy seas,
Nor thy blue-coifing air, encases thee
From prying of the stars, and the broad shafts
Of thrusting sunlight tempers? For, dropped near
From my removèd tour in the serene
Of utmost contemplation, I scent lives.
This is the efflux of thy rocks and fields,
And wind-cuffed forestage, and the souls of men,
And aura of all treaders over thee;
A sentient exhalation, wherein close
The odorous lives of many-throated flowers,
And each thing's mettle effused; that so thou wear'st,
Even like a breather on a frosty morn,
Thy proper suspiration. For I know,
Albeit, with custom-dulled perceivingness,
Nestled against thy breast, my sense not take
The breathings of thy nostrils, there's no tree,
No grain of dust, nor no cold-seeming stone,
But wears a fume of its circumfluous self.
Thine own life and the lives of all that live,
The issue of thy loins,

AN ANTHEM OF EARTH

Is this thy gaberdine,
Wherein thou walkest through thy large demesne
And sphery pleasances,—
Amazing the unstalèd eyes of Heaven,
And us that still a precious seeing have
Behind this dim and mortal jelly.
                              Ah!
If not in all too late and frozen a day
I come in rearward of the throats of song,
Unto the deaf sense of the agèd year
Singing with doom upon me; yet give heed!
One poet with sick pinion, that still feels
Breath through the Orient gateways closing fast,
Fast closing t'ward the undelighted night!

ANTHEM

IN nescientness, in nescientness,
Mother, we put these fleshly lendings on
Thou yield'st to thy poor children; took thy gift
Of life, which must, in all the after days,
Be craved again with tears,—
With fresh and still-petitionary tears.
Being once bound thine almsmen for that gift,
We are bound to beggary, nor our own can call
The journal dole of customary life,
But after suit obsequious for't to thee.
Indeed this flesh, O Mother,
A beggar's gown, a client's badging,
We find, which from thy hands we simply took,
Naught dreaming of the after penury,
In nescientness.

AN ANTHEM OF EARTH

In a little joy, in a little joy,
We wear awhile thy sore insignia,
Nor know thy heel o' the neck. O Mother ! Mother !
Then what use knew I of thy solemn robes,
But as a child to play with them ? I bade thee
Leave thy great husbandries, thy grave designs,
Thy tedious state which irked my ignorant years,
Thy winter-watches, suckling of the grain,
Severe premeditation taciturn
Upon the brooded Summer, thy chill cares,
And all thy ministries majestical,
To sport with me, thy darling. Thought I not
Thou set'st thy seasons forth processional
To pamper me with pageant,—thou thyself
My fellow-gamester, appanage of mine arms ?
Then what wild Dionysia I, young Bacchanal,
Danced in thy lap ! Ah for thy gravity !
Then, O Earth, thou rang'st beneath me,
Rocked to Eastward, rocked to Westward,
Even with the shifted
Poise and footing of my thought !
I brake through thy doors of sunset,
Ran before the hooves of sunrise,
Shook thy matron tresses down in fancies
Wild and wilful
As a poet's hand could twine them ;
Caught in my fantasy's crystal chalice
The Bow, as its cataract of colours
Plashed to thee downward ;
Then when thy circuit swung to nightward,
Night the abhorrèd, night was a new dawning,

AN ANTHEM OF EARTH

Celestial dawning
Over the ultimate marges of the soul;
Dusk grew turbulent with fire before me,
And like a windy arras waved with dreams.
Sleep I took not for my bedfellow,
Who could waken
To a revel, an inexhaustible
Wassail of orgiac imageries;
Then while I wore thy sore insignia
In a little joy, O Earth, in a little joy;
Loving thy beauty in all creatures born of thee,
Children, and the sweet-essenced body of woman;
Feeling not yet upon my neck thy foot,
But breathing warm of thee as infants breathe
New from their mother's morning bosom. So I,
Risen from thee, restless winnower of the heaven,
Most Hermes-like, did keep
My vital and resilient path, and felt
The play of wings about my fledgèd heel—
Sure on the verges of precipitous dream,
Swift in its springing
From jut to jut of inaccessible fancies,
In a little joy.

In a little thought, in a little thought,
We stand and eye thee in a grave dismay,
With sad and doubtful questioning, when first
Thou speak'st to us as men: like sons who hear
Newly their mother's history, unthought
Before, and say—' She is not as we dreamed:
Ah me! we are beguiled!' What art thou, then,

AN ANTHEM OF EARTH

That art not our conceiving ? Art thou not
Too old for thy young children ? Or perchance,
Keep'st thou a youth perpetual-burnishable
Beyond thy sons decrepit ? It is long
Since Time was first a fledgeling ;
Yet thou may'st be but as a pendant bulla
Against his stripling bosom swung. Alack !
For that we seem indeed
To have slipped the world's great leaping-time,
    and come
Upon thy pinched and dozing days : these weeds,
These corporal leavings, thou not cast'st us new,
Fresh from thy craftship, like the lilies' coats,
But foist'st us off
With hasty tarnished piecings negligent,
Snippets and waste
From old ancestral wearings,
That have seen sorrier usage ; remainder-flesh
After our father's surfeits ; nay with chinks,
Some of us, that, if speech may have free leave,
Our souls go out at elbows. We are sad
With more than our sires' heaviness, and with
More than their weakness weak ; we shall not be
Mighty with all their mightiness, nor shall not
Rejoice with all their joy. Ay, Mother ! Mother !
What is this Man, thy darling kissed and cuffed,
Thou lustingly engender'st,
To sweat, and make his brag, and rot,
Crowned with all honour and all shamefulness ?
From nightly towers
He dogs the secret footsteps of the heavens,

AN ANTHEM OF EARTH

Sifts in his hands the stars, weighs them as gold-dust,
And yet is he successive unto nothing
But patrimony of a little mold,
And entail of four planks. Thou hast made his mouth
Avid of all dominion and all mightiness,
All sorrow, all delight, all topless grandeurs,
All beauty, and all starry majesties,
And dim transtellar things ;—even that it may,
Filled in the ending with a puff of dust,
Confess—' It is enough.' The world left empty
What that poor mouthful crams. His heart is builded
For pride, for potency, infinity,
All heights, all deeps, and all immensities,
Arrased with purple like the house of kings,—
To stall the grey-rat, and the carrion-worm
Statelily lodge. Mother of mysteries !
Sayer of dark sayings in a thousand tongues,
Who bringest forth no saying yet so dark
As we ourselves, thy darkest ! We the young,
In a little thought, in a little thought,
At last confront thee, and ourselves in thee,
And wake disgarmented of glory : as one
On a mount standing, and against him stands,
On the mount adverse, crowned with westering rays,
The golden sun, and they two brotherly
Gaze each on each ;
He faring down
To the dull vale, his Godhead peels from him
Till he can scarcely spurn the pebble—
For nothingness of new-found mortality—
That mutinies against his gallèd foot.

AN ANTHEM OF EARTH

Littly he sets him to the daily way,
With all around the valleys growing grave,
And known things changed and strange ; but he
    holds on,
Though all the land of light be widowèd,
In a little thought.

In a little strength, in a little strength,
We affront thy unveiled face intolerable,
Which yet we do sustain.
Though I the Orient never more shall feel
Break like a clash of cymbals, and my heart
Clang through my shaken body like a gong ;
Nor ever more with spurted feet shall tread
I' the winepresses of song ; naught's truly lost
That moulds to sprout forth gain : now I have on me
The high Phœbean priesthood, and that craves
An unrash utterance ; not with flaunted hem
May the Muse enter in behind the veil,
Nor, though we hold the sacred dances good,
Shall the holy Virgins mænadize : ruled lips
Befit a votaress Muse.
Thence with no mutable, nor no gelid love,
I keep, O Earth, thy worship,
Though life slow, and the sobering Genius change
To a lamp his gusty torch. What though no more
Athwart its roseal glow
Thy face look forth triumphal ? Thou put'st on
Strange sanctities of pathos ; like this knoll
Made derelict of day,
Couchant and shadowèd

AN ANTHEM OF EARTH

Under dim Vesper's overloosened hair:
This, where embossèd with the half-blown seed
The solemn purple thistle stands in grass
Grey as an exhalation, when the bank
Holds mist for water in the nights of Fall.
Not to the boy, although his eyes be pure
As the prime snowdrop is
Ere the rash Phœbus break her cloister
Of sanctimonious snow;
Or Winter fasting sole on Himalay
Since those dove-nuncioed days
When Asia rose from bathing;
Not to such eyes,
Uneuphrasied with tears, the hierarchical
Vision lies unoccult, rank under rank
Through all create down-wheeling, from the Throne
Even to the bases of the pregnant ooze.
This is the enchantment, this the exaltation,
The all-compensating wonder,
Giving to common things wild kindred
With the gold-tesserate floors of Jove;
Linking such heights and such humilities
Hand in hand in ordinal dances,
That I do think my tread,
Stirring the blossoms in the meadow-grass,
Flickers the unwithering stars.
This to the shunless fardel of the world
Nerves my uncurbèd back: that I endure,
The monstrous Temple's moveless caryatid,
With wide eyes calm upon the whole of things,
In a little strength.

AN ANTHEM OF EARTH

In a little sight, in a little sight,
We learn from what in thee is credible
The incredible, with bloody clutch and feet
Clinging the painful juts of jaggèd faith.
Science, old noser in its prideful straw,
That with anatomising scalpel tents
Its three-inch of thy skin, and brags ' All 's bare '—
The eyeless worm, that, boring, works the soil,
Making it capable for the crops of God;
Against its own dull will
Ministers poppies to our troublous thought,
A Balaam come to prophecy,—parables,
Nor of its parable itself is ware,
Grossly unwotting; all things has expounded,
Reflux and influx, counts the sepulchre
The seminary of being, and extinction
The Ceres of existence : it discovers
Life in putridity, vigour in decay;
Dissolution even, and disintegration,
Which in our dull thoughts symbolize disorder,
Finds in God's thoughts irrefragable order,
And admirable the manner of our corruption
As of our health. It grafts upon the cypress
The tree of Life—Death dies on his own dart
Promising to our ashes perpetuity,
And to our perishable elements
Their proper imperishability; extracting
Medicaments from out mortality
Against too mortal cogitation; till
Even of the *caput mortuum* we do thus
Make a *memento vivere*. To such uses

AN ANTHEM OF EARTH

I put the blinding knowledge of the fool,
Who in no order seeth ordinance;
Nor thrust my arm in nature shoulder-high,
And cry—' There's naught beyond!' How should
 I so,
That cannot with these arms of mine engirdle
All which I am; that am a foreigner
In mine own region? Who the chart shall draw
Of the strange courts and vaulty labyrinths,
The spacious tenements and wide pleasances,
Innumerable corridors far-withdrawn,
Wherein I wander darkling, of myself?
Darkling I wander, nor I dare explore
The long arcane of those dim catacombs,
Where the rat memory does its burrows make,
Close-seal them as I may, and my stolen tread
Starts populace, a *gens lucifuga;*
That too strait seems my mind my mind to hold,
And I myself incontinent of me.
Then go I, my foul-venting ignorance
With scabby sapience plastered, aye forsooth!
Clap my wise foot-rule to the walls o' the world,
And vow—*A goodly house, but something ancient,
And I can find no Master?* Rather, nay,
By baffled seeing, something I divine
Which baffles, and a seeing set beyond;
And so with strenuous gazes sounding down,
Like to the day-long porer on a stream,
Whose last look is his deepest, I beside
This slow perpetual Time stand patiently,
In a little sight.

AN ANTHEM OF EARTH

In a little dust, in a little dust,
Earth, thou reclaim'st us, who do all our lives
Find of thee but Egyptian villeinage.
Thou dost this body, this enhavocked realm,
Subject to ancient and ancestral shadows ;
Descended passions sway it ; it is distraught
With ghostly usurpation, dinned and fretted
With the still-tyrannous dead ; a haunted tenement,
Peopled from barrows and outworn ossuaries.
Thou giv'st us life not half so willingly
As thou undost thy giving ; thou that teem'st
The stealthy terror of the sinuous pard,
The lion maned with curlèd puissance,
The serpent, and all fair strong beasts of ravin,
Thyself most fair and potent beast of ravin,
And thy great eaters thou, the greatest, eat'st.
Thou hast devoured mammoth and mastodon,
And many a floating bank of fangs,
The scaly scourges of thy primal brine,
And the tower-crested plesiosaure.
Thou fill'st thy mouth with nations, gorgest slow
On purple æons of kings ; man's hulking towers
Are carcase for thee, and to modern sun
Disglutt'st their splintered bones.
Rabble of Pharaohs and Arsacidæ
Keep their cold house within thee ; thou hast sucked down
How many Ninevehs and Hecatompyloi,
And perished cities whose great phantasmata
O'erbrow the silent citizens of Dis :—
Hast not thy fill ?

AN ANTHEM OF EARTH

Tarry awhile, lean Earth, for thou shalt drink,
Even till thy dull throat sicken,
The draught thou grow'st most fat on ; hear'st thou
   not
The world's knives bickering in their sheaths ? O
   patience !
Much offal of a foul world comes thy way,
And man's superfluous cloud shall soon be laid
In a little blood.

In a little peace, in a little peace,
Thou dost rebate thy rigid purposes
Of imposed being, and relenting, mend'st
Too much, with naught. The westering Phœbus'
   horse
Paws i' the lucent dust as when he shocked
The East with rising ; O how may I trace
In this decline that morning when we did
Sport 'twixt the claws of newly-whelped existence,
Which had not yet learned rending ? we did then
Divinely stand, not knowing yet against us
Sentence had passed of life, nor commutation
Petitioning into death. What 's he that of
The Free State argues ? Tellus, bid him stoop,
Even where the low *hic jacet* answers him ;
Thus low, O Man ! there 's freedom's seignory,
Tellus' most reverend sole free commonweal,
And model deeply-policied : there none
Stands on precedence, nor ambitiously
Woos the impartial worm, whose favours kiss
With liberal largesse all ; there each is free

AN ANTHEM OF EARTH

To be e'en what he must, which here did strive
So much to be he could not; there all do
Their uses just, with no flown questioning.
To be took by the hand of equal earth
They doff her livery, slip to the worm,
Which lacqueys them, their suits of maintenance,
And, that soiled workaday apparel cast,
Put on condition: Death's ungentle buffet
Alone makes ceremonial manumission;
So are the heavenly statutes set, and those
Uranian tables of the primal Law.
In a little peace, in a little peace,
Like fierce beasts that a common thirst makes brothers,
We draw together to one hid dark lake;
In a little peace, in a little peace,
We drain with all our burthens of dishonour
Into the cleansing sands o' the thirsty grave.
The fiery pomps, brave exhalations,
And all the glistering shows o' the seeming world,
Which the sight aches at, we unwinking see
Through the smoked glass of Death; Death, wherewith 's fined
The muddy wine of life; that earth doth purge
Of her plethora of man; Death, that doth flush
The cumbered gutters of humanity;
Nothing, of nothing king, with front uncrowned,
Whose hand holds crownets; playmate swart o' the strong;
Tenebrous moon that flux and refluence draws
Of the high-tided man; skull-housèd asp

AN ANTHEM OF EARTH

That stings the heel of kings ; true Fount of Youth,
Where he that dips is deathless ; being's drone-pipe ;
Whose nostril turns to blight the shrivelled stars,
And thicks the lusty breathing of the sun ;
Pontifical Death, that doth the crevasse bridge
To the steep and trifid God ; one mortal birth
That broker is of immortality.
Under this dreadful brother uterine,
This kinsman feared, Tellus, behold me come,
Thy son stern-nursed ; who mortal-motherlike,
To turn thy weanlings' mouth averse, embitter'st
Thine over-childed breast. Now, mortal-sonlike,
I thou hast suckled, Mother, I at last
Shall sustenant be to thee. Here I untrammel,
Here I pluck loose the body's cerementing,
And break the tomb of life ; here I shake off
The bur o' the world, man's congregation shun,
And to the antique order of the dead
I take the tongueless vows : my cell is set
Here in thy bosom ; my little trouble is ended
In a little peace.

MISCELLANEOUS ODES

LAUS AMARA DOLORIS

IMPLACABLE sweet dæmon, Poetry,
What have I lost for thee !
Whose lips too sensitively well
Have shaped thy shrivelling oracle.
So much as I have lost, O world, thou hast,
And for thy plenty I am waste ;
Ah, count, O world, my cost,
Ah, count, O world, thy gain,
For thou hast nothing gained but I have lost !
And ah, my loss is such,
If thou have gained as much
Thou hast even harvest of Egyptian years,
And that great overflow which gives thee grain—
The bitter Nilus of my risen tears !

I witness call the austere goddess, Pain,
Whose mirrored image trembles where it lies
In my confronting eyes,
If I have learned her sad and solemn scroll :—
Have I neglected her high sacrifice,
Spared my heart's children to the sacred knife,
Or turned her customed footing from my soul ?
Yea, thou pale Ashtaroth who rul'st my life,
Of all my offspring thou hast had the whole.
One after one they passed at thy desire
To sacrificial sword, or sacrificial fire ;
All, all,—save one, the sole.
One have I hid apart,
The latest-born and sweetest of my heart,
From thy requiring eyes.

MISCELLANEOUS ODES

O hope, most futile of futilities !
Thine iron summons comes again,
O inevadible Pain !
Not faithless to my pact, I yield :—'tis here,
That solitary and fair,
That most sweet, last, and dear ;
Swerv'st thou ? behold, I swerve not :—strike, nor spare !
Not my will shudders, but my flesh
In awful secrecy to hear
The wind of thy great treading sweep afresh
Athwart my face, and agitate my hair.
The ultimate unnerving dearness take,
The extreme rite of abnegation make,
And sum in one all renderings that were.

The agony is done,
Her footstep passes on ;—
The unchilded chambers of my heart rest bare.
The love, but not the loved, remains ;
As where a flower has pressed a leaf
The page yet keeps the trace and stains.
For thy delight, world, one more grief,
My world, one loss more for thy gains !

Yet, yet, ye few, to whom is given
This weak singing, I have learned
Ill the starry roll of heaven,
Were this all that I discerned
Or of Poetry or of Pain.
Song ! turn on thy hinge again !

LAUS AMARA DOLORIS

Thine alternate panel showed,
Give the Ode a Palinode !
Pain, not thou an Ashtaroth,
Glutted with a bloody rite,
But the icy bath that doth
String the slack sinews loosened with delight.
O great Key-bearer and Keeper
Of the treasuries of God !
Wisdom's gifts are buried deeper
Than the arm of man can go,
Save thou show
First the way, and turn the sod.
The poet's crown, with misty weakness tarnished,
In thy golden fire is burnished
To round with more illustrious gleam his forehead.
And when with sacrifice of costliest cost
On my heart's altar is the Eterne adorèd,
The fire from heaven consumes the holocaust.
Nay, to vicegerence o'er the wide-confined
And mutinous principate of man's restless mind
With thine anointing oils the singer is designed :
To that most desolate station
Thine is his deep and dolorous consecration.
Oh, where thy chrism shall dry upon my brow,
By that authentic sign I know
The sway is parted from this tenuous hand :
And all the wonted dreams that rankèd stand,
The high majestic state,
And cloud-consorting towers of visionary land,
To some young usurpation needs must go ;
And I am all unsceptred of command.

MISCELLANEOUS ODES

Disdiademed I wait
To speak with sieging Death, mine enemy, in the gate.

Preceptress in the wars of God !
His tyros draw the unmortal sword,
And their celestial virtue exercise,
Beneath thy rigorous eyes.
Thou severe bride, with the glad suit adored
Of many a lover whose love is unto blood ;
Every jewel in their crown
Thy lapidary hand does own ;
Nor that warm jacinth of the heart can put
Its lustres forth, till it be cut.
Thou settest thine abode
A portress in the gateways of all love,
And tak'st the toll of joys ; no maid is wed,
But thou dost draw the curtains of her bed.
Yea, on the brow of mother and of wife
Descends thy confirmation from above,
A Pentecostal flame ; love's holy bread,
Consecrated,
Not sacramental is, but through thy leaven.

Thou pacest either frontier where our life
Marches with God's ; both birth and death are given
Into thy lordship ; those debated lands
Are subject to thy hands :
The border-warden, thou, of Heaven—
Yea, that same awful angel with the glaive
Which in disparadising orbit swept
Lintel and pilaster and architrave

LAUS AMARA DOLORIS

Of Eden-gates, and forth before it drave
The primal pair, then first whose startled eyes,
With pristine drops o' the no less startled skies
Their own commingling, wept ;—
With strange affright
Sin knew the bitter first baptismal rite.

Save through thy ministry man is not fed ;
Thou uninvoked presid'st, and unconfest,
The mistress of his feast :
From the earth we gain our bread, and—like the bread
Dropt and regatherèd
By a child crost and thwart,
Whom need makes eat, though sorely weep he for't—
It tastes of dust and tears.

Iron Ceres of an earth where, since the Curse,
Man has had power perverse
Beside God's good to set his evil seed !
Those shining acres of the musket-spears—
Where flame and wither with swift intercease
Flowers of red sleep that not the corn-field bears—
Do yield thee minatory harvest, when
Unto the fallow time of sensual ease
Implacably succeed
The bristling issues of the sensual deed ;
And like to meteors from a rotting fen
The fiery pennons flit o'er the stagnation
Of the world's sluggish and putrescent life,
Misleading to engulfing desolation
And blind, retributive, unguessing strife,
The fatal footsteps of pursuing men.

MISCELLANEOUS ODES

Thy pall in purple sovereignty was dipt
Beneath the tree of Golgotha ;
And from the Hand, wherein the reed was clipt,
Thy bare and antique sceptre thou dost draw.
That God-sprung Lover to thy front allows,
Fairest, the bloody honour of His brows,
The great reversion of that diadem
Which did His drenched locks hem.
For the predestinated Man of Grief,
O regnant Pain, to thee
His subject sway elected to enfeoff ;
And from thy sad conferring to endure
The sanguine state of His investiture ;
Yea, at thy hand, most sombre suzerain,
That dreadful crown He held in fealty ;
O Queen of Calvary,
Holy and terrible, anointed Pain !

A CAPTAIN OF SONG

(ON A PORTRAIT OF COVENTRY PATMORE
BY J. S. SARGENT, R.A.)

LOOK on him. This is he whose works ye know ;
Ye have adored, thanked, loved him,—no, not him !
But that of him which proud portentous woe
To its own grim
Presentment was not potent to subdue,
Nor all the reek of Erebus to dim.
This, and not him, ye knew.
Look on him now. Love, worship if ye can,
The very man.
Ye may not. He has trod the ways afar,
The fatal ways of parting and farewell,
Where all the paths of painèd greatness are ;
Where round and always round
The abhorrèd words resound,
The words accursed of comfortable men,—
' For ever ' ; and infinite glooms intolerable
With spacious replication give again,
And hollow jar,
The words abhorred of comfortable men.
You the stern pities of the gods debar
To drink where he has drunk—
The moonless mere of sighs,
And pace the places infamous to tell,
Where God wipes not the tears from any eyes,
Where-through the ways of dreadful greatness are.

MISCELLANEOUS ODES

He knows the perilous rout
That all those ways about
Sink into doom, and sinking, still are sunk.
And if his sole and solemn term thereout
He has attained, to love ye shall not dare
One who has journeyed there ;
Ye shall mark well
The mighty cruelties which arm and mar
That countenance of control,
With minatory warnings of a soul
That hath to its own selfhood been most fell,
And is not weak to spare :
And lo, that hair
Is blanchèd with the travel-heats of hell.

If any be
That shall with rites of reverent piety
Approach this strong
Sad soul of sovereign Song,
Nor fail and falter with the intimidate throng ;
If such there be,
These, these are only they
Have trod the self-same way ;
The never-twice revolving portals heard
Behind them clang infernal, and that word
Abhorrèd sighed of kind mortality,
As he—
Ah, even as he !

AGAINST URANIA

LO, I, Song's most true lover, plain me sore
    That worse than other women she can deceive,
    For she being goddess, I have given her more
Than mortal ladies from their loves receive ;
And first of her embrace
She was not coy, and gracious were her ways,
That I forgot all virgins to adore ;
Nor did I greatly grieve
To bear through arid days
The pretty foil of her divine delays ;
And one by one to cast
Life, love, and health,
Content, and wealth,
Before her, thinking ever on her praise,
Until at last
Naught had I left she would be gracious for.
Now of her cozening I complain me sore,
Seeing her uses,
That still, more constantly she is pursued,
And straitlier wooed,
Her only-adorèd favour more refuses,
And leaves me to implore
Remembered boon in bitterness of blood.

From mortal woman thou may'st know full well,
O poet, that dost deem the fair and tall
Urania of her ways not mutable,
What things shall thee befall
When thou art toilèd in her sweet, wild spell.

MISCELLANEOUS ODES

Do they strow for thy feet
A little tender favour and deceit
Over the sudden mouth of hidden hell ?—
As more intolerable
Her pit, as her first kiss is heavenlier-sweet.
Are they, the more thou sigh,
Still the more watchful-cruel to deny ?—
Know this, that in her service thou shalt learn
How harder than the heart of woman is
The immortal cruelty
Of the high goddesses.
True is his witness who doth witness this,
Whose gaze too early fell—
Nor thence shall turn,
Nor in those fires shall cease to weep and burn—
Upon her ruinous eyes and ineludible.

TO THE ENGLISH MARTYRS

RAIN, rain on Tyburn tree,
   Red rain a-falling ;
   Dew, dew on Tyburn tree,
Red dew on Tyburn tree,
And the swart bird a-calling.
The shadow lies on England now
Of the deathly-fruited bough :
Cold and black with malison
Lies between the land and sun ;
Putting out the sun, the bough
Shades England now !

The troubled heavens do wan with care,
And burthened with the earth's despair
Shiver a-cold ; the starvèd heaven
Has want, with wanting man bereaven.
Blest fruit of the unblest bough,
Aid the land that smote you, now !
That feels the sentence and the curse
Ye died if so ye might reverse.
When God was stolen from out man's mouth,
Stolen was the bread ; then hunger and drouth
Went to and fro ; began the wail,
Struck root the poor-house and the jail.
Ere cut the dykes, let through that flood,
Ye writ the protest with your blood ;
Against this night—wherein our breath
Withers, and the toiled heart perisheth,—
Entered the *caveat* of your death.

MISCELLANEOUS ODES

Christ, in the form of His true Bride,
Again hung pierced and crucified,
And groaned, ' I thirst ! ' Not still ye stood,—
Ye had your hearts, ye had your blood ;
And pouring out the eager cup,—
' The wine is weak, yet, Lord Christ, sup ! '
Ah, blest ! who bathed the parchèd Vine
With richer than His Cana-wine,
And heard, your most sharp supper past :
' Ye kept the best wine to the last ! '

Ah, happy who
That sequestered secret knew,
How sweeter than bee-haunted dells
The blosmy blood of martyrs smells !
Who did upon the scaffold's bed,
The ceremonial steel between you, wed
With God's grave proxy, high and reverend Death ;
Or felt about your neck, sweetly,
(While the dull horde
Saw but the unrelenting cord)
The Bridegroom's arm, and that long kiss
That kissed away your breath, and claimed you His.
You did, with thrift of holy gain,
Unvenoming the sting of pain,
Hive its sharp heather-honey. Ye
Had sentience of the mystery
To make Abaddon's hookèd wings
Buoy you up to starry things ;
Pain of heart, and pain of sense,
Pain the scourge, ye taught to cleanse ;

TO THE ENGLISH MARTYRS

Pain the loss became possessing ;
Pain the curse was pain the blessing.
Chains, rack, hunger, solitude—these,
Which did your soul from earth release,
Left it free to rush upon
And merge in its compulsive Sun.
Desolated, bruised, forsaken,
Nothing taking, all things taken,
Lacerated and tormented,
The stifled soul, in naught contented,
On all hands straitened, cribbed, denied,
Can but fetch breath o' the Godward side.
Oh to me, give but to me
That flower of felicity,
Which on your topmost spirit ware
The difficult and snowy air
Of high refusal ! and the heat
Of central love which fed with sweet
And holy fire i' the frozen sod
Roots that had ta'en hold on God.

Unwithering youth in you renewed
Those rosy waters of your blood,—
The true *Fons Juventutis* ; ye
Pass with conquest that Red Sea,
And stretch out your victorious hand
Over the Fair and Holy Land.
O, by the Church's pondering art
Late set and named upon the chart
Of her divine astronomy,
Though your influence from on high

MISCELLANEOUS ODES

Long ye shed unnoted ! Bright
New cluster in our Northern night,
Cleanse from its pain and undelight
An impotent and tarnished hymn,
Whose marish exhalations dim
Splendours they would transfuse ! And thou
Kindle the words which blot thee now,
Over whose sacred corse unhearsed
Europe veiled her face, and cursed
The regal mantle grained in gore
Of genius, freedom, faith, and More !

Ah, happy Fool of Christ, unawed
By familiar sanctities,
You served your Lord at holy ease !
Dear Jester in the Courts of God—
In whose spirit, enchanting yet,
Wisdom and love, together met,
Laughed on each other for content !
That an inward merriment,
An inviolate soul of pleasure,
To your motions taught a measure
All your days ; which tyrant king,
Nor bonds, nor any bitter thing
Could embitter or perturb ;
No daughter's tears, nor, more acerb,
A daughter's frail declension from
Thy serene example, come
Between thee and thy much content.
Nor could the last sharp argument
Turn thee from thy sweetest folly ;

TO THE ENGLISH MARTYRS

To the keen *accolade* and holy
Thou didst bend low a sprightly knee,
And jest Death out of gravity
As a too sad-visaged friend ;
So, jocund, passing to the end
Of thy laughing martyrdom ;
And now from travel art gone home
Where, since gain of thee was given,
Surely there is more mirth in heaven !

Thus, in Fisher and in thee,
Arose the purple dynasty,
The anointed Kings of Tyburn tree ;
High in act and word each one :
He that spake—and to the sun
Pointed—' I shall shortly be
Above yon fellow.' He too, he
No less high of speech and brave,
Whose word was : ' Though I shall have
Sharp dinner, yet I trust in Christ
To have a most sweet supper.' Priced
Much by men that utterance was
Of the doomed Leonidas,—
Not more exalt than these, which note
Men who thought as Shakespeare wrote.

But more lofty eloquence
Than is writ by poets' pens
Lives in your great deaths : O these
Have more fire than poesies !
And more ardent than all ode,
The pomps and raptures of your blood !

MISCELLANEOUS ODES

By that blood ye hold in fee
This earth of England ; Kings are ye :
And ye have armies—Want, and Cold,
And heavy Judgements manifold
Hung in the unhappy air, and Sins
That the sick gorge to heave begins,
Agonies, and Martyrdoms,
Love, Hope, Desire, and all that comes
From the unwatered soul of man
Gaping on God. These are the van
Of conquest, these obey you ; these,
And all the strengths of weaknesses,
That brazen walls disbed. Your hand,
Princes, put forth to the command,
And levy upon the guilty land
Your saving wars ; on it go down,
Black beneath God's and heaven's frown ;
Your prevalent approaches make
With unsustainable Grace, and take
Captive the land that captived you ;
To Christ enslave ye and subdue
Her so bragged freedom : for the crime
She wrought on you in antique time,
Parcel the land among you : reign,
Viceroys to your sweet Suzerain !
Till she shall know
This lesson in her overthrow :
Hardest servitude has he
That 's jailed in arrogant liberty ;
And freedom, spacious and unflawed,
Who is walled about with God.

ODE *for the* DIAMOND JUBILEE OF QUEEN VICTORIA, 1897

NIGHT; and the street a corpse beneath the moon,
Upon the threshold of the jubilant day
That was to follow soon;
Thickened with inundating dark
'Gainst which the drowning lamps kept struggle; pole
And plank cast rigid shadows; 'twas a stark
Thing waiting for its soul,
The bones of the preluded pomp. I saw
In the cloud-sullied moon a pale array,
A lengthened apparition, slowly draw;
And as it came,
Brake all the street in phantom flame
Of flag and flower and hanging, shadowy show
Of the to-morrow's glories, as might suit
A pageant of the dead; and spectral bruit
I heard, where stood the dead to watch the dead,
The long Victorian line that passed with printless tread.

First went the holy poets, two on two,
And music, sown along the hardened ground,
Budded like frequence of glad daisies, where
Those sacred feet did fare;
Arcadian pipe, and psaltery, around,

MISCELLANEOUS ODES

And stringèd viol, sound
To make for them melodious due.
In the first twain of those great ranks of death
Went One, the impress recent on his hair
Where it was dinted by the Laureate wreath :
Who sang those goddesses with splendours bare
On Ida hill, before the Trojan boy ;
And many a lovely lay,
Where Beauty did her beauties unarray
In conscious song. I saw young Love his plumes deploy,
And shake their shivering lustres, till the night
Was sprinkled and bedropt with starry play
Of versicoloured light,
To see that Poet pass who sang him well ;
And I could hear his heart
Throb like the after-vibrance of a bell.

A Strength beside this Beauty, Browning went,
With shrewd looks and intent,
And meditating still some gnarlèd theme.
Then came, somewhat apart,
In a fastidious dream,
Arnold, with a half-discontented calm,
Binding up wounds, but pouring in no balm.
The fervid breathing of Elizabeth
Broke on Christina's gentle-taken breath.
Rossetti, whose heart stirred within his breast
Like lightning in a cloud, a Spirit without rest,
Came on disranked ; Song's hand was in his hair,
Lest Art should have withdrawn him from the band,
Save for her strong command ;

THE VICTORIAN ODE

And in his eyes high Sadness made its lair.
Last came a Shadow tall, with drooping lid,
Which yet not hid
The steel-like flashing of his armèd glance ;
Alone he did advance,
And all the throngs gave room
For one that looked with such a captain's mien.
A scornful smile lay keen
On lips that, living, prophesied of doom ;
His one hand held a lightning-bolt, the other
A cup of milk and honey blent with fire ;
It seemed as in that quire
He had not, nor desired not, any brother.
A space his alien eye surveyed the pride
Of meditated pomp, as one that much
Disdained the sight, methought ; then, at a touch,
He turned the heel, and sought with shadowy stride
His station in the dim,
Where the sole-thoughted Dante waited him.

What throngs illustrious next, of Art and Prose,
Too long to tell ! But other music rose
When came the sabre's children : they who led
The iron-throated harmonies of war,
The march resounding of the armèd line,
And measured movement of battalia :
Accompanied their tread
No harps, no pipes of soft Arcadia,
But—borne to me afar—
The tramp of squadrons, and the bursting mine,

MISCELLANEOUS ODES

The shock of steel, the volleying rifle-crack,
And echoes out of ancient battles dead.
So Cawnpore unto Alma thundered back,
And Delhi's cannon roared to Gujerat :
Carnage through all those iron vents gave out
Her thousand-mouthèd shout.
As balefire answering balefire is unfurled,
From mountain-peaks, to tell the foe's approaches,
So ran that battle-clangour round the world,
From famous field to field
So that reverberated war was tossed ;
And—in the distance lost—
Across the plains of France and hills of Spain
It swelled once more to birth,
And broke on me again,
The voice of England's glories girdling in the earth.

It caught like fire the main,
Where rending planks were heard, and broadsides
    pealed,
That shook were all the seas,
Which feared, and thought on Nelson. For with
    them
That struck the Russ, that brake the Mutineer,
And smote the stiff Sikh to his knee —with these
Came they that kept our England's sea-swept hem
And held afar from her the foreign fear.
After them came
They who pushed back the ocean of the Unknown
And fenced some strand of knowledge for our own
Against the outgoing sea

THE VICTORIAN ODE

Of ebbing mystery ;
And on their banner ' Science ' blazoned shone.
The rear were they that wore the statesman's fame,
From Melbourne, to
The arcane face of the much-wrinkled Jew.

Lo, in this day we keep the yesterdays,
And those great dead of the Victorian line.
They passed, they passed, but cannot pass away,
For England feels them in her blood like wine.
She was their mother, and she is their daughter,
This Lady of the water,
And from their loins she draws the greatness which
    they were.
And still their wisdom sways,
Their power lives in her.
Their thews it is, England, that lift thy sword,
They are the splendour, England, in thy song,
They sit unbidden at thy council-board,
Their fame doth compass all thy coasts from wrong,
And in thy sinews they are strong.
Their absence is a presence and a guest
In this day's feast ;
This living feast is also of the dead,
And this, O England, is thine All Souls' Day.
And when thy cities flake the night with flames,
Thy proudest torches yet shall be their names.

O royal England ! happy child
Of such a more than regal line ;
Be it said

MISCELLANEOUS ODES

Fair right of jubilee is thine ;
And surely thou art unbeguiled
If thou keep with mirth and play,
With dance, and jollity, and praise,
Such a To-day which sums such Yesterdays.
Pour to the joyless ones thy joy, thy oil
And wine to such as faint and toil.
And let thy vales make haste to be more green
Than any vales are seen
In less auspicious lands,
And let thy trees clap all their leafy hands,
And let thy flowers be gladder far of hue
Than flowers of other regions may ;
Let the rose, with her fragrance sweetened through,
Flush as young maidens do,
With their own inward blissfulness at play.
And let the sky twinkle an eagerer blue
Over our English isle
Than any otherwhere ;
Till strangers shall behold, and own that she is fair.
Play up, play up, ye birds of minstrel June,
Play up your reel, play up your giddiest spring,
And trouble every tree with lusty tune,
Whereto our hearts shall dance
For overmuch pleasance,
And children's running make the earth to sing.
And ye soft winds, and ye white-fingered beams,
Aid ye her to invest
Our queenly England, in all circumstance
Of fair and feat adorning to be drest ;
Kirtled in jocund green,

THE VICTORIAN ODE

Which does befit a Queen,
And like our spirits cast forth lively gleams :
And let her robe be goodly garlanded
With store of florets white and florets red,
With store of florets white and florets gold,
A fair thing to behold ;
Intrailed with the white blossom and the blue,
A seemly thing to view !
And thereunto,
Set over all a woof of lawny air,
From her head wavering to her sea-shod feet,
Which shall her lovely beauty well complete,
And grace her much to wear.

Lo, she is dressed, and lo, she cometh forth,
Our stately Lady of the North ;
Lo, how she doth advance,
In her most sovereign eye regard of puissance,
And tiar'd with conquest her prevailing brow,
While nations to her bow.
Come hither, proud and ancient East,
Gather ye to this Lady of the North,
And sit down with her at her solemn feast,
Upon this culminant day of all her days ;
For ye have heard the thunder of her goings-forth,
And wonder of her large imperial ways.
Let India send her turbans, and Japan
Her pictured vests from that remotest isle
Seated in the antechambers of the Sun :
And let her Western sisters for a while
Remit long envy and disunion,

MISCELLANEOUS ODES

And take in peace
Her hand behind the buckler of her seas,
'Gainst which their wrath has splintered ; come, for she
Her hand ungauntlets in mild amity.

Victoria ! Queen, whose name is victory,
Whose woman's nature sorteth best with peace,
Bid thou the cloud of war to cease
Which ever round thy wide-girt empery
Fumes, like to smoke about a burning brand,
Telling the energies which keep within
The light unquenched, as England's light shall be ;
And let this day hear only peaceful din.
For, queenly woman, thou art more than woman ;
Thy name the often-struck barbarian shuns :
Thou art the fear of England to her foemen,
The love of England to her sons.
And this thy glorious day is England's ; who
Can separate the two ?
She joys thy joys and weeps thy tears,
And she is one with all thy moods ;
Thy story is the tale of England's years,
And big with all her ills, and all her stately goods.
Now unto thee
The plenitude of the glories thou didst sow
Is garnered up in prosperous memory ;
And, for the perfect evening of thy day,
An untumultuous bliss, serenely gay,
Sweetened with silence of the after-glow.

THE VICTORIAN ODE

Nor does the joyous shout
Which all our lips give out
Jar on that quietude ; more than may do
A radiant childish crew,
With well-accordant discord fretting the soft hour,
Whose hair is yellowed by the sinking blaze
Over a low-mouthed sea. Exult, yet be not
    twirled,
England, by gusts of mere
Blind and insensate lightness ; neither fear
The vastness of thy shadow on the world.
If in the East
Still strains against its leash the unglutted beast
Of War ; if yet the cannon's lip be warm ;
Thou, whom these portents warn but not alarm,
Feastest, but with thy hand upon the sword,
As fits a warrior race :
Not like the Saxon fools of olden days,
With the mead dripping from the hairy mouth,
While all the South
Filled with the shaven faces of the Norman horde.

The NINETEENTH CENTURY

AS, fore-announced by threat of flame and smoke,
   Out of the night's lair broke
   The sun among the startled stars, whose blood
Looses its slow bright flood
Beneath the radiant onset of the sun ;
So crouches he anon,
With nostrils breathing threat of smoke and flame,
Back to the lairing night wherefrom he came.

Say, who is she,
With cloudy battle smoking round her feet,
That goes out through the exit-doors of death ;
And at the alternate limit of her path,
Where first her nascent footsteps troubled day,
Forgotten turmoil curls itself away ?
Who is she that rose
Tumultuous, and in tumult goes ?

This is she
That rose 'midst dust of a down-tumbled world,
And dies with rumour on the air
Of preparation
For a more ample devastation,
And death of ancient fairness no more fair.
First when she knew the day,
The holy poets sung her on her way :
The high, clear band that takes
Its name from heaven-acquainted mountain-lakes ;

THE NINETEENTH CENTURY

And he
That like a star set in Italian sea ;
And he that mangled by the jaws of our
Fierce London, from all frets
Lies balmed in Roman violets ;
And other names of power,
Too recent but for worship and regret,
On whom the tears lie wet.

But not to these
She gave her heart ; her heart she gave
To the blind worm that bores the mold,
Bloodless, pertinacious, cold,
Unweeting what itself upturns,
The seer and prophet of the grave.
It reared its head from off the earth
(Which gives it life and gave it birth)
And placed upon its eyeless head a crown,
Thereon a name writ new,
' Science,' erstwhile with ampler meanings known ;
And all the peoples in their turns
Before the blind worm bowed them down.
Yet, crowned beyond its due,
Working dull way by obdurate, slow degrees,
It is a thing of sightless prophecies ;
And glories, past its own conceit,
Wait to complete
Its travail, when the mounded time is meet.
Nor measured, fit renown,
When that hour paces forth,
Shall overlook those workers of the North

MISCELLANEOUS ODES

And West, those patient Darwins who forthdrew
From humble dust what truth they knew,
And greater than they knew, not knowing all they
    knew.
Yet was their knowledge in its scope a Might,
Strong and true souls to measure of their sight.
Behold the broad globe in their hands comprest,
As a boy kneads a pellet, till the East
Looks in the eyes o' the West ;
And as guest whispers guest
That counters him at feast,
The Northern mouth
Leans to the attent ear of the blended South.
The fur-skinned garb justling the Northern Bear
Crosses the threshold where,
With linen wisp girt on,
Drowses the next-door neighbour of the sun.
Such their laborious worth
To change the old face of the wonted earth.

Nor were they all o' the dust ; as witness may
Davy and Faraday ;
And they
Who clomb the cars
And learned to rein the chariots of the stars ;
Or who in night's dark waters dipt their hands
To sift the hid gold from its sands ;
And theirs the greatest gift, who drew to light
By their sciential might,
The secret ladder, wherethrough all things climb
Upward from the primeval slime.

THE NINETEENTH CENTURY

Nor less we praise
Him that with burnished tube betrays
The multitudinous diminutive
Recessed in virtual night
Below the surface-seas of sight ;
Him whose enchanted windows give
Upon the populated ways
Where the shy universes live
Ambushed beyond the unapprehending gaze :
The dusted anther's globe of spiky stars ;
The beetle flashing in his minute mail
Of green and golden scale ;
And every water-drop a-sting with writhing wars.
The unnoted green scale cleaving to the moist earth's face
Behold disclosed a conjugal embrace,
And womb—
Submitting to the tomb—
That sprouts its lusty issue :* everywhere·conjoins
Either glad sex, and from unguessed-at loins
Breeds in an opulent ease
The liberal earth's increase ;
Such Valentine's sweet unsurmisèd diocese.
Nor, dying Lady, of the sons
Whom proudly owns
Thy valedictory and difficult breath,
The least are they who followed Death
Into his obscure fastnesses,
Tracked to her secret lair Disease—

* The prothallus of the fern, for example, which contains in itself the two sexes, and decays as the young fern sprouts from it.

149

MISCELLANEOUS ODES

Under the candid-seeming and confederate Day
Venoming the air's pure lips to kiss and to betray;
Who foiled the ancient Tyrant's grey design
Unfathomed long, and brake his dusty toils,
Spoiling him of his spoils,
And man, the loud dull fly, loosed from his woven
    line.
Such triumph theirs who at the destined term
Descried the arrow flying in the day—
The age-long hidden Germ—
And threw their prescient shield before its deadly
    way.

Thou, spacious Century!
Hast seen the Western knee
Set on the Asian neck,
The dusky Africa
Kneel to imperial Europe's beck;
The West for her permitted while didst see
Stand mistress-wise and tutelar
To the grey nations dreaming on their days afar,
From old forgotten war
Folding hands whence has slid disusèd rule;
The while, unprescient, in her regent school
She shapes the ample days and things to be,
And large new empery.
Thence Asia shall be brought to bed
Of dominations yet undreamed;
Narrow-eyed Egypt lift again the head
Whereon the far-seen crown Nilotic gleamed.
Thou'st seen the Saxon horde whose veins run brine,

THE NINETEENTH CENTURY

Spawned of the salt wave, wet with the salt breeze,
Their sails combine,
Lash their bold prows together, and turn swords
Against the world's knit hordes ;
The whelps repeat the lioness' roar athwart the
    windy seas.

Yet let it grieve, grey Dame,
Thy passing spirit, God wot,
Thou wast half-hearted, wishing peace, but not
The means of it. The avaricious flame
Thou'st fanned, which thou should'st tame :
Cluck'dst thy wide brood beneath thy mothering
    plumes,
And coo'dst them from their fumes,
Stretched necks provocative, and throats
Ruffled with challenging notes ;
Yet all didst mar,
Flattering the too-much-pampered Boy of War :
Whence the far-jetting engine, and the globe
In labour with her iron progeny,—
Infernal litter of sudden-whelpèd deaths,
Vomiting venomous breaths ;
The growl as of long surf that draweth back
Half a beach in its rattling track,
When like a tiger-cat
The angry rifle spat
Its fury in the opposing foeman's eyes ;—
These are thy consummating victories,
For this hast thou been troubled to be wise !

MISCELLANEOUS ODES

And now what child is this upon thy lap,
Born in the red glow of relighted war ?
That draws Bellona's pap,
—Fierce foster-mother !—does already stare
With mimicked dark regard
And copied threat of brow whose trick it took from
    her :
Young Century, born to hear
The cannon talking at its infant ear—
The Twentieth of Time's loins, since that
Which in the quiet snows of Bethlehem he begat.
Ah ! with forthbringing such and so ill-starred,
After the day of blood and night of fate,
Shall it survive with brow no longer marred,
Lip no more wry with hate ;
With all thou hadst of good,
But from its blood
Washed thine hereditary ill,
Yet thy child still ?

PEACE

ON THE TREATY IN SOUTH AFRICA IN 1902

PEACE :—as a dawn that flares
Within the brazier of the barrèd East,
Kindling the ruinous walls of storm surceased
To rent and roughened glares,
After such night when lateral wind and rain
Torment the to-and-fro perplexèd trees
With thwart encounter ; which, of fixture strong,
Take only strength from the endurèd pain :
And throat by throat begin
The birds to make adventure of sweet din,
Till all the forest prosper into song :—
    Peace, even such a peace,
(O be my words an auspice !) dawns again
Upon our England, from her lethargies
Healed by that baptism of *her* cleansing pain.

Ended, the long endeavour of the land :
Ended, the set of manhood towards the sand
Of thirsty death ; and their more deadly death,
Who brought back only what they fain had lost,
No more worth-breathing breath,—
Gone the laborious and use-working hand.
Ended, the patient drip of women's tears,
Which joined the patient drip of faithful blood
To make of blood and water the sore flood
That pays our conquest's costliest cost.
This day, if fate dispose,
Shall make firm friends from firm and firm-met foes.

MISCELLANEOUS ODES

And now, Lord, since Thou hast upon hell's floor
Bound, like a snoring sea, the blood-drowsed bulk
    of War,
Shall we not cry, on recognising knees,
This is Thy peace ?

If, England, it be but to lay
The heavy head down, the old heavy way ;
Having a space awakened and been bold
To break from them that had thee in the snare,—
Resume the arms of thy false Dalila, Gold,
Shameful and nowise fair :
Forget thy sons who have lain down in bed
With Dingaan and old dynasties, nor heed
The ants that build their empires overhead ;
Forget their large in thy contracted deed,
And that thou stand'st twice-pledged to being great
For whom so many children greatly bleed,
Trusting thy greatness with their deaths : if thou,
England, incapable of proffered fate,
See in such deaths as these
But purchased pledges of unhindered mart,
And hirelings spent that in thy ringed estate
For some space longer now
Thou mayst add gain to gain, and take thine ease,—
God has made hard thy heart ;
Thou hast but bought thee respite, not surcease.
Lord, this is not Thy peace !

But wilt thou, England, stand
With vigilant heart and prescient brain ?—

PEACE

Knowing there is no peace
Such as fools deem, of equal-balanced ease :—
That they who build the State
Must, like the builders of Jerusalem,
The trowel in their hand,
Work with the sword laid ever nigh to them.
If thou hold Honour worthy gain
At price of gold and pain ;
And all thy sail and cannon somewhat more
Than the fee'd watchers of the rich man's store.
If thou discern the thing which all these ward
Is that imperishable thing, a Name,
And that Name, England, which alone is lord
Where myriad-armèd India owns with awe
A few white faces ; uttered forth in flame
Where circling round the earth
Has English battle roared ;
Deep in mid-forest African a Law ;
That in this Name's small girth
The treasure is, thy sword and navies guard :
If thou wilt crop the specious sins of ease,
Whence still is War's increase,—
Proud flesh which asks for War, the knife of God,
Save to thyself, thyself use cautery ;
Wilt stay the war of all with all at odd,
And teach thy jarring sons
Truth innate once,—
That in the whole alone the part is blest and great.
O should this fire of war thus purge away
The inveterate stains of too-long ease,
And yield us back our Empire's clay

MISCELLANEOUS ODES

Into one shoreless State
Compact and hardened for its uses : these
No futile sounds of joyance are to-day ;—
Lord, unrebuked we may
Call this Thy peace !

And in this day be not
Wholly forgot
They that made possible but shall not see
Our solemn jubilee.
Peace most to them who lie
Beneath unnative sky ;
In whose still hearts is dipt
Our reconciling script :
Peace ! But when shouts shall start the housetop
    bird,
Let these, that speak not, be the loudest heard !

CECIL RHODES
DIED MARCH 26, 1902

THEY that mis-said
This man yet living, praise him dead.
And I too praise, yet not the baser things
Wherewith the market and the tavern rings.
Not that high things for gold,
He held, were bought and sold,
That statecraft's means approved are by the end ;
Not for all which commands
The loud world's clapping hands,
To which cheap press and cheaper patriots bend ;
But for the dreams,
For those impossible gleams
He half made possible ; for that he was
Visioner of vision in a most sordid day :
This draws
Back to me Song long alien and astray.

In dreams what did he not,
Wider than his wide deeds? In dreams he wrought
What the old world's long livers must in act forego.
From the Zambesi to the Limpopo
He the many-languaged land
Took with his large compacting hand
And pressed into a nation : 'thwart the accurst
And lion-'larumed ways,
Where the lean-fingered Thirst
Wrings at the throat, and Famine strips the bone ;
A tawny land, with sun at sullen gaze,
And all above a cope of heated stone ;

MISCELLANEOUS ODES

He heard the shirted miner's rough halloo
Call up the mosquèd Cairene ; harkened clear
The Cairene's far-off summons sounding through
The sea's long noises to the Capeman's ear.

He saw the Teuton and the Saxon grip
Hands round the warded world, and bid it rock,
While they did watch its cradle. Like a ship
It swung, whileas the cabined inmates slept,
Secure their peace was kept,
Such arms of warranty about them lock.
Ophir* he saw, her long-ungazed-at gold,
Stirred from its deep
And often-centuried sleep,
Wink at the new Sun in an English hold ;
England, from Afric's swarthy loins
Drawing fecundity,
Wax to the South and North,
To East and West increase her puissant goings-
    forth,
And strike young emperies, like coins,
In her own recent effigy.
He saw the three-branched Teuton hold the sides
Of the round world, and part it as a dish
Whereof to each his wish
The amity of the full feast decides.

So large his dreams, so little come to act !
Who must call on the cannon to compact

* Rhodesia, according to some modern views.

CECIL RHODES

The hard Dutch-stubborned land,
Seditious even to such a potent hand ;
Who grasped and held his Ophir : held, no less,
The Northern ways, but never lived to see
The wing-foot messages
Dart from the Delta to the Southern Sea ;
Who, confident of gold,
A leaner on the statesman's arts
And the unmartial conquests of the marts,
Died with the sound of battle round him rolled,
And rumour of battle in all nations' hearts ;
Dying, saw his life a thing
Of large beginnings ; and for young
Hands yet untrained the harvesting,
Amid the iniquitous years if harvest sprung.

So in his death he sowed himself anew ;
Cast his intents over the grave to strike
In the left world of livers living roots,
And, banyan-like,
From his one tree raise up a wood of shoots.
The indestructible intents which drew
Their sap from him
Thus, with a purpose grim,
Into strange lands and hostile yet he threw,
That there might be
From him throughout the earth posterity :
And so did he—
Like to a smouldering fire by wind-blasts swirled—
His dying embers strew to kindle all the world.

MISCELLANEOUS ODES

Yet not for this I praise
The ending of his strenuous days ;
No, not alone that still
Beyond the grave stretched that imperial Will :
But that Death seems
To set the gateway wide to ampler dreams.
Yea, yet he dreams upon Matoppo hill,
The while the German and the Saxon see,
And seeing, wonder,
The spacious dreams take shape and be,
As at compulsion of his sleep thereunder.
Lo, young America at the Mother's knee,
Unlearning centuried hate,
For love's more blest extreme ;
And this is in his dream,
And sure the dream is great.
Lo, Colonies on Colonies,
The furred Canadian and the digger's shirt,
To the one Mother's skirt
Cling, in the lore of Empire to be wise ;
A hundred wheels a-turn
All to one end—that England's sons may learn
The glory of their sonship, the supreme
Worth that befits the heirs of such estate.
All these are in his dream,
And sure the dream is great.

So, to the last
A visionary vast,
The aspirant soul would have the body lie
Among the hills immovably exalt

CECIL RHODES

As he above the crowd that haste and halt,
' Upon that hill which I
Called " View of All the World " ' ; to show thereby
That still his unappeasable desires
Beneath his feet surveyed the peoples and empires.
Dreams, haply of scant worth,
Bound by our little thumb-ring of an earth ;
Yet an exalted thing
By the gross search for food and raimenting.
So in his own Matoppos, high, aloof,
The elements for roof,
Claiming his mountain kindred, and secure,
Within that sepulture
Stern like himself and unadorned,
From the loud multitude he ruled and scorned,
There let him cease from breath,—
Alone in crowded life, not lonelier in death.

OF NATURE: LAUD AND PLAINT

LO, here stand I and Nature, gaze to gaze,
   And I the greater. Couch thou at my feet,
   Barren of heart, and beautiful of ways,
Strong to weak purpose, fair and brute-brained beast.
I am not of thy fools
Who goddess thee with impious flatteries sweet,
Stolen from the little Schools
Which cheeped when that great mouth of Rydal ceased.
A little suffer that I try
What thou art, Child, and what am I—
Thy younger, forward brother, subtle and small,
As thou art gross and of thy person great withal.

Behold, the child
With Nature needs not to be reconciled.
The babe that keeps the womb
Questions not if with love
The life, distrainèd for its uses, come;
Nor we demand, then, of
The Nature who is in us and around us,
Whose life doth compass, feed, and bound us,
What prompteth her to bless
With gifts, unknown for gifts, our innocent thankless-
   ness.
Mother unguessed is she, to whom
We still are in the womb.
Then comes the incidental day
When our young mouth is weaned; and from her arms
   we stray.

OF NATURE : LAUD AND PLAINT

'Tis over ; not, mistake me not,
Those divine gleams forgot
Which one with a so ampler mouth hath sung ;
Not of these sings
My weak endeavouring tongue ;
But of those simpler things
Less heavenful : the unstrained integrity
Moving most natively,
As the glad customed lot
Of birthright privilege allows,
Through the domestic chambers of its Father's house ;
The virgin hills, provoking to be trod ;
The cloud, the stream, the tree,
The allowing bosom of the warm-breathed sod—
No alien and untemptable delight.
The wonder in a wondrous sight
Was wondrous simple, as our simple God—
Yet not dulled, daily, base,
But sweet and safe possession as our mother's face,
Which we knew not for sweet, but sweetly had ;
For who says—' Lo, how sweet ! ' has first said—' Lo,
    how sad ! '

This, not to be regained with utmost sighs,
This unconsidered birthright, is made void
As Edom's, and destroyed.
Grown man, we now despise
Thee, known for woman, nor too wise ;
As still the mother human
Is known for not too wise, and even woman.
We take ingrateful, for a blinded while,

MISCELLANEOUS ODES

Thine ignorant, sweet smile.
Yield maids their eyes unto their lovers' gaze ?—
Why, so dost thou. And is their gracious favour
Doled but to draw us on through warpèd ways,
Delays behind delays,
To tempt with scent,
And to deny the savour ?—
Ah, Lady, if that vengeance were thy bent,
Woman should 'venge thee for thy scornèd smiles :
Her ways are as thy ways,
Her wiles are as thy wiles.

No second joy ; one only first and over,
Which all life wanders from and looks back to ;
For sweet too sweet, till sweet is past recover :—
Let bitter Love and every bitter lover
Say, *Love's not bitter*, if I speak not true.
The first kiss to repeat !
The first ' Mine only Sweet ! '
Thine only sweet that sweetness, very surely,
And a sour truth thou spakest, if thou knew.
That first kiss to restore
By Nature given so frankly, taken so securely !
To knit again the broken chain ; once more
To run and be to the Sun's bosom caught ;
Over life's bended brows prevail
With laughters of the insolent nightingale,
Jocund of heart in darkness ; to be taught
Once more the daisy's tale,
And hear each sun-smote buttercup clang bold,
A beaten gong of gold ;

OF NATURE : LAUD AND PLAINT

To call delaying Phœbus up with chanticleer ;
Once more, once more to see the Dawn unfold
Her rosy bosom to the married Sun ;
Fulfilled with his delight,
Perfected in sweet fear—
Sweet fear, that trembles for sweet joy begun
As slowly drops the swathing night,
And all her barèd beauty lies warm-kissed and won !

No extreme rites of penitence avail
To lighten thee of knowledge, to impart
Once more the language of the daisy's tale,
And that doctorial Art
Of knowing-not to thine oblivious heart !
Of all the vain
Words of man's mouth, there are no words so vain
As ' once more ' and ' again ' !
Hope not of Nature ; she nor gives nor teaches ;
She suffers thee to take
But what thine own hand reaches,
And can itself make sovereign for thine ache.
Ah, hope not her to heal
The ills she cannot feel,
Or dry with many-businessed hand the tear
Which never yet was weak
In her unfretted eyes, on her uncarkèd cheek.

O heart of Nature ! did man ever hear
Thy yearned-for word, supposèd dear ?—
His pleading voice returns to him alone ;
He hears none other tone.

165

MISCELLANEOUS ODES

No, no;
Take back, O poets, your praises little-wise,
Nor fool weak hearts to their unshunned distress,
Who deem that even after your device
They shall lie down in Nature's holiness:
For it was never so;
She has no hands to bless.
Her pontiff thou; she looks to thee,
O man: she has no use, nor asks not, for thy knee,
Which but bewilders her,
Poor child; nor seeks thy fealty,
And those divinities thou wouldst confer.
If thou wouldst bend in prayer,
Arise, pass forth; thou must look otherwhere.
Thy travail all is null;
This Nature fair,
This gate is closèd, this Gate Beautiful,—
No man shall go in there,
Since the Lord God did pass through it;
'Tis sealed unto the King,
The King Himself shall sit
Therein, with them that are His following.
Go, leave thy labour null;
Ponder this thing.

Lady divine!
That giv'st to men good wine,
And yet the best thou hast
And nectarous, keepest to the last,
And bring'st not forth before the Master's sign:—
How few there be thereof that ever taste,

OF NATURE: LAUD AND PLAINT

Quaffing in brutish haste,
Without distinction of thy great repast!
For ah, this Lady I have much miscalled;
Nor fault in her, but in thy wooing is;
And her allowèd lovers that are installed,
Find her right frank of her sweet heart, y-wis.
Then if thy wooing thou aright wouldst 'gin,
Lo here the door; strait and rough-shapen 'tis,
And scant they be that ever here make stays,
But do the lintel miss,
In dust of these blind days.
Knock, tarry thou, and knock,
Although it seem but rock:
Here is the door where thou must enter in
To heart of Nature and of woman too,
And olden things made new.
Stand at the door and knock;
For it unlocked
Shall all locked things unlock,
And win but here, thou shalt to all things win,
And thou no more be mocked.
For know, this Lady Nature thou hast left,
Of whom thou fear'st thee reft,
This Lady is God's daughter, and she lends
Her hand but to His friends,
But to her Father's friends the hand which thou
    wouldst win;
Then enter in,
And here is that which shall for all make mends.

SONNETS

AD AMICAM

I

DEAR Dove, that bear'st to my sole-labouring ark
    The olive-branch of so long wishèd rest,
When the white solace glimmers through my dark
    Of nearing wings, what comfort in my breast!
Oh, may that doubted day not come, not come,
    When you shall fail, my heavenly messenger,
And drift into the distance and the doom
    Of all my impermissible things that were!
Rather than so, now make the sad farewell,
    Which yet may be with not too-painèd pain,
Lest I again the acquainted tale should tell
    Of sharpest loss that pays for shortest gain.
        Ah, if my heart should hear no white wings thrill
        Against its waiting window, open still!

SONNETS

II*

WHEN from the blossoms of the noiseful day
    Unto the hive of sleep and hushèd gloom
    Throng the dim-wingèd dreams—what dreams are they
That with the wildest honey hover home?
Oh, they that have from many thousand thoughts
  Stolen the strange sweet of ever-blossomy you,
A thousand fancies in fair-coloured knots
  Which you are inexhausted meadow to.
Ah, what sharp heathery honey, quick with pain,
  Do they bring home! It holds the night awake
To hear their lovely murmur in my brain;
  And Sleep's wings have a trouble for your sake.
    Day and you dawn together: for at end,
    With the first light breaks the first thought—
    'My friend!'

*Both in its theme and in its imagery this sonnet was written as a variation of Mrs. Meynell's verses 'At Night.'

AD AMICAM

III

O FRIEND, who mak'st that mis-spent word of 'friend'
   Sweet as the low note that a summer dove
Fondles in her warm throat! And shall it end,
   Because so swift on friend and friend broke love?
Lo, when all words to honour thee are spent,
   And fling a bold stave to the old bald Time
Telling him that he is too insolent
   Who thinks to rase thee from my heart or rhyme;
Whereof to one because thou life hast given,
   The other yet shall give a life to thee,
Such as to gain, the prowest swords have striven,
   And compassed weaker immortality:
      These spent, my heart not stinteth in her breast
      Her sweet 'Friend! friend!'—one note, and
        loves it best.

SONNETS

IV

NO, no, it cannot be, it cannot be,
   Because this love of close-affinèd friends
   In its sweet sudden ambush toilèd me
So swift, that therefore all as swift it ends.
For swift it was, yet quiet as the birth
   Of smoothest Music in a Master's soul,
Whose mild fans lapsing as she slides to earth
   Waver in the bold arms which dare control
Her from her lineal heaven ; yea, it was still
   As the young Moon that bares her nightly breast,
And smiles to see the Babe earth suck its fill.
   O Halcyon ! was thine auspice not of rest ?
      Shall this proud verse bid after-livers see
      How friends could love for immortality ?

AD AMICAM

V

WHEN that part heavenliest of all-heavenly you
    First at my side did breathe its blossomy air,
    What lovely wilderment alarmed me through!
On what ambrosial effluence did I fare,
And comforts Paradisal! What gales came,
    Through ports for one divinest space ajar,
Of rankèd lilies blown into a flame
    By watered banks where walks of young Saints are!
One attent space, my trembling locks did rise
    Swayed on the wind, in planetary wheel
Of intervolving sweet societies,
    From wavèd vesture and from fledgèd heel
        Odorous aspersion trailing. Then, alone
        In her eyes' central glory, God took throne.

TO A CHILD

WHENAS my Life shall time with funeral tread
    The heavy death-drum of the beaten hours,
Following, sole mourner, mine own manhood dead,
  Poor forgot corse, where not a maid strows flowers ;
When I you love am no more I you love,
  But go with unsubservient feet, behold
Your dear face through changed eyes, all grim
    change prove ;—
  A new man, mockèd with misname of old ;
When shamed Love keeps his ruined lodging, elf !
  When, ceremented in mouldering memory,
Myself is hearsèd underneath myself,
    And I am but the monument of me :—
      O to that tomb be tender then, which bears
      Only the name of him it sepulchres !

HERMES

SOOTHSAY. Behold, with rod twy-serpented,
   Hermes the prophet, twining in one power
   The woman with the man. Upon his head
The cloudy cap, wherewith he hath in dower
The cloud's own virtue—change and counterchange,
   To show in light, and to withdraw in pall,
As mortal eyes best bear. His lineage strange
   From Zeus, Truth's sire, and maiden May—the all
Illusive Nature. His fledged feet declare
   That 'tis the nether self transdeified,
And the thrice-furnaced passions, which do bear
   The poet Olympusward. In him allied
     Both parents clasp ; and from the womb of Nature
     Stern Truth takes flesh in shows of lovely feature.

HOUSE OF BONDAGE
I

WHEN I perceive Love's heavenly reaping still
    Regard perforce the clouds' vicissitude,
    That the fixed spirit loves not when it will,
But craves its seasons of the flawful blood;
When I perceive that the high poet doth
    Oft voiceless stray beneath the uninfluent stars,
That even Urania of her kiss is loth,
    And Song's brave wings fret on their sensual bars;
When I perceive the fullest-sailèd sprite
    Lag at most need upon the lethèd seas,
The provident captainship oft voided quite,
    And lamèd lie deep-draughted argosies;
        I scorn myself, that put for such strange toys
        The wit of man to purposes of boys.

HOUSE OF BONDAGE
II

THE spirit's ark sealed with a little clay
   Was old ere Memphis grew a memory;*
   The hand pontifical to break away
That seal what shall surrender? Not the sea
Which did englut great Egypt and his war,
   Nor all the desert-drownèd sepulchres.
Love's feet are stained with clay and travel-sore,
   And dusty are Song's lucent wing and hairs.
O Love, that must do courtesy to decay,
   Eat hasty bread standing with loins up-girt,
How shall this stead thy feet for their sore way?
   Ah, Song, what brief embraces balm thy hurt!
     Had Jacob's toil full guerdon, casting his
       Twice-seven heaped years to burn in Rachel's
         kiss?

* The Ark of the Egyptian temple was sealed with clay, which the Pontiff-King broke when he entered the inner shrine to offer worship.

THE HEART

To my Critic who had objected to the phrase—
'The heart's burning floors.'

I

THE heart you hold too small and local thing
  Such spacious terms of edifice to bear.
And yet, since Poesy first shook out her wing,
  The mighty Love has been impalaced there ;
That has she given him as his wide demesne,
  And for his sceptre ample empery ;
Against its door to knock has Beauty been
  Content ; it has its purple canopy,
A dais for the sovereign lady spread
  Of many a lover, who the heaven would think
Too low an awning for her sacred head.
    The world, from star to sea, cast down its brink—
      Yet shall that chasm, till He Who these did build
    An awful Curtius make Him, yawn unfilled.

THE HEART
II

O NOTHING, in this corporal earth of man,
    That to the imminent heaven of his high soul
    Responds with colour and with shadow, can
Lack correlated greatness. If the scroll
    Where thoughts lie fast in spell of hieroglyph
    Be mighty through its mighty habitants ;
If God be in His Name ; grave potence if
    The sounds unbind of hieratic chants ;
All's vast that vastness means. Nay, I affirm
    Nature is whole in her least things exprest,
Nor know we with what scope God builds the worm.
    Our towns are copied fragments from our breast ;
        And all man's Babylons strive but to impart
        The grandeurs of his Babylonian heart.

DESIDERIUM INDESIDERATUM

O GAIN that lurk'st ungainèd in all gain !
O love we just fall short of in all love !
O height that in all heights art still above !
O beauty that dost leave all beauty pain !
Thou unpossessed that mak'st possession vain,
See these strained arms which fright the simple air,
And say what ultimate fairness holds thee, Fair !
They girdle Heaven, and girdle Heaven in vain ;
They shut, and lo ! but shut in their unrest.
Thereat a voice in me that voiceless was :—
' Whom seekest thou through the unmarged arcane,
And not discern'st to thine own bosom prest ? '
I looked. My claspèd arms athwart my breast
Framed the august embraces of the Cross.

LOVE'S VARLETS

LOVE, he is nearer (though the moralist
   Of rule and line cry shame on me), more near
   To thee and to the heart of thee, be't wist,
Who sins against thee even for the dear
Lack that he hath of thee ; than who, chill-wrapt
   In thy light-thought-on customed livery,
Keeps all thy laws with formal service apt,
   Save that great law to tremble and to be
Shook to his heart-strings if there do but pass
   The rumour of thy pinions. Such one is
Thy varlet, guerdoned with the daily mass
   That feed on thy remainder-meats of bliss.
      More hath he of thy bosom, whose slips of
         grace
      Fell through despair of thy close gracious face

NON PAX—EXPECTATIO

HUSH! 'tis the gap between two lightnings. Room
Is none for peace in this thou callest peace,
This breathing-while wherein the breathings cease.
The pulses sicken, hearkening through the gloom.
Afar the thunders of a coming doom
Ramp on the cowering winds. Lo! at the dread,
Thy heart's tomb yawns and renders up its dead,—
The hopes 'gainst hope embalmèd in its womb.

Canst thou endure, if the pent flood o'erflows?
Who is estated heir to constancy?
Behold, I hardly know if I outlast
The minute underneath whose heel I lie;
Yet I endure, have stayed the minute passed,
Perchance may stay the next. Who knows, who knows?

NOT EVEN IN DREAM

THIS love is crueller than the other love :
    We had the Dreams for Tryst, we other pair ;
    But here there is no *we* ;—not anywhere
Returning breaths of sighs about me move.
No wings, even of the stuff which fancy wove,
    Perturb Sleep's air with a responsive flight
When mine sweep into dreams. My soul in fright
    Circles as round its widowed nest a dove.

One shadow but usurps another's place :
    And, though this shadow more enthralling is,
Alas, it hath no lips at all to miss !
    I have not even that former poignant bliss,
That haunting sweetness, that forlorn sad trace,
    The phantom memory of a vanished kiss.

MISCELLANEOUS POEMS

A HOLLOW WOOD

THIS is the mansion built for me
 By the sweating centuries ;
 Roofed with intertwinèd tree,
Woofed with green for my princelier ease.
Here I lie with my world about me,
Shadowed off from the world without me,
Even as my thoughts embosom me
From wayside humanity.
And here can only enter who
Delight me—the unpricèd few.
Come you in, and make you cheer,
It draweth toward my banquet-time.
Would you win to my universe,
Your thought must turn in the wards of rhyme.
Loose the chain of linkèd verse,
Stoop your knowledge, and enter here !

Here cushioned ivies you invite
To fall to with appetite.
What for my viands ?—Dainty thoughts.
What for my brows ?—Forget-me-nots.
What for my feet ?—A bath of green.
My servers ?—Phantasies unseen.
What shall I find me for feasting dress ?—
Your white disusèd childlikeness.
What hid music will laugh to my calls ?—
An orgy of mad bird-bacchanals.
Such meat, such music, such coronals !
From the cask which the summer sets aflow

MISCELLANEOUS POEMS

Under the roof of my raftered house,
The birds above, we below,
We carouse as they carouse.
Or have but the ear the ear within,
And you may hear, if you hold you mute,
You may hear by my amulet,
The wind-like keenness of violin,
The enamelled tone of shallow flute,
And the furry richness of clarinet.
These are the things shall make you cheer,
If you will grace my banquet-time.
Would you win to my universe,
Your thought must turn in the wards of rhyme.
Loose the chain of linkèd verse,
Stoop your knowledge, and enter here !

TO DAISIES

AH, drops of gold in whitening flame
   Burning, we know your lovely name—
   Daisies, that little children pull !
Like all weak things, over the strong
Ye do not know your power for wrong,
And much abuse your feebleness.
Weak maids, with flutter of a dress,
Increase most heavy tyrannies ;
And vengeance unto heaven cries
For multiplied injustice of dove-eyes.
Daisies, that little children pull,
As ye are weak, be merciful !
O hide your eyes ! they are to me
Beautiful insupportably.
Or be but conscious ye are fair,
And I your loveliness could bear ;
But, being fair so without art,
Ye vex the silted memories of my heart !

As a pale ghost yearning strays
With sundered gaze,
'Mid corporal presences that are
To it impalpable—such a bar
Sets you more distant than the morning-star.
Such wonder is on you and amaze,
I look and marvel if I be
Indeed the phantom, or are ye ?
The light is on your innocence
Which fell from me.

MISCELLANEOUS POEMS

The fields ye still inhabit whence
My world-acquainted treading strays,
The country where I did commence;
And though ye shine to me so near,
So close to gross and visible sense,
Between us lies impassable year on year.
To other time and far-off place
Belongs your beauty : silent thus,
Though to others naught you tell,
To me your ranks are rumorous
Of an ancient miracle.

Vain does my touch your petals graze,
I touch you not ; and, though ye blossom here,
Your roots are fast in alienated days.
Ye there are anchored, while Time's stream
Has swept me past them : your white ways
And infantile delights do seem
To look in on me like a face,
Dead and sweet, come back through dream,
With tears, because for old embrace
It has no arms. These hands did toy,
Children, with you when I was child,
And in each other's eyes we smiled :
Not yours, not yours the grievous-fair
Apparelling
With which you wet mine eyes ; you wear,
Ah me, the garment of the grace
I wove you when I was a boy ;
O mine, and not the year's, your stolen Spring !
And since ye wear it,

TO DAISIES

Hide your sweet selves ! I cannot bear it.
For, when ye break the cloven earth
With your young laughter and endearment,
No blossomy carillon 'tis of mirth
To me ; I see my slaughtered joy
Bursting its cerement.

TO THE SINKING SUN

How graciously thou wear'st the yoke
   Of use that does not fail!
   The grasses, like an anchored smoke,
  Ride in the bending gale;
This knoll is snowed with blosmy manna,
  And fire-dropt as a seraph's mail.

Here every eve thou stretchest out
  Untarnishable wing,
And marvellously bring'st about
  Newly an olden thing;
Nor ever through like-ordered heaven
  Moves largely thy grave progressing.

Here every eve thou goest down
  Behind the self-same hill,
Nor ever twice alike go'st down
  Behind the self-same hill;
Nor like-ways is one flame-sopped flower
  Possessed with glory past its will.

Not twice alike! I am not blind,
  My sight is live to see;
And yet I do complain of thy
  Weary variety.
O Sun! I ask thee less or more,
  Change not at all, or utterly!

TO THE SINKING SUN

O give me unprevisioned new,
    Or give to change reprieve!
For new in me is olden too,
    That I for sameness grieve.
O flowers! O grasses! be but once
    The grass and flower of yester-eve!

Wonder and sadness are the lot
    Of change: thou yield'st mine eyes
Grief of vicissitude, but not
    Its penetrant surprise.
Immutability mutable
    Burthens my spirit and the skies.

O altered joy, all joyed of yore,
    Plodding in unconned ways!
O grief grieved out, and yet once more
    A dull, new, staled amaze!
I dream, and all was dreamed before,
    Or dream I so? the dreamer says.

A MAY BURDEN

THROUGH meadow-ways as I did tread,
   The corn grew in great lustihead,
   And hey ! the beeches burgeonèd.
      By Goddès fay, by Goddès fay !
It is the month, the jolly month,
It is the jolly month of May.

God ripe the wines and corn, I say,
And wenches for the marriage-day,
And boys to teach love's comely play,
      By Goddès fay, by Goddès fay !
It is the month, the jolly month,
It is the jolly month of May.

As I went down by lane and lea,
The daisies reddened so, pardie !
' Blushets ! ' I said, ' I well do see,
      By Goddès fay, by Goddès fay !
The thing ye think of in this month,
Heigho ! this jolly month of May.'

As down I went by rye and oats,
The blossoms smelt of kisses ; throats
Of birds turned kisses into notes ;
      By Goddès fay, by Goddès fay !
The kiss it is a growing flower,
I trow, this jolly month of May !

A MAY BURDEN

God send a mouth to every kiss,
Seeing the blossom of this bliss
By gathering doth grow, certes !
   By Goddès fay, by Goddès fay !
Thy brow-garland pushed all aslant
Tells—but I tell not, wanton May !

   The first two stanzas are from a French original—I have forgotten what.

JULY FUGITIVE

CAN you tell me where has hid her
    Pretty Maid July ?
    I would swear one day ago
    She passed by,
I would swear that I do know
    The blue bliss of her eye :
'Tarry maid, maid,' I bid her ;
    But she hastened by.
Do you know where she has hid her,
    Maid July ?

Yet in truth it needs must be
    The flight of her is old ;
Yet in truth it needs must be,
    For her nest, the earth, is cold.
No more in the poolèd Even
    Wade her rosy feet,
Dawn-flakes no more plash from them
    To poppies 'mid the wheat.
She has muddied the day's oozes
    With her petulant feet ;
Scared the clouds that floated,
    As sea-birds they were,
Slow on the cœrule
    Lulls of the air,
Lulled on the luminous
    Levels of air :
She has chidden in a pet
    All her stars from her ;

JULY FUGITIVE

Now they wander loose and sigh
　　Through the turbid blue,
Now they wander, weep, and cry—
　　Yea, and I too—
' Where are you, sweet July,
　　Where are you ? '

Who hath beheld her footprints,
　　Or the pathway she goes ?
Tell me, wind, tell me, wheat,
　　Which of you knows ?
Sleeps she swathed in the flushed Arctic
　　Night of the rose ?
Or lie her limbs like Alp-glow
　　On the lily's snows ?
Gales, that are all-visitant,
　　Find the runaway ;
And for him who findeth her
　　(I do charge you say)
I will throw largesse of broom
　　Of this summer's mintage,
I will broach a honey-bag
　　Of the bee's best vintage.
Breezes, wheat, flowers sweet,
　　None of them knows !
How then shall we lure her back
　　From the way she goes ?
For it were a shameful thing,
　　Saw we not this comer
Ere Autumn camp upon the fields
　　Red with rout of Summer.

MISCELLANEOUS POEMS

When the bird quits the cage,
    We set the cage outside,
With seed and with water,
    And the door wide,
Haply we may win it so
    Back to abide.
Hang her cage of Earth out
    O'er Heaven's sunward wall,
Its four gates open, winds in watch
    By reinèd cars at all;
Relume in hanging hedgerows
    The rain-quenched blossom,
And roses sob their tears out
    On the gale's warm heaving bosom;
Shake the lilies till their scent
    Over-drip their rims;
That our runaway may see
    We do know her whims:
Sleek the tumbled waters out
    For her travelled limbs;
Strew and smooth blue night thereon:
    There will—O not doubt her!—
The lovely sleepy lady lie,
    With all her stars about her!

FIELD-FLOWER
A PHANTASY

GOD took a fit of Paradise-wind,
   A slip of cœrule weather,
   A thought as simple as Himself,
And ravelled them together.
Unto His eyes He held it there,
To teach it gazing debonair
   With memory of what, perdie,
A God's young innocences were.
His fingers pushed it through the sod—
It came up redolent of God,
Garrulous of the eyes of God
   To all the breezes near it ;
Musical of the mouth of God
   To all had ears to hear it ;
Mystical with the mirth of God,
   That glow-like did ensphere it.
      And—' Babble ! babble ! babble ! ' said ;
   ' I'll tell the whole world one day ! '
   There was no blossom half so glad,
      Since sun of Christ's first Sunday.

A poet took a flaw of pain,
   A hap of skiey pleasure,
A thought had in his cradle lain,
   And mingled them in measure.
That chrism he laid upon his eyes,
And lips, and heart, for euphrasies,
   That he might see, feel, sing, perdie,

MISCELLANEOUS POEMS

The simple things that are the wise.
Beside the flower he held his ways,
And leaned him to it gaze for gaze—
He took its meaning, gaze for gaze,
  As baby looks on baby ;
Its meaning passed into his gaze,
  Native as meaning may be ;
He rose with all his shining gaze
  As children's eyes at play be.
      And—' Babble ! babble ! babble ! ' said :
       ' I'll tell the whole world one day ! '
    There was no poet half so glad,
      Since man grew God that Sunday.

TO A SNOWFLAKE

WHAT heart could have thought you ?—
    Past our devisal
     (O filigree petal !)
Fashioned so purely,
Fragilely, surely,
From what Paradisal
Imagineless metal,
Too costly for cost ?
Who hammered you, wrought you,
From argentine vapour ?—
  God was my shaper.
Passing surmisal,
He hammered, He wrought me,
From curled silver vapour,
To lust of His mind :—
Thou could'st not have thought me !
So purely, so palely,
Tinily, surely,
Mightily, frailly,
Insculped and embossed,
With His hammer of wind,
And His graver of frost.'

A QUESTION

O BIRD with heart of wassail,
    That toss the Bacchic branch,
    And slip your shaken music,
An elfin avalanche ;

Come tell me, O tell me,
  My poet of the blue !
What 's *your* thought of me, Sweet ?—
  Here 's *my* thought of you.

A small thing, a wee thing,
  A brown fleck of naught ;
With winging and singing
  That who could have thought ?

A small thing, a wee thing,
  A brown amaze withal,
That fly a pitch more azure
  Because you 're so small.

Bird, I'm a small thing—
  My angel descries ;
With winging and singing
  That who could surmise ?

Ah, small things, ah, wee things,
  Are the poets all,
Whose tour 's the more azure
  Because they 're so small.

A QUESTION

The angels hang watching
    The tiny men-things :—
' The dear speck of flesh, see,
    With such daring wings !

' Come, tell us, O tell us,
    Thou strange mortality !
What 's *thy* thought of us, Dear ?—
    Here 's *our* thought of thee.'

' Alack ! you tall angels,
    I can't think so high !
I can't think what it feels like
    Not to be I.'

Come tell me, O tell me,
    My poet of the blue !
What 's *your* thought of me, Sweet ?—
    Here 's *my* thought of you.

THE CLOUD'S SWAN-SONG

THERE is a parable in the pathless cloud,
    There's prophecy in heaven,—they did not lie,
    The Chaldee shepherds,—sealèd from the proud,
To cheer the weighted heart that mates the seeing eye.

A lonely man, oppressed with lonely ills,
And all the glory fallen from my song,
Here do I walk among the windy hills ;
The wind and I keep both one monotoning tongue.

Like grey clouds one by one my songs upsoar
Over my soul's cold peaks ; and one by one
They loose their little rain, and are no more ;
And whether well or ill, to tell me there is none.

For 'tis an alien tongue, of alien things,
From all men's care, how miserably apart !
Even my friends say : ' Of what is this he sings ? '
And barren is my song, and barren is my heart.

For who can work, unwitting his work's worth ?
Better, meseems, to know the work for naught,
Turn my sick course back to the kindly earth,
And leave to ampler plumes the jetting tops of thought.

And visitations that do often use,
Remote, unhappy, inauspicious sense
Of doom, and poets widowed of their muse,
And what dark 'gan, dark ended, in me did commence.

THE CLOUD'S SWAN-SONG

I thought of spirit wronged by mortal ills,
And my flesh rotting on my fate's dull stake ;
And how self-scornèd they the bounty fills
Of others, and the bread, even of their dearest, take.

I thought of Keats, that died in perfect time,
In predecease of his just-sickening song ;
Of him that set, wrapt in his radiant rhyme,
Sunlike in sea. Life longer had been life too long.

But I, exanimate of quick Poesy,—
O then no more but even a soulless corse !
Nay, my Delight dies not ; 'tis I should be
Her dead, a stringless harp on which she had no force.

Of my wild lot I thought ; from place to place,
Apollo's song-bowed Scythian, I go on ;
Making in all my home, with pliant ways,
But, provident of change, putting forth root in none.

Now, with starved brain, sick body, patience galled
With fardels even to wincing ; from fair sky
Fell sudden little rain, scarce to be called
A shower, which of the instant was gone wholly by.

What cloud thus died I saw not ; heaven was fair.
Methinks my angel plucked my locks : I bowed
My spirit, shamed ; and looking in the air :—
' Even so,' I said, ' even so, my brother the good
    Cloud ? '

MISCELLANEOUS POEMS

It was a pilgrim of the fields of air,
Its home was allwheres the wind left it rest,
And in a little forth again did fare,
And in all places was a stranger and a guest.

It harked all breaths of heaven, and did obey
With sweet peace their uncomprehended wills;
It knew the eyes of stars which made no stay,
And with the thunder walked upon the lonely hills.

And from the subject earth it seemed to scorn,
It drew the sustenance whereby it grew
Perfect in bosom for the married Morn,
And of his life and light full as a maid kissed new.

Its also darkness of the face withdrawn,
And the long waiting for the little light,
So long in life so little. Like a fawn
It fled with tempest breathing hard at heel of flight;

And having known full East, did not disdain
To sit in shadow and oblivious cold,
Save what all loss doth of its loss retain,
And who hath held hath somewhat that he still must hold.

Right poet! who thy rightness to approve,
Having all liberty, didst keep all measure,
And with a firmament for ranging, move
But at the heavens' uncomprehended pleasure.

THE CLOUD'S SWAN-SONG

With amplitude unchecked, how sweetly thou
Didst wear the ancient custom of the skies,
And yoke of used prescription; and thence how
Find gay variety no licence could devise!

As we the quested beauties better wit
Of the one grove our own than forests great,
Restraint, by the delighted search of it,
Turns to right scope. For lovely moving intricate

Is put to fair devising in the curb
Of ordered limit; and all-changeful Hermes
Is Terminus as well. Yet we perturb
Our souls for latitude, whose strength in bound and
    term is.

How far am I from heavenly liberty,
That play at policy with change and fate,
Who should my soul from foreign broils keep free,
In the fast-guarded frontiers of its single state!

Could I face firm the Is, and with To-be
Trust Heaven; to Heaven commit the deed, and do;
In power contained, calm in infirmity,
And fit myself to change with virtue ever new;

Thou hadst not shamed me, cousin of the sky,
Thou wandering kinsman, that didst sweetly live
Unnoted, and unnoted sweetly die,
Weeping more gracious song than any I can weave;

MISCELLANEOUS POEMS

Which these gross-tissued words do sorely wrong.
Thou hast taught me on powerlessness a power;
To make song wait on life, not life on song;
To hold sweet not too sweet, and bread for bread
    though sour;

By law to wander, to be strictly free.
With tears ascended from the heart's sad sea,
Ah, such a silver song to Death could I
Sing, Pain would list, forgetting Pain to be,
And Death would tarry marvelling, and forget to die!

OF MY FRIEND

THE moonlight cloud of her invisible beauty,
    Shook from the torrent glory of her soul
    Its aëry spray, hangs round her; love grows duty,
If you that angel-populous aureole
      Have the glad power to feel;
      As all our longings kneel
To the intense and cherub-wingèd stole
Orbing a painted Saint: and through control
      Of this sweet faint
      Veil, my unguessing Saint
Celestial ministrations sheds which heal.

    *   *   *   *

Now, Friend, short sweet outsweetening sharpest woes!
    In wintry cold a little, little flame—
So much to me that little!—here I close
      This errant song. O pardon its much blame!
      Now my grey day grows bright
      A little ere the night;
Let after-livers who may love my name,
And gauge the price I paid for dear-bought fame,
      Know that at end,
      Pain was well paid, sweet Friend,
Pain was well paid which brought me to your sight.

TO MONICA : AFTER NINE YEARS

IN the land of flag-lilies,
  Where burst in golden clangours
  The joy-bells of the broom,
You were full of willy-nillies,
Pets, and bee-like angers :
Flaming like a dusky poppy,
In a wrathful bloom.

You were full of sweet and sour,
Like a dish of strawberries
Set about with curd.
In your petulant foot was power,
In your wilful innocences,
Your wild and fragrant word.
O, was it you that sweetly spake,
Or I that sweetly heard ?

Yellow were the wheat-ways,
The poppies were most red ;
And all your meet and feat ways,
Your sudden bee-like snarlings,—
Ah, do you remember,
Darling of the darlings ?
Or is it but an ember,
A rusted peal of joy-bells,
Their golden buzzings dead ?

TO MONICA: AFTER NINE YEARS

Now at one, and now at two,
Swift to pout and swift to woo,
The maid I knew :
Still I see the duskèd tresses—
But the old angers, old caresses ?
Still your eyes are autumn thunders,
But where are *you*, child, you ?

This your beauty is a script
Writ with pencil brightest-dipt—
Oh, it is the fairest scroll
For a young, departed soul !—
Thus you say :
' Thrice three years ago to-day,
There was one
Shall no more beneath the sun
Darkle, fondle, featly play.
If to think on her be gloom,
Rejoice she has so rich a tomb ! '

But there's he—
Ask thou not who it may be !—
That, until Time's boughs are bare,
Shall be unconsoled for her.

A DOUBLE NEED
(*To W—*)

AH, gone the days when for undying kindness
I still could render you undying song !
You yet can give, but I can give no more
Fate, in her extreme blindness,
Has wrought me so great wrong.
I am left poor indeed ;
Gone is my sole and amends-making store,
And I am needy with a double need.

Behold that I am like a fountained nymph,
Lacking her customed lymph,
The longing parched in stone upon her mouth,
Unwatered of its ancient plenty. She
(Remembering her irrevocable streams),
A Thirst made marble, sits perpetually
With sundered lips of still-memorial drouth.

GRIEF'S HARMONICS

AT evening, when the lank and rigid trees,
 To the mere forms of their sweet day-selves
  drying,
On heaven's blank leaf seem pressed and flattenèd ;
Or rather, to my sombre thoughts replying,
Of plumes funereal the thin effigies ;
That hour when all old dead things seem most dead,
And their death instant most and most undying,
That the flesh aches at them ; there stirred in me
The babe of an unborn calamity,
Ere its due time to be deliverèd.
Dead sorrow and sorrow unborn so blent their pain,
That which more present was were hardly said,
But both more *now* than any Now can be.
My soul like sackcloth did her body rend,
And thus with Heaven contend :—
' Let pass the chalice of this coming dread,
Or that fore-drained O bid me not re-drain ! '
So have I asked, who know my asking vain ;
Woe against woe in antiphon set over,
That grief's soul transmigrates, and lives again,
And in new pang old pang's incarnatèd.

MEMORAT MEMORIA

COME you living or dead to me, out of the silt of the Past,
   With the sweet of the piteous first, and the shame of the shameful last?
Come with your dear and dreadful face through the passes of Sleep,
The terrible mask, and the face it masked—the face you did not keep?
You are neither two nor one—I would you were one or two,
For your awful self is embalmed in the fragrant self I knew:
And Above may ken, and Beneath may ken, what I mean by these words of whirl,
But by my sleep that sleepeth not,—O Shadow of a Girl!—
Naught here but I and my dreams shall know the secret of this thing :—
For ever the songs I sing are sad with the songs I never sing,
Sad are sung songs, but how more sad the songs we dare not sing!

Ah, the ill that we do in tenderness, and the hateful horror of love!
It has sent more souls to the unslaked Pit than it ever will draw above.
I damned you, girl, with my pity, who had better by far been thwart,

MEMORAT MEMORIA

And drave you hard on the track to hell, because I was
    gentle of heart.
I shall have no comfort now in scent, no ease in dew, for
    this ;
I shall be afraid of daffodils, and rose-buds are amiss ;
You have made a thing of innocence as shameful as a sin,
I shall never feel a girl's soft arms without horror of the
    skin.
My child ! what was it that I sowed, that I so ill should
    reap ?
You have done this to me. And I, what I to you ?—It
    lies with Sleep.

NOCTURN

I WALK, I only,
Not I only wake;
Nothing is, this sweet night,
But doth couch and wake
For its love's sake;
Everything, this sweet night,
Couches with its mate.
For whom but for the stealthy-visitant sun
Is the naked moon
Tremulous and elate?
The heaven hath the earth
Its own and all apart;
The hushèd pool holdeth
A star to its heart.
You may think the rose sleepeth,
But though she folded is,
The wind doubts her sleeping;
Not all the rose sleeps,
But smiles in her sweet heart
For crafty bliss.
The wind lieth with the rose,
And when he stirs, she stirs in her repose:
The wind hath the rose,
And the rose her kiss.
Ah, mouth of me!
Is it then that this
Seemeth much to thee?—
I wander only.
The rose hath her kiss.

HEAVEN AND HELL

'TIS said there were no thought of hell,
　　Save hell were taught ; that there should be
A Heaven for all's self-credible.
　　Not so the thing appears to me.
'Tis Heaven that lies beyond our sights,
　　And hell too possible that proves ;
For all can feel the God that smites,
　　But ah, how few the God that loves !

'CHOSE VUE'

A Metrical Caprice

UP she rose, fair daughter—well she was graced,
As a cloud her going, stept from her chair,
As a summer-soft cloud in her going paced,
Down dropped her riband-band, and all her waving
   hair
Shook like loosened music cadent to her waist ;—
Lapsing like music, wavery as water,
   Slid to her waist.

ST MONICA

AT the Cross thy station keeping
   With the mournful Mother weeping,
   Thou, unto the sinless Son,
Weepest for thy sinful one.
Blood and water from His side
Gush; in thee the streams divide:
From thine eyes the one doth start,
But the other from thy heart.

Mary, for thy sinner, see,
To her Sinless mourns with thee:
Could that Son the son not heed,
For whom two such mothers plead?
So thy child had baptism twice,
And the whitest from thine eyes.

The floods lift up, lift up their voice,
With a many-watered noise!
Down the centuries fall those sweet
Sobbing waters to our feet,
And our laden air still keeps
Murmur of a Saint that weeps.

Teach us but, to grace our prayers,
Such divinity of tears,—
Earth should be lustrate again
With contrition of that rain:
Till celestial floods o'er-rise
The high tops of Paradise.

MARRIAGE IN TWO MOODS

I

LOVE that's loved from day to day
   Loves itself into decay :
   He that eats one daily fruit
Shrivels hunger at the root.
Daily pleasure grows a task ;
Daily smiles become a mask.
Daily growth of unpruned strength
Expands to feebleness at length.
Daily increase thronging fast
Must devour itself at last.
Daily shining, even content,
Would with itself grow discontent ;
And the sun's life witnesseth
Daily dying is not death.
So Love loved from day to day
Loves itself into decay.

II

Love to daily uses wed
Shall be sweetly perfected.
Life by repetition grows
Unto its appointed close :
Day to day fulfils one year—
Shall not Love by Love wax dear ?
All piles by repetition rise—
Shall not then Love's edifice ?

MARRIAGE IN TWO MOODS

Shall not Love, too, learn his writ,
Like Wisdom, by repeating it ?
By the oft-repeated use
All perfections gain their thews ;
And so, with daily uses wed,
Love, too, shall be perfected.

ALL FLESH

I DO not need the skies'
Pomp, when I would be wise;
For pleasaunce nor to use
Heaven's champaign when I muse.
One grass-blade in its veins
Wisdom's whole flood contains:
Thereon my foundering mind
Odyssean fate can find.

O little blade, now vaunt
Thee, and be arrogant!
Tell the proud sun that he
Sweated in shaping thee;
Night, that she did unvest
Her mooned and argent breast
To suckle thee. Heaven fain
Yearned over thee in rain,
And with wide parent wing
Shadowed thee, nested thing,
Fed thee, and slaved for thy
Impotent tyranny.
Nature's broad thews bent
Meek for thy content.
Mastering littleness
Which the wise heavens confess,
The frailty which doth draw
Magnipotence to its law—
These were, O happy one, these
Thy laughing puissances!

ALL FLESH

Be confident of thought,
Seeing that thou art naught;
And be thy pride thou'rt all
Delectably safe and small.
Epitomized in thee
Was the mystery
Which shakes the spheres conjoint—
God focussed to a point.

All thy fine mouths shout
Scorn upon dull-eyed doubt.
Impenetrable fool
Is he thou canst not school
To the humility
By which the angels see!
Unfathomably framed
Sister, I am not shamed
Before the cherubin
To vaunt my flesh thy kin.
My one hand thine, and one
Imprisoned in God's own,
I am as God; alas,
And such a god of grass!
A little root clay-caught,
A wind, a flame, a thought,
Inestimably naught!

THE KINGDOM OF GOD

' In no Strange Land '

O WORLD invisible, we view thee,
   O world intangible, we touch thee,
   O world unknowable, we know thee,
Inapprehensible, we clutch thee!

Does the fish soar to find the ocean,
The eagle plunge to find the air—
That we ask of the stars in motion
If they have rumour of thee there?

Not where the wheeling systems darken,
And our benumbed conceiving soars!—
The drift of pinions, would we hearken,
Beats at our own clay-shuttered doors.

The angels keep their ancient places;—
Turn but a stone and start a wing!
'Tis ye, 'tis your estrangèd faces,
That miss the many-splendoured thing.

But when so sad thou canst not sadder)
Cry;—and upon thy so sore loss
Shall shine the traffic of Jacob's ladder
Pitched betwixt Heaven and Charing Cross.

THE KINGDOM OF GOD

Yea, in the night, my Soul, my daughter,
Cry,—clinging Heaven by the hems;
And lo, Christ walking on the water
Not of Gennesareth, but Thames!

[THIS POEM (found among his papers when he died) Francis Thompson might yet have worked upon to remove, here a defective rhyme, there an unexpected elision. But no altered mind would he have brought to the purport of it;—the prevision of ' Heaven in Earth and God in Man, pervading his earlier published verse, is here accented by poignantly local and personal allusion. For in these triumphing stanzas he held in retrospect those days and nights of human dereliction he spent beside London's River, and in the shadow—but all radiance to him—of Charing Cross.]

THE SINGER SAITH OF HIS SONG

THE touches of man's modern speech
   Perplex her unacquainted tongue;
   There seems through all her songs a sound
Of falling tears. She is not young.

Within her eyes' profound arcane
   Resides the glory of her dreams;
Behind her secret cloud of hair,
   She sees the Is beyond the Seems.

Her heart sole-towered in her steep spirit,
   Somewhat sweet is she, somewhat wan;
And she sings the songs of Sion
   By the streams of Babylon.

NOTES

THE ODE TO THE ENGLISH MARTYRS:
Some three hundred in all, of whom one hundred suffered at Tyburn; the first, John Houghton, Carthusian, (4th May 1535); the last, Archbishop Oliver Plunket (1st July 1681). Their names, including More and Fisher, were added to the Roman Martyrology in 1886. To Ralph Sherwin and John Sugar are set down the sayings quoted on page 135.

THE VICTORIAN ODE: The 'holy Poets' who had died during the latter part of Queen Victoria's reign were Tennyson, Browning, Matthew Arnold, Elizabeth Barrett Browning, Christina Rossetti, Dante Gabriel Rossetti and Coventry Patmore.

The Notes in the Text are the Poet's own, except where they are enclosed in brackets.
W. M.

BIBLIOGRAPHY

I. POEMS PUBLISHED IN FRANCIS THOMPSON'S LIFETIME

(The Letters in brackets mean that the poem was reprinted either in *Poems* 1893, or *New Poems* 1897, or the *Works* 1913.)

In *Merry England*

1888 Apr. 'The Passion of Mary' (*Eyes of Youth* 1910, and *W*)
May 'Dream-Tryst' (*P*)
Dec. 'Not even in dream' (*W*)
1889 July 'Non Pax—Expectatio' (*W*)
Sept 'Ode to the Setting Sun' (*NP*)
1890 Jan. 'Song of the Hours' (*W*)
Mar. 'Daisy' (*P*)
Apr. 'A Dead Astronomer' (*NP*)
May 'Daphne' (*W*)
July 'The Hound of Heaven' (*P*)
Aug. 'To-day': sonnet (*not reprinted*)
1891 Jan. 'The Sere of the Leaf' (*W*)
Feb. 'A Hymn to Snow' (92 lines, of which 22 were printed as 'To a Snow-flake,' *NP*)

In *Ushaw Magazine*

Mar. 'Lines for a Drawing of Our Lady of the Night' (*W*)

In *Merry England*

Mar. 'A Corymbus for Autumn' (*P*)
June 'To my Godchild' (*P*)
Aug. 'The Poppy' (*P*)
Sept. 'Laus Legis' (*not reprinted*)
Oct. 'A Song of Youth and Age' (reprinted only in Wilfrid Meynell's anthology, *The Child set in the Midst*, 1892)
Nov. 'A Broom Branch at Twilight' (*not reprinted*)
1892 Jan. 'A Fallen Yew' (*P*)
Feb. 'To the Dead of Westminster' (*P*, with title amended)
Apr. 'Marriage in Two Moods' (*W*)
May 'The Making of Viola' (*P*)

BIBLIOGRAPHY

1892 Aug. 'To a Child': sonnet (*NP*)
Sept. 'To a Traveller: from Victor Hugo'
Nov. 'How the Singer's Singing wailed for the Singer'
1893 Jan. 'Leonidas to the Three Hundred': sonnet
(*These three last have not been reprinted*)
May 'Ex Ore Infantium' ('Little Jesus') (*NP*)
June 'Desiderium Indesideratum' (*W*)
July 'In her Paths' (*W*)
Aug. 'To a Poet breaking Silence' (*P*)
Sept. 'A Carrier-Song' (*P*)

In *Franciscan Annals*

Oct. 'Franciscus Christificatus' (*not reprinted*)

In *Merry England*

Oct. 'A Judgment in Heaven' (*P*)
Nov. 'Elevaverunt Flumina' ('St. Monica') (*W*)
Dec. 'Assumpta Maria' (*NP*)

(Dec.)   POEMS (Contents in full)
'Dedication to Wilfrid and Alice Meynell'
'Love in Dian's Lap'
    I. Before her Portrait in youth
   II. To a Poet breaking Silence (from *ME*, Aug. 1893)
  III. Manus Animam pinxit
  IV. A Carrier-Song (from *ME*, Sept. 1893)
   V. Scala Jacobi Portaque Eburnea
  VI. Gilded Gold
 VII. Her Portrait
    An Epilogue to the Poet's Sitter

Miscellaneous Poems (from *ME*)
To the Dead Cardinal at Westminster (Feb. 1892)
A Fallen Yew (Jan. 1892)
Dream-Tryst (May 1888)
A Corymbus for Autumn (Mar. 1891)
The Hound of Heaven (July 1890)
A Judgment in Heaven (Oct. 1893)

Poems on Children (from *ME*, except the last)
Daisy (March 1890)
The Making of Viola (May 1892)

231

BIBLIOGRAPHY

1893 To my Godchild (June 1891)
   The Poppy (Aug. 1891)
   To Monica thought Dying
     In *Merry England*
1894 Jan. 'Any Saint' (*NP*)
     In *Illustrated London News*
 Feb. 3. 'An Echo of Victor Hugo' (*W*)
     In *Merry England*
 July 'Cuckoo: verses for a boy with Cuckoo for his pet-name'
   (*not reprinted*)
 Nov. 'An Anthem of Earth' (*NP*)
1895 Mar. 'A Chorus from Isaiah' (*not reprinted*)
 (June) SISTER SONGS
   Introductory Poem to translation of Leopold de Cherance's *St. Anthony of Padua* (*not reprinted*)
    In *Catholic World* (New York)
1896 June 'Love and the Child' (*W*)
     In *The Athenæum*
 Dec. 5. 'A Captain of Song' (*NP*)
1897 (May) NEW POEMS (Contents in full)
 Dedication to Coventry Patmore

  Sight and Insight
   The Mistress of Vision
   Contemplation
   'By Reason of Thy Law'
   The Dread of Height
   Orient Ode
   New Year's Chimes
   From the Night of Forebeing
   Any Saint (from *ME* Jan. 1894)
   Assumpta Maria (from *ME* Dec. 1893)
   The After Woman
   Grace of the Way
   Retrospect

  A Narrow Vessel
   A Girl's Sin—in her Eyes

BIBLIOGRAPHY

1897 A Girl's Sin—in his Eyes
Love Declared
The Way of a Maid
Beginning of the End
Penelope
The End of It
Epilogue

Miscellaneous Odes
 Ode to the Setting Sun (from *ME* Sept. 1889)
 A Captain of Song (from *Athenæum* 5 Dec. 1896)
 Against Urania
 An Anthem of Earth (from *ME* Nov. 1894)

Miscellaneous Poems
 'Ex Ore Infantium' (from *ME* May 1893)
 A Question
 Field-Flower
 The Clouds Swan-Song
 To the Sinking Sun
 Grief's Harmonics
 Memorat Memoria
 July Fugitive
 To a Snow-flake (from *ME* Feb. 1891)
 Nocturn
 A May Burden
 A dead Astronomer (from *ME* Apr. 1890)
 'Chose Vue'
 'Whereto art thou come'
 Heaven and Hell
 To a Child (from *ME* Aug. 1892)
 Hermes
 House of Bondage
 The Heart
 A Sunset
 Heard on the Mountain

Ultima
 Love's Almsman plaineth his Fare
 A Holocaust
 Beneath a Photograph

BIBLIOGRAPHY

1897   After her Going
        My Lady the Tyranness
        Unto this Last
        Ultimum
        Envoy

(*From this point all the poems to be mentioned were reprinted in Works 1913 unless marked as 'Not reprinted'.*)

In the *Daily Chronicle*
1897 June   'Ode for the Diamond Jubilee of Queen Victoria'

In *The Dome*
1898 May 1   'Tom of Bedlam's Song' (*not reprinted*)
1899 Jan.   'Arab Love Song' (*Eyes of Youth*, 1910)

In *The Academy*
1900 Dec. 29. 'The Nineteenth Century'
1901 Jan. 26. 'Victoria' (*not reprinted*)

In the *Monthly Review*
Aug.   'To Monica: after nine Years'

In *The Academy*
1902 Apr. 12. 'Cecil Rhodes'

In '*Health and Holiness*'
1905   'Body and Spirit' (*Works*, vol. iii, Prose)

In the *Dublin Review*
1906 Apr.   'To the English Martyrs'

In *The Nation*
1907 Apr. 6. 'The Fair Inconstant'

II. POEMS FIRST PUBLISHED POSTHUMOUSLY

In the *Dublin Review*
1908 Jan.   'Motto and Invocation' (in Alice Meynell's 'Some Memories of Francis Thompson': reprinted in *Works*, vol. iii, Prose)

In *Selected Poems*
'To Olivia'
'To W——'

BIBLIOGRAPHY

                In *Catholic World* (*New York*)
1908 Feb.   'Rejected Lovers' (*not reprinted*)
                In *The Academy*
    Mar. 19. 'To England' (*not reprinted*)
                In *Cornhill Magazine*
    July   'At Lord's': 36 lines (ll. 1-10: *W*)
            Imitation of FitzGerald's 'Omar': 18 quatrains (not reprinted in *W*)
            (In E. V. Lucas's 'Francis Thompson's Cricket Verses,' reprinted as 'A Rhapsodist at Lord's in *One Day and Another* 1909.)
                In *The Athenæum*
    Aug. 8. 'In no strange Land' ('The Kingdom of God')
1909 July 10. 'Buona Notte' (*Eyes of Youth* 1910)
    Nov. 13. 'Threatened Tears' (*Eyes of Youth* 1910)
                In the *English Review*
1910 Jan.   'Absence'
                In the *Dublin Review*
    Jan.   'Ecclesiastical Ballads. I. The Veteran of Heaven. II. Lilium Regis.'
    Apr.   'Orison-Tryst'
    July   'Ad Castitatem'
                In the *English Review*
    July   'To Daisies'
                In the *Dublin Review*
    Oct.   'Carmen Genesis'
                In *The Athenæum*
    Nov. 12. 'To Two Friends' (part of 'Proemion' to 'Love in Dian's Lap')
                In the *Dublin Review*
1911 Jan.   'The House of Sorrows'
                In the *Century Magazine*
    June   'Cheated Elsie'

BIBLIOGRAPHY

In the *Dublin Review*
1912 Apr.   'Holy Ground' (*not reprinted*)

•   In *The Athenæum*
1913 Mar. 29. 'Messages'

(June)   In *Works, Vol. I*
'Domus Tua' (cancelled in proofs of *Poems* 1893)
To Stars
Pastoral
Past Thinking of Solomon

In *Vol. II*
Laus Amara Doloris
Peace
Of Nature: Laud and Plaint
Sonnets:
  Ad Amicam
  Love's Varlets
A Hollow Wood
Of my Friend (2 stanzas: a third is given in the *Life*, 1925 edition, p. 229)
A Double Need
All Flesh
The Singer saith of his Song

In *Vol. III*
Motto and Invocation
Prologue to a Pastoral

In Everard Meynell's *Life of Francis Thompson*, with other fragments
  Caudated Sonnet ('With dawn and children risen would he run')
  'Degraded Poor'
  'On the Anniversary of Rossetti's death': a fragment (23 lines)
(In the revised edition of 1926 the first of these was omitted, and the last shortened to 15 lines. None are printed elsewhere.)

236

INDEX OF TITLES

Absence v. 1, 178
Ad Amicam v. 2, 171
Ad Castitatem v. 2, 60
After her going v. 1, 102
After Woman, The v. 2, 64
Against Urania v. 2, 129
All Flesh v. 2, 224
Anthem of Earth, An v. 2, 105
Any Saint v. 2, 45
Arab Love-Song v. 1, 168
Assumpta Maria v. 2, 52

Before her Portrait in Youth v. 1, 77
Beginning of End v. 2, 85
Beneath a Photograph v. 1, 104
Body and Spirit v. 3, 250
Buona Notte v. 1, 169
'By Reason of Thy Law' v. 2, 15

Captain of Song, A v. 2, 127
Carmen Genesis v. 2, 56
Carrier Song, A v. 1, 85
Cecil Rhodes v. 2, 157
Cheated Elsie v. 1, 216
Child, To a v. 2, 176
Chose vue v. 2, 220
Cloud's Swan-Song, The v. 2, 206
Contemplation v. 2, 12
Corymbus for Autumn, A v. 1, 141

Daisies, To v. 2, 191
Daisy v. 1, 3
Daphne v. 1, 176
Dead Astronomer, A v. 1, 215

Dead Cardinal, To the v. 1, 131
Dedication of *New Poems* v. 2, vii
    Poems v. 1, xiii
Desiderium Indesideratum v. 2, 182
Diamond Jubilee, Ode for the v. 2, 137
Domus Tua v. 1, 100
Double Need, A v. 2, 214
Dread of Height, The v. 2, 17
Dream-Tryst v. 1, 167

Echo of Victor Hugo, An v. 1, 163
End of It, The v. 2, 88
English Martyrs, To the v. 2, 131
Envoy v. 1, 226
Epilogue to 'A Judgment in Heaven' v. 1, 190
    'A narrow Vessel' v. 2, 89
    The Poet's Sitter v. 1, 98
'Ex Ore Infantium' v. 1, 121

Fair Inconstant, The v. 1, 220
Fallen Yew, A v. 1, 181
Field-Flower, A v. 2, 201
Friend, Of my v. 2, 211
From the Night of Forebeing v. 2, 32

Gilded Gold v. 1, 90
Girl's Sin, A v. 2, 75
Godchild, To my v. 2, 17
Grace of the Way v. 2, 67
Grief's Harmonics v. 2, 215

INDEX OF TITLES

Heard on the Mountain v. 1, 158
Heart, The v. 2, 180
Heaven and Hell v. 2, 219
Her Portrait v. 1, 92
Hermes v. 2, 177
Hollow Wood, A v. 2, 189
Holocaust, A. v. 2, 95
Hound of Heaven, The v. 1, 107
House of Bondage v. 2, 178
House of Sorrows, The v. 1, 222
Hugo, Victor, An Echo of v. 1, 163

In Her Paths v. 1, 101
'In no strange Land' v. 2, 226
Insentience v. 1, 225

Judgment in Heaven, v. 1, 185
July Fugitive v. 2, 198

Kingdom of God, The v. 2, 226
Laus Amara Doloris v. 2, 121
Lilium Regis v. 1, 151
Lines for a Drawing of Our Lady v. 1, 200
Little Jesus v. 1, 21
Lord's, At v. 1, 174
Love and the Child v. 1, 175
Love Declared v. 2, 82
Love in Dian's Lap v. 1, 69
Love's Almsman plaineth his Fare v. 2, 93
Love's Varlets v. 2, 183

Making of Viola, The v. 1, 13
'Manus Animam Pinxit' v. 1, 82
Marriage in two Moods v. 2, 222
May Burden, A v. 2, 196
Memorat Memoria v. 2, 216

Messages v. 1, 173
Mistress of Vision, The v. 2, 3
Monica, St. v. 2, 221
Monica, To: after Nine Years v. 2, 212
   thought Dying so v. 1, 10
Motto and Invocation v. 3, vii
My Lady the Tyranness v. 2, 96

Narrow Vessel, A v. 2, 73
Nature, Of: Laud and Plaint v. 2, 162
New Year's Chimes v. 2, 29
Night of Forebeing, From the v. 2, 32
Night, Our Lady of the v. 1, 200
Nineteenth Century, The v. 2, 146
Nocturn v. 2, 218
Non Pax—Expectatio v. 2, 184
Not even in Dream v. 2, 185

Ode for the Diamond Jubilee v. 2, 137
   Orient v. 2, 21
   to the Setting Sun v. 1, 117
Olivia, To v. 1, 20
Orient Ode v. 2, 21
Orison-Tryst v. 1, 201

Passion of Mary, The v. 1, 171
Past Thinking of Solomon v. 1, 213
Pastoral v. 1, 211
Peace v. 2, 153
Penelope v. 2, 86
Photograph, Beneath a v. 1, 104
Poet breaking Silence, To a v. 1, 79

INDEX OF TITLES

Poppy, The v. 1, 6
Portrait in Youth, Before her v. 1, 77

Question, A v. 2, 204

Retrospect v. 2, 70
Rhodes, Cecil v. 2, 157

Scala Jacobi Portaque Eburnea v. 1, 89
Sere of the Leaf, The v. 1, 192
Sight and Insight v. 2, 1
Singer saith of his Song, The v. 2, 228
Sinking Sun, To the v. 2, 194
Sister Songs v. 1, 23
Snowflake, To a v. 2, 203
Song of the Hours v. 1, 204

Sonnets v. 2, 169
Stars, To v. 1, 198
Sunset, A v. 1, 158

Threatened Tears v. 1, 221
Translations v. 1, 153

Ultima v. 2, 91
Ultimum v. 2, 101
Unto this Last v. 2, 99
Urania, Against v. 2, 129

Veteran of Heaven, The v. 1, 149

Way of a Maid, The v. 2, 84
'Whereto art thou come?' v. 1, 203
W. M., To v. 1, 180

INDEX OF FIRST LINES

A boy's young fancy taketh love	v. 2, 99
A perfect woman—Thine be laud	v. 1, 100
Ah, drops of gold in whitening flame	v. 2, 191
Ah, gone the days when for undying kindness	v. 2, 214
Alas, and I have sung	v. 2, 70
Alas! now wilt thou chide, and say (I deem)	v. 1, 98
And she has trod before me in these ways	v. 1, 101
Ariel to Miranda:—Hear	v. 1, 169
As, fore-announced by threat of flame and smoke	v. 2, 146
As lovers, banished from their lady's face	v. 1, 77
At evening, when the lank and rigid trees	v. 2, 215
At the Cross thy station keeping	v. 2, 221
Athwart the sod which is treading for God	v. 1, 185
Can I forget her cruelty	v. 2, 80
Can you tell me where has hid her	v. 2, 198
Cast wide the folding doorways of the East	v. 2, 32
Come you living or dead to me, out of the silt of the Past	v. 2, 216
Cross child! red, and frowning so	v. 2, 75
Daughter of the ancient Eve	v. 2, 64
Dear Dove, that bear'st to my sole-labouring ark	v. 2, 171
Do not loose those rains thy wet	v. 1, 221
Dost thou still hope thou shalt be fair	v. 1, 220
Elsie was a maiden fair	v. 1, 216
'Friend, whereto art thou come?' Thus Verity	v. 1, 203
Go, songs, for ended is our brief, sweet play	v. 1, 226
God took a fit of Paradise-wind	v. 2, 201
Have you sometimes, calm, silent	v. 1, 158
Hear, my Muses, I demand	v. 1, 71
Hearken my chant, 'tis	v. 1, 141
Her soul from earth to Heaven lies	v. 1, 89
Here I make oath	v. 2, 15
His shoulder did I hold	v. 2, 45

INDEX OF FIRST LINES

How graciously thou wear'st the yoke	v. 2, 194
Hush! 'tis the gap between two lightnings. Room	v. 2, 184
I do not need the skies'	v. 2, 224
I fear to love thee, Sweet, because	v. 1, 20
I fled Him, down the nights and down the days	v. 1, 107
I looked, she drooped, and neither spake, and cold	v. 2, 82
I love the evenings, passionless and fair	v. 1, 158
I walk, I only	v. 2, 218
I will not perturbate	v. 1, 131
If I have studied here in part	v. 2, 89
If the rose in meek duty	v. 1, xiii
Immeasurable Earth	v. 2, 105
Implacable sweet dæmon, Poetry	v. 2, 121
In curbed expanses our wheeling dances	v. 1, 204
In nescientness, in nescientness	v. 2, 105
In the land of flag-lilies	v. 2, 212
It is little I repair	v. 1, 174
It seemed corrival of the world's great prime	v. 1, 181
Lady who hold'st on me dominion	v. 1, 81
Life's a veil the real has	v. 1, 163
Little Jesus, wast thou shy	v. 1, 21
Lo, here stand I and Nature, gaze to gaze	v. 2, 162
Lo, I, Song's most true lover, plain me sore	v. 2, 129
Lo, in the sanctuaried East	v. 2, 21
Lo, my book thinks to look Time's leaguer down	v. 2, vii
Look on him. This is he whose works ye know	v. 2, 127
Love, he is nearer (though the moralist)	v. 2, 183
Love, like a wind, shook wide your blossomy eyes	v. 2, 86
Love that's loved from day to day	v. 2, 222
Me since your fair ambition bows	v. 2, 96
Mortals, that behold a Woman	v. 2, 52
'My brother!' spake she to the sun	v. 2, 67
Night; and the street a corpse beneath the moon	v. 2, 137
No, no, it cannot be, it cannot be	v. 2, 174
Not the Circean wine	v. 2, 17
Now in these last spent drops, slow, slower shed	v. 2, 101

241

INDEX OF FIRST LINES

O bird with heart of wassail	v. 2, 204
O captain of the wars	v. 1, 149
O friend, who mak'st that mis-spent word of 'friend'	v. 2, 173
O gain that bark'st ungained in all gain	v. 2, 182
O Lady Mary, thy bright crown	v. 1, 171
O Lily of the King! low lies thy silver wing	v. 1, 151
O nothing, in this corporeal earth of man	v. 2, 181
O sweet is Love, and sweet is Lack	v. 1, 225
O tree of many branches! One thou hast	v. 1, 180
O world invisible, we view thee	v. 2, 226
Of the white purity	v. 1, 222
Oh, but the heavenly grammar did I hold	v. 1, 92
Pan-imbued	v. 1, 211
Pardon, O Saint John divine	v. 3, vii
Peace:—as a dawn that flares	v. 2, 153
Phoebus, who taught me art divine	v. 1, 104
Rain, rain on Tyburn tree	v. 2, 131
Said sprite o' me to body o' me	v. 3, 250
Secret was the garden	v. 2, 3
She did not love to love, but hated him	v. 2, 88
She told me, in the morning her white thought	v. 1, 201
She was aweary of the hovering	v. 2, 85
Shrewd winds and shrill—were these the speech of May	v. 1, 25
Since you have waned from us	v. 1, 85
Sing how the uncreated Light	v. 2, 56
Soothsay, Behold, with rod twy-serpented	v. 2, 177
Spin, daughter Mary, spin	v. 1, 13
Starry amorist, starward gone	v. 1, 215
Summer set lip to earth's bosom bare	v. 1, 6
The after-event! Ah, did I walk	v. 1, 102
The breaths of kissing night and day	v. 1, 167
The heart you hold too small and local thing	v. 2, 180
The hunchèd camels of the night	v. 1, 168
The leaves dance, the leaves sing	v. 1, 27
The lover whose soul shaken is	v. 2, 84

INDEX OF FIRST LINES

The moonlight cloud of her invisible beauty	v. 2, 211
The river-god's daughter,—the sun-god sought her	v. 1, 176
The spirit's ark sealed with a little clay	v. 2, 179
The touches of man's modern speech	v. 2, 228
The wailful sweetness of the violin	v. 1, 117
There is a parable in the pathless cloud	v. 2, 206
They that mis-said	v. 2, 157
This, could I paint my inward sight	v. 1, 200
This is the mansion built for me	v. 2, 189
This labouring, vast, Tellurian galleon	v. 2, 17
This love is crueller than the other love	v. 2, 185
This morning saw I, fled the shower	v. 2, 12
Thou dost to rich attire a grace	v. 1, 90
Through meadow-ways as I did tread	v. 2, 196
Through thee, Virginity, endure	v. 2, 60
'Tis said there were no thought of hell	v. 2, 219
Too wearily had we and song	v. 1, 79
Up she rose, fair daughter—well she was graced	v. 2, 220
Virtue may unlock hell, or even	v. 1, 190
What heart could have thought you	v. 2, 203
What is the song the stars sing	v. 2, 29
What shall I your true-love tell	v. 1, 173
When from the blossoms of the noiseful day	v. 2, 172
When I perceive Love's heavenly reaping still	v. 2, 178
When I presage the time shall come—yea, now	v. 2, 95
When music's fading's faded	v. 1, 178
When that part heavenliest of all-heavenly you	v. 2, 175
When as my life shall time with funeral tread	v. 2, 176
Where the thistle lifts a purple crown	v. 1, 3
Why do you so clasp me	v. 1, 175
Winter wore a flapping wind	v. 1, 192
Wise-unto-hell Ecclesiast	v. 1, 213
You, Love's mendicancy who never tried	v. 2, 93
You, my unrest, and Night's tranquillity	v. 1, 198
You, O the piteous you	v. 1, 10

FRANCIS THOMPSON
Poems and Essays

———

THREE VOLUMES IN ONE
VOLUME THREE: *Essays*

THE CONTENTS

	Page	
The Literary Executor's Preface		v
The Author's Motto and Invocation		vii
Shelley		1
Paganism Old and New		38
In Darkest England		52
The Fourth Order of Humanity		66
Form and Formalism		71
Nature's Immortality		78
Sanctity and Song		89
Don Quixote		93
The Way of Imperfection		97
A Renegade Poet on the Poet		105
Moestitiae Encomium		110
Finis Coronat Opus		116
The Poets' Poet		140
Sidney's Prose		147
Shakespeare's Prose		153
Ben Jonson's Prose		159
Seventeenth Century Prose		164
Goldsmith's Prose		170
Crashaw		175
Coleridge		181
Bacon		190
Milton		195
Pope		203
James Thomson		209
Thomas De Quincey		215

CONTENTS

Macaulay	222
Emerson	231
Dante	238
The Nibelungen Lied	245
Health and Holiness	249
Notes	283

The Preface by Francis Thompson's Literary Executor

IF Francis Thompson's concern for the Prose of Poets is the Reader's too, this volume carries its own proper passport on its title-page. Of this Poet's prose, his *Shelley* Essay stands first among even his own writings. Yet the same ease with which he turns one of its passages of imagery into verse for *An Anthem of Earth* is equally evident in the case of other essays and other poems : a sign of a general closer kinship than is common between the less and the more imaginative modes of expression.

Poetry and Prose he began to write simultaneously. His *Paganism Old and New* (composed before he left the London streets, as one of its allusions betrays) was sent in the same envelope as his *Dream Tryst* to the office of the magazine which produced them ; and the *Shelley* Essay and *The Hound of Heaven* were contemporaries—one could say twins. But whereas his Poetry was written, at intervals, almost wholly during the decade of years 1888 to 1897, he continued to write Prose, if a little fitfully, during the remaining decade of his life. To the earlier period belong the imaginative papers : such as the *Moestitiae Encomium*, written when he had been reading Blake and De Quincey, his ' very own Thomas De Quincey ' ; and the *Finis Coronat Opus*, a fantasia which he might appropriately have produced in competition with Mary Shelley, but one which, for all its artificiality, and its hardly hidden

PREFACE

irony, has hints of that slaying of domesticities which went to his own making of ' a poet out of a man.'

Later his literary criticisms had a friendly welcome in several quarters, notably in *The Academy*, under Charles Lewis Hind, and in *The Athenæum*, first under Norman Maccoll and finally under Vernon Rendall. The reprinting of such articles and reviews, written in haste, must be something of a hazardous adventure. But I am fortified in making it by the fact that he himself projected a Prose volume; appointing for it some of the articles here printed, and even formally correcting them for the Press. And if my choice, where left unaided, is a faulty one, I know that the very failures and unexpectednesses of a man of genius serve a sound purpose, though a biographical, rather than a literary one.

W.M.

May 1913.

MOTTO & INVOCATION

OMNIA PER IPSUM, ET SINE IPSO NIHIL
St John's Gospel, chap. 1, *v.* 3, *abbreviated.*

PARDON, O Saint John Divine,
   That I change a word of thee—
   None the less, aid thou me!
And Siena's Catharine!
Lofty Doctor, Augustine,
Glorious penitent! And be
Assisi's Francis also mine!
Mine be Padua's Anthony:
And that other Francis, he
Called of Sales! Let all combine
To counsel (of great charity)
What I write! Thy wings incline,
Ah, my Angel, o'er the line!
Last and first, O Queen Mary,
Of thy white Immaculacy,
If my work may profit aught,
Fill with lilies every thought!
I surmise
What is white will then be wise.

To which I add: Thomas More,
Teach (thereof my need is sore)
What thou showedst well on earth—
Good writ, good wit, make goodly mirth!

                F.T.

SHELLEY

THE Church, which was once the mother of poets no less than of saints, during the last two centuries has relinquished to aliens the chief glories of poetry, if the chief glories of holiness she has preserved for her own. The palm and the laurel, Dominic and Dante, sanctity and song, grew together in her soil: she has retained the palm, but forgone the laurel. Poetry in its widest sense,* and when not professedly irreligious, has been too much and too long either misprised or distrusted; too much and too generally the feeling has been that it is at best superfluous, at worst pernicious, most often dangerous. Once poetry was, as she should be, the lesser sister and helpmate of the Church; the minister to the mind, as the Church to the soul. But poetry sinned, poetry fell; and, in place of lovingly reclaiming her, Catholicism cast her from the door to follow the feet of her pagan seducer. The separation has been ill for poetry; it has not been well for religion.

Fathers of the Church (we would say), pastors of the Church, pious laics of the Church: you are taking from its walls the panoply of Aquinas; take also from its walls the psaltery of Alighieri. Unrol the precedents of the Church's past; recall to your minds that Francis of Assisi was among the precursors of Dante; that sworn to

* That is to say, taken as the general animating spirit of the Fine Arts.

SHELLEY

Poverty he forswore not Beauty, but discerned through the lamp Beauty the Light God; that he was even more a poet in his miracles than in his melody; that poetry clung round the cowls of his Order. Follow his footsteps; you who have blessings for men, have you no blessing for the birds? Recall to your memory that, in their minor kind, the love poems of Dante shed no less honour on Catholicism than did the great religious poem which is itself pivoted on love; that in singing of heaven he sang of Beatrice—this supporting angel was still carven on his harp even when he stirred its strings in Paradise. What you theoretically know, vividly realize: that with many the religion of beauty must always be a passion and a power, that it is only evil when divorced from the worship of the Primal Beauty. Poetry is the preacher to men of the earthly as you of the Heavenly Fairness; of that earthly fairness which God has fashioned to His own image and likeness. You proclaim the day which the Lord has made, and she exults and rejoices in it. You praise the Creator for His works, and she shows you that they are very good. Beware how you misprise this potent ally, for hers is the art of Giotto and Dante: beware how you misprise this insidious foe, for hers is the art of modern France and of Byron. Her value, if you know it not, God knows, and know the enemies of God. If you have no room for her beneath the wings of the Holy One, there is place for her beneath the webs of the

SHELLEY

Evil One : whom you discard, he embraces ; whom you cast down from an honourable seat, he will advance to a haughty throne ; the brows you dislaurel of a just respect, he will bind with baleful splendours ; the stone which you builders reject, he will make his head of the corner. May she not prophesy in the temple ? then there is ready for her the tripod of Delphi. Eye her not askance if she seldom sing directly of religion : the bird gives glory to God though it sings only of its innocent loves. Suspicion creates its own cause ; distrust begets reason for distrust. This beautiful, wild, feline poetry, wild because left to range the wilds, restore to the hearth of your charity, shelter under the rafter of your Faith ; discipline her to the sweet restraints of your household, feed her with the meat from your table, soften her with the amity of your children ; tame her, fondle her, cherish her—you will no longer then need to flee her. Suffer her to wanton, suffer her to play, so she play round the foot of the Cross !

There is a change of late years : the Wanderer is being called to her Father's house, but we would have the call yet louder, we would have the proffered welcome more unstinted. There are still stray remnants of the old intolerant distrust. It is still possible for even a French historian of the Church to enumerate among the articles cast upon Savonarola's famous pile, *poésies érotiques, tant des anciens que des modernes, livres impies ou corrupteurs, Ovide,*

SHELLEY

Tibulle, Properce, pour ne nommer que les plus connus, Dante, Pétrarque, Boccace, tous ces auteurs Italiens qui déjà souillaient les âmes et ruinaient les mœurs, en créant ou perfectionnant la langue. Blameworthy carelessness, at the least, which can class the *Vita Nuova* with the *Ars Amandi* and the *Decameron!* With few exceptions, whatsoever in our best poets is great and good to the non-Catholic, is great and good also to the Catholic; and though Faber threw his edition of Shelley into the fire and never regretted the act; though, moreover, Shelley is so little read among us that we can still tolerate in our churches the religious parody which Faber should have thrown after his three-volumed Shelley;*—in spite of this, we are not disposed to number among such exceptions that straying spirit of light.

We have among us at the present day no lineal descendant, in the poetical order, of Shelley; and any such offspring of the aboundingly spontaneous Shelley is hardly possible, still less likely, on account of the defect by which (we think) contemporary poetry in general, as compared with the poetry of the early nineteenth century, is mildewed. That defect is the predominance of art over inspiration, of body over soul. We do not say the *defect* of inspiration. The warrior is there, but he is hampered by his armour. Writers of high aim in

* The hymn, 'I rise from dreams of time.'

SHELLEY

all branches of literature, even when they are not—as Mr Swinburne, for instance, is—lavish in expression, are generally over-deliberate in expression. Mr Henry James, delineating a fictitious writer clearly intended to be the ideal of an artist, makes him regret that he has sometimes allowed himself to take the second-best word instead of searching for the best. Theoretically, of course, one ought always to try for the best word. But practically, the habit of excessive care in word-selection frequently results in loss of spontaneity ; and, still worse, the habit of always taking the best word too easily becomes the habit of always taking the most ornate word, the word most removed from ordinary speech. In consequence of this, poetic diction has become latterly a kaleidoscope, and one's chief curiosity is as to the precise combinations into which the pieces will be shifted. There is, in fact, a certain band of words, the Prætorian cohorts of poetry, whose prescriptive aid is invoked by every aspirant to the poetical purple, and without whose prescriptive aid none dares aspire to the poetical purple ; against these it is time some banner should be raised. Perhaps it is almost impossible for a contemporary writer quite to evade the services of the freelances whom one encounters under so many standards.* But it is at any rate curious to note

* We are a little surprised at the fact, because so many Victorian poets are, or have been, prose-writers as well. Now, according to our theory, the practice of prose should main-

SHELLEY

that the literary revolution against the despotic diction of Pope seems issuing, like political revolutions, in a despotism of its own making.

This, then, we cannot but think, distinguishes the literary period of Shelley from our own. It distinguishes even the unquestionable treasures and masterpieces of to-day from similar treaures and masterpieces of the precedent day; even *The Lotus-Eaters* from *Kubla Khan*; even Rossetti's ballads from *Christabel*. It is present in the restraint of Matthew Arnold no less than in the exuberance of Swinburne, and affects our writers who aim at simplicity no less than those who seek richness. Indeed, nothing is so artificial as our simplicity. It is the simplicity of the French stage *ingénue*. We are self-conscious to the finger-tips; and this inherent quality, entailing on our poetry the inevitable loss of spontaneity, ensures that whatever poets, of whatever excellence, may be born to us from the Shelleian stock, its founder's spirit can take among us no reincarnation. An age that is ceasing to produce child-like children cannot

tain fresh and comprehensive a poet's diction, should save him from falling into the hands of an exclusive coterie of poetic words. It should react upon his metrical vocabulary to its beneficial expansion, by taking him outside his aristocratic circle of language, and keeping him in touch with the great commonalty, the proletariat of speech. For it is with words as with men: constant intermarriage within the limits of a patrician clan begets effete refinement; and to reinvigorate the stock, its veins must be replenished from hardy plebeian blood.

SHELLEY

produce a Shelley. For both as poet and man he was essentially a child.

Yet, just as in the effete French society before the Revolution the Queen played at Arcadia, the King played at being a mechanic, every one played at simplicity and universal philanthropy, leaving for most durable outcome of their philanthropy the guillotine, as the most durable outcome of ours may be execution by electricity;—so in our own society the talk of benevolence and the cult of childhood are the very fashion of the hour. We, of this self-conscious, incredulous generation, sentimentalize our children, analyse our children, think we are endowed with a special capacity to sympathize and identify ourselves with children; we play at being children. And the result is that we are not more child-like, but our children are less child-like. It is so tiring to stoop to the child, so much easier to lift the child up to you. Know you what it is to be a child? It is to be something very different from the man of to-day. It is to have a spirit yet streaming from the waters of baptism; it is to believe in love, to believe in loveliness, to believe in belief; it is to be so little that the elves can reach to whisper in your ear; it is to turn pumpkins into coaches, and mice into horses, lowness into loftiness, and nothing into everything, for each child has its fairy godmother in its own soul; it is to live in a nutshell and to count yourself the king of infinite space; it is

SHELLEY

> To see a world in a grain of sand,
> And a heaven in a wild flower,
> Hold infinity in the palm of your hand,
> And eternity in an hour;

it is to know not as yet that you are under sentence of life, nor petition that it be commuted into death. When we become conscious in dreaming that we dream, the dream is on the point of breaking; when we become conscious in living that we live, the ill dream is but just beginning. Now if Shelley was but too conscious of the dream, in other respects Dryden's false and famous line might have been applied to him with very much less than its usual untruth.* To the last, in a degree uncommon even among poets, he retained the idiosyncrasy of childhood, expanded and matured without differentiation. To the last he was the enchanted child.

This was, as is well known, patent in his life. It is as really, though perhaps less obviously, manifest in his poetry, the sincere effluence of his life. And it may not, therefore, be amiss to consider whether it was conditioned by anything beyond his congenital nature. For our part, we believe it to have been equally largely the outcome of his early and long isolation. Men given to retirement and abstract study are

* Wordsworth's adaptation of it, however, is true. Men are not 'children of a larger growth,' but the child *is* father of the man, since the parent is only partially reproduced in his offspring.

SHELLEY

notoriously liable to contract a certain degree of childlikeness : and if this be the case when we segregate a man, how much more when we segregate a child ! It is when they are taken into the solution of school-life that children, by the reciprocal interchange of influence with their fellows, undergo the series of reactions which converts them from children into boys and from boys into men. The intermediate stage must be traversed to reach the final one.

Now Shelley never could have been a man, for he never was a boy. And the reason lay in the persecution which overclouded his schooldays. Of that persecution's effect upon him he has left us, in *The Revolt of Islam*, a picture which to many or most people very probably seems a poetical exaggeration ; partly because Shelley appears to have escaped physical brutality, partly because adults are inclined to smile tenderly at childish sorrows which are not caused by physical suffering. That he escaped for the most part bodily violence is nothing to the purpose. It is the petty malignant annoyance recurring hour by hour, day by day, month by month, until its accumulation becomes an agony ; it is this which is the most terrible weapon that boys have against their fellow boy, who is powerless to shun it because, unlike the man, he has virtually no privacy. His is the torture which the ancients used, when they anointed their victim with honey and exposed him naked to the restless fever of the

SHELLEY

flies. He is a little St Sebastian, sinking under the incessant flight of shafts which skilfully avoid the vital parts.

We do not, therefore, suspect Shelley of exaggeration: he was, no doubt, in terrible misery. Those who think otherwise must forget their own past. Most people, we suppose, *must* forget what they were like when they were children : otherwise they would know that the griefs of their childhood were passionate abandonment, *déchirants* (to use a characteristically favourite phrase of modern French literature) as the griefs of their maturity. Children's griefs are little, certainly ; but so is the child, so is its endurance, so is its field of vision, while its nervous impressionability is keener than ours. Grief is a matter of relativity; the sorrow should be estimated by its proportion to the sorrower ; a gash is as painful to one as an amputation to another. Pour a puddle into a thimble, or an Atlantic into Etna ; both thimble and mountain overflow. Adult fools ! would not the angels smile at *our* griefs, were not angels too wise to smile at them ?

So beset, the child fled into the tower of his own soul, and raised the drawbridge. He threw out a reserve, encysted in which he grew to maturity unaffected by the intercourses that modify the maturity of others into the thing we call a man. The encysted child developed until it reached years of virility, until those later Oxford days in which Hogg encountered

SHELLEY

it; then, bursting at once from its cyst and the university, it swam into a world not illegitimately perplexed by such a whim of the gods. It was, of course, only the completeness and duration of this seclusion—lasting from the gate of boyhood to the threshold of youth—which was peculiar to Shelley. Most poets, probably, like most saints, are prepared for their mission by an initial segregation, as the seed is buried to germinate : before they can utter the oracle of poetry, they must first be divided from the body of men. It is the severed head that makes the seraph.

Shelley's life frequently exhibits in him the magnified child. It is seen in his fondness for apparently futile amusements, such as the sailing of paper boats. This was, in the truest sense of the word, child-like ; not, as it is frequently called and considered, childish. That is to say, it was not a mindless triviality, but the genuine child's power of investing little things with imaginative interest ; the same power, though differently devoted, which produced much of his poetry. Very possibly in the paper boat he saw the magic bark of Laon and Cythna, or

> That thinnest boat
> In which the mother of the months is borne
> By ebbing night into her western cave.

In fact, if you mark how favourite an idea, under varying forms, is this in his verse, you will perceive that all the charmed boats which glide

SHELLEY

down the stream of his poetry are but glorified resurrections of the little paper argosies which trembled down the Isis.

And the child appeared no less often in Shelley the philosopher than in Shelley the idler. It is seen in his repellent no less than in his amiable weaknesses ; in the unteachable folly of a love that made its goal its starting-point, and firmly expected spiritual rest from each new divinity, though it had found none from the divinities antecedent. For we are clear that this was no mere straying of sensual appetite, but a straying, strange and deplorable, of the spirit ; that (contrary to what Coventry Patmore has said) he left a woman not because he was tired of her arms, but because he was tired of her soul. When he found Mary Shelley wanting, he seems to have fallen into the mistake of Wordsworth, who complained in a charming piece of unreasonableness that his wife's love, which had been a fountain, was now only a well:

> Such change, and at the very door
> Of my fond heart, hath made me poor.

Wordsworth probably learned, what Shelley was incapable of learning, that love can never permanently be a fountain. A living poet, in an article* which you almost fear to breathe upon lest you should flutter some of the frail pastel-like bloom, has said the thing : ' Love

* *The Rhythm of Life*, by Alice Meynell.

SHELLEY

itself has tidal moments, lapses and flows due to the metrical rule of the interior heart.' Elementary reason should proclaim this true. Love is an affection, its display an emotion: love is the air, its display is the wind. An affection may be constant; an emotion can no more be constant than the wind can constantly blow. All, therefore, that a man can reasonably ask of his wife is that her love should be indeed a well. A well; but a Bethesda-well, into which from time to time the angel of tenderness descends to trouble the waters for the healing of the beloved. Such a love Shelley's second wife appears unquestionably to have given him. Nay, she was content that he should veer while she remained true; she companioned him intellectually, shared his views, entered into his aspirations, and yet—yet, even at the date of *Epipsychidion*, the foolish child, her husband, assigned her the part of moon to Emilia Viviani's sun, and lamented that he was barred from final, certain, irreversible happiness by a cold and callous society. Yet few poets were so mated before, and no poet was so mated afterwards, until Browning stooped and picked up a fair-coined soul that lay rusting in a pool of tears.

In truth, his very unhappiness and discontent with life, in so far as it was not the inevitable penalty of the ethical anarch, can only be ascribed to this same childlike irrationality—though in such a form it is irrationality hardly peculiar to Shelley. Pity, if you will, his

SHELLEY

spiritual ruins, and the neglected early training which was largely their cause; but the pity due to his outward circumstances has been strangely exaggerated. The obloquy from which he suffered he deliberately and wantonly courted. For the rest, his lot was one that many a young poet might envy. He had faithful friends, a faithful wife, an income small but assured. Poverty never dictated to his pen; the designs on his bright imagination were never etched by the sharp fumes of necessity.

If, as has chanced to others—as chanced, for example, to Mangan—outcast from home, health and hope, with a charred past and a bleared future, an anchorite without detachment, and self-cloistered without self-sufficingness, deposed from a world which he had not abdicated, pierced with thorns which formed no crown, a poet hopeless of the bays, and a martyr hopeless of the palm, a land cursed against the dews of love, an exile banned and proscribed even from the innocent arms of childhood—he were burning helpless at the stake of his unquenchable heart, then he might have been inconsolable, then might he have cast the gorge at life, then have cowered in the darkening chamber of his being, tapestried with mouldering hopes, and hearkened to the winds that swept across the illimitable wastes of death. But no such hapless lot was Shelley's as that of his own contemporaries—Keats, half-chewed in the jaws of London and spit dying

SHELLEY

on to Italy; De Quincey, who, if he escaped, escaped rent and maimed from those cruel jaws; Coleridge, whom they dully mumbled for the major portion of his life. Shelley had competence, poetry, love; yet he wailed that he could lie down like a tired child and weep away his life of care! Is it ever so with you, sad brother? is it ever so with me? and is there no drinking of pearls except they be dissolved in biting tears? 'Which of us has his desire, or having it, is satisfied?'

It is true that he shared the fate of nearly all the great poets contemporary with him, in being unappreciated. Like them, he suffered from critics who were for ever shearing the wild tresses of poetry between rusty rules, who could never see a literary bough project beyond the trim level of its day but they must lop it with a crooked criticism, who kept indomitably planting in the defile of fame the 'established canons' that had been spiked by poet after poet. But we decline to believe that a singer of Shelley's calibre could be seriously grieved by want of vogue. Not that we suppose him to have found consolation in that senseless superstition, 'the applause of posterity.' Posterity, posterity! posterity which goes to Rome, weeps large-sized tears, carves beautiful inscriptions, over the tomb of Keats; and the worm must wriggle her curtsey to it all, since the dead boy, wherever he be, has quite other gear to tend. Never a bone less dry for all the tears!

SHELLEY

A poet must to some extent be a chameleon, and feed on air. But it need not be the musty breath of the multitude. He can find his needful support in the judgement of those whose judgement he knows valuable, and such support Shelley had:

> La gloire
> Ne compte pas toujours les voix ;
> Elle les pèse quelquefois.

Yet if this might be needful to him as support, neither this, nor the applause of the present, nor the applause of posterity, could have been needful to him as motive : the one all-sufficing motive for a great poet's singing is that expressed by Keats :

> I was taught in Paradise
> To ease my breast of melodies.

Precisely so. The overcharged breast can find no ease but in suckling the baby-song. No enmity of outward circumstances, therefore, but his own nature, was responsible for Shelley's doom.

A being with so much about it of childlike unreasonableness, and yet withal so much of the beautiful attraction luminous in a child's sweet unreasonableness, would seem fore-fated by its very essence to the transience of the bubble and the rainbow, of all things filmy and fair. Did some shadow of this destiny bear part in his sadness ? Certain it is that, by a curious

SHELLEY

chance, he himself in *Julian and Maddalo* jestingly foretold the manner of his end. 'O ho! You talk as in years past,' said Maddalo (Byron) to Julian (Shelley); 'if you can't swim, Beware of Providence.' Did no unearthly *dixisti* sound in his ears as he wrote it? But a brief while, and Shelley, who could not swim, was weltering on the waters of Lerici. We know not how this may affect others, but over us it is a coincidence which has long tyrannized with an absorbing inveteracy of impression (strengthened rather than diminished by the contrast between the levity of the utterance and its fatal fulfilment)—thus to behold, heralding itself in warning mockery through the very lips of its predestined victim, the Doom upon whose breath his locks were lifting along the coasts of Campania. The death which he had prophesied came upon him, and Spezzia enrolled another name among the mournful Marcelli of our tongue; Venetian glasses which foamed and burst before the poisoned wine of life had risen to their brims.

Coming to Shelley's poetry, we peep over the wild mask of revolutionary metaphysics, and we see the winsome face of the child. Perhaps none of his poems is more purely and typicallg Shelleian than *The Cloud*, and it is interestiny to note how essentially it springs from the faculty of make-believe. The same thing is conspicuous, though less purely conspicuous, throughout his singing; it is the child's faculty of make-believe raised to the nth power. He is still at play, save only that his play is such as manhood stops to watch, and his playthings are those which the gods give their children. The universe is his box of toys. He dabbles his fingers in the day-fall. He is gold-dusty with tumbling amidst the stars. He makes bright mischief with the moon. The meteors nuzzle their noses in his hand. He teases into growling the kennelled thunder, and laughs at the shaking of its fiery chain. He dances in and out of the gates of heaven: its floor is littered with his broken fancies. He runs wild over the fields of ether. He chases the rolling world. He gets between the feet of the horses of the sun. He stands in the lap of patient Nature, and twines her loosened tresses after a hundred wilful fashions, to see how she will look nicest in his song.

This it was which, in spite of his essentially modern character as a singer, qualified Shelley to be the poet of *Prometheus Unbound*, for it made him, in the truest sense of the word, a mythological poet. This child-like quality assimilated him to the child-like peoples among whom mythologies have their rise. Those Nature myths which, according to many, are the basis of all mythology, are likewise the very basis of Shelley's poetry. The lark that is the gossip of heaven, the winds that pluck the grey from the beards of the billows, the clouds that are snorted from the sea's broad nostril, all the

SHELLEY

elemental spirits of Nature, take from his verse perpetual incarnation and reincarnation, pass in a thousand glorious transmigrations through the radiant forms of his imagery.

Thus, but not in the Wordsworthian sense, he is a veritable poet of Nature. For with Nature the Wordsworthians will admit no tampering: they exact the direct interpretative reproduction of her; that the poet should follow her as a mistress, not use her as a handmaid. To such following of Nature, Shelley felt no call. He saw in her not a picture set for his copying, but a palette set for his brush; not a habitation prepared for his inhabiting, but a Coliseum whence he might quarry stones for his own palaces. Even in his descriptive passages the dream-character of his scenery is notorious; it is not the clear, recognizable scenery of Wordsworth, but a landscape that hovers athwart the heat and haze arising from his crackling fantasies. The materials for such visionary Edens have evidently been accumulated from direct experience, but they are recomposed by him into such scenes as never mortal eye beheld. 'Don't you wish you had?' as Turner said. The one justification for classing Shelley with the Lake poet is that he loved Nature with a love even more passionate, though perhaps less profound. Wordsworth's *Nightingale and Stockdove* sums up the contrast between the two, as though it had been written for such a purpose. Shelley is the 'creature of ebullient heart,' who

SHELLEY

> Sings as if the god of wine
> Had helped him to a valentine.

Wordsworth's is the

> —Love with quiet blending,
> Slow to begin and never ending,

the 'serious faith and inward glee.'

But if Shelley, instead of culling Nature, crossed with its pollen the blossoms of his own soul, that Babylonian garden is his marvellous and best apology. For astounding figurative opulence he yields only to Shakespeare, and even to Shakespeare not in absolute fecundity but in range of images. The sources of his figurative wealth are specialized, while the sources of Shakespeare's are universal. It would have been as conscious an effort for him to speak without figure as it is for most men to speak with figure. Suspended in the dripping well of his imagination the commonest object becomes encrusted with imagery. Herein again he deviates from the true Nature poet, the normal Wordsworth type of Nature poet: imagery was to him not a mere means of expression, not even a mere means of adornment, it was a delight for its own sake.

And herein we find the trail by which we would classify him. He belongs to a school of which not impossibly he may hardly have read a line—the Metaphysical School. To a large extent, he *is* what the Metaphysical School

SHELLEY

should have been. That school was a certain kind of poetry trying for a range. Shelley is the range found. Crashaw and Shelley sprang from the same seed; but in the one case the seed was choked with thorns, in the other case it fell on good ground. The Metaphysical School was in its direct results an abortive movement, though indirectly much came of it—for Dryden came of it. Dryden, to a greater extent than is (we imagine) generally perceived, was Cowley systematized; and Cowley, who sank into the arms of Dryden, rose from the lap of Donne.

But the movement was so abortive that few will thank us for connecting with it the name of Shelley. This is because to most people the Metaphysical School means Donne, whereas it ought to mean Crashaw. We judge the direction of a development by its highest form, though that form may have been produced but once, and produced imperfectly. Now the highest product of the Metaphysical School was Crashaw, and Crashaw was a Shelley *manqué*; he never reached the Promised Land, but he had fervid visions of it. The Metaphysical School, like Shelley, loved imagery for its own sake: and how beautiful a thing the frank toying with imagery may be, let *The Skylark* and *The Cloud* witness. It is only evil when the poet, on the straight way to a fixed object, lags continually from the path to play. This is commendable neither in poet nor errand-boy. The Metaphysical School failed, not because it toyed with

SHELLEY

imagery, but because it toyed with it frostily. To sport with the tangles of Neæra's hair may be trivial idleness or caressing tenderness, exactly as your relation to Neæra is that of heartless gallantry or of love. So you may toy with imagery in mere intellectual ingenuity, and then you might as well go write acrostics: or you may toy with it in raptures, and then you may write a *Sensitive Plant*. In fact, the Metaphysical poets when they went astray cannot be said to have done anything so dainty as is implied by *toying* with imagery. They cut it into shapes with a pair of scissors. From all such danger Shelley was saved by his passionate spontaneity; no trappings are too splendid for the swift steeds of sunrise. His sword-hilt may be rough with jewels, but it is the hilt of an Excalibur. His thoughts scorch through all the folds of expression. His cloth of gold bursts at the flexures, and shows the naked poetry.

It is this gift of not merely embodying but apprehending everything in figure which co-operates towards creating one of his rarest characteristics, so almost preternaturally developed in no other poet, namely, his well-known power to condense the most hydrogenic abstraction. Science can now educe threads of such exquisite tenuity that only the feet of the tiniest infant-spiders can ascend them; but up the filmiest insubstantiality Shelley runs with agile ease. To him, in truth, nothing is abstract. The dustiest abstractions

SHELLEY

Start, and tremble under his feet,
And blossom in purple and red.

The coldest moon of an idea rises haloed through his vaporous imagination. The dimmest-sparked chip of a conception blazes and scintillates in the subtle oxygen of his mind. The most wrinkled Æson of an abstruseness leaps rosy out of his bubbling genius. In a more intensified signification than it is probable that Shakespeare dreamed of, Shelley gives to airy nothings a local habitation and a name. Here afresh he touches the Metaphysical School, whose very title was drawn from this habitual pursuit of abstractions, and who failed in that pursuit from the one cause omnipresent with them, because in all their poetic smithy they had left never a place for a forge. They laid their fancies chill on the anvil. Crashaw, indeed, partially anticipated Shelley's success, and yet further did a later poet, so much further that we find it difficult to understand why a generation that worships Shelley should be reviving Gray, yet almost forget the name of Collins. The generality of readers, when they know him at all, usually know him by his *Ode on the Passions*. In this, despite its beauty, there is still a *soupçon* of formalism, a lingering trace of powder from the eighteenth century periwig, dimming the bright locks of poetry. Only the literary student reads that little masterpiece, the *Ode to Evening*, which sometimes heralds the Shelleian strain, while other passages are

SHELLEY

the sole things in the language comparable to the miniatures of *Il Penseroso*. Crashaw, Collins, Shelley—three ricochets of the one pebble, three jets from three bounds of the one Pegasus! Collins's Pity, ' with eyes of dewy light,' is near of kin to Shelley's Sleep, ' the filmy-eyed '; and the ' shadowy tribes of mind ' are the lineal progenitors of ' Thought's crowned powers.' This, however, is personification, wherein both Collins and Shelley build on Spenser : the dizzying achievement to which the modern poet carried personification accounts for but a moiety, if a large moiety, of his vivifying power over abstractions. Take the passage (already alluded to) in that glorious chorus telling how the Hours come

> From those skiey towers
> Where Thought's crowned powers
> Sit watching your dance, ye happy Hours ;
> * * * * * *
> From the temples high
> Of Man's ear and eye,
> Roofed over Sculpture and Poesy,
> Our feet now, every palm,
> Are sandalled with calm,
> And the dew of our wings is a rain of balm ;
> And beyond our eyes
> The human love lies
> Which makes all it gazes on Paradise.

Any partial explanation will break in our hands before it reaches the root of such a power. The

SHELLEY

root, we take it, is this. He had an instinctive perception (immense in range and fertility, astonishing for its delicate intuition) of the underlying analogies, the secret subterranean passages, between matter and soul; the chromatic scales, whereat we dimly guess, by which the Almighty modulates through all the keys of creation. Because, the more we consider it, the more likely does it appear that Nature is but an imperfect actress, whose constant changes of dress never change her manner and method, who is the same in all her parts.

To Shelley's ethereal vision the most rarefied mental or spiritual music traced its beautiful corresponding forms on the sand of outward things. He stood thus at the very junction-lines of the visible and invisible, and could shift the points as he willed. His thoughts became a mounted infantry, passing with baffling swiftness from horse to foot or foot to horse. He could express as he listed the material and the immaterial in terms of each other. Never has a poet in the past rivalled him as regards this gift, and hardly will any poet rival him as regards it in the future: men are like first to see the promised doom lay its hand on the tree of heaven and shake down the golden leaves.*

The finest specimens of this faculty are probably to be sought in that Shelleian treasury,

* 'And the stars of heaven fell unto the earth, even as a fig-tree casteth her untimely figs, when she is shaken of a mighty wind.' (Rev. vi, 13.)

SHELLEY

Prometheus Unbound. It is unquestionably the greatest and most prodigal exhibition of Shelley's powers, this amazing lyric world, where immortal clarities sigh past in the perfumes of the blossoms, populate the breathings of the breeze, throng and twinkle in the leaves that twirl upon the bough; where the very grass is all a-rustle with lovely spirit-things, and a weeping mist of music fills the air. The final scenes especially are such a Bacchic reel and rout and revelry of beauty as leaves one staggered and giddy; poetry is spilt like wine, music runs to drunken waste. The choruses sweep down the wind, tirelessly, flight after flight, till the breathless soul almost cries for respite from the unrolling splendours. Yet these scenes, so wonderful from a purely poetical standpoint that no one could wish them away, are (to our humble thinking) nevertheless the artistic error of the poem. Abstractedly, the development of Shelley's idea required that he should show the earthly paradise which was to follow the fall of Zeus. But dramatically with that fall the action ceases, and the drama should have ceased with it. A final chorus, or choral series, of rejoicings (such as does ultimately end the drama where Prometheus appears on the scene) would have been legitimate enough. Instead, however, the bewildered reader finds the drama unfolding itself through scene after scene which leaves the action precisely where it found it, because there is no longer an action to advance. It is as if the

SHELLEY

choral *finale* of an opera were prolonged through two acts.

We have, nevertheless, called *Prometheus* Shelley's greatest poem, because it is the most comprehensive storehouse of his power. Were we asked to name the most *perfect* among his longer efforts, we should name the poem in which he lamented Keats; under the shed petals of his lovely fancy giving the slain bird a silken burial. Seldom is the death of a poet mourned in true poetry. Not often is the singer coffined in laurel-wood. Among the very few exceptions to such a rule, the greatest is *Adonais*. In the English language only *Lycidas* competes with it; and when we prefer *Adonais* to *Lycidas*, we are following the precedent set in the case of Cicero : *Adonais* is the longer. As regards command over abstraction, it is no less characteristically Shelleian than *Prometheus*. It is throughout a series of abstractions vitalized with daring exquisiteness, from Morning who sought

> Her eastern watch-tower, and her hair unbound,
> Wet with the tears which should adorn the ground,

and who

> Dimmed the aerial eyes that kindle day,

to the Dreams that were the flock of the dead shepherd, the Dreams

SHELLEY

> Whom near the living streams
> Of his young spirit he fed ; and whom he taught
> The love that was its music ;

of whom one sees, as she hangs mourning over him,

> Upon the silken fringe of his faint eyes,
> Like dew upon a sleeping flower, there lies
> A tear some Dream has loosened from his brain !
> Lost angel of a ruined Paradise !
> She knew not 'twas her own ; as with no stain
> She faded like a cloud which had outwept its rain.

In the solar spectrum, beyond the extreme red and extreme violet rays, are whole series of colours, demonstrable, but imperceptible to gross human vision. Such writing as this we have quoted renders visible the invisibilities of imaginative colour.

One thing prevents *Adonais* from being ideally perfect : its lack of Christian hope. Yet we remember well the writer of a popular memoir on Keats proposing as " the best consolation for the mind pained by this sad record " Shelley's inexpressibly sad exposition of Pantheistic immortality :

> He is a portion of the loveliness
> Which once he made more lovely, etc.

What utter desolation can it be that discerns comfort in this hope, whose wan countenance is as the countenance of a despair ? Nay, was not

SHELLEY

indeed *wanhope* the Saxon for despair ? What deepest depth of agony is it that finds consolation in this immortality : an immortality which thrusts you into death, the maw of Nature, that your dissolved elements may circulate through her veins ?

Yet such, the poet tells me, is my sole balm for the hurts of life. I am as the vocal breath floating from an organ. I too shall fade on the winds, a cadence soon forgotten. So I dissolve and die, and am lost in the ears of men : the particles of my being twine in newer melodies, and from my one death arise a hundred lives. Why, through the thin partition of this consolation Pantheism can hear the groans of its neighbour, Pessimism. Better almost the black resignation which the fatalist draws from his own hopelessness, from the fierce kisses of misery that hiss against his tears.

With some gleams, it is true, of more than mock solace, *Adonais* is lighted ; but they are obtained by implicitly assuming the personal immortality which the poem explicitly denies ; as when, for instance, to greet the dead youth,

> The inheritors of unfulfilled renown
> Rose from their thrones, built beyond mortal thought
> Far in the unapparent.

And again the final stanza of the poem :

> The breath whose might I have invoked in song
> Descends on me ; my spirit's bark is driven

SHELLEY

Far from the shore, far from the trembling throng
Whose sails were never to the tempest given :
The massy earth, the spherèd skies are riven ;
I am borne darkly, fearfully afar,
Whilst, burning through the inmost veil of heaven,
The soul of Adonais like a star
Beacons from the abode where the eternal are.

The soul of Adonais ?—Adonais, who is but

> A portion of that loveliness
> Which once he made more lovely.

After all, to finish where we began, perhaps the poems on which the lover of Shelley leans most lovingly, which he has oftenest in his mind, which best represent Shelley to him, and which he instinctively reverts to when Shelley's name is mentioned, are some of the shorter poems and detached lyrics. Here Shelley forgets for a while all that ever makes his verse turbid ; forgets that he is anything but a poet, forgets sometimes that he is anything but a child ; lies back in his skiff, and looks at the clouds. He plays truant from earth, slips through the wicket of fancy into heaven's meadow, and goes gathering stars. Here we have that absolute virgin-gold of song which is the scarcest among human products, and for which we can go to but three poets—Coleridge, Shelley, Chopin,*

* Such analogies between masters in sister-arts are often interesting. In some respects, is not Brahms the Browning of music ?

SHELLEY

and perhaps we should add Keats:—*Christabel* and *Kubla Khan*; *The Skylark*, *The Cloud*, and *The Sensitive Plant* (in its first two parts); *The Eve of Saint Agnes* and *The Nightingale*; certain of the Nocturnes; these things make very quintessentialized loveliness. It is attar of poetry.

Remark, as a thing worth remarking, that, although Shelley's diction is at other times singularly rich, it ceases in these poems to be rich, or to obtrude itself at all; it is imperceptible; his Muse has become a veritable Echo, whose body has dissolved from about her voice. Indeed, when his diction is richest, nevertheless the poetry so dominates the expression that we only feel the latter as an atmosphere until we are satiated with the former; then we discover with surprise to how imperial a vesture we had been blinded by gazing on the face of his song. A lesson, this, deserving to be conned by a generation so opposite in tendency as our own: a lesson that in poetry, as in the Kingdom of God, we should not take thought too greatly wherewith we shall be clothed, but seek first* the spirit, and all these things will be added unto us.

On the marvellous music of Shelley's verse we need not dwell, except to note that he avoids that metronomic beat of rhythm which Edgar Poe introduced into modern lyric measures, as Pope introduced it into the

* Seek *first*, not seek *only*.

SHELLEY

rhyming heroics of his day. Our varied metres are becoming as painfully over-polished as Pope's one metre. Shelley could at need sacrifice smoothness to fitness. He could write an anapæst that would send Mr Swinburne into strong shudders (e.g., 'stream did glide') when he instinctively felt that by so forgoing the more obvious music of melody he would better secure the higher music of harmony. If we have to add that in other ways he was far from escaping the defects of his merits, and would sometimes have to acknowledge that his Nilotic flood too often overflowed its banks, what is this but saying that he died young?

It may be thought that in our casual comments on Shelley's life we have been blind to its evil side. That, however, is not the case. We see clearly that he committed grave sins, and one cruel crime; but we remember also that he was an Atheist from his boyhood; we reflect how gross must have been the moral neglect in the training of a child who *could* be an Atheist from his boyhood: and we decline to judge so unhappy a being by the rules which we should apply to a Catholic. It seems to us that Shelley was struggling—blindly, weakly, stumblingly, but still struggling—towards higher things. His Pantheism is an indication of it. Pantheism is a half-way house and marks ascent or descent according to the direction from which it is approached. Now Shelley came to it from

SHELLEY

absolute Atheism; therefore in his case it meant rise. Again, his poetry alone would lead us to the same conclusion, for we do not believe that a truly corrupted spirit can write consistently ethereal poetry. We should believe in nothing if we believed that, for it would be the consecration of a lie. Poetry is a thermometer: by taking its average height you can estimate the normal temperature of its writer's mind. The devil can do many things. But the devil cannot write poetry. He may mar a poet, but he cannot make a poet. Among all the temptations wherewith he tempted St Anthony, though we have often seen it stated that he howled, we have never seen it stated that he sang.

Shelley's anarchic principles were as a rule held by him with some misdirected view to truth. He disbelieved in kings. And is it not a mere fact—regret it if you will—that in all European countries, except two, monarchs are a mere survival, the obsolete buttons on the coat-tails of rule, which serve no purpose but to be continually coming off? It is a miserable thing to note how every little Balkan State, having obtained liberty (save the mark!) by Act of Congress, straightway proceeds to secure the service of a professional king. These gentlemen are plentiful in Europe. They are the 'noble Chairmen' who lend their names for a consideration to any enterprising company which may be speculating in Liberty. When we see these things, we revert to the old lines in which

SHELLEY

Persius tells how you cannot turn Dama into a freeman by twirling him round your finger and calling him Marcus Dama.

Again, Shelley desired a religion of humanity, and that meant, to him, a religion for humanity, a religion which, unlike the spectral Christianity about him, should permeate and regulate the whole organization of men. And the feeling is one with which a Catholic must sympathize, in an age where—if we may say so without irreverence—the Almighty has been made a constitutional Deity, with certain state-grants of worship, but no influence over political affairs. In these matters Shelley's aims were generous, if his methods were perniciously mistaken. In his theory of Free Love alone, borrowed like the rest from the Revolution, his aim was as mischievous as his method. At the same time he was at least logical. His theory was repulsive, but comprehensible. Whereas from our present *via media*—facilitation of divorce—can only result the era when the young lady in reduced circumstances will no longer turn governess, but will be open to engagement as wife at a reasonable stipend.

We spoke of the purity of Shelley's poetry. We know of but three passages to which exception can be taken. One is happily hidden under a heap of Shelleian rubbish. Another is offensive because it presents his theory of Free Love in its most odious form. The third is very much a matter, we think, for the individual

SHELLEY

conscience. Compare with this the genuinely corrupt Byron, through the cracks and fissures of whose heaving versification steam up perpetually the sulphurous vapours from his central iniquity. We cannot credit that any Christian ever had his faith shaken through reading Shelley, unless his faith were shaken before he read Shelley. Is any safely-havened bark likely to slip its cable, and make for a flag planted on the very reef where the planter himself was wrecked?

Why indeed (one is tempted to ask in concluding) should it be that the poets who have written for us the poetry richest in skiey grain, most free from admixture with the duller things of earth—the Shelleys, the Coleridges, the Keats'—are the very poets whose lives are among the saddest records in literature? Is it that (by some subtle mystery of analogy) sorrow, passion, and fantasy are indissolubly connected, like water, fire, and cloud; that as from sun and dew are born the vapours, so from fire and tears ascend the 'visions of aërial joy'; that the harvest waves richest over the battlefields of the soul; that the heart, like the earth, smells sweetest after rain; that the spell on which depend such necromantic castles is some spirit of pain charm-prisoned at their base?*

* We hope that we need not refer the reader, for the methods of magic architecture, to Ariosto and that Atlas among enchanters, Beckford.

SHELLEY

Such a poet, it may be, mists with sighs the window of his life until the tears run down it; then some air of searching poetry, like an air of searching frost, turns it to a crystal wonder. The god of golden song is the god, too, of the golden sun; so peradventure songlight is like sunlight, and darkens the countenance of the soul. Perhaps the rays are to the stars what thorns are to the flowers; and so the poet, after wandering over heaven, returns with bleeding feet. Less tragic in its merely temporal aspect than the life of Keats or Coleridge, the life of Shelley in its moral aspect is, perhaps, more tragical than that of either; his dying seems a myth, a figure of his living; the material shipwreck a figure of the immaterial.

Enchanted child, born into a world unchildlike; spoiled darling of Nature, playmate of her elemental daughters; 'pard-like spirit, beautiful and swift,' laired amidst the burning fastnesses of his own fervid mind; bold foot along the verges of precipitous dream; light leaper from crag to crag of inaccessible fancies; towering Genius, whose soul rose like a ladder between heaven and earth with the angels of song ascending and descending it;—he is shrunken into the little vessel of death, and sealed with the unshatterable seal of doom, and cast down deep below the rolling tides of Time. Mighty meat for little guests, when the heart of Shelley was laid in the cemetery of Caius Cestius! Beauty, music, sweetness, tears—the

SHELLEY

mouth of the worm has fed of them all. Into that sacred bridal-gloom of death where he holds his nuptials with eternity let not our rash speculations follow him ; let us hope rather that as, amidst material nature, where our dull eyes see only ruin, the finer eye of science has discovered life in putridity and vigour in decay, seeing dissolution even and disintegration, which in the mouth of man symbolize disorder, to be in the works of God undeviating order, and the manner of our corruption to be no less wonderful than the manner of our health,—so, amidst the supernatural universe, some tender undreamed surprise of life in doom awaited that wild nature, which, worn by warfare with itself, its Maker, and all the world, now

> Sleeps, and never palates more the dug,
> The beggar's nurse, and Cæsar's.

PAGANISM OLD AND NEW

PAGANISM, a natural religion obviously capable of accommodating itself to widely different natures by reason of its flexibility, can also surround itself with the prestige of a great past—though a dead past; of a poetry—though a dead poetry; of a sculpture—though a dead sculpture; of an idealizing retrospection which is *not* dead. And it can proclaim that, with the revival of dead Paganism, these other dead things too shall live. The old gods, say its advocates, were warm with human life, and akin to human sympathy: beautiful gods whose names were poetry. Then the daily gracefulness of Pagan life and religion! The ceremonial pageants, with the fluent grace of their processional maidens, as they

—— shook a most divine dance from their feet;

or the solemn chastity of their vestal virgins; the symmetry of their temples with their effigies of benignant powers; the street, adorned with noble statuary, invested with a crystal air, and bright with its moving throng in garments of unlaboured elegance; and the theatre unroofed to the smokeless sky, where an audience, in which the merest cobbler had some vision beyond his last, heard in the language of Æschylus or Sophocles the ancestral legends of its native land.

PAGANISM OLD AND NEW

With all this, these advocates contrast the condition of to-day : the cold formalities of an outworn worship; our *ne plus ultra* of pageantry, a Lord Mayor's Show ; the dryadless woods regarded chiefly as potential timber ; the grimy street, the grimy air, the disfiguring statues, the Stygian crowd ; the temple to the reigning goddess Gelasma, which mocks the name of theatre ; last and worst, the fatal degradation of popular perception, which has gazed so long on ugliness that it takes her to its bosom. In our capitals the very heavens have lost their innocence. Aurora may rise over our cities, but she has forgotten how to blush.

And those who, like the present writer, tread as on thorns amidst the sordidness and ugliness, the ugly sordidness and the sordid ugliness, the dull materiality and weariness of this unhonoured old age of the world,—cannot but sympathize with these feelings ; nay, even look back with a certain passionate regret to the beauty which invested at least the outward life of those days. But, in truth, with this outward life the vesture of beauty ceases : the rest is a day-dream, lovely it is true, but none the less a dream. Heathenism is lovely *because* it is dead. To read Keats is to grow in love with Paganism ; but it is the Paganism of Keats. Pagan Paganism was not poetical.

Literally, this assertion is untenable. Almost every religion becomes a centre of poetry. But, if not absolutely true, it is at least true with

PAGANISM OLD AND NEW

relation to Christianity. The poetry of Paganism is chiefly a modern creation; in the hands of the Pagans themselves it was not even developed to its full capabilities. The gods of Homer are braggarts and gluttons; and the gods of Virgil are cold and unreal. The kiss of Dian was a frigid kiss till it glowed in the fancy of the barbarian Fletcher: there was little halo around Latmos' top, till it was thrown around it by the modern Keats. No pagan eye ever visioned the nymphs of Shelley. In truth there was around the Olympian heaven no such halo and native air of poetry as, for Christian singers, clothed the Christian heaven. To the heathen mind its divinities were graceful, handsome, noble gods; powerful, and therefore to be propitiated with worship; cold in their sublime selfishness, and therefore unlovable. No Pagan ever loved his god. Love he might, perhaps, some humble rustic or domestic deity,—but no Olympian. Whereas, in the Christian religion, the Madonna, and a greater than the Madonna, were at once high enough for worship and low enough for love. Now, without love no poetry can be beautiful; for all beautiful poetry comes from the heart. With love it was that Wordsworth and Shelley purchased the right to sing sweetly of Nature. Keats wrote lovingly of his Pagan hierarchy, because what he wrote about he loved. Hence for no antique poet was it possible to make, or even conceive, a Pagan Paradise. We, who love the gods, do not worship them.

PAGANISM OLD AND NEW

The ancients, who worshipped the gods, did not love them. Whence is this?

Coleridge, in those beautiful lines from *Wallenstein*, has given us his explanation. It is true, yet only half the truth. For in very deed that beautiful mythology has a beauty beyond anything it ever possessed in its worshipped days; and that beauty came to it in dower when it gave its hand to Christianity. Christianity it was that stripped the weeds from that garden of Paganism, broke its statue of Priapus, and delivered it smiling and fair to the nations for their pleasure-ground. She found Mars the type of brute violence, and made of him the god of valour. She took Venus, and made of her the type of Beauty,—Beauty, which the average heathen hardly knew. There is no more striking instance of the poetizing influence exerted on the ancient mythology by Christianity than the contrast between the ancient and modern views of this goddess. Any school-boy will tell you that she was the Goddess of Love and Beauty. 'Goddess of Love,' is true only in the lowest sense—but 'Goddess of Beauty'? It exhibits an essentially modern attitude towards Venus, and would be hard to support from the ancient poets. No doubt there are passages in which she is styled the beautiful goddess; but the phrases are scarcely to my point. If, in the early days of the Second Empire, you came across a writer who described the Empress Eugénie as 'the beautiful Empress,'

PAGANISM OLD AND NEW

you would hardly be fair in deducing from *that* his devotion to her as the Empress of Beauty. No; when Heine, addressing the Venus of Melos, called her 'Our Lady of Beauty,' the idea, no less than the expression, was centrally modern. I will go further. It was centrally Christian.

To the average Pagan, Venus was simply the personification of the generative principle in nature; and her offspring was Cupid,—Desire, Eros—sexual passion. Far other is she to the modern. To him she is the Principle of Earthly Beauty, who, being of necessity entirely pure, walks naked and is not ashamed, garmented in the light of her unchanging whiteness. This worship of Beauty in the abstract, this conception of the Lady Beauty as an all-amiable power, to register the least glance of whose eye, to catch the least trail of whose locks, were worth the devotion of a life,—all this is characteristic of the Christian and Gothic poet, unknown to the Pagan poet. No antique singer ever saw Sibylla Palmifera; no antique artist's hand ever shook in her pursuit.* The sculptors, I suspect, had known something of Sibylla, in the elder days, before Praxiteles made of the Queen of Beauty merely the Queen of Fair Women. The

---

* Philosophers and 'dreaming Platonists,' perhaps, had scaled her craggy heights after their own manner, but none will pretend that Platonic dreams of the 'First and Only Fair' were the offspring of Paganism. Rather were they a contravention of it.

42

PAGANISM OLD AND NEW

Venus of Melos remains to hint so much. But, besides that Greek sculpture is virtually dead and unrevivable in civilized lands, I do not purpose in this narrow space to deal with subjects so wide as Sculpture or Art. Suffice it if I can suggest a few of the irreparable losses to Poetry which would result from the supersession of the Christian by the Pagan spirit.

If there are two things on which the larger portion of our finest modern verse may be said to hinge, they are surely Nature and Love. Yet it would be the merest platitude to say that neither the one nor the other, as glorified by our great modern poets, was known to the singers of old. Their insensibility to landscape was accompanied and perhaps conditioned by an insensibility to all the subtler and more spiritual qualities of beauty; so that it would hardly be more than a pardonable exaggeration to call Christianity (in so far as it has influenced the arts) the religion of beauty, and Paganism the religion of form and sense. Perhaps it is incorrect to say that the ancients were indifferent to landscape: rather they were indifferent to Nature. Cicero luxuriates in his 'country,' Horace in his Socrate and fitful glimpses of scenery; but both merely as factors in the composition of enjoyment: the bees, the doves, of Virgil are mere ministers to luxury and sleep. 'The fool,' says Blake in a most pregnant aphorism, 'The fool sees not the same tree as a wise man sees.' And assuredly no heathen

PAGANISM OLD AND NEW

ever saw the same tree as Wordsworth. For it is a noteworthy fact that the intellect of man seems unable to seize the divine beauty of Nature, until moving beyond that outward beauty it gazes on the spirit of Nature : even as the mind seems unable to appreciate the beautiful face of woman until it has learned to appreciate the more beautiful beauty of her soul.

That Paganism had no real sense of the exquisite in female features is evident from its statues and few extant paintings : mere regularity of form is all it sees. Or again, compare the ancient erotic poets, delighting in the figure and bodily charms of their mistresses, with the modern love-poets, whose first care is to dwell on the heavenly breathings of their ladies' faces. Significant is it, from this point of view, that the very word in favourite use among the Latin poets to express beauty should be *forma*, form, grace of body and line. When Catullus pronounces on the charms of a rival to his mistress, he never even mentions her face. ' Candida, longa, recta ; ' that is all : ' She is fair, tall, straight.'

But the most surprising indication of this blindness to the subtler qualities of beauty is the indifference of the ancient singers to what in our estimation is the most lovely and important feature in woman—the eye. This may have some connexion with their apparent deadness to colour. But so it is. In all Catullus there is only a single *indirect* allusion to the

PAGANISM OLD AND NEW

colour of Lesbia's eyes. There is, to the best of my recollection, no such allusion at all throughout Tibullus, Propertius, or Ovid. This one fact reveals a desert of arid feeling in the old erotic poets which a modern imagination refuses to traverse. In the name of all the Muses, what treason against Love and Beauty! Why, from the poetical Spring of Chaucer to the Indian-Summer of William Morris, their ladies' eyes have been the cynosure of modern love-poets!

> Debonair, good, glad, and sad,

are the admirably chosen words in which Chaucer describes his Duchess' eyes; and this is the beautiful passage in which Morris sets *his* lady's eyes before us:

> Her great eyes, standing far apart,
> *Draw up some memory from her heart,*
> And gaze out very mournfully;
>   Beata mea Domina!—
> So beautiful and kind they are,
> But most times looking out afar,
> Waiting for something, not for me.
>   Beata mea Domina!

The value which Morris' master, Rossetti, had for this feature in feminine attraction is conspicuous. Witness his Blessed Damozel, whose

> — Eyes were deeper than the depth
> Of waters stilled at even.

In his mistress' portrait he notes that

> The shadowed eyes remember and forget.

PAGANISM OLD AND NEW

Tennyson's Isabel has

> Eyes not down-dropt nor over-bright, but fed
> With the clear-pointed flame of chastity.

And almost all his heroines have their characteristic eyes : the Gardener's Daughter, violet, Amy of Locksley Hall, hazel,

> All the spirit deeply dawning in the dark of hazel eyes;

Enid, meek blue eyes; and so on. Wordsworth, again, notes his wife's

> Eyes like stars of twilight fair;

and has many a beautiful passage on female eyes. Shelley overflows with such passages, showing splendid power in conveying the idea of *depth :* the following is a random example :

> —— deep her eyes as are
> Two openings of unfathomable night
> Seen through a tempest's cloven roof.

Will any one forget the eyes of the dreaming Christabel ?

> Both blue eyes, more bright than clear,
> Each about to have a tear.

One could multiply instances; but take as a last one those magnificent eyes of De Quincey's *Mater Suspiriarum :* ' Her eyes were filled with perishing dreams, and wrecks of forgotten delirium.'

Again, what a magnificent means of characterization—especially in personification—do

PAGANISM OLD AND NEW

our poets make of the eye. Could anything be more felicitous than Collins' Pity

> With eyes of dewy light ?

And equally marvellous is Shelley's epithet for sleep :

> Thy sweet child Sleep, the *filmy-eyed*.

Yet all this superfluity of poetic beauty remained a sealed fountain for the Pagan poets ! After such a revelation it can excite little surprise that, compared with Christian writers, they lay little stress on the grace of female hair.

But, after all, the most beautiful thing in love-poetry is Love. Now Love is the last thing any scholar will look for in ancient erotic poetry.* Body differs not more from soul than the Amor of Catullus or Ovid differs from the Love of Dante or Shelley ;† and the root of this difference is the root of the whole difference between this class of poetry in antique and contemporary periods. The rite of marriage was to the Pagan the goal and attainment of Love—Love, which he regarded as a transitory and

* It will not do to say that this was solely owing to the impossibility of what we call courtship in heathen society ; and that heathen love was postnuptial. It is sufficiently apparent from Martial's allusions that the married poems of Sulpicia, styled and considered ' chaste ' because addressed to her husband, would have justly incurred among us the reproach of licentiousness in treatment.

† An Anti-Christian in ethics. But the blood in the veins of his Muse was Christian. The spirit of his treatment of Love is—with few, if any, exceptions—entirely Christian.

PAGANISM OLD AND NEW

perishable passion, born of the body and decaying with the body. On the wings of Christianity came the great truth that Love is of the soul, and with the soul coeval.

It was most just and natural, therefore, that from the Christian poets should come the full development of this truth. To Dante and the followers of Dante we must go for its ripe announcement. Not in marriage, they proclaim, is the fulfilment of Love, though its earthly and temporal fulfilment may be therein ; for how can Love, which is the desire of soul for soul, attain satisfaction in the conjunction of body with body ? Poor, indeed, if this were all the promise which Love unfolded to us—the encountering light of two flames from within their close-shut lanterns. Therefore sings Dante, and sing all noble poets after him, that Love in this world is a pilgrim and a wanderer, journeying to the New Jerusalem : not here is the consummation of his yearnings, in that mere knocking at the gates of union which we christen marriage, but beyond the pillars of death and the corridors of the grave, in the union of spirit to spirit within the containing Spirit of God.

The distance between Catullus and the *Vita Nuova*, between Ovid and the *House of Life*, can be measured only by Christianity. And the lover of poetry owes a double gratitude to his Creator, Who, not content with giving us salvation on the cross, gave us also, at the marriage in Cana of Galilee, Love. For there

PAGANISM OLD AND NEW

Love was consecrated, and declared the child of Jehovah, not of Jove; there virtually was inaugurated the whole successive order of those love-poets who have shown the world that passion, in putting on chastity, put on also tenfold beauty. For purity is the sum of all loveliness, as whiteness is the sum of all colours.

A detailed comparison would be possible between the treatment of the Pagan Olympus by the ancients and by the moderns, with Keats at their head, in order to demonstrate what I have in these pages merely advanced. One point, however, I must briefly notice. This is the false idea that a modern Paganism could perpetuate, from a purely artistic sense, the beauty proper to Christian literature: that it is possible for the imaginative worker, like the conspirator in Massinger, to paint and perfume with the illusion of life a corpse. For refutation, witness the failure of our English painters, with all their art, to paint a Madonna which can hang beside the simplest old Florentine Virgin without exhibiting the absence of the ancient religious feeling.* And what has befallen the loveliness of Catholicity would—in a few generations, when Christianity had faded out of the blood of men —befall the loveliness of Christianity.

Bring back, then, even the best age of Paganism, and you smite beauty on the cheek.

*Rossetti is perhaps an exception. But he had Catholic blood in his veins, and could not escape from it. His heart worshipped.

PAGANISM OLD AND NEW

But you *cannot* bring back the best age of Paganism, the age when Paganism was a faith. None will again behold Apollo in the forefront of the morning, or see Aphrodite in the upper air loose the long lustre of her golden locks. But you *may* bring back—*dii avertant omen*—the Paganism of the days of Pliny, and Statius, and Juvenal; of much philosophy and little belief; of superb villas and superb taste; of banquets for the palate in the shape of cookery, and banquets for the eye in the shape of art; of poetry singing dead songs on dead themes with the most polished and artistic vocalization; of everything most polished, from the manners to the marble floors; of Vice carefully drained out of sight, and large fountains of Virtue springing in the open air;—in one word, a most shining Paganism indeed—as putrescence also shines.

This Paganism it is which already stoops on Paris,* and wheels in shadowy menace over England. Bring back *this*—and make of poetry a dancing-girl, and of art a pandar. This is the Paganism which is formidable, and not the

---

* Paris, it may be said, is not scrupulous as to draining her vice underground. But it is kept underground exactly to the same extent as vice was in the Plinian days. Private vice is winked at with a decorous platitude about ' the sanctity of private life.' If evil literature is openly written, what Roman or Italian of the younger Pliny's day thought anything of writing '*facetiae*'? If indecent pictures are displayed in the windows, what, I should like to know, if photography had flourished under Rome, would have been the state of the shop-windows of Pompeii?

PAGANISM OLD AND NEW

antique lamp whose feeding oil is spent, whose light has not outlasted the damps of its long sepulture. She who created Zeus and Here, Phœbus and Artemis, Pallas Athene and the fair-haired Aphrodite, is dead, and lives only in her corruption ; nor have we lost by her death one scintillation of beauty. For the poetry of Paganism (with reference to England) was born in the days of Elizabeth, and entered on its inheritance in the days of Keats. But could Paganism indeed grow supple in her cere-cloths, and open her tarnished eyes to the light of our modern sun— in that same hour the poetry of Paganism would sicken and fall to decay. For Pagan Paganism was not poetical.

IN DARKEST ENGLAND

I

IN certain all too frequent moods, when I behold in the sphinx Life not so much that inscrutable face of hers, nor yet her nurturing breasts, but rather her lion's claws; in such moods, a contrast rises before me. I see, as it were, upon my right hand and upon my left, two regions; separated only by a few hours' journey along our iron roads. I see upon my right hand a land of lanes, and hedgerows, and meadowed green; whose people's casual tread is over blossoming yellow, white, and purple, far-shining as the constellations that sand their nightly heaven; where the very winter rains, into which the deciduous foliage rots, cover the naked boughs with a vividness of dusted emerald.

I look upon my left hand, and I see another region—is it not rather another universe ? A region whose hedgerows have set to brick, whose soil is chilled to stone; where flowers are sold and women, where the men wither and the stars; whose streets to me on the most glittering day are black. For I unveil their secret meanings. I read their human hieroglyphs. I diagnose from a hundred occult signs the disease which perturbs their populous pulses. Misery cries out to me from the kerb-stone, despair passes me by in the ways; I discern limbs laden with fetters impalpable, but not imponderable;

IN DARKEST ENGLAND

I hear the shaking of invisible lashes, I see men dabbled with their own oozing life. This contrast rises before me ; and I ask myself whether there be indeed an Ormuzd and an Ahriman, and whether Ahriman be the stronger of the twain. From the claws of the sphinx my eyes have risen to her countenance which no eyes read.

Because, therefore, I have these thoughts ; and because also I have knowledge, not indeed great or wide, but within certain narrow limits more intimate than most men's, of this life which is not a life ; to which food is as the fuel of hunger ; sleep, our common sleep, precious, costly, and fallible, as water in a wilderness ; in which men rob and women vend themselves— for fourpence ; because I have such thoughts and such knowledge, I read with painful sympathy the book just put forward by a singular personality.* I rise from the reading of it with a strong impression that here is a proposal which they who will not bless would do well to abstain from banning. Here is at last a man who has formulated a comprehensive scheme, and has dared to take upon himself its execution. That the terrible welter of London misery has not been left undealt with during recent years, that a multitude of agencies have long been making on it a scattered guerilla warfare, I know. But from their efforts I derived not hope, but despair ; they served only to render darkness

* *In Darkest England*, by General Booth.

IN DARKEST ENGLAND

visible. Before me stretched an immense, soundless, bitter ocean. On its shore stood a string of benevolent children, equipped with sugar-basins. What were they doing? They were throwing lumps of sugar into the waves, to sweeten the sea. Here was this vast putrescence strangling the air at our very doors, and what scavengers of charity might endeavour its removal? Now comes by a man, and offers to take on himself the responsibility of that removal; in God's name, give him the contract! one inclines to exclaim.

What, then, is his book? The first part is an unexaggerated statement of the facts—too surely facts—regarding the existence of our London outcasts. It is the kind of thing which the public has had so often lately, under one form or another, that I suppose it has ceased to be roused by it. I will therefore only note in it a single point, which for more than one reason I cannot here dwell upon. Let those who are robust enough not to take injury from the terrible directness with which things are stated read the chapter entitled *The Children of the Lost*. For it drives home a truth which I fear the English public, with all its compassion for our destitute children, scarcely realizes, knows but in a vague, general way; namely, that they are brought up in sin from their cradles, that they know evil before they know good, that the boys are ruffians and profligates, the girls harlots in the mother's womb. This, to me the

IN DARKEST ENGLAND

most nightmarish idea in all the nightmare of those poor little lives, I have never been able to perceive that people had any true grasp on. And having mentioned it, though it is a subject very near my heart, I will say no more; nor enforce it, as I might well do, from my own sad knowledge.

In the name of the Mother of Sorrows, our derelict Catholic men and women shall not have to wait till the Salvation Army has bruised our heel. We have done much already, considering our means; therefore it is that we shall do more. Take, for instance, General Booth's Slum Sisters, themselves living in a house like the tenements around them, cleaning in the dwellings of the poor, and nursing their sick. Then read the constitution given by St Vincent de Paul to his Sisters of Charity. They were ' to consist of girls, and widows unencumbered with children, destined to seek out the poor in the alleys and streets of cities. They were to have for monastery the houses of the sick; for cell, a hired room; for their chapel, the parish church; for their cloister, the streets of the town or the wards of the hospital; for enclosure, obedience; for grating, the fear of God; for veil, holy modesty.'* The genesis of the Slum Sisters is

---

* The Little Sisters of the Assumption, who have houses in London, as a matter of fact were founded within late years exclusively to nurse and work for the poor in their own homes. They are debarred from going to any but the entirely destitute who can procure no other help.

IN DARKEST ENGLAND

evident. It would appear that we have forgotten what manner of men we are; let us look, then, into this Salvation glass and see. When Professor Huxley incidentally compared the Salvation Army to the Franciscans, in an article in the *Pall Mall*, I took up the comparison with alacrity, and extended it.

The very chivalrous militarism of St Francis has been caught and vulgarized in the outward military symbolism of the Salvation Army. That joyous spirit which St Francis so peculiarly fostered is claimed by General Booth as an integral and essential feature in his own followers. The street-preaching, in which the Salvationists are so energetic, received its first special extension from the Franciscans. Mother of street-preaching, where are your street-preachers? To gather the multitude into our churches something more than the sound of a bell has become necessary; let us go forth into the highways and byways like the Franciscan Friars of old. And it is for the Friars to do it. The priest, worn almost to breaking by the cares of his own poor parish, has no strength or time to go forth among that nomad population which is of no parish and of all parishes. Why should the Franciscans hide behind their caricatures? The scarf and scarlet jersey is crying in street, in slum-dwelling, in common lodging-house, such God's truth as is in it to cry; where is the brown frock and the cord?

But the preaching Friar can only subserve a

IN DARKEST ENGLAND

portion of the uses subserved by the Salvation Army. Consider what the Salvation Army is. It is not merely a sect, it is virtually a Religious Order, but a Religious Order of a peculiar kind. It consists of men and women living in the world the life of the world, pursuing their businesses, marrying, bringing up families; yet united by rule and discipline, and pushing forward active work of charity and religious influence among the forsaken poor. It possesses, moreover, the advantage of numerous recruits from the ranks of the poor, through whom it can obtain intimate knowledge of the condition and requirements of their class.

May it be that here, too, the Salvation Army has but studied St Francis? Here, too, has the Assisian left us a weapon which but needs a little practice to adapt it to the necessity of the day? Even so. Our army is in the midst of us, enrolled under the banner of the Stigmata, quartered throughout the kingdom; an army over 13,000 strong, following the barrack routine of religious peace, diligently pipe-claying its spiritual accoutrements, practising what that other Army calls 'knee-drill,' turning out for periodical inspection, and dreaming of no conflict at hand. Sound to it the trumpet. Sound to the militia of Assisi that the enemy is about them, that they must take the field; sound to the Tertiaries of St Francis. Yes, the Franciscan Tertiaries are this army. They are men and women who live in the world the life of the world—though not

IN DARKEST ENGLAND

a worldly life; who marry, rear their families, attend to their worldly vocations; yet they are a Religious Order, with rule and observance. They include numbers of men and women among the poor. Nay, the resemblance extends to minor matters. Like the Salvationists, they exact from their women plainness of dress; though unlike the Salvationists, and most like their Poet-founder, they do not exact ugliness of dress. Like the Salvationists, again, they are an essentially democratic body: a Tertiary peeress, writing to a Tertiary factory girl, addresses her as 'sister.'

It rests with themselves to complete the resemblance in the one point now lacking. They are saying their Office, holding their monthly meetings, sanctifying themselves; it is excellent, but only half that for which their Founder destined them. He intended them likewise for active works of charity. They are the Third Order of St Francis; their founder's spirit should be theirs; and with the ecstatic of Alverno, contemplation was never allowed to divert him from activity. He who penanced Brother Ruffino because the visionary was overpowering in him the worker, with what alacrity would he have thrown his Tertiaries on the battle-field where reserves are so needed; with what alacrity would he have bidden them come down from Alverno, and descend into the streets! Nay, Pope Leo XIII, as if he had foreseen the task which might call upon them, has released them from the weight of fasts and prayers which burdened them, reducing their fasts to two in the year, their prayers to twelve daily *Paters* and *Aves*. They are freed from their spiritual austerities, and at liberty for external labours. They, therefore, if their founder live at all in them, seem the organization ready constituted for this work. In whatever town there was a Congregation of Tertiaries, they would endeavour to combine for the establishment of Shelters, and whatever, in the process of development, might ultimately grow out of them.

Let us, then, put this thing to the test, in God's name! And, except in God's name, it were indeed wanton to try it. It may fail, true; it may be much of a leap in the dark, true; but every community must make its leaps in the dark, and make them often for far less clamorous cause. We English at large were nigh on bringing our Home Rule prodigy to birth; though astrologers hardly cast its horoscope alike, though there were not wanting prophets who boded the apparition of an armed head from our seething Irish cauldron. But long and crying suffering waited redress, we had tried palliatives which fell short, and we had all but determined (wisely, I think, determined) to test a heroic remedy. Here, at your own lintel, is long and crying suffering, worse than that of the Irish peasant, who has at least the consolation of his God, his priest, his neighbour, and his conscience; here, too, you have tried palliatives

IN DARKEST ENGLAND

which have fallen short ; here, too, then, venture a heroic remedy. The most disastrous daring is better in such a matter than but-too-certainly-disastrous quiescence. I do not like Mohammed, but I like less Moloch : the code of the Koran is ill ; is the code of Cotytto better ? But to this it shall not come.

Things hard, not unachievable, I have set before you, children of Assisi ; not unachievable, much less unattemptable. Scorn you may have, contumely you may have : but witness that these Salvationists, being of a verity blind prophets, yet endured all this; and you, who know whereof you prophesy, shall you not endure it ? Can men conjure in the ways with the name of Booth, and not with the name of Manning ? If they are shielded by the red jersey, you shall be shielded by the reflex of that princely red at Westminster. But rather will I cry to you, lineage of Alverno : Gird on your weakness as a hauberk of proof ! *They* have grown strong because they were weak, and esteemed because they were despised ; you shall grow stronger because weaker, and more esteemed because more despised. What sword have they, but you have a keener ? For blood and fire, gentle humility ; for the joy of a religious alcoholism, the joy of that peace which passeth understanding ; for the tumults, the depths of the spirit ; for the discipline of trumpets, the discipline of the Sacraments ; for the chiming of tambourines, Mary's name pensile like a bell-tongue in men's

IN DARKEST ENGLAND

resonant souls ; for hearts clashed open by a whirlwind, the soft summons of Him Who stands at the door and knocks. If with these you cannot conquer, then you could not with chariots and horsemen.

II

THIS is a day which, with all its admitted and most lamentable evils, many of us are most glad that we have lived to see: for it is a day wherein a bad old order is fast giving place to a new ; and the new, we trust, through whatever struggle and gradual transformation, will finally prove a higher order than the old. Free education is in the air. It is one among many signs of the common tendency. It involves the negation of individualism. The hearts of men are softening to each other : we will no longer suffer unchecked the rehatched 'dragons of the prime' : many minds, with many thoughts, many aims, are uniting with a common watchword against a common foe.

> We, are we not formed as notes of music are
> For one another, though dissimilar ?

We are raising from the dust a fallen standard of Christianity : not in phrase merely, but in practice, not by lips only, but by lives also, we are re-affirming the Brotherhood of Man.

IN DARKEST ENGLAND

Rousseau said it. But so did Jesus Christ. It is the doctrine of the red cap. But it is likewise the doctrine of the red cassock. While on the antagonistic side is the conspicuous and significant figure of Professor Huxley, the map of life is crumpled between the convolutions of Darwin's brain : he cannot so much as attack Rousseau-ism, without unconsciously postulating as his argumentative basis the omnigenous truth of Darwinism. Now, Individualism was simply Natural Selection applied to the social order.

The Individualist theory had its scaffolding of excellence ; O let us confess it ! The walls of no theory can rise far from the ground without that. Our neighbours have this in common with heaven—they only help those who are perfectly able to help themselves. In the days when the blatant beast of Individualism held the field, that was a truth. It is now almost a cynicism—a cynicism with the whiff of truth which makes most cynicisms piquant; but, thank God, fast becoming cynicism. This was the scaffolding whereby the Individualist edifice arose ; the precept, always true within rigid limitations and safeguards, of self-help. But, in practice, the script of self-help has been the script of selfishness, has been the maxim of Cain ; in practice, self-help has meant ' devil take the hindmost.' By its fruits you shall know it. Look at your darkest England ; look at your darkest London. Zohar-snakes which guard

IN DARKEST ENGLAND

the flesh they grow from ; your Goths, O Rome of the sea-ways, your Goths within your own gates. You have sown your dragon's teeth, and you shall reap—armed men ? Nay, I tell you, but dragons. From dragon's teeth, dragons; and from devil's teaching, devils. His evangel you have preached, by word and deed, throughout this century ; do you fear his kingdom at hand ? You have prepared the way of your lord, you have made straight his paths ; and now you tremble at his coming. For diabolical this doctrine of Individualism is ; it is the outcome of the proud teaching which declares it despicable for men to bow before their fellow-men. It has meant, not that a man should be individual, but that he should be independent. Now this I take to be an altogether deadly lie. A man *should* be individual, but not independent. The very laws of Nature forbid independence, which have made man in a thousand ways inevitably dependent on his fellows.

Vain is the belief that man can convert to permanent evil that which is in itself good. It has been sought to do so with science ; and some of us have been seriously frightened at science. Folly. Certain temporary evil has been wrought through it in the present, which seems very great because it *is* present. That will pass, the good will remain ; and men will wonder how they with whom was truth could ever have feared research. Scientists, those eyeless worms who loosen the soil for the crops of God, have declared that they are proving miracles false, because they are contrary to the laws of Nature. I can see that in fifty years' time they will have proved miracles true, because they are based on the laws of Nature. So much good, at least, will come from the researches of Nancy and the Charité, of the followers of Bernheim and the followers of Charcot. If any, being evil, offer to us good things, I say: Take; for ours must be the ultimate harvest from them. Good steel wins in the hands that can wield it longest; and those hands are ours.

No scheme, be it General Booth's or another's, will avail to save more than a fraction—may it be a large fraction—out of that drift of adult misery wherewith the iniquitous neglect of our forefathers has encumbered the streets. But the children! There is the chance; there, alas, also is the fear. Think of it! If Christ stood amidst your London slums, He could not say: 'Except ye become as one of *these* little children.' For better your children were cast from the bridges of London than they should become as one of those little ones. Could they be gathered together and educated in the truest sense of the word; could the children of the nation at large be so educated as to cut off future recruits to the ranks of Darkest England; then it would need no astrology to cast the horoscope of to-morrow. *La tête de l'homme du peuple,* or rather, *de l'enfant du peuple*—around

IN DARKEST ENGLAND

that sways the conflict. Who grasps the child grasps the future.

The grim old superstition was right. When man would build to a lasting finish, he must found his building over a child. There is not a secret society in Europe, there is not a Secularist in France, in Germany, in Italy, in England, but knows it; everywhere these gangs of coiners are at their work of stamping and uttering base humanity. We, too, have recognized it; we on our part have not been idle, we least of all; but we are hard put to it for labourers in the task. In the school-satchel lie the keys of to-morrow. What gate shall be opened into that morrow, whether a gate of horn, or the gate of ivory wherethrough the inheritors of our own poor day passed surrounded by so many vain dreams into their inheritance, must rest with them who are still

> In that sweet age
> When Heaven's our side the lark.

THE FOURTH ORDER OF HUMANITY

IN the beginning of things came man, sequent to him woman; on woman followed the child, and on the child the doll. It is a climax of development; and the crown of these is the doll.

To the doll's supremacy in beauty woman's self bears testimony, implicit, if unconscious. For ages has she tricked her face in pigment, and her brows in alien hair; her *contours* she has filled to counterfeit roundness, her eyes and lashes tinged: and all in a frustrate essay to compass by Art what in the doll is right of Nature. Even the child exhibits distinct inferiorities. It is full of thwartness and eating and drinking, and selffulness (selfishness were a term too dully immitigate), and a plentiful lack of that repose wherein the doll is nearest to the quiet gods. For my own part, I profess that much acquaintance only increases my consideration for this fourth order of humanity: always excepting the very light-blue-eyed doll, in whose regard there is a certain chill *hauteur* against which my diffidence is not proof.

Consider the life of dolls. At the whim of some *debonair* maternal tyranness, they veer on every wind of mutability; are the sport of imputed moods, suffer qualities over which they have no election,—are sorry or glad, indocile

THE FOURTH ORDER OF HUMANITY

or amiable, at their mistress' whim and mandate; they are visited with stripes, or the soft aspersion of kisses; with love delectably persecuted, or consigned to the clement quiet of neglect; exalted to the dimple of their mistress' cheek, or dejected to the servile floor; rent and mutilated, or rocked and murmured over; blamed or petted, be-rated or loved. Nor why it is thus or thus with them, are they any wise witting; wherefore these things should be, they know not at all.

> Consider the life of us—
> Oh, my cousins the dolls!

Some consciousness, I take it, there was; some secret sense of this occult co-rivalry in fate, which withheld me even in childhood from the youthful male's contempt for these short-lived parasites of the nursery. I questioned, with wounded feelings, the straitened feminine intolerance which said to the boy : ' Thou shalt not hold a baby; thou shalt not possess a doll.' In the matter of babies, I was hopeless to shake the illiberal prejudice; in the matter of dolls, I essayed to confound it. By eloquence and fine diplomacy I wrung from my sisters a concession of dolls; whence I date my knowledge of the kind.

But ineluctible sex declared itself. I dramatized them, I fell in love with them; I did not father them; intolerance was justified of its children. One in particular I selected, one with

THE FOURTH ORDER OF HUMANITY

surpassing fairness crowned, and bowed before the fourteen inches of her skirt. She was beautiful. She was one of Shakespeare's heroines. She was an amity of inter-removed miracles; all wrangling excellencies at paƈt in one sole doll; the frontiers of jealous virtues marched in her, yet trespassed not against her peace. I desired for her some worthy name; and asked of my mother: Who was the fairest among living women? Laughingly was I answered that I was a hard questioner, but that perhaps the Empress of the French bore the bell for beauty. Hence, accordingly, my Princess of puppetdom received her style; and at this hour, though she has long since vanished to some realm where all sawdust is wiped for ever from dolls' wounds, I cannot hear that name but the Past touches me with a rigid agglomeration of small china fingers.

But why with childhood and with her should I close the blushing recital of my puppet-loves? Men are but children of a larger growth; and your statue, I warrant me, is but your crescent doll. Wherefore, then, should I leave unmemorized the statue which thralled my youth in a passion such as feminine mortality was skill-less to instigate? Nor at this let any boggle; for *she* was a goddess. Statue I have called her; but indeed she was a bust, a head, a face—and who that saw that face could have thought to regard further? She stood nameless in the gallery of sculptural casts which she

THE FOURTH ORDER OF HUMANITY

strangely deigned to inhabit; but I have since learned that men called her the Vatican Melpomene. Rightly stood she nameless, for Melpomene she never was: never went words of hers from bronzèd lyre in tragic order; never through *her* enspelled lips moaned any syllables of woe. Rather, with her leaf-twined locks, she seemed some strayed Bacchante, indissolubly filmed in secular reverie. The expression which gave her divinity resistless I have always suspected for an accident of the cast; since in frequent engravings of her prototype I never met any such aspect. The secret of this indecipherable significance, I slowly discerned, lurked in the singularly diverse set of the two corners of the mouth; so that her profile wholly shifted its meaning according as it was viewed from the right or left. In one corner of her mouth the little languorous firstling of a smile had gone to sleep; as if she had fallen a-dream, and forgotten that it was there. The other had drooped, as of its own listless weight, into a something which guessed at sadness; guessed, but so as indolent lids are easily grieved by the pricks of the slate-blue dawn. And on the full countenance those two expressions blended to a single expression inexpressible; as if pensiveness had played the Mænad, and now her arms grew heavy under the cymbals. Thither each evening, as twilight fell, I stole to meditate and worship the baffling mysteries of her meaning: as twilight fell, and the blank noon surceased

THE FOURTH ORDER OF HUMANITY

arrest upon her life, and in the vaguening countenance the eyes broke out from their day-long ambuscade. Eyes of violet blue, drowsed-amorous, which surveyed me not, but looked ever beyond, where a spell enfixed them,

Waiting for something, not for me.

And I was content. Content; for by such tenure of unnoticedness I knew that I held my privilege to worship: had she beheld me, she would have denied, have contemned my gaze. Between us, now, are years and tears: but the years waste her not, and the tears wet her not; neither misses she me or any man. There, I think, she is standing yet; there, I think, she will stand for ever: the divinity of an accident, awaiting a divine thing impossible, which can never come to her, and she knows this not.

For I reject the vain fable that the ambrosial creature is really an unspiritual compound of lime, which the gross ignorant call plaster of Paris. If Paris indeed had to do with her, it was he of Ida. And for him, perchance, she waits.

FORM AND FORMALISM

MANY think in the head; but it is the thinking in the heart that is most wanted. Theology and philosophy are the soul of truth; but they must be clothed with flesh, to create an organism which can come down and live among men. Therefore Christ became incarnate, to create Christianity. Be it spoken with reverence, a great poet, for example, who is likewise a great thinker, does for truth what Christ did for God, the Supreme Truth. And though the world may be loath to admit it, the saint does for truth even more; for he gives to truth his own flesh. What of the man who—like the illustrious English Canon of Loreto—should be poet and saint? Ah, 'hard and rarest union' indeed! for he is a twofold incarnation of truth. He gives to it one body which has the life of man, another which has the life of humanity and the diuturnal hills.

This is a concrete example of an abstract principle—the supreme necessity under which truth is bound to give itself a definite shape. Of such immutable importance is form that without this effigy and witness of spirit, spirit walks invisible among men. Yet, except in literature (and possibly in art), where a materialistic worship of form curiously prevails, form is a special object of the age's blasphemy. In politics, music, society, ethics, the cry is: '*Dirumpamus vincula eorum!*' I am led to this

FORM AND FORMALISM

reflection by the strange miscomprehensions which have beset even so wise and sympathetic a teacher as Mr Ruskin, when he has touched on Religious Orders; and the passage which led to it is a passage in one of his most wise and charming books, the *Ethics of the Dust.*

' Half the monastic system,' he says, ' rose out of the notion of future reward acting on the occult pride and ambition of good people. . . . There is always a considerable quantity of pride, to begin with, in what is called " giving oneself to God." As if one had ever belonged to anybody else ! . . . When it had become the principal amusement, and the most admired art, of Christian men, to cut one another's throats, and burn one another's towns, of course the few feeble or reasonable persons left, who desired quiet, safety, and kind fellowship, got into cloisters; and the gentlest, thoughtfullest, noblest men and women shut themselves up, precisely where they could be of least use.'

It is a most representative passage, for many reasons. Mr Ruskin is, as he truly says, a witness favourable to the monasteries. So it comes about that his words represent not mere Protestant prejudice, but the current secular prejudice of the age. ' All the good people,' as he says further on, ' getting themselves hung up out of the way of mischief.' That then, as now, it was only the minority, even of ' good people,' who became monks; that, numerous though monks were, the world must have been in a worse way than in the days

FORM AND FORMALISM

of Sodom and Gomorrah, if these were all its just; that the majority of monks by no means let the world slide, but very actively combated it;—on all this a professed thinker might have been expected to think.

But confine monasticism, if you will, to contemplative monasticism. Not by the good in general, but by the good with a contemplative bent, are contemplative Orders entered. Is it unlawful to lead the life contemplative, only when the object of contemplation is God? Was Wordsworth right, St Bernard wrong? Or does Mr Ruskin consider the poet's contemplation fruitful, but the saint's unfruitful? Yes, there is the root of it; and there again is Mr Ruskin representative. The modern world profoundly and hopelessly disbelieves the power of prayer. It is not always scornful, this modern world; it simply does not comprehend, and is doubtful whether anything may lawfully be supposed to exist which it cannot comprehend. Yet I would sooner be prayed for by John of Patmos than written for by John of Coniston.

But Mr Ruskin's words indicate that not only the Religious Orders, but the Religious life itself is held by him 'suspect.' In what is called 'giving oneself to God' he sees pride. He desires life, in fact, to be religious without the form of religion; even as, in his own later tendencies, he has apparently aimed to be a Catholic without Catholic belief. One sees this revolt from form, with its inevitable con-

FORM AND FORMALISM

sequences, in his teaching and in his thought. In his teaching, which is full of insulated and capricious beauty, but has little unity beyond that of his own individuality. And that makes artistic, not ethical, unity. In his thought, which is often strangely unprecise. He can, for instance, as the basis of his diatribe against monasticism, assert that 'nothing is ever done so as really to please our Great Father, unless we would also have done it, though we had had no Father to know of it.' Why, then, are we to do it? 'Because it is right,' Mr Ruskin implies. Which is so dearly fine in sound, that it is a pity it should be so childishly empty in sense. We are not to do a thing for the pleasure of God; but we are to do it because it is right—i.e., the pleasure of God. For what is right, but the pleasure of God? If Mr Ruskin had asked himself that question, he would not have spun this Penelope-web. It is an example, not of thinking in the heart (which I have averred to be so much needed), but of thinking *with* the heart, which is quite another thing, and the peculiar curse of sentimentalists.

But in such utterances, and in his protest against the formal 'giving oneself to God,' Mr Ruskin has latter-day feeling at his back. Formalism is the repressor of vitality: therefore let us away with form. Let us all stop short where the young man stopped, who went to Christ for a counsel of perfection, and departed sad at heart. When a maid takes a man

FORM AND FORMALISM

to husband, she goes forth from her father's house; and none cries out upon the inhuman sundering of family ties by the relentless system of marriage. But when a soul takes Christ to husband, and goes forth from her father's house, we will cry, like them that cried Diana great. Christ alone we admit not to have His spouse all to Himself. Without form, formalism is impossible; then let us give short shrift to dogma! The letter killeth, but the spirit quickeneth; then let us have the Essence without the Word!

What, you builders of futurity! You will have life, yet not form? Such thing is not known to man as life without form. To avoid formalism by destroying form, is to remedy carnality by committing suicide. You have the spirit freed from the letter then, with a vengeance; but the spirit, somehow, no longer quickens. Yet may not form change? Yes, in so far as the life changes, not otherwise. The Church is like man's body: which grows to completion altering or adding a little in superficialities and details of figure, but unchanging in essential line and structure. Each bone, muscle, nerve, and blood-vessel, though it have increase, is in form, position, and constitution immutable. And with the Church, also, which is Christ's body, you may add in non-essentials, you may develop in essentials; but you shall not alter in essentials by so much as a clause of its dogmatic theology. 'That the Scripture may

FORM AND FORMALISM

be fulfilled: You shall not break a bone of Him.'

In things more general, the same confusion of form with its abuse, the same uncomprehending iconoclasm, is patent. What is the widest ideal of this age? 'The parliament of man, the federation of the world.' Universal federation, in government or in no government, in religion or in no religion. And the decided tendency of what are called 'popular leaders' is towards federation with the minimum of government, and no religion. Yet when it comes (as come I believe it will), it can only be federation in both government and religion of plenary and ordered dominance. I see only two religions constant enough to effect this: each based upon the past—which is stability; each growing according to an interior law—which is strength. Paganism and Christianism; the religion of the queen of heaven* who is Astarte, and of the queen of heaven who is Mary.

'Under which king?' For under a king it must be, not merely a flag. No common aim can triumph, till it is crystallized in an individual, at once its child and ruler. Man himself must become incarnate in a man before his cause can triumph. Thus the universal Word became the individual Christ; that total God

---

* 'We offer sacrifice to the queen of heaven.' (Jer. xliv, 19.) The Phœnicians represented Astarte with a veil blown out by the wind, and the crescent moon under her feet.

FORM AND FORMALISM

and total man being particularized in a single symbol, the cause of God and man might triumph. In Christ, therefore, centres and is solved that supreme problem of life—the marriage of the Unit with the Sum. In Him is perfectly shown forth the All for one and One for all, which is the justificatory essence of that substance we call Kingship; and from which, in so far as each particular kingship derogates, it forfeits justificatory right. When the new heavens and the new earth, which multitudinous Titans are so restlessly forging, at length stand visible to resting man, it needs no prophecy to foretell that they will be like the old, with head, and form, and hierarchic memberment, as the six-foot bracken is like the bracken at your knee. For out of all its disintegrations and confusion earth emerges, like a strong though buffeted swimmer, nearer to the unseen model and term of all social growth; which is the civil constitution of angeldom, and Uranian statecraft of imperatorial God.

NATURE'S IMMORTALITY

IN the days when days were fable, before the grim Tartar fled from Cathay,* or the hardy Goth from the shafted Tartar; before the hardy Goth rolled on the hot Kelt, or the hot Kelt on Italy; before the wolf-cubs lolled tongues of prey, or Rhodian galleys sheered the brine, an isle there was which has passed into the dreams of men, itself

Full of sweet dreams, and health, and quiet breathing.

* [This passage Francis Thompson translated into verse, as the Prologue of a Pastoral that was, however, never finished.]

> Ere the fierce Tartar fled Cathay,
>   The stark Goth shafted Tartary,
> The fiery Kelt the Gothic fray,—
>   And the Kelt rolled on Italy;
> Ere the wolf-cubs lolled tongues of prey,
>   Or Rhodian galleys sheered the sea,
> An isle there was—where is't to-day?—
>   The Muses called it Sicily.
> Was it, and is it not?—Aye me,
> Where's Eden, or Taprobane?
>
> Where now does old Simæthus flow?
>   You take a map (great Poesy,
> Have they mapped Heaven!) and thereon show—
>   What?—the dust-heap of Italy!
> The Ausonian mainland from its toe
>   Spurns it aside contemptuously.
> You point to it, you man that know,
>   And this, you say, is Sicily.—
> I know not how the thing may be—
> It is not Sicily to me!

NATURE'S IMMORTALITY

And when the Muses talked, they named it Sicily. Was it, and is it not? Alas, where's Eden, or Taprobane? Where flows Alpheus now? You take a map (great Poetry! have they mapped Heaven?) and show me—what? The dust-heap of Italy; a thing spurned contemptuously from the toe of the Ausonian mainland; you point to it, you man of knowledge, and this, you say, is Sicily. You may be right, I know not; but it is not Sicily to me.

Yet that olden Sicily could not, cannot pass. Dew but your eyes with the euphrasy of fancy, and purge your ears with the poet's singing; then, to the ear within the ear, and the eye within the eye, shall come the green of the ever-vernal forests, the babble of the imperishable streams. For within this life of ache and dread, like the greenness in the rain, like the solace in the tear, we may have each of us a dreamful Sicily. And since we can project it where we will, for me, seeking those same 'sweet dreams, and health, and quiet breathing,' for me perchance, Sicily may be Little Cloddington.

What balm, then, for hurt minds has my Sicily? In the old Sicily, 'Shepherds piped on oaten straws,' and the inhabitants were entirely worthy of their surroundings. But that cultivating influence of beauty which our æsthetes preach has somehow broken down in the case of Little Cloddington, and one begins to have an uneasy suspicion that the constant imbibing of beauty, like the constant imbibing of wine,

NATURE'S IMMORTALITY

dulls the brain which it is supposed to stimulate. Yet, to commune with the heart of Nature—this has been the accredited mode since the days of Wordsworth. Nature, Coleridge assures us, has ministrations by which she heals her erring and distempered child; and it is notorious how effectual were her ministrations in the case of Coleridge.

Well, she is a very lovely Nature in this Sicily of mine; yet I confess a heinous doubt whether rustic stolidity may not be a secret effluence from her. You speak, and you think she answers you. It is the echo of your own voice. You think you hear the throbbing of her heart, and it is the throbbing of your own. I do not believe that Nature has a heart; and I suspect that, like many another beauty, she has been credited with a heart because of her face. You go to her, this great, beautiful, tranquil, self-satisfied Nature, and you look for—sympathy? Yes; the sympathy of a cat, sitting by the fire and blinking at you. What, indeed, does she want with a heart or brain? She knows that she is beautiful, and she is placidly content with the knowledge; she was made to be gazed on, and she fulfils the end of her creation. After a careful anatomization of Nature, I pronounce that she has nothing more than a lymphatic vesicle. She cannot give what she does not need; and if we were but similarly organized, we should be independent of sympathy. A man cannot go straight to his objects, because he has a

NATURE'S IMMORTALITY

heart; he cannot eat, drink, sleep, make money, and be satisfied, because he has a heart. It is a mischievous thing, and wise men accordingly take the earliest opportunity of giving it away.

Yet the thing is, after all, too deep for jest. What is this heart of Nature, if it exist at all? Is it, according to the conventional doctrine derived from Wordsworth and Shelley, a heart of love, according with the heart of man, and stealing out to him through a thousand avenues of mute sympathy? No; in this sense I repeat seriously what I said lightly: Nature has no heart.

I sit now, alone and melancholy, with that melancholy which comes to all of us when the waters of sad knowledge have left their ineffaceable delta in the soul. As I write, a calm, faint-tinted evening sky sinks like a nestward bird to its sleep. At a little distance is a dark wall of fir-wood; while close at hand a small group of larches rise like funeral plumes against that tranquil sky, and seem to say, 'Night cometh.' They alone are in harmony with me. All else speaks to me of a beautiful, peaceful world in which I have no part. And did I go up to yonder hill, and behold at my feet the spacious amphitheatre of hill-girt wood and mead, overhead the mighty aerial *velarium*, I should feel that my human sadness was a higher and deeper and wider thing than all. O Titan Nature! a petty race, which has dwarfed its spirit in dwellings, and bounded

NATURE'S IMMORTALITY

it in selfish shallows of art, may find you too vast, may shrink from you into its earths: but though you be a very large thing, and my heart a very little thing, yet Titan as you are, my heart is too great for you. Coleridge—speaking, not as Wordsworth had taught him to speak, but from his own bitter experience—said the truth:

> O Lady! we receive but what we give,
> And in our life alone does Nature live:
> Ours is her wedding garment, ours her shroud!
> . . . .
> I may not hope from outward forms to win
> The passion and the life, whose fountains are within.

The truth, in relation to ourselves; though not the truth with regard to Nature absolutely. Absolute Nature lives not in our life, nor yet is lifeless, but lives in the life of God: and in so far, and so far merely, as man himself lives in that life, does he come into sympathy with Nature, and Nature with him. She is God's daughter, who stretches her hand only to her Father's friends. Not Shelley, not Wordsworth himself, ever drew so close to the heart of Nature as did the Seraph of Assisi, who was close to the Heart of God.

Yet higher, yet further let us go. Is this daughter of God mortal; can her foot not pass the grave? Is Nature, as men tell us, but a veil concealing the Eternal,

> A fold
> Of Heaven and earth across His Face,

NATURE'S IMMORTALITY

which we must rend to behold that Face ? Do our eyes indeed close for ever on the beauty of earth when they open on the beauty of Heaven ? I think not so ; I would fain beguile even death itself with a sweet fantasy, if it be no more than fantasy : I believe that in Heaven is earth. Plato's doctrine of Ideals, as I conceive, laid its hand upon the very breast of truth, yet missed her breathing. For beauty —such is my faith—is beauty for eternity.

If the Trinity were not revealed, I should nevertheless be induced to suspect the existence of such a master-key by the trinities through which expounds itself the spirit of man. Such a trinity is the trinity of beauty—Poetry, Art, Music. Although its office is to create beauty, I call it the trinity of beauty, because it is the property of earthly as of the heavenly beauty to create everything to its own image and likeness. Painting is the eye of passion, Poetry is the voice of passion, Music is the throbbing of her heart. For all beauty is passionate, though it may be a passionless passion. So absolutely are these three the distinct manifestations of a single essence that, in considering the general operation of any one of them we consider the general operation of all ; and hence, as most easily understood because most definitely objective in its result, I take Art. Not the so-called Art which aims at the mere photographic representation of external objects, for that can only reproduce ; but the creative Art

NATURE'S IMMORTALITY

which alone is one essence with Poetry and Music.

In the artist's creation there are two distinct stages or processes, the second of which is but a revelation of the first. There is the ideal and the image of the ideal, the painting. To be more exact I should distinguish an intermediate stage, only theoretically separable in order of process from the first stage, with which it is, or may be, practically synchronous. There is first the ideal, secondly the mental image of the ideal (i.e., the picture of it in form and colour formed on the mental eye*), thirdly the external or objective reproduction of the mental image in material form and colour, in pigments. Now of these three stages, which is the most perfect creation, and therefore the most beautiful? They lessen in perfection as they become material; the ideal is the most perfect; the mental image less perfect; the objective image, the painting, least perfect.

'But,' you say, 'this ideal is an abstract thing, without real existence.' The commonest of errors, that the ideal is the unreal; and the more pernicious because founded on a truth. It is impossible to speak here with the distinctions and modifications necessary for accuracy; but generally I may say this:—The

---

* *On the mental eye.*—I use the popular expression. In reality this image is as really, as physically (I do not say as vividly) seen as is a ray of sunlight. It is therefore material, not spiritual. But this is not the place for a physiological discussion, and the popular phrase subserves my object, if it does not subserve accuracy.

NATURE'S IMMORTALITY

reality of the artist's ideal is not the reality of, e.g., a star; for one is man's creation, the other directly from God. Nor is the reality of the artist's ideal the same in kind as the reality of its objective image, of the painting. The one exists externally, and the senses are cognizant of it; the other within his spirit, and the senses can take no account of it. Yet both are real, actual. If there be an advantage, it is not on the side of the painting; for in no true sense can the image be more real than the thing imaged. I admit that in man the ideal has not the continuous vividness of its objective image. The ideal may be dimmed or even forgotton; though I hold that in such a case it is merely put away from spiritual cognizance as the painting might be put out of physical sight, and that it still exists in the soul. But were the artist omniscient, so that he could hold all things in perpetual and simultaneous contemplation, the ideal would have an existence as unintermittent as that of the painting, and, unlike that of the painting, coeval with the artist's soul.

In Painting and Music the same thing holds good. In both there is the conception (a term perhaps less suggesting unreality than the term 'ideal') with its material expression; and between these two stages a mental expression which the material expression cannot realize. The mental expression in its turn cannot represent all the qualities of the conception; and

NATURE'S IMMORTALITY

the conception, whose essence is the same in all three arts, has a subtlety which the expressional union of all three could not adequately render, because expression never fully expresses. Yet (and it is on this that I insist) the conception is an actually existent thing, an existence within an existence, real as the spirit in which it exists, *the* reality of which the objective reality is but the necessarily less perfect image, and transcending in beauty the image as body is transcended by soul. Can it be adequately revealed by one mortal to another? No. Could it be so revealed? Yes. If the spirit of man were untrammelled by his body, conception could be communicated by the interpenetration of soul and soul.

Let us apply this.* The Supreme Spirit, creating, reveals His conceptions to man in the material forms of Nature. There is no necessity here for any intermediate process, because nobody obstructs the free passage of conception into expression. An ideal wakes in the Omnipotent Painter; and straightway over the eternal dikes rush forth the flooding tides of night, the blue of Heaven ripples into stars; Nature, from Alp to Alpine flower, rises lovely with the betrayal of the Divine thought. An ideal wakes in the Omnipotent Poet; and there

---

* Be it observed that I am not trying to *explain* anything, metaphysically or otherwise, and consequently my language is not to be taken metaphysically. I am merely endeavouring analogically to *suggest* an idea. And the whole thing is put forward as a fantasy, which the writer likes to think may be a dim shadowing of truth.

NATURE'S IMMORTALITY

chimes the rhythm of an ordered universe. An ideal wakes in the Omnipotent Musician; and Creation vibrates with the harmony, from the palpitating throat of the bird to the surges of His thunder as they burst in fire along the roaring strand of Heaven; nay, as Coleridge says,

> The silent air
> Is Music slumbering on her instrument.

Earthly beauty is but heavenly beauty taking to itself flesh. Yet, though this objective presentment of the Divine Ideal be relatively more perfect than any human presentment of a human ideal, though it be the most flawless of possible embodiments; yet is even the Divine embodiment transcendently inferior to the Divine Ideal.

Within the Spirit Who is Heaven lies Earth; for within Him rests the great conception of Creation. There are the woods, the streams, the meads, the hills, the seas that we have known in life, but breathing indeed 'an ampler ether, a diviner air,' themselves beautiful with a beauty which, for even the highest created spirit utterly to apprehend were 'swooning destruction.'

> Yet there the soul shall enter which hath earned
> That privilege by virtue.

As in the participation of human spirits some are naturally more qualified for interpenetration

NATURE'S IMMORTALITY

than others—in ordinary language, as one man is more able than his fellows to enter into another's mind, so in proportion as each of us by virtue has become kin to God, will he penetrate the Supreme Spirit, and identify himself with the Divine Ideals. There is the immortal Sicily, there the Elysian Fields, there all visions, all fairness engirdled with the Eternal Fair. This, my faith, is laid up in my bosom.

SANCTITY AND SONG

THREE Canticles are assigned to St Francis in his collected writings. It is dubious whether they are actually his; it is not dubious that they are early Franciscan work. Of these, the *Canticle of the Sun* is well known, and generally admired. The other two, which are never likely to win general admiration, may or may not be the work of the Saint, but certainly they are the work of *a* saint, and a saint admitted to the highest privileges of Divine Love. The manifest personal experience which notes them, the intimate secrets of that experience, are sufficient proofs of this. Because of that intimate secrecy of personal experience it is that I have said they are never likely to be generally admired. 'The fool,' says Lord Verulam, 'the fool receives not the words of the wise, unless thou speakest the things that are in his heart.' And not only the fool. By the law of Nature, no man can admire, for no man can understand, that of which he has no echo in himself. Such an echo implies an experience kindred, if not equal, to that of the utterer. Now, to the majority of men, Saintship is an uncomprehended word,

> A doubtful tale from fairyland,
> Hard for the non-elect to understand.

Tell them its meaning, and your words will be to them a sound, signifying nothing. Saintship

SANCTITY AND SONG

is the touch of God. To most, even good people, God is a belief. To the saints He is an embrace. They have felt the wind of His locks, His Heart has beaten against their side. They do not believe in Him, for they know Him.

Therefore to the many these Canticles must seem strained and fantastic things, touching in them no corresponding realities of their own experience. If it is hard for such men to seize the aloofness of the purely lyrical poet, how much harder for them to seize the aloofness of the lyrical saint! Take the first of the two Canticles to which I have referred. Saint Francis recounts the purifying struggles of Divine Love under the image of a warfare with Christ. Christ strikes him with dart and lance, overwhelms him with stones, until he falls with pierced heart, dying on the ground.

> But lo! I did not die;
> For my belovèd Lord,
> To crown His victory,
> My life anew restored,
> So keen and fresh that I
> That moment could have soared
> To join the saints on high.

How many will see in this finely daring allegory anything but the bizarre and tortured fancy of an 'ascetic'—word of reprobation! Yet mark. A young poet has recently revived in happy verse a mediæval fable—'Le Chevalier Malheur.' He is encountered by an armed

SANCTITY AND SONG

knight, who overthrows him, and then, as his
'poor heart lies dead,' pierces his bosom and
thrusts in a gauntleted hand. Whereupon

> A new, a noble heart
> Within me woke.

The coincidence is striking; but it is the result
of both poems being based upon a fact of human
nature. The purifying power of suffering was
known even to the heathen. In the Egyptian
obsequies, the removal of the most perishable
parts of the body, the preservation of the rest
by steeping and burning nitre, signified the
cleansing of the human being by pain; and the
symbolism was emphasized by the words
spoken over the embalmed corpse: 'Thou art
pure, Osiris, thou art pure.'

Now grace does not supersede, but acts along
the lines of, Nature. This mysterious strife of
the soul with Christ is manifestly prefigured in
the Old Testament by the struggle of Jacob
with the angel. Yet St Francis has a higher
mystery to symbolize. Revivified and strengthened, he hastens again to the heavenly contest, and in that final strife,

> I conquered Christ my Lord;

he has passed beyond the ken of profane eyes;
to saints and a few readers of the mystics only
is the meaning of that final triumphant image
known. 'My dwelling,' says Wisdom, 'is in a
pillar of a cloud.'

SANCTITY AND SONG

The second Canticle, less profoundly mystical, is perhaps to many even more profoundly unreal. It emphasizes the fire and torments of that Love which the Saint has rashly tempted—to find, alas! that the gates of the beatific Love are guarded by the purgatorial Love.

> Though held, I run; I rise, yet fall;
> I speak, though mute I am become;
> Pursue, and am pursued withal.
> O Love eternal, why
> Am I a fool for Thee?
> Wherefore hast Thou cast me
> In such a fire to die?

Christ answers in rebuke: Francis suffers because his love has broken rule, within which Charity, like all other virtues, should contain itself. Then, with a daring born of the love which casteth out fear, the Saint turns on his Lord, and tells Him that his own follies are Christ's, since Christ is transformed to him: nay, no folly to which love can lead him may equal the folly to which it led Christ:

> Was that Love wise, O Saviour mine,
> Which drew Thee down to earth below?
> . . . . .
> This Love which makes me foolish, lo!
> It took away Thy Wisdom quite;
> This love which makes me languish so,
> It robbed Thee of Thy very might.

And the poem ends in transports which are veritable foolishness to men.

DON QUIXOTE

WAS there ever so strange a book as this *Don Quixote!* To what class shall we assign it ? Solitary, singular, it will not be pigeon-holed ; your literary entomologists shall ticket it, *genus* and *sub-genus* it, at their peril. It is complex beyond measure. It is a piece of literary duplicity without precedent or succession ; nay, duplicity within duplicity, a sword turning all ways, like that which guarded 'unpermitted Eden,' to quote a cancelled verse of Rossetti's *Love's Nocturn*.

Let not Swift say that he was born to introduce and refine irony. The irony of Cervantes is refined and dangerous beyond the irony of Swift ; Swift's is obvious beside it. All irony is double-tongued ; but whether it be the irony of Swift, or Swift's predecessors, or Swift's successors, it has this characteristic : that its duplicity is (so to speak) a one-sided duplicity ; if you do not take the inner meaning, you read baffled, without pleasure, without admiration, without comprehension. But this strange irony, this grave irony, this broadly-laughing irony, of the strange, grave, humorous Spaniard, delights even those who have not a touch of the ironic in their composition. They laugh at the comic mask, who cannot see the melancholy face behind it. It is the Knight of the Rueful Countenance in the vizard of Sancho Panza ; and all laugh, while some few have tears in

DON QUIXOTE

their laughter. And they know not that their derision is derided; that they are trapped and cozened into jeers; that Cervantes, from behind his mask, beholds their grins with a sardonic smile.

A core of scornful and melancholy protest, set about with a pulp of satire and outside all a rind of thick burlesque—that is *Don Quixote*. It never 'laughed Spain's chivalry away.' Chivalry was no more, in a country where it could be written. Where it could be thought an impeachment of idealism, idealism had ceased to be. Against this very state of things its secret but lofty contempt is aimed. Herein lies its curious complexity. Outwardly Cervantes falls in with the waxing materialism of the day, and professes to satirize everything that is chivalrous and ideal. Behind all that, is subtle, suppressed, mordant satire of the material spirit in all its forms: the clownish materialism of the boor; the comfortable materialism of the *bourgeois;* the pedantic materialism of the scholar and the mundane cleric; the idle, luxurious, arrogant materialism of the noble—all agreeing in derisive conceit of superiority to the poor madman who still believes in grave, exalted, heroic ideas of life and duty. Finally, at the deepmost core of the strange and wonderful satire, in which the hidden mockery, is so opposite to the seeming mockery, lies a sympathy even to tears with all height and heroism insulated and out of date,

DON QUIXOTE

mad to the eyes of a purblind world : nay, a bitter confession that such nobility is, indeed, mad and phantasmal, in so much as it imputes its own greatness to a petty and clay-content society. Even Sancho is held up to admiration mixed with smiles, because he has the dim yet tough insight to follow what he does not understand, yet obscurely feels to be worthy of love and following. The author of the heroic *Numantia* a contemner of the lofty and ideal! It could not be. Surely Don Quixote has much of the writer's self ; of his poetic discontent with the earthy and money-seeking society around him. There is no true laughter in literature with such a hidden sadness as that of Cervantes.

Yet it is laughter, and not all sad. The man is a humorist, and feels that if the world be full of mournful humour, yet life would go nigh to madness if there were not some honest laughter as well—laughter from the full lungs. Therefore he gives us Sancho—rich, unctuous, Shakespearean humour to the marrow of him. The mockers of the Don, with their practical jests on him, furnish the understanding reader with but pitying and half-reluctant laughter ; but the faithful compost of fat and flesh who cleaves to the meagre visionary allows us mirth unstinted and unqualified. Many a touch in this creation of the great Spaniard reminds us of like touches in the greatest of Englishmen. Sancho's blunt rejection of titles, for

DON QUIXOTE

example: 'Don does not belong to me, nor ever did to any of my family: I am called plain Sancho Panza, my father was a Sancho, and my grandfather a Sancho, and they were all Panzas, without any addition of Dons or Donnas.' Who does not remember at once the drunken tinker's 'What! am I not Christopher Sly?' etc. The two passages are delightfully kindred in style and humour. How like, too, are Sancho's meandering telling of his story at the Duke's table, and Dame Quickly's narrative style, when she recounts Falstaff's promise of marriage! Unadulterated peasant nature both—the same in Spain as in Eastcheap. What more gloriously characteristic than Sancho's rebutting of the charge that he may prove ungrateful in advancement to high station? 'Souls like mine are covered four inches thick with the grease of the old Christian.'

But enough. With all the inward gravity of his irony, Cervantes has abundantly provided that we need not take his seriousness too seriously: there is laughter even for those who enter deepest into that grave core.

THE WAY OF IMPERFECTION

OVID, with the possible exception of Catullus, is the most modern-minded of Latin poets. It is therefore with delight that we first encounter his dictum, so essentially modern, so opposed to the æsthetic feeling of the ancient world, *decentiorem esse faciem in quâ aliquis nœvus esset.* It was a dictum borne out by his own practice, a practice at heart essentially romantic rather than classic; and there can therefore be little wonder that the saying was scouted by his contemporaries as an eccentricity of genius. The dominant cult of classicism was the worship of perfection, and the Goth was its iconoclast. Then at length literature reposed in the beneficent and quickening shadow of imperfection, which gave us for consummate product Shakespeare, in whom greatness and imperfection reached their height. Since him, however, there has been a gradual decline from imperfection. Milton, at his most typical, was far too perfect; Pope was ruined by his quest for the quality; and if Dryden partially escaped, it was because of the rich faultiness with which Nature had endowed him. The stand made by the poets of the early part of the nineteenth century was only temporarily successful; and now [1889], we suppose, no thoughtful person can contemplate without alarm the hold which the renascent principle has gained over the contemporary mind. Unless some voice be raised

THE WAY OF IMPERFECTION

in timely protest, we feel that English art (in its widest sense) must soon dwindle to the extinction of unendurable excellence.

Over the whole contemporary mind is the trail of this serpent perfection. It even affects the realm of colour, where it begets cloying, enervating harmonies, destitute of those stimulating contrasts by which the great colourists threw into relief the general agreement of their hues. It leads in poetry to the love of miniature finish, and *that* in turn (because minute finish is most completely attainable in short poems) leads to the tyranny of sonnet, ballade, rondeau, triolet, and their kind. The principle leads again to æstheticism; which is simply the aspiration for a hot-house seclusion of beauty in a world which Nature has tempered by bracing gusts of ugliness.

The most nobly conceived character in assuming *vraisemblance* takes up a certain quantity of imperfection; it is its water of crystallization: expel this, and far from securing, as the artist fondly deems, a more perfect crystal, the character falls to powder. We by no means desire those improbable incongruities which, frequent enough in actual life, should in art be confined to comedy. But even incongruities may find their place in serious art, if they be artistic incongruities, not too glaring or suggestive of unlikelihood; incongruities which are felt by the reader to have a whimsical hidden keeping with the congruities of the

THE WAY OF IMPERFECTION

character, which enhance the consent of the general qualities by an artistically modulated dissent; which just lend, and no more than lend, the ratifying seal of Nature to the dominating regularities of characterization.

From the neglect of all this have come the hero and heroine; and among all prevalent types of heroine, *the* worst is one apparently founded on Pope's famous dictum,

<blockquote>Most women have no characters at all—</blockquote>

a dictum which we should denounce with scorn, if so acute an observer as De Quincey did not stagger us by defending it. He defends it to attack Pope. Pope (says De Quincey) did not see that what he advances as a reproach against women constitutes the very beauty of them. It is the absence of any definite character which enables their character to be moulded by others: and it is this soft plasticity which renders them such charming companions as wives. We should be inclined to say that the feminine characteristic which De Quincey considered plasticity was rather elasticity. Now the most elastic substance in Nature is probably ivory. What are the odds, you subtle, paradoxical, delightful ghost of delicate thought, what *are* the odds on your moulding a billiard ball?

Does anyone believe in Patient Grizzel? Still more, does anyone believe in the Nut-brown Maid? Yet their descendants infest literature, from Spenser to Dickens and Tennyson, from

THE WAY OF IMPERFECTION

Una to Enid; made tolerable in the poem only by their ideal surroundings. The dream of 'a perfect woman nobly planned' underlies the thing; albeit Wordsworth goes on to show that his 'perfect woman' had her little failings. Shakespeare was not afraid to touch with such failings his finest heroines; he knew that these defects serve only to enhance the large nobilities of character, as the tender imperfections and wayward wilfulnesses of individual rose-petals enhance the prevalent symmetry of the rose. His most consummate woman, Imogen, possesses her little naturalizing traits. Take the situation where she is confronted with her husband's order for her murder. What the Patient Grizzel heroine would have done we all know. She would have behaved with unimpeachable resignation, and prepared for death with a pathos ordered according to the best canons of art. What does this glorious Imogen do? Why (and we publicly thank Heaven for it), after the first paroxysm of weeping, which makes the blank verse sob, she bursts into a fit of thoroughly feminine and altogether charming jealousy. A perfect woman indeed, for she is imperfect! Imogen, however, it may be urged, is not a Patient Grizzel. Take, then, Desdemona, who is. That is to say, Desdemona represents the type in nature which Patient Grizzel misrepresents. Mark now the difference in treatment. Shakespeare knew that these gentle, affectionate, yielding, all-submissive and all-suffering dis-

THE WAY OF IMPERFECTION

positions are founded on weakness, and accordingly he gave Desdemona the defects of her qualities. He would have no perfection in *his* characters. Rather than face the anger of the man whom she so passionately loves, Desdemona will lie—a slight lie, but one to which the ideal distortion of her would never be allowed to yield. Yet the weakness but makes Shakespeare's lady more credible, more piteous, perhaps even more lovable.

From the later developments of contemporary fiction the faultless hero and heroine have, we admit, relievingly disappeared. So much good has been wrought by the craze for 'human documents.' But alas! the disease expelled, who will expel the medicine? And the hydra perfection merely shoots up a new head. It is now a desire for the perfect reproduction of Nature, uninterfered with by the writer's ideals or sympathies; so that we have novelists who stand coldly aloof from their characters, and exhibit them with passionless countenance. We all admire the representations which result: 'How beautifully drawn! how exactly like Nature!' Yes, beautifully drawn; but they do not live. They resemble the mask in *Phaedrus* —a cunning semblance, *at animam non habet.* This attitude of the novelist is fatal to artistic illusion: his personages do not move us because they do not move him. Partridge believed in the ghost because ' the little man on the stage was more frightened than I'; and in novel-

THE WAY OF IMPERFECTION

reading we are all Partridges, we only believe in the novelist's creations when he shows us that he believes in them himself. Finally, this pestilence attacks in literature the form no less than the essence, the integuments even more than the vitals. Hence arises the dominant belief that mannerism is vicious; and accordingly critics have erected the ideal of a style stripped of everything special or peculiar, a style which should be to thought what light is to the sun. Now this pure white light of style is as impossib e as undesirable; it *must* be splintered into colour by the refracting media o the individual mind, and humanity will always prefer the colour. Theoretically we ought to have no mannerisms; practically we cannot help having them, and without them style would be flavourless—' faultily faultless, icily regular, splendidly null.' Men will not drink distilled water; it is entirely pure and entirely insipid. The object of writing is to communicate individuality, the object of style adequately to embody that individuality; and since in every individuality worth anything there are characteristic peculiarities, these must needs be reproduced in the embodiment. So reproduced we call them mannerisms. They correspond to those little unconscious tricks of voice, manner, gesture, in a friend which are to us the friend himself, and which we would not forgo. It is affected to imitate another's tricks of demeanour : similarly, it is affected to imitate another's mannerisms.

THE WAY OF IMPERFECTION

We should avoid as far as possible in conversation passing conventionalities of speech, because they are brainless; similarly, we should avoid as far as possible in writing the mannerisms of our age; because they corrupt originality. But in essence, mannerisms—individual mannerisms, are a season of style, and happily unavoidable. It is, for instance, stated in the *Encyclopædia Britannica* that De Quincey is not a manneristic writer; and, so put, the assertion has much truth. Yet he is full of mannerisms, mannerisms which every student lovingly knows, and without which the essayist would not be our very own De Quincey.

We say, therefore: Guard against this seductive principle of perfection. Order yourselves to a wise conformity with that Nature who cannot for the life of her create a brain without making one half of it weaker than the other half, or even a fool without a flaw in his folly; who cannot set a nose straight on a man's face, and whose geometrical drawing would be tittered at by half the pupils of South Kensington. Consider who is the standing modern oracle of perfection, and what resulted from *his* interpretation of it. 'Trifles make perfection, and perfection is no trifle.' No; it is half a pound of muscle to the square inch—and *that* is no trifle. One satisfactory reflection we have in concluding. Wherever else the reader may be grieved by perfection, this article, at least, is sacred from the accursed thing.

THE WAY OF IMPERFECTION

Now, how much of all this do we mean? Hearken, O reader, to an apologue.

Once on a time there was a hypochondriac, who—though his digestion was excellent—believed that his delicate system required a most winnowed choice of viands. His physician, in order to humour him, prescribed a light and carefully varied diet. But the hypochondriac was not satisfied.

'I want to know, Doctor,' he said, 'how much of this food really contributes to the building up of my system, and how much is waste material!'

'That,' observed the sage physician, 'I cannot possibly tell you without recondite analysis and nice calculation.'

'Then,' said the hypochondriac, in a rage, I will not eat your food. You are an impostor Sir, and a charlatan, and I believe now your friends who told me that you were a homœopath in disguise.'

'My dear Sir' replied the unmoved physician, 'if you will eat nothing but what is entire nutriment, you will soon need to consult, not a doctor, but a chameleon. To what purpose are your digestive organs, unless to secrete what is nutritious, and excrete what is innutritious!'

And the moral is—no, the reader shall have a pleasure denied to him in his outraged childhood. He that hath understanding, let him understand.

A RENEGADE POET ON THE POET

A POET is one who endeavours to make the worst of both worlds. For he is thought seldom to make provision for himself in the next life, and 'tis odds if he gets any in this. The world will have nothing with his writings because they are not of the world; nor the religious, because they are not of religion. He is suspect of the worldly, because of his unworldliness, and of the religious for the same reason. For there is a way of the world in religion, no less than in irreligion. Nay, though he should frankly cast in his lot with the profane, he is in no better case with them; for he alone of men, though he travel to the Pit, picks up no company by the way; but has a contrivance to evade Scripture, and find out a narrow road to damnation. Indeed, if the majority of men go to the nether abodes, 'tis the most hopeful argument I know of his salvation; for 'tis inconceivable he should ever do as other men.

Mr Robert Louis Stevenson does not stick to affirm that the *littérateur* in general is but a poor devil of a fellow, who lives to please, and earns his bread by doing what he likes. Let this mere son of joy, says Mr Stevenson, sleek down his fine airs before men who are of some use in the world. Yet if religion be useful, so is poetry.

A RENEGADE POET ON THE POET

For poetry is the teacher of beauty; and without beauty men would soon lose the conception of a God, and exchange God for the devil: as indeed happens at this day among many savages where the worships of ugliness and of the devil flourish together. Whence it was, doubtless, that poetry and religion were of old so united, as is seen in the prophetic books of the Bible. Where men are not kept in mind of beauty they become lower than the beasts; for a dog, I will maintain, s a very tolerable judge of beauty, as appears from the fact that any liberally educated dog does, in a general way, prefer a woman to a man. The instinct of men is against this *renegado* of a Robert Louis. Though Butler justly observes that all men love and admire clothes, but scorn and despise him that made them, 'tis of tailors that he speaks. A *modiste* is held in as fair a reverence as any tradesman; and 'tis evident that the ground of the difference is because a *modiste* has some connexion with art and beauty, but a tailor only with ugliness and utility. There is no utilitarian but will class a soapmaker as a worthy and useful member of the community; yet is there no necessity why a man should use soap. Nay, if necessity be any criterion of usefulness (and surely that is useful which is necessary), the universal practice of mankind will prove poetry to be more useful than soap; since there is no recorded age in which men did not use poetry, but for some odd thousand years the world got

A RENEGADE POET ON THE POET

on very tolerably well without soap. Look closely into the matter, and there are no people really useful to a man, in the strict utilitarian sense, but butchers and bakers, for they feed man; builders, for they house a man; women, for they help him into the world; and doctors and soldiers, for they help him out of it.

Then, too, this rogue of an R. L. S., I doubt me (plague on him! I cannot get him out of my head), has found writing pretty utilitarian—to himself; and utility begins at home, I take it. Does he not eat and drink romances, and has he not dug up Heaven knows what riches (the adventurer!) in *Treasure Island?* And as for usefulness to other men, since we must have that or be ignoble, it seems—is there no utility in pleasure, pray you, when it makes a man's heart the better for it; as do, I am very certain, sun, and flowers, and Stevensons?

Did we give in to that sad dog of a Robert Louis, we must needs set down the poor useless poet as a son of joy. But the title were an irony more mordant than the title of the hapless ones to whom it likens him. *Filles de joie?* O rather *filles d'amertume!* And if the pleasure they so mournfully purvey were lofty and purging as it is abysmal and corrupting then would Stevenson's parallel be just; but *then*, too, from ignoble victims they would become noble ministrants. 'Tis a difference which vitiates the whole comparison, O careless player with the toys of the gods! whom we have taken, I warrant

A RENEGADE POET ON THE POET

me, more gravely than you take your whimsical self in this odd pleasantry!

Like his sad sisters, but with *that* transfiguring distinction, the poet sows in sorrow that men may reap in joy. He serves his pleasure, say you, R. L. S.? 'Tis a strange pleasure, if so it be. He loves his art? No, his art loves *him;* cleaves to him when she has become unwelcome, a very weariness of the flesh. He is the sorry sport of a mischievous convention. The traditions of his craft, fortified by the unreasonable and misguiding lessons of those sages who have ever instructed the poet in the things that make for his better misery, persuade him that he can be no true singer except he slight the world. Wordsworth has taught him a most unnecessary apprehension lest the world should be too much with him; which, to be sure, was very singular in Wordsworth, who never had the world with him till he was come near to going out of it. The poor fool, therefore, devotes assiduous practice to acquiring an art which comes least natural to him of all men; and, after employing a world of pains to scorn the world, is strangely huffed that it should return the compliment in kind. There is left him no better remedy but, having spent his youth in alienating its opinion, to spend his manhood in learning to despise its opinion. And though it be a hard matter to contemn the world, 'tis a yet harder matter to contemn its contempt. I regard the villainous misleaders of poets who have preached up these doctrines as

A RENEGADE POET ON THE POET

all one for selfish cruelty with those who maintained the tradition of operatic eunuchs; and would have them equally suppressed by Christian sentiment. For they have procured the severance of the one from his kind to gratify their understanding, as of the other to gratify their ear.

MOESTITIAE ENCOMIUM

MARSH, and night. There are sounds; no man shall say what sounds. There are shadows; no man shall say what shadows. There is light; were there not shadow, no man should call it light. The landscape is a sketch blotted in with smoke of Erebus, and greys from the cheek of death : those trees which threaten from the horizon—they are ranked apparitions, no boon of gracious God. The heaven is a blear copy of the land. Athwart the saturnine marsh, runs long, pitilessly straight, ghastly with an inward pallor (for no gleam dwells on it from the sky), the leprous, pined, infernal watercourse ; a water for the Plutonian naiads—exhaling cold perturbation. It is a stream, a land, a heaven, pernicious to the heart of man ; created only for

> The abhorred estate
> Of empty shades, and disembodied elves.

Over this comes up of a sudden an unlawful moon. My very heart blanches. But a voice which is not the voice of reed, or sedge, or flag, or wind, yet is as the voice of each, says : ' Fear not ; it is I, whom you know.' I know her, this power that has parted from the side of Terror ; she is Sadness, and we are companions of old. Yet not here am I most familiar with her presence ; far oftener have I found her lurking in the blocked-out, weighty shadows which fall

MOESTITIAE ENCOMIUM

from the tyrannous sun. We love the tyrannous sun, she and I.

I know her, for I am of the age, and the age is hers. Alas for the nineteenth century, with so much pleasure, and so little joy; so much learning, and so little wisdom; so much effort, and so little fruition; so many philosophers, and such little philosophy; so many seers, and such little vision; so many prophets, and such little foresight; so many teachers, and such an infinite wild vortex of doubt! the one divine thing left to us is Sadness. Even our virtues take her stamp; the intimacy of our loves is born of despair; our very gentleness to our children is because we know how short their time. ' Eat, we say, ' eat, drink, and be merry; for to-morrow ye are men.'

I know her; and praise, knowing. Foolishly we shun this shunless Sadness; fondly we deem of her as but huntress of men, who is tender and the bringer of tenderness to those she visits with her fearful favours. A world without joy were more tolerable than a world without sorrow. Without sadness where were brotherliness ? For in joy is no brotherliness, but only a boon-companionship. She is the Spartan sauce which gives gusto to the remainder-viands of life, the broken meats of love. ' The full soul loatheth an honeycomb; but to the hungry soul every bitter thing is sweet.' Her servitors rise in the hierarchy of being : to woman, in particular, hardly comes the gracious gift of sweetness till her soul has been excavated by pain. Even

MOESTITIAE ENCOMIUM

a dog in sadness is nearer to the level and the heart of man. She has her dark *accolade*, her sombre patents of nobility; but the titles of that abhorred peerage are clemently and benignly unsuccessive. Our sweetest songs are from her, Shelley knew; but he needed not to have limited the benefaction by song. She is not fair, poor Grief yet in her gift is highest fairness. Love, says Plato, is unbeaut.ful: yet Love makes all things beautiful. And all things take on beauty which pass into the hueless flame of *her* aureole. It may chance to one, faring through a wet grey day-fall, that suddenly from behind him spurts the light of the sinking sun. Instantly, the far windows of unseen homesteads break into flash through the rain-smoke the meads run over with yellow light, the scattered trees are splashed with saffron He turns about towards the fountain of the splendorous surprise —sees but a weeping sundown of pallid and sickly gold. So, throughout humanity, my eyes discern a mourning loveliness; so I turn expectant—' What, pale Sorrow? Could all this have been indeed from you? And give you so much beauty that no dower of it remains for your own?' Nay, but my vision was unversed when I disvalued her comeliness, and I looked not with the looking of her lovers.

Nay, but to our weak mortality the extremity of immitigate beauty is inapprehensible save through reflection and dilution. Sorrow is fair with an unmortal fairness, which we see not till

MOESTITIAE ENCOMIUM

it is humanized in the sorrowful. The sweetest smiles I know, her rod draws forth from the rock of an abiding melancholy; the faces which haunt me from canvas attest that *she* prescribed to the painter's hand; of the most beautiful among the sons of men it is recorded that, though many had seen Him weep, no man had seen Him smile. Nor with beauty end her gifts to men Solomon, who found in knowledge but increase of sorrow, might have found in sorrow increase of knowledge: it is less wisdom that reveals mourning, than mourning that reveals wisdom—as the Hindoo gathers secret things from gazing in the pool of ink. Power is the reward of sadness. It was after the Christ had wept over Jerusalem that He uttered some of His most august words; it was when His soul had been sorrowful even unto death that His enemies fell prostrate before His voice. Who suffers, conquers. The bruised is the breaker. By torture the Indians try their braves; by torture Life, too, tries the elected victors of her untriumphal triumphs, and of cypress is the commemoration on their brows. Sadness the king-maker, *morituri te salutant!*

Come, therefore, O Sadness, fair and froward and tender; dolorous coquette of the Abyss, who claspest them that shun thee, with fierce kisses that hiss against their tears; wraith of the mists of sighs; mermaid of the flood Cocytus, of the waves which are salt with the weeping of the generations; most menacing seductress,

MOESTITIAE ENCOMIUM

whose harp is stringed with lamentations, whose voice is fatal with disastrous prescience; draw me down, merge me, under thy waters of wail! Of thy undesired loveliness am I desirous, for I have looked long on thy countenance, and can forget it not, nor the footfalls of thy majesty which still shake the precincts of my heart: under the fringed awnings of the sunsets thou art throned, and *thy* face parts the enfolding pavilions of the Evens; thou art very dear to the heart of Night; thou art mistress of the things unmetable which are dreadful to meted life, mistress of the barren hearth and the barren soul of man, mistress of the weepings of death and of birth; the cry of the bride is thine and the pang of the first k ss, the pain which is mortise to delight, the flowers which trail between the ruined chaps of mortality, the over-foliaging death which chequers all human suns. Of thy beauty undesired am I desirous, for knowledge is with thee, and dominion, and piercing, and healing; thou woundest with a thorn of light; thou sittest portress by the gates of hearts; and a sceptred quiet rests regal in thine eyes' sepulchral solitudes, in the tenebrous desolations of thine eyes.

'The over-foliaging death which chequers all human suns.' Even so. Not by Cocytus is delimited her delimitless realm. For I have a vision; and the manner of the vision is this. I see the Angel of life. It (for it may be of either sex) is a mighty grey-winged Angel, with bowed

MOESTITIAE ENCOMIUM

and hidden face, looking into the river of life. And sometimes a waver of sunshine rests upon its grey wings and folded veil, so that I seem to see its face, and to see it exceeding beautiful; and then again the sunlight fades, and I dare not attempt to penetrate that veil, for I imagine the countenance exceeding awful. And I see that within its sad drapery the Angel weeps, and its tears fall into the water of life: but whether they be tears of joy or sorrow, only its Creator knows, not I. I have tasted the water of life where the tears of the Angel fell; and the taste was bitter as brine.

Then, say you, they were tears of sorrow? The tears of joy are salt, as well as the tears of sorrow. And in that sentence are many meanings.

FINIS CORONAT OPUS

IN a city of the future, among a people bearing a name I know not, lived Florentian the poet, whose place was high in the retinue of Fortune. Young, noble, popular, influential, he had succeeded to a rich inheritance, and possessed the natural gifts which gain the love of women. But the seductions which Florentian followed were darker and more baleful than the seductions of women; for they were the seductions of knowledge and intellectual pride. In very early years he had passed from the pursuit of natural to the pursuit of unlawful science; he had conquered power where conquest is disaster, and power servitude.

But the ambition thus gratified had elsewhere suffered check. It was the custom of this people that among their poets he who by universal acclaim outsoared all competitors should be crowned with laurel in public ceremony. Now between Florentian and this distinction there stood a rival. Seraphin was a spirit of higher reach than Florentian, and the time was nearing fast when even the slow eyes of the people must be opened to a supremacy which Florentian himself acknowledged in his own heart. Hence arose in his lawless soul an insane passion; so that all which he had seemed to him as nothing beside that which he had not, and the compassing of this barred achievement became to him the one worthy object of existence. Repeated

FINIS CORONAT OPUS

essay only proved to him the inadequacy of his native genius, and he turned for aid to the power which he served. Nor was the power of evil slow to respond. It promised him assistance that should procure him his heart's desire, but demanded in return a crime before which even the unscrupulous selfishness of Florentian paled. For he had sought and won the hand of Aster, daughter to the Lady Urania, and the sacrifice demanded from him was no other than the sacrifice of his betrothed, the playmate of his childhood. The horror of such a suggestion prevailed for a time over his unslacked ambition. But he, who believed himself a strong worker of ill, was in reality a weak follower of it; he believed himself a Vathek, he was but a Faust : continuous pressure and gradual familiarization could warp him to any sin. Moreover his love for Aster had been gradually and unconsciously sapped by the habitual practice of evil. So God smote Florentian, that his antidote became to him his poison, and love the regenerator love the destroyer. A strong man, he might have been saved by love : a weak man, he was damned by it.

The palace of Florentian was isolated in the environs of the city ; and on the night before his marriage he stood in the room known to his domestics as the Chamber of Statues. Both its appearance, and the sounds which (his servants averred) sometimes issued from it, contributed to secure for him the seclusion that he desired

FINIS CORONAT OPUS

whenever he sought this room. It was a chamber in many ways strongly characteristic of its owner, a chamber 'like his desires lift upwards and exalt,' but neither wide nor far-penetrating; while its furnishing revealed his fantastic and somewhat childish fancy. At the extremity which faced the door there stood, beneath a crucifix, a small marble altar, on which burned a fire of that strange greenish tinge communicated by certain salts. Except at this extremity, the walls were draped with deep violet curtains bordered by tawny gold, only half displayed by the partial illumination of the place. The light was furnished from lamps of coloured glass, sparsely hung along the length of the room, but numerously clustered about the altar: lamps of diverse tints, amber, peacock-blue, and changefully mingled harmonies of green like the scales on a beetle's back. Above them were coiled thinnest serpentinings of suspended crystal, hued like the tongues in a wintry hearth, flame-colour, violet, and green; so that, as in the heated current from the lamps the snakes twirled and flickered, and their bright shadows twirled upon the wall, they seemed at length to undulate their twines and the whole altar became surrounded with a fiery fantasy of sinuous stains.

On the right hand side of the chamber there rose—appearing almost animated in the half lustre—three statues of colossal height, painted to resemble life; for in this matter Florentian followed the taste of the ancient Greeks. They

FINIS CORONAT OPUS

were statues of three poets, and, not insignificantly, of three pagan poets. The first two, Homer and Æschylus, presented no singularity beyond their Titanic proportions; but it was altogether otherwise with the third statue, which was unusual in conception. It was the figure of Virgil; not the Virgil whom *we* know, but the Virgil of mediæval legend, Virgil magician and poet. It bent forwards and downwards towards the spectator; its head was uncircled by any laurel, but on the flowing locks was an impression as of where the wreath had rested; its lowered left hand proffered the magician's rod, its outstretched right poised between light finger-tips the wreath of gilded metal whose impress seemed to linger on its hair: the action was as though it were about to place the laurel on the head of some one beneath. This was the carved embodiment of Florentian's fanatical ambition, a perpetual memento of the double end at which his life was aimed. On the necromancer's rod he could lay his hand, but the laurel of poetic supremacy hung yet beyond his reach. The opposite side of the chamber had but one object to arrest attention: a curious head upon a pedestal, a head of copper with a silver beard, the features not unlike those of a Pan, and the tongue protruded as in derision. This, with a large antique clock completed the noticeable garniture of the room.

Up and down this apartment Florentian

FINIS CORONAT OPUS

paced for long, his countenance expressive of inward struggle, till his gaze fell upon the figure o Virgil. His face grew hard; with an air of sudden decision he began to act. Taking from its place the crucifix he threw it on the ground; taking from its pedestal the head he set it on the altar; and it seemed to Florentian as if he reared therewith a demon on the altar of his heart, round which also coiled burning serpents. He sprinkled, in the flame which burned before the head, some drops from a vial; he wounded his arm, and moistened from the wound the idol's tongue, and, stepping back, he set his foot upon the prostrate cross.

A darkness rose like a fountain from the altar, and curled downward through the room as wine through water, until every light was obliterated. Then from out the darkness grew gradually the visage of the idol, soaked with fire; its face was as the planet Mars, its beard as white-hot wire that seethed and crept with heat; and there issued from the lips a voice that threw Florentian on the ground: 'Whom seekest thou?' Twice was the question repeated; and then, as if the display of power were sufficient, the gloom gathered up its edges like a mantle and swept inwards towards the altar; where it settled in a cloud so dense as to eclipse even the visage of fire. A voice came forth again; but a voice that sounded not the same; a voice that seemed to have withered in crossing the confines of existence,

FINIS CORONAT OPUS

and to traverse illimitable remotenesses beyond the imagining of man; a voice melancholy with a boundless calm, the calm not of a crystalline peace but of a marmoreal despair, ' Knowest thou me; what I am ? '

Vanity of man! He who had fallen prostrate before this power now rose to his feet with the haughty answer, ' My deity and my slave! '

The unmoved voice held on its way :

' Scarce high enough for thy deity; too high for thy slave, I am pain exceeding great; and the desolation that is at the heart of things, in the barren heath and the barren soul. I am terror without beauty, and force without strength, and sin without delight. I beat my wings against the cope of Eternity, as thou thine against the window of Time. Thou knowest me not, but I know thee, Florentian, what thou art and what thou wouldst. Thou wouldst have and wouldst not give, thou wouldst not render, yet wouldst receive. This cannot be with me. Thou art but half baptized with my baptism, yet wouldst have thy supreme desire. In thine own blood thou wast baptized, and I gave my power to serve thee; thou wouldst have my spirit to inspire thee— thou must be baptized in blood not thine own! '

' Any way but one way! ' said Florentian, shuddering.

' One way : no other way. Knowest thou not that in wedding thee to her thou givest me a rival ? Thinkest thou my spirit can dwell

FINIS CORONAT OPUS

beside her spirit ? Thou must renounce her or me : aye, thou wilt lose not only all thou dreadest to sin for, but all thou hast already sinned for. Render me her body for my temple, and I render thee my spirit to inhabit it. This supreme price thou must pay for thy supreme wish. I ask not her soul. Give that to the God Whom she serves, give her body to me whom thou servest. Why hesitate ? It is too late to hesitate, for the time is at hand to act. Choose, before this cloud dissolve which is now dissolving. But remember : thine ambition thou mightest have had ; love thou art too deep damned to have.'

The cloud turned from black to grey. ' I consent ! ' cried Florentian, impetuously.

* * * * *

Three years—what years ! since I planted in the grave the laurel which will soon now reach its height ; and the fatal memory is heavy upon me, the shadow of my laurel is as the shadow of funeral yew. If confession indeed give ease, I, who am deprived of all other confession, may yet find some appeasement in confessing to this paper. I am not penitent ; yet I w ll do fiercest penance. With the scourge of inexorable recollection I will tear open my scars. With the cuts of a pitiless analysis I make the post-mortem examen of my crime.

Even now can I feel the passions of that moment when (since the forefated hour was

FINIS CORONAT OPUS

not till midnight), leaving her under the influence of the merciful potion which should save *her* from the agony of knowledge and *me* from the agony of knowing that she knew, I sought, in the air of night and in hurrying swiftness, the resolution of which she had deprived me. The glow-worm lamps went out as I sped by, the stars in rainy pools leaped up and went out, too, as if both worm and star were quenched by the shadow of my passing, until I stopped exhausted on the bridge, and looked down into the river. How dark it ran, how deep, how pauseless; how unruffled by a memory of its ancestral hills! Wisely unruffled, perchance. When it first danced down from its native source, did it not predestine all the issues of its current, every darkness through which it should flow, every bough which it should break, every leaf which it should whirl down in its way? Could it, if it would, revoke its waters, and run upward to the holy hills? No; the first step includes all sequent steps; when I did my first evil, I did also this evil; years ago had this shaft been launched, though it was but now curving to its mark; years ago had I smitten her, though she was but now staggering to her fall. Yet I hesitated to act who had already acted, I ruffled my current which I could not draw in. When at length, after long wandering, I retraced my steps, I had not resolved, I had recognized that I could resolve no longer.

FINIS CORONAT OPUS

She only cried three times. Three times, O my God!—no, not *my* God.

It was close on midnight, and I felt her only, (she was not visible,) as she lay at the feet of Virgil, magician and poet. The lamp had fallen from my hand, and I dared not relume it. I even placed myself between her and the light of the altar, though the salt-green fire was but the spectre of a flame. I reared my arm; I shook; I faltered. At that moment, with a deadly voice, the accomplice-hour gave forth its sinister command.

I swear I struck not the first blow. Some violence seized my hand, and drove the poniard down. Whereat she cried; and I, frenzied, dreading detection, dreading, above all, her wakening,—I struck again, and again she cried; and yet again, and yet again she cried. Then—her eyes opened. I *saw* them open, through the gloom I saw them; through the gloom they were revealed to me, that I might see them to my hour of death. An awful recognition, an unspeakable consciousness grew slowly into them. Motionless with horror they were fixed on mine, motionless with horror mine were fixed on them, as she wakened into death.

How long had I seen them? I saw them still. There was a buzzing in my brain as if a bell had ceased to toll. How long had it ceased to toll? I know not. Has any bell been tolling? I know not. All my senses are resolved into one sense, and that is frozen to those eyes. Silence

FINIS CORONAT OPUS

now, at least; abysmal silence; except the sound (or is the sound in me?), the sound of dripping blood; except that the flame upon the altar sputters, and hisses, and bickers, as if it licked its jaws. Yes, there is another sound—hush, hark!—It is the throbbing of my heart. Not—no, nevermore the throbbing of *her* heart! The loud pulse dies slowly away, as I hope my life is dying; and again I hear the licking of the flame.

A mirror hung opposite to me, and for a second, in some mysterious manner, without ever ceasing to behold the eyes, I beheld also the mirrored flame. The hideous, green, writhing tongue was streaked and flaked with *red!* I swooned, if swoon it can be called; swooned to the mirror, swooned to all about me, swooned to myself, but swooned not to those eyes.

Strange, that no one has taken me, me for such long hours shackled in a gaze! It is night again, is it not? Nay, I remember, I have swooned; what now stirs me from my stupor? Light; the guilty gloom is shuddering at the first sick rays of day. Light? not that, not that; anything but that. Ah! the horrible traitorous light, that will denounce me to myself, that will unshroud to me my dead, that will show me all the monstrous fact. I swooned indeed.

When I recovered consciousness, It was risen from the ground, and kissed me with the kisses of Its mouth.

FINIS CORONAT OPUS

They told me during the day that the great bell of the cathedral, though no man rang it, had sounded thrice at midnight. It was not a fancy, therefore, that I heard a bell toll *there*, where—when she cried three times. And they asked me jestingly if marriage was ageing me already. I took a mirror to find what they meant. On my forehead were graven three deep wrinkles; and in the locks which fell over my right shoulder I beheld, long and prominent, three white hairs. I carry those marks to this hour They and a dark stain on the floor at the feet of Virgil are the sole witnesses to that night.

It is three years, I have said, since then; and how have I prospered! Has Tartarus fulfilled its terms of contract, as I faithfully and frightfully fulfilled mine? Yes. In the course which I have driven through every obstacle and every scruple, I have followed at least no phantom-lure. I have risen to the heights of my aspiration, I have overtopped my sole rival. True, it is a tinsel renown; true, Seraphin is still the light-bearer, I but a dragon vomiting infernal fire and smoke which sets the crowd a-gaping. But it is your nature to gape, my good friend of the crowd, and I would have you gape at me. If you prefer to Jove Jove's imitator, what use to be Jove? 'Gods,' you cry; 'what a clatter of swift-footed steeds, and clangour of rapid rolling brazen wheels, and vibrating glare of lamps! Surely, the

FINIS CORONAT OPUS

thunder-maned horses of heaven, the chariot of Olympus; and you must be the mighty Thunderer himself, with the flashing of his awful bolts!' Not so, my short-sighted friend: very laughably otherwise. It is but vain old Salmoneus, gone mad in Elis. I know you, and I know myself. I have what I would have. I work for the present: let Seraphin have the moonshine future, if he lust after it. Present renown means present power; it suffices me that I am supreme in the eyes of my fellowmen. A year since was the laurel decreed to me, and a day ordained for the ceremony: it was only postponed to the present year because of what they thought my calamity. They accounted it calamity, and knew not that it was deliverance. For, my ambition achieved, the compact by which I had achieved it ended, and the demon who had inspired forsook me. Discovery was impossible. A death sudden but natural: how could men know that it was death of the Two-years-dead? I drew breath at length in freedom. For two years It had spoken to me with her lips, used her gestures, smiled her smile:—ingenuity of hell!—for two years the breathing Murder wrought before me, and tortured me in a hundred ways with the living desecration of her form.

Now, relief unspeakable! that vindictive sleuth-hound of my sin has at last lagged from the trail; I have had a year of respite, of release

FINIS CORONAT OPUS

from all torments but those native to my breast; in four days I shall receive the solemn gift of what I already virtually hold; and now, surely, I exult in fruition. If the approach of possession brought not also the approach of recollection, if— Rest, O rest, sad ghost! Is thy grave not deep enough, or the world wide enough, that thou must needs walk the haunted precincts of my heart? Are not spectres there too many, without thee?

Later in the same day. A strange thing has happened to me—if I ought not rather to write a strange nothing. After laying down my pen, I rose and went to the window. I felt the need of some distraction, of escaping from myself. The day, a day in the late autumn, a day of keen winds but bright sunshine, tempted me out: so, putting on cap and mantle, I sallied into the country, where winter pitched his tent on fields yet reddened with the rout of summer. I chose a sheltered lane, whose hedge-rows, little visited by the gust, still retained much verdure; and I walked along, gazing with a sense of physical refreshment at the now rare green. As my eyes so wandered, while the mind for a time let slip its care, they were casually caught by the somewhat peculiar trace which a leaf-eating caterpillar had left on one of the leaves I carelessly outstretched my hand, plucked from the hedge the leaf, and examined it as I strolled. The marking—a large marking

FINIS CORONAT OPUS

which traversed the greater part of the surface —took the shape of a rude but distinct figure, the figure 3. Such a circumstance, thought I, might by a superstitious man be given a personal application; and I fell idly to speculating how it might be applied to myself.

Curious!—I stirred uneasily; I felt my cheek pale, and a chill which was not from the weather creep through me. Three years since *that;* three strokes—three cries—three tolls of the bell—three lines on my brow—three white hairs in my head! I laughed: but the laugh rang false. Then I said, 'Childishness,' threw the leaf away, walked on, hesitated, walked back, picked it up, walked on again, looked at it again. Then, finding I could not laugh myself out of the fancy, I began to reason myself out of it. Even were a supernatural warning probable, a warning refers not to the past but to the future. This referred only to the past, it told me only what I knew already. *Could* it refer to the future? To the bestowal of the laurel? No; that was four days hence, and on the same day was the anniversary of what I feared to name, even in thought. Suddenly I stood still, stabbed to the heart by an idea. I was wrong. The enlaurelling had been postponed to a year from the day on which my supposed affliction was discovered. Now this, although it took place on the day of terrible anniversary, was not known till the day ensuing. Consequently, though it wanted four

FINIS CORONAT OPUS

days to the bestowal of the laurel, it lacked but three days to the date of my crime. The chain of coincidence was complete. I dropped the leaf as if it had death in it, and strove to evade, by rapid motion and thinking of other things, the idea which appalled me. But, as a man walking in a mist circles continually to the point from which he started, so, in whatever direction I turned the footsteps of my mind, they wandered back to that unabandonable thought. I returned trembling to the house.

Of course it is nothing; a mere coincidence, that is all. Yes; a mere coincidence, perhaps, if it had been *one* coincidence. But when it is seven coincidences! Three stabs, three cries, three tolls, three lines, three hairs, three years, three days; and on the very date when these coincidences meet, the key to them is put into my hands by the casual work of an insect on a casual leaf, casually plucked. This day alone of all days in my life the scattered rays converge; they are instantly focussed and flashed on my mind by a leaf! It may be a coincidence, only a coincidence; but it is a coincidence at which my marrow sets. I will write no further till the day comes. If by that time anything has happened to confirm my dread, I will record what has chanced.

One thing broods over me with the oppression of certainty. If this incident be indeed a warning that but three days stand as barriers between me and nearing justice, then doom

FINIS CORONAT OPUS

will come upon me at the unforgettable minute when it came on her.

The third day.—It is an hour before midnight, and I sit in my room of statues. I dare not sleep if I could sleep; and I write, because the rushing thoughts move slower through the turnstile of expression. I have chosen this place to make what may be my last vigil and last notes, partly from obedience to an inexplicable yet comprehensible fascination, partly from a deliberate resolve. I would face the lightning of vengeance on the very spot where I most tempt its stroke, that if it strike not I may cease to fear its striking. Here then I sit to tease with final questioning the Sibyl of my destiny. With *final* questioning; for never since the first shock have I ceased to question her, nor she to return me riddling answers. She unrolls her volume till my sight and heart ache at it together. I have been struck by innumerable deaths; I have perished under a fresh doom every day, every hour—in these last hours, every minute. I write in black thought; and tear, as soon as written, guess after guess at fate till the floor of my brain is littered with them.

That the deed has been discovered—that seems to me most probable, that is the conjecture which oftenest recurs. Appallingly probable! Yet how improbable, could I only reason it. Aye, but I cannot reason it. What reason will be left me, if I survive this hour?

FINIS CORONAT OPUS

What, indeed, have I to do with reason, or has reason to do with this, where all is beyond reason, where the very foundation of my dread is unassailable simply because it is unreasonable? What crime can be interred so cunningly, but it will toss in its grave, and tumble the sleeked earth above it? Or some hidden witness may have beheld me, or the prudently-kept imprudence of this writing may have encountered some unsuspected eye. In any case the issue is the same; the hour which struck down her will also strike down me: I shall perish on the scaffold or at the stake, unaided by my occult powers; for I serve a master who is the prince of cowards, and can fight only from ambush. Be it by these ways, or by any of the countless intricacies that my restless mind has unravelled, the vengeance will come: its occasion may be an accident of the instant, a wandering mote of chance; but the vengeance is pre-ordained and inevitable. When the Alpine avalanche is poised for descent, the most trivial cause—a casual shout—will suffice to start the loosened ruin on its way; and so the mere echoes of the clock that beats out midnight will disintegrate upon me the precipitant wrath.

Repent? Nay, nay, it could not have been otherwise than it was; the defile was close behind me, I could but go forward, forward. If I was merciless to her, was I not more merciless to myself; could I hesitate to sacrifice her life,

FINIS CORONAT OPUS

who did not hesitate to sacrifice my soul? I do not repent, I cannot repent; it is a thing for inconsequent weaklings. To repent your purposes is comprehensible, to repent your deeds most futile. To shake the tree, and then not gather the fruit—a fool's act! Aye, but if the fruit be not worth the gathering? If this fame was not worth the sinning for—this fame, with the multitude's clapping hands half-drowned by the growl of winds that comes in gusts through the unbarred gate of hell? If I am miserable with it, and might have been happy without it? With her, without ambition —yes, it might have been. Wife and child! I have more in my heart than I have hitherto written. I have an intermittent pang of loss. Yes, I, murderer, worse than murderer, have still passions that are not deadly, but tender.

I met a child to-day; a child with great candour of eyes. They who talk of children's instincts are at fault: she knew not that hell was in my soul, she knew only that softness was in my gaze. She had been gathering wild flowers, and offered them to me. To me, to *me!* I was inexpressibly touched and pleased, curiously touched and pleased. I spoke to her gently, and with open confidence she began to talk. Heaven knows it was little enough she talked of! Commonest common things, pettiest childish things, fondest foolish things. Of her school, her toys, the strawberries in her garden, her little brothers and sisters—nothing, surely,

FINIS CORONAT OPUS

to interest any man. Yet I listened enchanted. How simple it all was ; how strange, how wonderful, how sweet ! And she knew not that my eyes were anhungered of her, she knew not that my ears were gluttonous of her speech, she could not have understood it had I told her ; none could, none. For all this exquisiteness is among the commonplaces of life to other men, like the raiment they indue at rising, like the bread they weary of eating, like the daisies they trample under blind feet ; knowing not what raiment is to him who has felt the ravening wind, knowing not what bread is to him who has lacked all bread, knowing not what daisies are to him whose feet have wandered in grime. How can these elves be to such men what they are to me, who am damned to the eternal loss of them ? Why was I never told that the laurel could soothe no hunger, that the laurel could staunch no pang, that the laurel could return no kiss ? But needed I to be told it, did I not know it ? Yes, my brain knew it, my heart knew it not. And now——

At half-past eleven.

    O lente, lente currite, noctis equi !

Just ! they are the words of that other trafficker in his own soul.* Me, like him, the time tracks swiftly down ; I can fly no farther, I fall

---

* Faustus, in the last scene of Marlowe's play.

FINIS CORONAT OPUS

exhausted, the fanged hour fastens on my throat: they will break into the room, my guilt will burst its grave and point at me; I shall be seized, I shall be condemned, I shall be executed; I shall be no longer I, but a nameless lump on which they pasture worms. Or perhaps the hour will herald some yet worser thing, some sudden death, some undreamable, ghastly surprise—ah! what is that at the door there, that, that with *her* eyes? Nothing: the door is shut. Surely, surely, I am not to die now? Destiny steals upon a man asleep or off his guard, not when he is awake, as I am awake, at watch, as I am at watch, wide-eyed, vigilant, alert. Oh, miserable hope! Watch the eaves of your house, to bar the melting of the snow; or guard the gateways of the clouds, to bar the forthgoing of the lightning; or guard the four quarters of the heavens, to bar the way of the winds: but what prescient hand can close the Hecatompyloi of fate, what might arrest the hurrying retributions whose multitudinous tramplings converge upon me in a hundred presages, in a hundre shrivelling menaces, down all the echoing avenues of doom? It is but a question of which shall arrive the fleetest and the first. I cease to think. I am all a waiting and a fear. *Twelve!*

At half-past two. Midnight is stricken, and I am unstricken. Guilt, indeed, makes babies of the wisest. Nothing happened; absolutely

FINIS CORONAT OPUS

nothing. For two hours I watched with lessening expectance: still nothing. I laughed aloud between sudden light-heartedness and scorn. Ineffable fool that I was, I had conjured up death, judgement, doom—heaven knows what, all because a caterpillar had crawled along a leaf! And then, as I might have done before had not terror vitiated my reason, I made essay whether I still retained my power. I retain it. Let me set down for my own enhardiment what the oracle replied to my questioning.

'Have I not promised and kept my promise, shall I not promise and keep? You would be crowned and you shall be crowned. Does your way to achievement lie through misery?—is not that the way to all worth the achieving? Are not half the mill-wheels of the world turned by waters of pain? Mountain summit that would rise into the clouds, can you not suffer the eternal snows? If your heart fail you, turn; I chain you not. I will restore you your oath. I will cancel your bond. Go to the God Who has tenderness for such weaklings: *my* service requires the strong.'

What a slave of my fancy was I! Excellent fool, what! pay the forfeit of my sin and forgo the recompense, recoil from the very gates of conquest? I fear no longer: the crisis is past, the day of promise has begun, I go forward to my destiny; I triumph.

* * * *

FINIS CORONAT OPUS

Florentian laid down his pen, and passed into dreams. He saw the crowd, the throne, the waiting laurel, the sunshine, the flashing of rich robes; he heard the universal shout of acclaim, he felt the flush of intoxicating pride. He rose, his form dilating with exultation, and passed, lamp in hand, to the foot of the third statue. The colossal figure leaned above him with its outstretched laurel, its proffered wand, its melancholy face and flowing hair; so lifelike was it that in the wavering flame of the lamp the laurel seemed to move. 'At length, Virgil,' said Florentian, 'at length I am equal with you; Virgil, magician and poet, your crown shall descend on me!'

One.. Two.. Three! The strokes of the great clock shook the chamber, shook the statues; and after the strokes had ceased, the echoes were still prolonged. Was it only an echo?

Boom!

Or—*was it the cathedral bell?*

Boom!

It *was* the cathedral bell. Yet a third time, sombre, surly, ominous as the bay of a nearing bloodhound, the sound came down the wind.

Boom!

Horror clutched his heart. He looked up at the statue. He turned to fly. But a few hairs, tangled round the lowered wand, for a single instant held him like a cord. He knew, without seeing, that they were the three white hairs.

FINIS CORONAT OPUS

When, later in the day, a deputation of officials came to escort Florentian to the place fixed for his coronation, they were informed that he had been all night in his Chamber of Statues, nor had he yet made his appearance. They waited while the servant left to fetch him. The man was away some time, and they talked gaily as they waited: a bird beat its wings at the window; through the open door came in a stream of sunlight, and the fragmentary song of a young girl passing:

> Oh, syne she tripped, and syne she ran
> (The water-lily's a lightsome flower),
> All for joy and sunshine weather
> The lily and Marjorie danced together,
> As he came down from Langley Tower.

> There's a blackbird sits on Langley Tower,
> And a throstle on Glenlindy's tree;
> The throstle sings ' Robin, my heart's love!'
> And the blackbird, ' Bonnie, sweet Marjorie!'

The man came running back at last, with a blanched face and a hushed voice. 'Come,' he said, ' and see!'

They went and saw.

At the feet of Virgil's statue Florentian lay dead. A dark pool almost hid that dark stain on the ground, the three lines on his forehead were etched in blood, and across the shattered brow lay a ponderous gilded wreath; while over

FINIS CORONAT OPUS

the extinguished altar-fire the idol seemed to quiver its derisive tongue.

'He is already laurelled,' said one, breaking at length the silence ; ' we come too late.'

Too late. The crown of Virgil, magician and poet, had descended on him.

THE POETS' POET

HERE s a poet who is just poetry, and the stuff of poetry; whose narrative—a mere vehicle for his ideas—is a tissue of romantic fancy, careless of manners or character, of interest epic or dramatic. He has been much beloved of poets, and little of that vague entity, the ' general reader.' Shakespeare had read him much: Milton called him master; he made Cowley a poet two hundred years ago, Keats a poet the other day, and who shall say how many in the illustrious line between? Raleigh and Sidney were his lovers in life; for they also were poets. Raleigh might hail in him a double kinship, as poet and explorer. Was not Spenser indeed a great explorer, among the greatest in that age of adventure, when a man got up in the morning and said, ' I have an idea. If you have nothing better to do, let us go continent-hunting.' And he that had not found an island or so was accounted a fellow of no spirit.

Well, Spenser for his share rediscovered Poetry; or, at least, made Poetry possible. It is among the strangest of strange things that the early sixteenth century should have lisped and stammered where the fourteenth had sung with full mouth; that where the middle ages had led with Chaucer, it should follow with Skelton; that Surrey, Wyatt, and Spenser's immediate forerunners should doubtfully experiment in an art of which Chaucer had been consummate master. The tongue of Chaucer was changed;

THE POETS' POET

the methods of Chaucer held good. Yet the poets were a people of a stammering tongue; their art had gone back to infancy; and things were at such a pass that the egregious Harvey was for setting the English Muses to their *gradus ad Parnassum* and the penning (singing were a misnomer) of obscene horrors styled hexameters, elegiacs, and the like. Then came Spenser, and found again that land of Poetry, more golden than any El Dorado towards which Raleigh ever set his bold-questing keel. He joined hands with Chaucer across the years: even the metre of his earlier poems is Chaucer's. A swarm of adventurers followed their Columbus; and English Poetry was.

For all which, outside the poets, he got little more recognition than he gets now. To a cultured Queen and her Court he cried, in new and unmatched verse, that:

> Fame with golden wings aloft doth fly
> Above the reach of ruinous decay,
> And with brave plumes doth beat the azure sky
> Admired of base-born men from far away:
> Then who so will with virtuous deeds essay
> To mount to heaven, on Pegasus must ride,
> And with sweet poets' verse be glorified.
>
> For not to have been dipt in Lethe lake
> Could save the son of Thetis from to die;
> But that blind bard did him immortal make
> With verses dipt in dew of Castaly:
> Which made the Eastern Conqueror to cry—
> ' O fortunate young man, whose virtue found
> So brave a trump, thy noble acts to sound!'

THE POETS' POET

What deaf adder could withstand such charming ? ' With verses dipt in dew of Castaly '—can you not hear the delicate dewy drip of that exquisitely musical line ?

> Provide, therefore, ye Princes, while ye may,
> That of the Muses ye may honoured be,

exhorted the poet in logical conclusion : and the Princes ' provided '—on the cheap. The Cecils and Elizabeths rated their ' immortality ' a good deal below the pay of a foreign spy.

' Greatest Gloriane,' like a many be-rhymed ladies, probably yawned over her *Faëry Queen* and one may be sure never got to the end of it. It would be curious to inquire how many lovers of poetry have read through it or *The Excursion*. The *Faëry Queen* is in truth a poem that no man can read through save as a duty, and in a series of arduous campaigns (so to speak). The later books of it steadily fail in power ; but that is not all. The Spenserian stanza, beautiful for a time, in the course of four hundred or so pages becomes a very wearisome and cumbrous narrative form. The repetition of it grows monotonous ; it fatigues by the perpetual discontinuity. Spenser himself seems to find it sometimes cumbrous, in the end. You have occasional lines like—

> Until they both do hear what she to them will say.

No, the *Faëry Queen* must not be read on end ; it is a poem to linger over and dip into. It

THE POETS' POET

is, indeed, as much a series of poems as the *Idylls of the King*. It is not a great poem as its model, Ariosto's *Orlando Furioso*, is a great poem; for Spenser has planned on a scale beyond his physical power of endurance, and its completion would have been only so much superfluous evidence of the fact. Its waning power was not caused by waning genus; for in the same year with the latest books he published his magnificent lyrical poems. But if not a great poem it is great poetry; nay, we might say it contains great poems.

The obvious qualities of it and its author are grown mere truisms. He is princely in fancy rather than imagination. His gift of vision (in a specialized sense of the word) is unapproached. Every one has remarked upon that faculty of seeing visions, and presenting them as before the bodily eye: the *Faëry Queen* is a gallery hung with the rarest tapestries, an endless procession of dream-pictures. There is no emotion, save the emotion of beauty. Yet incidentally, like the exclamations of a dreaming man, he will utter brief passages of tenderest pathos, or exultant joy:

> Nought is there under heaven's wide hollowness
> That moves more dear compassion of mind,
> Than beauty brought to unworthy wretchedness.

The mournful sweetness of those lines is insurpassable; and they are quintessential Spenser. Yet it is unluckily characteristic of

THE POETS' POET

him, too, that he mars half the effect of this perfect passage by not stopping with its completion, but following it with a line which makes an anti-climax, and is too manifestly inserted for rhyme's sake:

Through envy's snares, or fortune's freaks unkind.

One might almost take that little passage as a text for one's whole disquisition on Spenser. For, after all, it is not in the richly luxuriant descriptive embroidery, or the pictures brushed in with words as with line and colour, which are traditionally quoted by this poet's critics, that the highest Spenser lies. The secret of him is shut in those three lines.

Wherein lies their power? The language is so utterly plain that an uninspired poet would have fallen upon baldness. Yet Spenser is a mine of diction (as was remarked to us by a poet who had worked in that mine). But here he had no need for his gorgeous opulence of diction: a few commonest words, and the spell was worked. It is all a matter of relation: the words take life from each other, and become an organism, as with Coleridge. And it is a matter of music; an integral element in the magic of the passage is its sound. In this necromancy, by which the most elementary words, entering into a secret relation of sense and sound, acquire occult property, Spenser is a master. And that which gives electric life to their relation is the Spenserian subtlety of

THE POETS' POET

emotion. Here it is specifically pathos, at another time it is joyous exultation, or again the pleasure of beauty. But behind and underneath all these emotional forms, the central and abiding quality, the essence of his emotion, is peace, and the radiance of peace. The final effect of all, in this and kindred passages, is lyrical.

Yes, lyrical. We are well-nigh minded to write ourselves down arch-heretics, and say that the *Faëry Queen* is a superb error. Spenser, it almost seems to us, was a supreme lyric poet who, by the influence of tradition and example, was allured to spend his strength in narrative poetry, and found his true path only at the close of his literary career. Throughout the *Faëry Queen* he is happy when he drops narration to dream dreams, and touches his serenest height in some brief, casual access of lyric feeling such as we have quoted. And in his last years, before misfortune silenced him, he wrote an all-too-small, precious handful of lyrics, which cover but a few pages, yet are greater than all his 'great' poem together, flowing with milk and honey of poetry though it be.

In those grand Platonic *Hymns to Beauty*, in the *Prothalamion* and *Epithalamion*, all his finest qualities are gathered into organic wholes, sublimated by a lyric ardour which is the radiant effluence of central peace. Joy never had such expression as in the *Epithalamion*,

THE POETS' POET

so serenely noble that its intensity of joy may almost be missed, as the swift interflux of the blue heaven cheats us with the aspect of perfect calm. To express supreme joy is the most difficult of tasks (as a critic has remarked), far more difficult than to express intense sadness, which is the chosen aim of most modern poetry. Here it is supremely expressed, in connexion with the culminating point of natural joy; and is ennobled by the interfused presence of something loftier and more perfect than joy— that static joy which is peace. How well could we have forgone the full latter half of the *Faëry Queen* for some twenty more of such consummate lyrics! But Spenser found his greatest gift, his truest line of work, all too late, when the night was closing on him wherein no man can work—the night of poverty, ruin, and sorrow-hastened age.

SIDNEY'S PROSE

AMONG prose-writers a peculiar interest attaches to the poets who have written prose, who can both soar and walk. For to this case the image will not apply of the eagle overbalanced in walking by the weight of his great wings. Nay, far from the poets' being astray in prose-writing, it might plausibly be contended that English prose, as an art, is but a secondary stream of the Pierian fount, and owes its very origin to the poets. The first writer one remembers with whom prose became an art was Sir Philip Sidney. And Sidney was a poet.

If Chaucer, as has been said, is Spring, it is modern, premature Spring, followed by an interval of doubtful weather. Sidney is the very Spring—the later May. And in prose he is the authentic, only Spring. It is a prose full of young joy, and young power, and young inexperience, and young melancholy, which is the wilfulness of joy; full of young fertility, wantoning in its own excess. Every nerve of it is steeped in deliciousness, which one might confuse with the softness of a decadent and effeminate age like our own, so much do the extremes of the literary cycle meet. But there is all the difference between the pliancy of youthful growth and the languor of decay. This martial and fiery progeny of a martial and fiery age is merely relaxing himself

SIDNEY'S PROSE

to the full in the interval of his strenuous life's campaign, indulging the blissful dreams of budding manhood—a virile Keats, one might say. You feel these martial spirits revelling in the whole fibre of his style. It is, indeed, the writing of a child; or, perhaps, of an exceptional boy, who still retains the roaming, luxuriant sweetness of a child's fancy; who has broken into the store-closet of literary conserves, and cloyed himself in delicious contempt of law and ignorance of satiety, tasting all capricious dainties as they come. The *Arcadia* runs honey; with a leisurely deliberation of relish, epicureanly savoured to the full, all alien to our hurried and tormented age.

Sidney's prose is treasurable, not only for its absolute merits, but as the bud from which English prose, that gorgeous and varied flower, has unfolded. It is in every way the reverse of modern prose. Our conditions of hurry carry to excess the abrupt style, resolved into its ultimate elements of short and single sentences. Sidney revels in the periodic style—long sentences, holding in suspension many clauses, which are shepherded to a full and sonorous close. But with him this style is inchoate: it is not yet logically compacted, the clauses do not follow inevitably, are not gradually evolved and expanded like the blossom from the seed. The sentences are loose, often inartificial and tyro-like, tacked together by a profuse employment of relatives and present participles. At times the grammar

SIDNEY'S PROSE

becomes confused, and falls to pieces. But this looseness has a characteristic effect : it conduces to the general quality of Sidney's style. Here, truly, the style is the man. The long, fluctuant sentences, impetuously agglomerated rather than organically grown, have a copious and dissolving melody, quite harmonious with the subject-matter and the nature of the man. Jeremy Taylor, too, mounds his magnificent sentences rather than constructs them : but the effect is different and more masculine; nay, they are structural compared with Sidney's —so far had prose travelled during the interim.

The *Arcadia* is tedious to us in its unvarying chivalrous fantasy and unremittent lusciousness long drawn-out. Yet it has at moments a certain primitive tenderness, natural and captivating in no slight degree. No modern romancer could show us a passage like this, so palpitating in its poured-out feminine compassion. The hero has attempted suicide by his mistress's couch :

> Therefore, getting with speed her weak, though well-accorded, limbs out of her sweetened bed, as when jewels are hastily pulled out of some rich coffer, she spared not the nakedness of her tender feet, but, I think, borne as fast with desire as fear carried *Daphne*, she came running to *Pyrocles*, and finding his spirits something troubled with the fall, she put by the bar that lay close to him, and straining him in her well-beloved embracements ; ' My comfort, my joy, my life,' said she, ' what haste have you to kill your *Philoclea* with the most cruel torment that ever lady suffered ? '

SIDNEY'S PROSE

What a delightful chivalry of heart there is in it all! How exquisitely felt that phrase, ' her sweetened bed '! How charmingly fancied the image which follows it; and how beautiful—' she spared not the nakedness of her tender feet '! How womanly Philoclea's outburst, and the tender eagerness of the whole picture! In other passages Sidney shows his power over that pastoral depiction dear to the Elizabethans—artificial, if you will, refined and courtly, yet simple as the lisp of babes :

> There were hills which garnished their proud heights with trees ; humble valleys, whose bare estate seemed comforted with the refreshing of silver rivers; meadows, enamelled with all sorts of eye-pleasing flowers ; thickets, which, being lined with most pleasant shade, were witnessed so, too, by a cheerful disposition of many well-tuned birds ; each pasture stored with sheep, feeding with sober security ; while the lambs, with bleating oratory craved the dam's comfort. Here a shepherd's boy piping, as though he should never be old ; there a young shepherdess knitting, and withal singing ; and it seemed that her voice comforted her hands to work and her hands kept time to her voice-music.

Sidney is not without that artificial balance and antithesis which, in its most excessive form, we know as euphuism. This, and the other features of his style, appear where we should least expect them ; for his style has not the flexibility which can adjust itself to varying themes. How shall an age accustomed to the direct battle-music of Kipling and Steevens

SIDNEY'S PROSE

admit such tortuous narratives of conflict as his? Assuredly he might have learned much from the forthright old Northern sagas, if he had known them, in the art of warlike narrative. But his best prose is, after all, to be found, not in the romantic *Arcadia*, but in the *Defence of Poesy*. There he has had a set purpose of conviction, of attack and defence before him, and is not constantly concerned with artistic writing. The result is more truly artistic for having less explicit design of art. We get not only melodiously-woven sentences, but also touches of true fire and vigour: he is even homely on occasion. It is from the *Defence of Poesy* that critics mostly choose their 'Sidneian showers of sweet discourse.'

Very plainly Sidney was no believer in that modern fanaticism—art for art's sake. But from his own standpoint, which is the eternal standpoint, no finer apology for poetry has ever been penned. The construction has not the perfection of subsequent prose—of Raleigh at his best, or Browne. The sentences do not always stop at their climax, but are weakened by a tagged-on continuation. But, for all the partial inexpertness, it is splendid writing, with already the suggestion of the arresting phrase and stately cadences presently to be in English prose. He is specially felicitous in those sayings of direct and homely phrase which have become household words: 'A tale which holdeth children from play, and old men from

SIDNEY'S PROSE

the chimney-corner,' or that other well-known saying that Chevy-Chase moved him ' like the sound of a trumpet. It was a great and original genius, perhaps in prose (where he had no models) even more than in poetry, which was cut short on the field of Zutphen; even as the Spanish Garcilaso, also young, noble, and a pastoral poet, fell in the breach of a northern town.

SHAKESPEARE'S PROSE

IT might almost be erected into a rule that a great poet is, if he please, also a master of prose. Tennyson in modern times is the great example of a poet who never spoke without his singing-robes. But we feel an instinctive conviction that Tennyson's prose would have been worth having; that it would have been terse, strong, and picturesque—in another fashion from the pictorial English of the Anglo-Saxon revivalists. Indeed, there is manifest reason why a poet should have command over ' that other harmony of prose,' as a great master of both has called it. The higher includes the lower, the more the less. He who has subdued to his hand all the resources of language under the exaltedly difficult and specialized conditions of metre should be easy lord of them in the unhindered forms of prose. Perhaps it is lack of inclination rather than of ability which indisposes a poet for the effort. Perhaps, also, the metrical restraints are to him veritable aids and pinions, the lack of which is severely felt in prose. Perhaps he suffers, like Claudio, ' from too much liberty.'

Though Shakespeare bequeathed us neither letters nor essays, nor so much as a pamphlet, he has not left us without means of estimating what his touch would have been in prose. The evidences of it are scattered through his plays. There is, of course, the plentiful prose-dialogue.

SHAKESPEARE'S PROSE

But this can only indirectly give us any notion of what might have been his power as a prose-writer. Dramatic and impersonal, it is directed to reproducing the conversational style of his period, as developed among the picturesque and varying classes of Elizabethan men and women. It is one thing with Rosalind, another with Orlando, another with Beatrice, another with Mistress Ford or Master Page, and yet another with his fools or clowns. Thersites differs from Apemantus, plain-spoken old Lafeu from plain-spoken Kent. At the most we might conjecture hence how Shakespeare talked. And if there be anywhere a suggestion of Shakespeare's talk, we would look for it not so much in the overpowering richness of Falstaff, as in the light, urbane, good-humoured pleasantry of Prince Hal. Prince Hal is evidently a model of the cultivated, quick-witted, intelligent gentleman unbending himself in boon society. In his light dexterity, his high-spirited facility, one seems to discern a reminder of the nimble-witted Shakespeare, as Fuller portrays him in the encounters at the 'Mermaid.' No less do the vein of intermittent seriousness running through his talk, the touches of slightly scornful melancholy, conform to one's idea of what Shakespeare may have been in society. One can imagine him, in some fit of disgust with his companions such as prompted the sonnets complaining of his trade, uttering the contemptuous retort of Prince Hal to Poins:

SHAKESPEARE'S PROSE

'It would be every man's thought, and thou art a blessed fellow to think as every man thinks; never a man's thought in the world keeps the roadway better than thine.'

The noble speech of Brutus to the Romans would alone prove that Shakespeare had a master's touch in prose. The balance, the antithesis, the terseness, the grave simplicity of diction make it a model in its kind. Yet one can hardly say that this is the fashion in which Shakespeare would have written prose, had he used that vehicle apart from the drama. It was written in this manner for a special purpose—to imitate the laconic style which Plutarch records that Brutus affected. Its laconisms, therefore, exhibit no tendency of the poet's own. To find a passage which we do believe to show his native style we must again go to Prince Hal, in his after-character of Henry V. The whole of the King's encounter with the soldiers, who lay on his shoulders the private consequences of war, affords admirable specimens of prose. But in particular we quote his chief defensive utterance:

There is no king, be his cause never so spotless, if it come to the arbitrament of swords, can try it out with all unspotted soldiers. Some, peradventure, have on them the guilt of premeditated and contrived murder; some, of beguiling virgins with the broken seals of perjury; some, making the wars their bulwark, that have before gored the gentle bosom of peace with pillage and robbery. Now, if these men have defeated the law, and outrun native punishment, though they can outstrip men, they have no wings to fly from God: war is His beadle, war is His vengeance; so that here men are punished, for before-breach of the King's laws, is now the King's quarrel: where they feared the death, they have borne life away; and where they would be safe, they perish. Then if they die unprovided, no more is the King guilty of their damnation, than he was before guilty of those impieties for the which they are now visited. Every subject's duty is the King's, but every subject's soul is his own. Therefore should every soldier in the wars do as every sick man in his bed, wash every mote out of his conscience; and dying so, death is to him advantage: or not dying, the time was blessedly lost, wherein such preparation was gained: and in him that escapes, it were not sin to think that, making God so free an offer, He let him outlive that day to see His greatness, and to teach others how they should prepare.

The whole is on a like level, and it is obvious that Shakespeare's interest in his theme has caused him for the moment to forsake dramatic propriety by adopting a structure much more complete and formal than a man would use in unpremeditated talk. It is Shakespeare defending a thesis with the pen, rather than Henry with the tongue. And you have, in consequence, a fine passage of prose, quite original in movement and style, unlike other prose of the period, and characteristic (we venture to think) of Shakespeare himself. You would know that style again. Close-knit, pregnant, with a dexterous use of balance and antithesis,

SHAKESPEARE'S PROSE

it is yet excellently direct, fluent, and various, the rhetorical arts carefully restrained, and all insistence on them avoided. Despite its closeness, it is not too close; there s space for free motion : and it has a masculine ring, a cut-and-thrust fashion, which removes it far alike from pedantry on the one hand and poetized prose on the other. Such, or something after this manner, would (we think) have been Shakespeare's native style in prose : not the ultra-formal style he put (for a reason) into the mouth of Brutus.

With the Baconian dispute revived, it is interesting to ask how such passages compare with the known prose of Bacon. The speech of Brutus might possibly be Bacon's, who loved the sententious. But surely not a typical passage such as we have quoted. Take an average extract from Bacon's *Essays*:

> It is worth observing that there is no passion in the mind of man so weak, but it mates and masters the fear of death; and, therefore, death is no such terrible enemy when a man hath so many attendants about him that can win the combat of him. Revenge triumphs over death ; Love delights in it ; Honour aspireth to it ; Grief flieth to it ; nay, we read, after Otho, the Emperor, had slain himself, Pity (which is the tenderest of affections) provoked many to die, out of mere compassion to their Sovereign, and as the truest sort of followers.

Grave, cold, slow, affecting an aphoristic brevity, and erring (when it does err) on the

SHAKESPEARE'S PROSE

side of pedantry, could this style take on the virile energy and freedom of movement, the equipoise of concision and fluency, which we discern in Henry's speech, as in all Shakespeare's characteristic passages? We cannot think it. And that other style of Bacon's, exemplified in the *Reign of Henry VII*, expanded, formal, in the slow-moving and rather cumbersome periods which he deems appropriate to historic dignity, is yet more distant from Shakespeare. The more one studies Shakespeare, the more clearly one perceives in him a latent but quite individual prose-style, which, had he worked it out, would have been a treasurable addition to the great lineage of English prose.

BEN JONSON'S PROSE

ASKED haphazard to name the poets who were also prose-writers (why have we not developed a single term for the thing, like the French *prosateur?*), few, probably, would think of including Ben Jonson. There is some reason for not thinking of Ben as a prose-writer: he never produced any set and continuous work in prose—not so much as a pamphlet. All he has left us is a collection called *Sylva* or *Timber*, corresponding to the *memorabilia* of what we now call a commonplace book—apparently because it contains the observations which a man thinks are not commonplace. We English have small relish for apophthegms and prose-brevities in general: not among us would a La Rochefoucauld, a Pascal of the *Pensées*, a La Bruyère, have found applause. Selden, or Coleridge's *Table-Talk*, the exceedingly witty ' Characters ' of ' Hudibras ' Butler, and other admirable literature of the kind, go virtually unread. We want expansion and explanation ; we like not being asked to complement the author's wit by our own. So that *Sylva* has small chance, were it better than it is.

We know two Ben Jonsons, it may be said— the Ben of the plays, rugged, strong, pedantic, unsympathetic, often heavy, coarse and repellent even in his humour, where he is strongest ; and the Ben of those surprisingly

BEN JONSON'S PROSE

contrasting lyrics, all too few; small, delicate, and exquisite. It is a though Vulcan took to working in filigree. Here, in *Sylva* is another Ben, who increases our estimation of the man. We have often thought there was a measure of affinity between the two Johnsons—Ben and Sam. Their surnames are the same save in spelling; both have a scriptural Christian name; both were large and burly men, of strong, unbeautiful countenance—'a mountain belly and a rocky face' the dramatist ascribed to himself. Both were convivial spirits, with a magnetic tendency to form a personal following; 'the tribe of Ben' was paralleled by the tribe of Samuel. Both were men distinguished for learning unusual among the literary men of their time. Both carried it over the verge of pedantry, and at the same time had strong sense. Both were notably combative. Both were mighty talkers, and founded famous literary clubs which made the 'Mermaid' and the 'Mitre' illustrious among taverns. Both, it seems pretty sure, were overbearing. You can imagine Benjamin as ready to browbeat a man as Samuel. There the parallel ends; Ben was not distinguished for religiosity or benevolence, Ben was never cited as a moralist. But in *Sylva*, it seems to us, we pick it up again.

There is the strong common-sense, and the uncommon sense, which we find in the Doctor's talk; there is the directness, the straightness

BEN JONSON'S PROSE

to the point. There is, moreover, a robust manliness, an eye which discerns, and a hand which strikes for the pith of any matter, a contained vigour which wastes no stroke. Even the style is not without analogies to the spoken style of the great conversationalist— so different from his written style. It has nothing of the occasional stateliness, the latinities, which appeared even in the Doctor's talk. But on the Doctor's vernacular side it has its kinships. It is clean, hardy, well-knit, excellently idiomatic; pithy and well-poised as an English cudgel. Its marked tendency to the use of balance is a further Johnsonian affinity. We would not, however, be understood to say that it is like the style of Johnson's talk. It is individual, and has the ring common to the Elizabethan style. But it has certain qualities which seem to us akin to the spirit of Johnson's talk. One striking feature is its modernity. It is more modern than Shakespeare's prose. There are many sentences which, with the alteration of a word or so, the substitution of a modern for an archaic inflection, would pass for very good and pure modern prose. It is singular that prose so vernacular should have had no successor, and that so wide an interval should have elapsed between him and Dryden.

Yet, if Jonson influenced no follower, it certainly deserves more notice than it has received that, thus early, prose so native,

BEN JONSON'S PROSE

showing so much the mettle of its English pasture, could be written. The average style is seen at once in such a passage as this:

> No man is so foolish, but may give another good counsel sometimes; and no man is so wise, but may easily err, if he will take no other counsel but his own. But very few men are wise by their own counsel or learned by their own teaching. For he that was only taught by himself, hath a fool for a master.

Save for the antiquated inflection of 'hath,' that is modern enough. Johnson could put a thing with almost—or quite—brutal terseness; but Ben is still more uncompromisingly effective, as in the last sentence of the following quotation:

> Many men believe not themselves what they would persuade others, and less do the things which they would impose on others . . . only they set the sign of the Cross over their outer doors, and sacrifice to their guts and their groin in their inner closets.

It has not the sweetness and light of modern culture; it is ursine: but it sticks in the memory. It is interesting, in reading *Sylva*, to note that Jonson had already formed an opinion on the contest between the Ancients and Moderns, long before it became a burning question in the latter Seventeenth, and brought forth Swift's *Battle of the Books* in the Eighteenth Century. If any man might have been looked for to be a bigoted champion of the Ancients, it was Jonson, who marred his own work and

BEN JONSON'S PROSE

would have gone hard to mar that of others by his pedantic insistence on classical authority, and lamented Shakespeare's 'little Latin and less Greek.' Yet he maintains a clear-sighted attitude of respectful independence.

One cannot but smile a little, none the less, at Ben's disclaimer of sects, his ' I will have no man addict himself to me ' : Ben, the focus of disciples and leader in many a literary *fracas*. Yet, despite his upholding of the just rights of the present against the past, he was not satisfied with the present. It is a strange fact that the complaints of decadence in letters, which we hear now, come to us like an echo from the pages of the *Sylva*. In one passage he observes :

> I cannot think Nature is so spent and decayed, that she can bring forth nothing worth her former years. She is always the same, like herself, and when she collects her strength, is abler still. Men are decayed, and studies ; she is not.

Who could conceive that this last pessimist sentence was written by the friend of Shakespeare, the sharer in the glorious prime of English literature, and one of the great literary periods of the world ? Even in his day he evidently felt the scarcity of true appreciation.

SEVENTEENTH CENTURY PROSE

IGNORED by the general voice of the Eighteenth Century, championed by Coleridge, De Quincey, Ruskin, and other writers of the early or middle Nineteenth Century, Seventeenth Century prose has again suffered some eclipse as a profitable model through the more recent revulsion towards the prose of Queen Anne and her immediate successors. And now its claims are again zealously urged by the writer of a very knowledgeable article in the *Quarterly Review*, whose views are sound and discerning, though we cannot say the same of his *obiter dicta*. What, for example, are we to think of the pronouncement that 'of all our writers of great merit, from the Restoration to the present century, Newman alone succeeded in recovering that mastery of rhythm which was the characteristic' of pre-Restoration prose ? Was there no 'mastery of rhythm' in Ruskin, none in De Quincey—to name but two ? De Quincey's rhythm was not that of the Seventeenth Century, indeed, though based on the rhythm of the Seventeenth Century; but it was a better thing—it was characteristically and recognizably his own. Consider merely that passage in the 'Confessions,' ending with the words 'I awoke . . . and cried, " I will sleep no more ! " '—which

SEVENTEENTH CENTURY PROSE

for superbly marshalled complexity of structure and choric intricacy of sound, for mastery over the counterpoint of rhythmic prose, is perhaps the most amazing in the language. The congregating sentences throng like the assembling of armies, with growing innumerable agitation herded and precipitantly accelerated to the multitudinous crash of the close.

But the writer does not simply extol the prose of the Seventeenth Century for those qualities generally confessed. He seeks to show that it possessed likewise the secret of a vernacular style, available for workaday use. It has been said that the Seventeenth Century men, with all their pomps and splendours, worked out no style fit for average use; whereas the writers who underwent French influence after the Restoration did achieve this aim. To which he answers that the average style of the Restoration and the earlier Eighteenth Century was as bad as it could be. The eminent writers, most of them, were largely dominated by the Seventeenth Century—Swift, for instance, who went back to those earlier writers to get marrow for his style. It was Johnson who founded the average prose style which (in decadence enough) still sways the average man when he takes up his pen; and Johnson based himself on Sir Thomas Browne. But the tradition of a truly vernacular style had never failed from the time of Elizabeth (though the prevalent belief is that it became extinct with the Seventeenth Century giants); and it could have been developed into an excellent common style but for the irruption of French influences. In tracing this vernacular current in the Seventeenth Century to which he mainly devotes his article, the writer fixes with acute perception on Ben Jonson as the restorer and upholder of the Tudor tradition, the popular element in the style of his day.

The resemblance between the sturdy vernacular of Jonson and the sturdy vernacular of Dryden was not, it seems, accidental. Dryden makes express reference to the principles advocated in Jonson's *Sylva*. And Jonson had a chain of successors. One need not, however, go further than Browne himself to show that pre-Restoration prose was not always a tissue of long periodic sentences, now unduly loose, now unduly latinized in construction. Browne was more idiomatic in structure than the Ciceronian Hooker. But the admirable knitting of his sentences was not due merely to a better study of English idiom. He was steeped in classic models more compact and pregnant than Cicero. Like his French contemporaries, he was influenced by the great Latin rhetoricians, Lucan, Ovid, and Seneca; whose rivalry it was to put an idea into the fewest possible words. Lucan, Browne quotes more than any other Latin poet. His style is usually represented by passages such as the opening or closing paragraphs in the famous last chapter of the

SEVENTEENTH CENTURY PROSE

Urn-Burial; passages which combine severely logical structure with a motion like the solemn winging of many seraphim. But the greater portion of that same chapter is terse and sententious, an aphoristic style. When his thought moves him to eloquent rhetoric, the sentence dispreads like a mounting pinion. But the level style is brief and serried, like this :

> There is no antidote against the opium of time, which temporarily considereth all things; our fathers find their graves in our short memories, and sadly tell us how we may be buried in our survivors. Grave-stones tell truth scarce forty years. Generations pass while some trees stand, and old families last not three oaks.

Or again :

> To be nameless in worthy deeds, exceeds an infamous history. The Canaanitish woman lives more happily without a name than Herodias with one.

This style is a far better foundation for a general style than the ponderous structure which Johnson reared upon it. Nor, with all his latinities (the supposed excessive proportion of which is grossly exaggerated) was Browne to seek in the vulgar tongue. On the contrary, he blends it in his prose with an excellent mastery, as may partly be seen even in these brief extracts.

But for direct use of the vernacular, the *Quarterly* reviewer points with justice to men like Fuller, South, Chillingworth, and especially Baxter—whose vigour and plainness he compares to Cobbett's. He points, also, to the neglected writers of 'Characters,' and, in particular, the best of them—'Hudibras' Butler. It is another point on which we commend his acumen. We cannot go the length of decrying Butler's verse in order to enhance his prose, as the reviewer does: we are scandalized by the assertion that *Hudibras* is written in ' a clever mechanical kind of verse.' But that the 'Characters' are most undeservedly neglected we have long held. They are witty and full of Hudibrastic point; while the style is vernacular, clear, and strong—though we will not add (with the reviewer) ' as Swift's.' But these, and Izaak Walton, though they prove that vernacular prose was maintained in the Seventeenth Century, do not disturb the fact that the loftier style was in the ascendant, the style of Hooker, Bacon, Taylor, Browne, Milton. There was no Shakespeare of prose in that day, says the reviewer, who wedded and wielded both styles equally. But is a Gallic uniformity of basic style necessary or desirable in English? Does it matter what style is written by the unliterary? Is not the wide latitude and freedom of style among the masters of modern prose, wherein each is free to follow his own affinities, a thing more precious, more suited to our English individualism, than the finished but after all limited perfection of style which France has attained by a contrary method? We think it

SEVENTEENTH CENTURY PROSE

is. We think it better that we should bring forth out of our treasuries new things and old, than develop on a fixed and contracting line, however perfect the results secured by such narrowing. Individual freedom is the English heritage, in letters as in life.

GOLDSMITH'S PROSE

IN the prose style of that delightful poet and universal man of letters, Oliver Goldsmith, the man himself counts for so much that it is impossible to write of one without the other. One can trace the derivations of that style it is true; one can discern that it owes much to French influence. Style does not come out of the blue, be it ever so native to the man, and however authentic his genius. But when you have recognized its Gallic derivation, that which gives it breath of life, and radiates from it in personal fascination, is Goldsmith himself —the careless Goldsmith, the much-tried Goldsmith, the sweet-natured Goldsmith, the Goldsmith who took his troubles like a happy-go-lucky child: an Irish child withal, bright, emotional, and candid.

Yet all this would not have produced the inexpressibly exhilarating mixture we call Goldsmith, limpid and effervescent, touched with the simplest sentiment, enriched with the most varied experience, unfailing in dexterous grace, had this Irish child not been also a child of the eighteenth century. Into this artificial, unruffled eighteenth century, which made composure not merely an inward ideal but an external law was borne this Celtic child, uttering himself right out with a modern sincerity, and an unconsciousness not often modern. The result, at its best, is a combination of qualities singularly piquant and unreproducible. Born into the nineteenth century with such a temperament, a life so troublous and largely *manqué*, Goldsmith would have had the *weltschmerz* pretty badly. He would have wailed the impossibility of things; he would have taken the bandage from his sores; his gaiety would have been dashed with some eclipse. Born into the eighteenth century, he had no encouragement to the indulgence of world-smart. He kept his sores under decent covering, knowing there was small sympathy for literary groans; he looked neither back nor forward, took the hour as it came, and piped against his troubles if Fate gave him half a chance. That European tour, when, half scholarly impostor, half minstrel, he alternately challenged disputant (not forthcoming) and fluted for a living, is a type of his whole career. The Irishman of that character no longer exists: and if personal dignity gains by his vanishing, the gaiety of nations suffers. No wonder that the dignifiedly Britannic, and a trifle priggish, Johnsonian circle was half scandalized by the advent amongst it of this improvident creature of Nature.

Johnson, sternly moralizing under adversity, meets Goldie piping against it, and shakes his unambrosial wig. Yet it says much for the formidable old Doctor that he seems to have appreciated the simple, sweet-natured genius better than did the rest of his circle. It is the

GOLDSMITH'S PROSE

fashion to discredit Boswell's stories of Goldsmith on the ground of envy. Jealous they self-evidently are, but they are too racy of the Goldsmith soil not to be true. The *naïf* vanity is the vanity of a child. One can imagine Goldie breaking his shins in imitating a mountebank— and laugh with kindly amusement. Where talk was upremely valued, he would plunge in, sink or swim. But only that bewigged eighteenth century circle could sneer at him for the harmless weakness. He knew he had the brilliance in him, and pathetically hoped he could teach it to shine at the call of the moment. A little ugly man, slow-tongued and unattractive to women, he sought indemnity for his maimed life in plum-coloured coats, Tokay, and the sorry loves of Covent Garden. ' Goldie was wild, sir,' and small cause for wonder.

But all that weakness is strength in his charming pro,e. There was valiance, could the Doctor have seen it, in that clear fountain of gaiety which turned all his misfortunes to brightness and favour. It is his sunny wit and sweet heart which clarifies his style ; his lovable humour draws for us perpetual refreshment from the vicissitudes of a life as hard as ever fell to struggling poet. What modern writer is brave child enough to extract sunshine from the recollection of his own darkest hours ? A more admirable example you could not have of Goldsmith's prose than that exquisitely sly description of George's search for a l ving in the

GOLDSMITH'S PROSE

Vicar of Wakefield. Yet small was the laughter in the experiences which furnished it to poor Goldie; and it was written when he was still struggling for bread. The narrative s saturated with humour as delicate as it is buoyant, and kindly with large good nature towards the very rogues and blockheads who have set their heels on the helpless seeker for bread. The mere technique is that of a master: every sentence deftly shaped, yet easy as the song of a bird; the phrasing unobtrusively perfect, as we have lost the art of perfecting it in our self-conscious age. He had, indeed, the great heritage of eighteenth century prose, which a succession of masters had shaped to the purposes of wit and humour. But he had lightened it, made it nimble and touched it with an artless-seeming grace, as t never was before. This in the very day when Johnson had compelled English prose to the following of his own deep-draughted movement. Yet, by a singular stretch of blind jealousy, Boswell and others accused him of imitating the Gargantuan Doctor!

Perhaps Johnson may have had some influence on his serious and 'elevated' style, which is antithetic and not a little rhetorical. Perhaps Johnson, also, taught him compactness of structure and grammatical accuracy, which are invaluable even in his lightest style. But, though he 'touched nothing he did not adorn,' and was as irresistible in the pathos of poor

GOLDSMITH'S PROSE

Olivia as in the humours of Mr Jenkinson or Miss Carolina Wilhelmina Skeggs, it is as a comedian that one loves him best. That gay humour could pass from demure slyness to the most buoyant farce; and the combination of extravagance with the deftest delicacy is perhaps his most characteristic and felicitous achievement. Beau Tibbs, in the *Citizen of the World*, is farce; but farce which nowadays would pass for comedy. But Beau Tibbs is too great to be displayed in a mere extract; he must be read entire. Why is Goldsmith unknown at the present day by that delightful series of papers? If the cream of his comedy be in the plays and the *Vicar*, yet, for the sake of Beau Tibbs alone, the *Citizen* should be resuscitated. And if this inadequate article sends one fresh reader to those neglected essays, it will not have been written uselessly.

CRASHAW

MODERN poets have singled Crashaw as a man of genius and a source of inspiration. Coleridge declared that Crashaw's *Hymn to St Teresa* was present to his mind while he was writing the second part of *Christabel;* ' if, indeed, by some subtle process of the mind it did not suggest the first thought of the whole poem.'

Lyric poetry is a very nclusive term. It includes Milton and Herrick, Burns and Shelley, *Tintern Abbey* and *The Grecian Urn* the odes of Coventry Patmore and the songs of Tennyson. But its highest form—that which is to other lyric forms what the epic is to the narrative poem or the ballad—is the form typically represented by the ode. This order of lyric may again be divided into such lyrics as are distinguished by stately structure, and such as are distinguished by ardorous abandonment. In the former kind ardour *may* be present, though under the continual curb of the structure ; and this is the highest species of the lyric. In the latter kind the ardour is naked and predominant : it is to the former kind what the flight of the skylark is to the flight of the eagle. The conspicuous first appearance of the former kind in English poetry was the monumental *Epithalamion* of Spenser. Ardour cannot, as a rule, be predicated of Spenser ; but *there* is ardour of the most ethereal impulse, equipoised throughout with the most imperial and imperious structure. For the development of the latter kind English poetry had to await the poet of *Prometheus Unbound*. But its first, almost unnoticed and unperfected appearance, was in the work of Richard Crashaw. His age gave the preference to Cowley, in whose odes there is unlimited ostentation of dominating ardour without the reality, the result being mere capricious and unmeaning dislocation of form. Too much of the like is there in Crashaw; but every now and again he ascends into real fervour, such as makes metre and diction plastic to its own shaping spirit of inevitable rightness. This is the eminent praise of Crashaw, that he marks an epoch, a turn of the tide in English lyric, though the crest of the tide was not to come till long after, though—like all first innovators —he not only suffered present neglect, but has been overshadowed by those who came a century after him.

He is fraught with suggestion—infinite suggestion More than one poet has drawn much from him, yet much remains to be drawn. But it is not only for poets he exists. Those who read for enjoyment can find in him abundant delight, if they will be content (as they are content with Wordsworth) to grope through his plenteous infelicity. He is no poet of the human and household emotions; he has not pathos, or warm love, or any of the qualities

CRASHAW

which come home to the natural kindly race of men. But how fecund is his brilliant imagery, rapturous ethereality! He has, at his best, an extraordinary cunning of diction, cleaving like gold-leaf to its object. In such a poem as *The Musician and the Nightingale* the marvel of diction becomes even too conscious; in the moment of wondering at the miracle, we feel that the miracle is too researched: it is the feat of an amazing gymnast in words rather than of an unpremeditating angel. Yet this poem is an extraordinary verbal achievement, and there are numerous other examples in which the miracle seems as unconscious as admirable.

For an example of his sacred poems, take the *Nativity*, which has less deforming conceit than most. Very different from Milton's great Ode, which followed it, yet it has its own characteristic beauty. The shepherds sing it turn by turn—as thus:

> Gloomy night embraced the place
>   Where the noble Infant lay.
> The Babe looked up and showed His face;
>   In spite of darkness, it was day.
> It was Thy day, Sweet! and did rise,
> Not from the East, but from Thine eyes.

Here is seen one note of Crashaw—the human and lover-like tenderness which informs his sacred poems, differentiating them from the conventional style of English sacred poetry, with its solemn aloofness from celestial things.

CRASHAW

I saw the curled drops, soft and slow
    Come hovering o'er the place's head;
Offering their whitest sheets of snow
    To furnish the fair Infant's bed:
Forbear, said I; be not too bold,
Your fleece is white, but 'tis too cold.

I saw the obsequious Seraphim
    Their rosy fleece of fire bestow,
For well they now can spare their wings,
    Since heaven itself lies here below.
Well done, said I; but are you sure
Your down so warm will pass for pure?

In the second stanza is shown the fire of his fancy; in 'The curled drops,' etc., the happiness of his diction. In *The Weeper* (a poem on the Magdalen), amid stanzas of the most frigid conceit, are others of the loveliest art in conception and expression:

    The dew no more will weep
        The primrose's pale cheek to deck:
    The dew no more will sleep
        Nuzzled in the Lily's neck;
    Much rather would it be thy tear,
    And leave them both to tremble here.

        ·   ·   ·   ·

    Not in the Evening's eyes
        When they red with weeping are
    For the Sun that dies,
        Sits Sorrow with a face so fair.
    Nowhere but here did ever meet
        Sweetness sad, sadness so sweet.

CRASHAW

Two more alien poets could not be conceived than Crashaw and Browning. Yet in the last couplet of these most exquisite stanzas we have a direct coincidence with Browning's line :

> Its sad in sweet, its sweet in sad.

In the *Hymn to St Teresa* are to be found the most beautiful delicacies of language and metre. Listen to this (*à propos* of Teresa's childish attempt to run away and become a martyr among the Moors) :

> She never undertook to know
> What Death with Love should have to do ;
> Nor has she e'er yet understood
> Why to show love she should shed blood ;
> Yet though she cannot tell you why,
> She can love, and she can die.

The wonderfully dainty *Wishes to a Supposed Mistress* shows what Crashaw might have been as an amative poet :

> Whoe'er she be,
> That not impossible She,
> That shall command my heart and me ;
>
> Where'er she lie,
> Locked up from mortal eye
> In shady leaves of Destiny :

CRASHAW

And so on through a series of unequal but often lovely stanzas. So, too, does *Love's Horoscope.* His epitaphs are among the sweetest and most artistic even of that age, so cunning in such kind of verse. For instance, that on a young gentleman :

> Eyes are vocal, tears have tongues,
> And there be words not made with lungs—
> Sententious showers ; O let them fall !
> Their cadence is rhetorical !

With what finer example can I end than the close of *The Flaming Heart,* Crashaw's second hymn to St Teresa ?

> Oh, thou undaunted daughter of desires !
> By all thy dower of lights and fires ;
> By all the eagle in thee, all the dove ;
> By all thy lives and deaths of love ;
> By thy large draughts of intellectual day,
> And by thy thirsts of love more large than they ;
> By all thy brim-filled bowls of fierce desire,
> By thy last morning's draught of liquid fire ;
> By the full kingdom of that final kiss,
> That seized thy parting soul, and sealed thee His ;
> By all the Heaven thou hast in Him
> (Fair Sister of the seraphim !)
> By all of Him we have in thee ;
> Leave nothing of myself in me.
> Let me so read thy life, that I
> Unto all life of mine may die.

It has all the ardour and brave-soaring transport of the highest lyrical inspiration.

COLERIDGE

COLERIDGE is (with the exception of Pope) perhaps the only poet who was a genius to his schoolfellows—and, more wonderful still, to his schoolmaster. At Christ's Hospital his Greek and philosophy were things sensational to all. How he afterwards left Cambridge and enlisted, how he made an indifferent trooper and was bought out, how he came in contact with Southey and later with Wordsworth; of the Pantisocratic scheme and its failure; of the *Lyrical Ballads* and their failure, Macaulay's schoolboy would think it trite to speak. Those were the golden days of the *Ancient Mariner* and *Christabel;* the days when even women like Dorothy Wordsworth sat entranced while the young man eloquent poured out talk the report of which is immortal.

Of that Coleridge one could wish a Sargent or Watts to have left us a portrait, to settle, for one thing, whether his eyes were brown, as some observers say, or grey, as others declare—though it is by a curious error that even De Quincey attaches to him the famous line of Wordsworth about the 'noticeable man with large grey eyes.'* Then came ill-health and opium. Laudanum by the wine-glassful and half-pint at a time soon reduced him to the jour-

---

* As De Quincey himself shows elsewhere, the passage in question refers probably to Sir Humphry Davy—certainly not to Coleridge.

COLERIDGE

nalist lecturer and philosopher who projected all things, executed nothing; only the eloquent tongue left. So he perished—the mightiest intellect of his day; and great was the fall thereof. There remain of him his poems, and a quantity of letters painful to read. They show him wordy, full of weak lamentation, deplorably strengthless.

No other poet, perhaps, except Spenser, has been an initial influence, a generative influence, on so many poets. Having with that mild Elizabethan much affinity, it is natural that he also should be 'a poets' poet' in the rarer sense—the sense of fecundating other poets. As with Spenser, it is not that other poets have made him their model, have reproduced essentials of his style (accidents no great poet will consciously perpetuate). The progeny are sufficiently unlike the parent. It is that he has incited the very sprouting in them of the laurel-bough, has been to them a fostering sun of song. Such a primary influence he was to Rossetti—Rossetti, whose model was far more Keats than Coleridge. Such he was to Coventry Patmore, in whose work one might trace many masters rather than Coleridge. 'I did not try to imitate his style,' said that great singer. 'I can hardly explain *how* he influenced me: he was rather an ideal of perfect style than a model to imitate; but in some indescribable way he did influence my development more than any other poet.'

COLERIDGE

No poet, indeed, has been senseless enough to imitate the inimitable. One might as well try to paint air as to catch a style so void of all manner that it is visible, like air, only in its results. All other poets have not only a style, but a manner; not only style, but features of style. The style of Coleridge is bare of manner, without feature, not ' distinguishable in member, joint, and limb'; it is, in the Roman sense of *merum*, mere style; style unalloyed and integral. Imitation has no foothold; it would tread on glass. Therefore poets, diverse beyond other men in their appreciation of poets, have agreed with a single mind in their estimate of this poet; no artist could refrain his homage to the miracle of such utterance. To the critic has been left the peculiar and purblind shame of finding eccentricity in this speech unflawed. It seems beyond belief; yet we could point to an edition of Coleridge, published during his lifetime, and preceded by a would-be friendly memoir, which justifies our saying, ' Be thou as chaste as ice, as pure as snow, thou shalt not escape calumny.' The admiring critic complains of Mr Coleridge's affectations and wilful fantasticalness of style; and he dares to cite as example that wonderfully perfect union of language and metre:

> The night is chill, the forest bare;
> Is it the wind that moaneth bleak?
> There is not wind enough in the air

COLERIDGE

To move away the ringlet curl
From the lovely lady's cheek—
There is not wind enough to twirl
The one red leaf, the last of its clan,
That dances as often as dance it can,
Hanging so light, and hanging so high,
On the topmost twig that looks up at the sky.

Critics wrapped in ' cocksureness '—to warn, not to discourage you, poets branded with affectation—to give you heart, not recklessness, we recall the fact that this lovely passage was once thought affected and fantastic. There is not one great poet who has escaped the charge of obscurity, fantasticalness, or affectation of utterance. It was hurled, at the outset of their careers, against Coleridge, Wordsworth, Shelley, Keats, Tennyson, Browning. Wordsworth wrote simple diction, and his simplicity was termed affected; Shelley gorgeous diction, and his gorgeousness was affected; Keats rich diction, and his richness was affected; Tennyson cunning diction, and his cunning was affected; Browning rugged diction, and his ruggedness was affected. Why Coleridge was called affected passes the wit of man, except it be that he did not write like Pope or the elegant Mr Rogers—or, indeed, that all critical tradition would be outraged if a mere recent poet were not labelled with the epithet made and provided for him by wise critical precedent. If this old shoe were not thrown at the

COLERIDGE

wedding of every poet with the Muse, what would become of our ancient English customs?

But critic and poet, lion and lamb, have now lain down together in their judgement of Coleridge; and abundance of the most excellent appreciation has left no new word about him possible. The critic, it is to be supposed, feels much the same delicacy in praising a live poet as in eulogizing a man to his face: when the poet goes out of the room, so to speak, and the door of the tomb closes behind him, the too sensitive critic breathes freely, and finds vent for his suppressed admiration. For at least thirty years criticism has unburdened its suppressed feelings about Coleridge, which it considerately spared him while he was alive; and his position is clear, unquestioned; his reputation beyond the power of wax or wane. Alone of modern poets, his fame sits above the power of fluctuation. Wordsworth has fluctuated; Tennyson stands not exactly as he did; there is reaction in some quarters against the worship of Shelley; though all are agreed Keats is a great poet, not all are agreed as to his place. But around Coleridge the clamour of partisans is silent: none attacks, none has need to defend. *The Ancient Mariner, Christabel, Kubla Khan, Genevieve,* are recognized as perfectly unique masterpieces of triumphant utterance and triumphant imagination of a certain kind. They bring down magic to the earth. Shelley has followed it to the skies; but not all can

COLERIDGE

companion him in that rarefied ether, and breathe. Coleridge brings it in to us, floods us round with it, makes it native and apprehensible as the air of our own earth. To do so he seeks no remote splendours of language, uses no brazier of fuming imagery. He waves his wand, and the miracle is accomplished before our eyes in the open light of day; he takes words which have had the life used out of them by the common cry of poets, puts them into relation, and they rise up like his own dead mariners, wonderful with a supernatural animation.

The poems take the reason prisoner, and the spell is renewed as often as they are read. The only question on which critics differ is the respective places of the two longer poems. *The Ancient Mariner* has the advantage of completion, and its necromancy is performed, so to speak, more in the sight of the reader, with a more absolutely simple diction, and a simpler metre. The apparatus—if we may use such a degrading image—is less. *Christabel* is not only a fragment, but incapable of being anything else. Not even Coleridge, we do believe, could have maintained through the intricacies of plot and in *dénouement* the expectations aroused by the opening. The second part, as has been said, declines its level in portions. Yet, in opposition to the general opinion, we think that a more subtle magic is effected in the first part than in *The Ancient Mariner*—marvellous though that be. *The Ancient*

COLERIDGE

Mariner passes in a region of the supernatural; *Christabel* brings the supernatural into the regions of everyday. Nor can we see, as some critics have seen, any flaw in the success with which this is done. Yet, perhaps, there are a few—chiefly poetic—readers to whom the most unique and enthralling achievement of all is *Kubla Khan*. The words, the music—one and indivisible—come through the gates of dream as never has poem come before or since. This, we believe, might have been completed, so far as a dream is ever completed; that is to say, there might have been more of it. Obviously, the thing has no plot, difficult sustainedly to execute. It is pure lyrism; and the tapestry of shifting vision might unroll indefinitely to the point at which the dream melted. For, unlike many, we have no difficulty in believing Coleridge's account of how the poem arose. We should feel it difficult to believe any other origin. We could no more see a shower without postulating a cloud than we could doubt this poem to have been rained out of dream. If there were a day of judgement against the preventers of poetry, heavy would be the account of that unnamed visitor who interrupted Coleridge in the transcription of his dream-music, and lost to the world for ever the remainder of *Kubla Khan*. In the other world, we trust, this wretched individual will be condemned eternally to go out of ear-shot when the angels prelude on

COLERIDGE

their harps; together with all those who by choice enter concert-rooms during the divinest passage of a symphony.

The minor poems of this great poet are minor indeed. *Youth and Age*, *Frost at Midnight*, passages of *The Nightingale* and one or two more which might be named, in spite of a real measure of quiet beauty, could never support a great reputation. The *Ode to Dejection* has unquestionably fine passages, but hardly aims at sustained power. The Odes *To France* and *The Departing Year* are terrible bombast, though here again occur fine lines. The fingers of one hand number the poems on which Coleridge's fame is adamantinely based; and they were all written in about two years of his youth.

A portrait shows the Coleridge of those younger days, with the poet not yet burned out in him; when we are told his face had beauty in the eyes of many women. But it is of the later Coleridge that we possess the most luminous descriptions. A slack, shambling man, flabby in face and form and character, redeemed by noble brow and dim yet luminous eyes; womanly and unstayed of nature, torrentuous of golden talk, the poet submerged and feebly struggling in opium-darkened oceans of German philosophy, amid which he finally foundered, striving to the last to fish up gigantic projects from the bottom of a daily half-pint of laudanum. And over that wreck

COLERIDGE

most piteous and terrible in all our literary history, shines, and will shine for ever, the five-pointed star of his glorious youth; those poor five resplendent poems, for which he paid the devil's price of a desolated life and unthinkably blasted powers. Other poets may have done greater things; none a thing more perfect and uncompanioned. Other poets belong to this class or that; he to the class of Samuel Taylor Coleridge.

BACON

FIRST and before all things, Francis Bacon, Lord Verulam, was a great philosopher. In saying this we make no pretension to estimate the value of his philosophy, regarded as an exposition of truth. But it is the acknowledged fact that he is the founder, the *fons et origo*, of that utilitarian school of philosophy which is peculiarly English. We do not say that without him we should have had no Scottish school of philosophy; no Hume, no Bain, no Reid; that without him we should have had no Locke, no John Stuart Mill, no Herbert Spencer—who, though very different from the utilitarian school, is nevertheless essentially English, and could not have arisen without the various English philosophers (whether strictly English or Scottish) who had preceded him. That school was in the air, and was bound to come. It is perhaps only in the case of a Shakespeare that we can say a whole literature—nay, almost a whole nation—would have been different if he had not appeared. But as things have been arranged, the whole temper of the British school of philosophy looks back to Bacon as its starting-point.

Far more, in our opinion, must it be said that the whole of English physical science must acknowledge Bacon as its very Adam and progenitor. Not because Bacon was himself a great physical investigator; but because he first pointed out the aims and the temper of the physical investigator. Cowley stated the truth, with the usual perspicacity of the poet. Bacon did not enter the Promised Land, but he had the vision of it, and pointed the way to it. His whole aim was to start a new philosophical school, which should antithesize the philosophy of the scholastics and the ancients by proceeding from without inwards, instead of from within outwards; from phenomena to essence, not from essence to phenomena. Physical investigation was but a branch of this new departure, as he conceived it. Yet, in laying down this principle, he unwittingly became the patriarch of our modern scientists. Huxley was bred from his loins, and men greater in physical science than Huxley. This, we unhesitatingly aver, seems to us a greater achievement than the authorship of the British school of philosophy. Already there is a reaction towards the recognition of that very scholastic school which Bacon, the philosopher, lived only to destroy and bring into contempt. But there is not, nor ever will be, any reaction from the temper of physical research which he first inculcated. Other views may arise as to the value of the principle he laid down in regard to philosophy. There can be no other view as to the value of the principle he laid down in regard to physical science.

Here, however, we are not concerned with

BACON

him on these grounds. We are concerned with him solely as one of the explorers in English prose. And here his name is not so great. He wrote many things, including the not very successful attempt to follow the path of Plato and Sir Thomas More, in the *New Atlantis*. But he survives chiefly by his Essays. They mainly show Bacon the chancellor, the courtier, and man of the world. They are full of very shrewd wisdom, of a devious and not over-principled kind. No attempt is there in them at deep truths, such as you might expect from a philosopher. Not truth, but expediency; the truth of self-interest and worldly consideration is their aim. They show Bacon as an opportunist of the first water, a respectable British Machiavel. If to be a sage in the art of 'getting on' constitutes greatness, then, and not otherwise, they are great. As regards their style, they are doubtless what he would himself call very pithy, pregnant, and sententious. The sentences are short, clear, well-knit, unsuperfluous. But there is no attempt at the more complex evolutions of style; and the succession of short barks (so to speak) is apt to get as tiresome as the utterances of a dog, though he barked like the hoariest sage in kenneldom. There is one exception; and that (if we remember rightly) is the first essay in the collection. But though the earliest (or almost the earliest, if our memory should deceive us) in the book, it is stated by editors to be the latest written. We can well believe it. For here Bacon ascends to an altogether higher level in subject-matter; and naturally, therefore, to an altogether higher level in style. In the sustained dignity of its sentences, as in the sustained dignity of its thought, it is altogether worthy of Sir Thomas Browne, and might not unhappily be taken for the work of that later and greater master of prose.

Otherwise, even as regards the terseness and weight of wisdom in individual sentences (the excellence in which Bacon excels), the palm must be given to his philosophical works, in spite of their alien language. For example:

> Present justice is in your power; for that which is to come you have no security.

Or again:

> Men believe that their reason governs words. But it is also true that words, like the arrows from a Tartar bow, are shot back, and react on the mind.

And yet again (though it is a precept which has its exceptions, in the case of intuitional minds):

> Let every student of Nature take this as a fact, that whatever the mind seizes and dwells on with peculiar satisfaction is to be held in suspicion.

Consider also this most practical maxim:

> In attempts to improve your character, know what is in your power and what beyond it.

Or finally, the saying in the *De Amicitia*,

BACON

which we quote in the original language on account of its superior terseness :

> Magna civitas, magna solitudo.

It might be a saying from Seneca or St Augustine, so pregnant and sparse in wording is it. And if we have somewhat deprecated the excessive praise usually given to Bacon as a writer of prose, let it be acknowledged that, compared with the average modern writer, he is fine and full of matter indeed. It is only by comparison with the great writers of the seventeenth century that he appears less a master of his art. But then, he preceded them ; and perhaps even Sir Thomas Browne learned something from him.

MILTON

THE most apocalyptic of English poets was appropriately a 'John'; more inappropriately, one of the richest of all poets was a Puritan. The facts of his life are common history. He is almost the sole great poet we recollect who was a strict Londoner; being born in that city, of a scrivener, on December 9, 1608. He was educated at Christ's College, Cambridge—the beauty of the reserved and haughty student procuring him the name of 'the lady of Christ's.' All things considered, he was one of the most truly precocious of English poets; for in his twenty-first year he wrote the *Hymn on the Nativity*—in spite of some too ingenious and 'conceited' stanzas, as grand a lyric as was ever penned. Perhaps Rossetti, with his *Blessed Damozel* at nineteen, is the nearest parallel; for a fine stanza or two at an early age cannot be paralleled with this sustainedly consummate achievement. In 1637 was published the *Comus*, and in the same year the *Lycidas*, which from its subject should seem to belong to his college years. These, with *L'Allegro*, *Il Penseroso*, and the *Arcades* marked him in his youth for one of the most perfect lyrical geniuses ever born.

How, after a tour in Italy, where he won golden opinions from the Italian *literati*, he thenceforward devoted himself to the defence,

MILTON

in prose, of the Puritan cause, holding a position as Latin Secretary to the Council of State, is well known; nor was it until the Restoration that he gave himself again wholly to poetry. Twenty-four years of prose drudgery, immortalized only through a genius which turned to gold whatever it touched, is a record of self-command not matched in the history of poets, or matched only partially by Goethe. In 1658, when the Latin Secretaryship was divided with Marvell, he began *Paradise Lost*. It is the custom to think of this as a work carried on steadily at intervals throughout the bulk of Milton's later life; but, as a mater of fact, it was the work of seven years—a brief enough time for the magnitude of the task. Published in 1665, it met with an instant success. Thirteen hundred copies were sold in two years. Practically, his contemporaries—let it be recorded to their credit—pronounced the verdict of posterity. Six years later he closed his record with *Paradise Regained* and *Samson Agonistes*. In 1674 he died; having been blind for the last twenty-two years of his life.

Of his three wives, and his relations with them, enough has been written. It was a hard thing to be Milton's wife or Milton's daughter. He was stern, he was austere, he was self-centred; his impeccable strength was purchased by a sublime and monotonous egoism—which is the name they give to selfishness in poets. Very chill must have been the life of his girls

MILTON

in that Puritan house, reading to the inwrapped Puritan father from languages they did not understand, and taking down from his lips poetry they understood still less. Milton found them undutiful. Poor little ' undutiful ' daughters ! Fathers had terrible conceptions of duty in those days. Did anyone ever want to know Milton ? Did anyone ever not want to know Shakespeare ? Doubtless there are readers of the Exeter Hall class who would have yearned for the godly company of the ' great Christian poet.' But, on the whole, how thankful one should be that Shakespeare was not a ' Christian poet ' ! ' Les vrais artistes sont toujours un peu païens,' said poor Stephen Heller to Sir Charles Hallé ; in no invidious sense, for was he not a Catholic writing to a Catholic ?

But, in truth, this Sunday-school tradition apart, Milton was more than ' un peu païen.' An extraordinary *mélange* of Hebrew and heathen, this Milton—something of Job, something of Æschylus, not a little of Plato, with an infusion of the Ancient Fathers to ' make the gruel thick and slab.' That ' Dorique delicacy ' which ravished Sir Henry Wotton in the lyrics of *Comus* was indeed a gift from the Greeks ; yet even in *Il Penseroso* one comes across a fragment from St Athanasius. All learning was fuel to this fire ; and what fire it was that could fuse all learning into such poetry ! A like burthen of knowledge clogged even Goethe ; but, with occasional exceptions, Milton moves under it freely as in festal garlands. As he borrowed from all learning, so he took from all poets. In particular, to an extent not fully realized, the style of *Comus* is based on Shakespeare. In structure, *Comus* is obviously indebted to Fletcher and the Elizabethan masque-writers. But its diction and the very music of its blank verse follow Shakespeare with a superb and unique felicity, which excludes no jot of Milton's own genius. Shakespeare's magic here, at least, is copied. Such a passage as this has the very ring of Shakespeare's softer style in versification :

> Some say, no evil thing that walks by night,
> In fog or fire, by lake or moorish fen,
> Blue meagre hag, or stubborn unlaid ghost
> That breaks his magic chains at curfew-time ;
> No goblin, or swart faery of the mine,
> Hath hurtful power o'er true virginity.

Compare Titania's speech :

> Never, since the middle summer's spring,
> Met we on hill, in dale, forest, or mead,
> By pavèd fountain or by rushy brook,
> Or on the beachèd margent of the sea,
> To dance our ringlets to the whistling wind,
> But with thy brawls thou hast disturbed our sport.

And one expression, ' the porch and inlet of each sense,' is suggested by ' the porches of my sear ' in Hamlet. But not in Shakespeare's

MILTON

self is there such a distillation of sheer beauty, combined with perfect form and stately philosophy, as in this wonderful masque. With the monumental *Lycidas* and the other minor poems, it makes an achievement which Milton has not surpassed in kind. The ' bowery loneliness' of *Paradise Lost* is less lovelily beautiful. The special greatness of that epic is, first and last, sublimity—unmatched outside the Scriptures. It widened the known bounds of the sublime. De Quincey has described how, in his opium-dreams, the sense of space was portentously enlarged. Such a tyrannous extension of the spatial sense presides over *Paradise Lost*. But the source of sublimity is not in mere vastness. Henry Vaughan has at once expounded and exemplified it in two lines :

> There is in God, some say,
> A deep, but dazzling, darkness.

That is not only sublime—it is sublimity. Mystery impelling awe is the fountain of this quality. Accordingly, Milton's imagery is not simply spacious, but undefined. The immediate suggestion of the image we grasp ; but the associations stirred by it ascend and descend through interminable reverberations.

Mr Coventry Patmore considered Milton even a greater thaumaturge in words than Shakespeare. It is disputable ; but to those who, like Mr Patmore, lean rather towards the classic

MILTON

and Greek than towards the romantic and Gothic school, it may be conceded that Milton is unapproached for his union of Gothic richness with the sculpturesqueness of classic form. Mr Patmore, who was himself a reconciler of yet more impossible opposites, might well incline a little to Milton. It is impossible to question another opinion of his, that the three chief fountains of wonderful diction are Spenser, Shakespeare, and Milton. 'What a mine he is of words!' he once exclaimed, regarding Spenser; and Milton himself 'mined for words' in both his predecessors, most of all, we think, in Spenser.

Mr Patmore remarks truly that from Spenser Milton derived even some of the metres thought to be peculiarly his own—for example, the metre of *Lycidas*. To a minor extent he used more primitive sources, as in 'the swinked hedger' of *Comus*. As with all great poets, no soil came amiss to him in prospecting for diction; in spite of his ruling tendency towards the exotic, the polysyllabic, the grandiose, he could use 'homespun Saxon' with an enchantment not surpassed by Shakespeare. This needs the more insistence, because his contributions to (as apart from what he drew out of) the treasury of English are notoriously latinized and stately. The successful, the wonderful latinisms of Shakespeare have been grossly overlooked. 'All the abhorrèd births below crisp heaven'; 'The replication of your sounds made in his concave shores'; 'The intertissued robe of gold and pearl'; 'Not all these, laid in bed majestical'; here is but a random handful of the supreme latinities, some become current, others unimitated in poetry, which are first found in Shakespeare. But it is Milton who has been the great lapidary of Latin splendours in the English tongue; solemnities of diction, indeed, so exotic that for the most part they remain among the unprofaned insignia of poetry when she goes forth in state; words never journalized by the 'base mechanical hand' of prose. In *Comus* alone can we justly compare him with his great dramatic predecessor, and there we find this essential contrast in the matter of diction; the words of Shakespeare seem to flower from the line, while the Miltonic line is inlaid with rich and chosen words. The distinction may seem —but we think is not—fanciful.

Of his blank verse two men alone could have written with full perception; both have left but slight and casual utterances. One was De Quincey, the other Coventry Patmore. Were the critic fool enough to rush in where the most gifted have feared to tread, not in a journalistic summary could he analyse its colossal harmonies. *Paradise Lost* is the treasury and supreme display of metrical counterpoint. It is to metre what the choruses of Handel are to music.

A poet (to conclude, where we have ventured

little more than a prelude) for sheer accomplishment not equalled in our language; in youth capable of luxuriant beauty, in age of 'severe magnificence,' yet in youth or age without humaneness or heart-blood in his greatness; of overawing sublimity, yet not ethereal; of concrete solidity, yet not earthly; a poet to whom all must bow the knee, few or none the heart; 'the second name of men' in English song, who had gone near to being the first, if his grandeurs, his majesties, his splendours, his august solemnities, had been humid with a tear or a smile. The most inspired artificer in poetry, he lacked, perhaps (or was it a perfecting fault?), a little poetic poverty of soul, a little detachment from his artistic riches. He could not forget, nor can we forget, that he was Milton. And, after all, one must confess it was worth remembering. An art so conscious and consummate was never before joined with such plenitude of the spirit.

POPE

THERE was born in eighteenth century England a pale little diseased wretch of a boy. Since it was evident that he would never be fit for any healthy and vigorous trade, and that he must all his life be sickly and burdensome to himself, and since it is the usual way of such unhappy beings to add to their unhappiness by their own perversities of choice, he naturally became a poet. And after living for long in a certain miserable state called glory, reviled and worshipped and laughed at and courted, despised by the women he loved, very ill looked after, amid the fear and malignity of many and the affection of very few, the wizened little suffering monstrosity died, and was buried in Westminster Abbey, by way of encouraging others to follow in his footsteps. And though a large number of others have done so with due and proper misfortune, in all the melancholy line there is, perhaps, no such destined a wretch as Alexander Pope. What fame can do to still the cravings of such a poor prodigal of song, in the beggarly raiment of his tattered body, that it did for him. The husks of renown he had in plenty, and had them all his life, as no other poet has had. But Voltaire testified that the author of that famous piece of philosophy, 'Whatever is, is right,' was the most miserable man he had ever known.

This king of the eighteenth century is still

the king of the eighteenth century by general consent. Dryden was a greater poet, *meo judicio*, but he did not represent the eighteenth century so well as Pope. All that was elegant and airy in the polished artificiality of that age reaches its apotheosis in the *Rape of the Lock*. It is Pope's masterpiece, a Watteau in verse. The poetry of manners could no further go than in this boudoir epic, unmatched in any literature. It is useless, I may here say, to renew the old dispute whether Pope was a poet. Call his verse poetry or what you will, it is work in verse which could not have been done in prose, and, of its kind, never equalled. Then the sylph machinery in the *Rape of the Lock* is undoubted work of fancy: the fairyland of powder and patches, *A Midsummer Night's Dream* seen through chocolate-fumes. The *Essay on Man* is naught to us nowadays, as a whole. It has brilliant artificial passages. It has homely aphorisms such as only Pope and Shakespeare could produce—the quintessence of pointed common sense: many of them have passed into the language, and are put down, by three out of five who quote them, to Shakespeare. But, as a piece of reasoning in verse, the *Essay on Man* is utterly inferior to Dryden's *Hind and Panther*. Even that brilliant achievement could not escape the doom which hangs over the didactic poem pure and simple; and certain, therefore, was the fate of the *Essay on Man*.

POPE

The *Dunciad* De Quincey ranked even above the *Rape of the Lock*. At my peril I venture to question a judgement backed by all the ages. The superb satire of parts of the poem I admit; I admit the exceedingly fine close, in which Pope touched a height he never touched before or after; I admit the completeness of the scheme. But from that completeness comes the essential defect of the poem. He adapted the scheme from Dryden's *MacFlecknoe*. But Dryden's satire is at once complete and succinct: Pope has built upon the scheme an edifice greater than it will bear; has extended a witty and ingenious idea to a portentous extent at which it ceases to be amusing. The mock solemnity of Dryden's idea becomes a very real and dull solemnity when it is extended to liberal epic proportions. A serious epic is apt to nod, with the force of a Milton behind it; an epic satire fairly goes to sleep. A pleasantry in several books is past a pleasantry. And it is bolstered out with a great deal which is sheer greasy scurrility. The mock-heroic games of the poets are in large part as dully dirty as the waters into which Pope makes them plunge.

If the poem had been half as long, it might have been a masterpiece. As it is, unless we are to reckon masterpieces by avoirdupois weight, or to assign undue value to mere symmetry of scheme, I think we must look for Pope's satirical masterpiece elsewhere. Not in the satire on women, where Pope seems hardly to

POPE

have his heart in his work; but in the imitations from Horace, those generally known as Pope's *Satires*. Here he is at his very best and tersest. They are as brilliant as anything in the *Dunciad*, and they are brilliant right through; the mordant pen never flags. It matters not that they are imitated from Horace. They gain by it: their limits are circumscribed, their lines laid down, and Pope writes the better for having these limits set him, this tissue on which to work. Not a whit does he lose in essential originality: nowhere is he so much himself. It is very different from Horace, say the critics. Surely that is exactly the thing for which to thank poetry and praise Pope. It has not the pleasant urbane good humour of the Horatian spirit. No, it has the spirit of Pope—and satire is the gainer. Horace is the more charming companion; Pope is the greater satirist. In place of an echo of Horace (and no verse translation was ever anything but feeble which attempted merely to echo the original), we have a new spirit in satire; a fine series of English satirical poems, which in their kind are unapproached by the Roman, and in his kind wisely avoid the attempt to approach him. *Satires after Horace* would have been a better title than *Imitations;* for less imitative poems in essence were never written. These and the *Rape of the Lock* are Pope's finest title to fame. The *Elegy on an Unfortunate Lady* has at least one part which shows a pathos little to have been surmised from his later work; and so, perhaps (in a much less degree, I think), have fragments of the once famous *Eloisa to Abelard*. But the *Pastorals*, and the *Windsor Forest*, and the *Ode on St Cecilia's Day*, and other things in which Pope tried the serious or natural vein, are only fit to be remembered with Macpherson's Ossian and the classical enormities of the French painter David.

On the whole, it is as a satirist we must think of him, and the second greatest in the language. The gods are in pairs, male and female; and if Dryden was the Mars of English satire, Pope was the Venus—a very eighteenth century Venus, quite as conspicuous for malice as for elegance. If a woman's satire were informed with genius, and cultivated to the utmost perfection of form by lifelong and exclusive literary practice, one imagines it would be much like Pope's. His style seems to me feminine in what it lacks; the absence of any geniality, any softening humour to abate its mortal thrust. It is feminine in what it has, the malice, the cruel dexterity, the delicate needle point which hardly betrays its light and swift entry, yet stings like a bee. Even in his coarseness—as in the *Dunciad*—Pope appears to me female. It is the coarseness of the fine ladies of that material time, the Lady Maries and the rest of them. Dryden is a rough and thick-natured man, cudgelling his adversaries with coarse speech in the heat and brawl and the bluntness of his sensibilities ; a country squire, who is apt at times to use the heavy end of his cutting whip ; but when Pope is coarse he is coarse with effort, he goes out of his way to be nasty, in the evident endeavour to imitate a man. It is a girl airing the slang of her schoolboy brother.

The one thing, perhaps, which differentiates him from a woman, and makes it possible to read his verse with a certain pleasure, without that sense of unrelieved cruelty which repels one in much female satire, is his artist's delight in the exercise of his power. You feel that, if there be malice, intent to wound, even spite, yet none of these count for so much with him as the exercise of his superb dexterity in fence. He is like Ortheris fondly patting his rifle after that long shot which knocked over the deserter, in Mr Kipling's story. After all, you reflect, it is fair fight ; if his hand was against many men, many men's hands were against him. So you give yourself up to admire the shell-like epigram, the rocketing and dazzling antithesis, the exquisitely deft play of point, by which the little invalid kept in terror his encompassing cloud of enemies—many of them adroit and formidable wits themselves. And you think, also, that the man who was loved by Swift, the professional hater, was not a man without a heart ; though he wrote the most finished and brilliant satire in the language.

JAMES THOMSON

WHAT are the chances of the poet as against the practical man—the politician, for instance—in the game of Fame ? The politician sees his name daily in the papers, until even he is a little weary of seeing it there. The poet's name appears so rarely that the sight of it has a certain thrill for its owner. But time is all on the side of the poet. The politician's name is barely given a decent burial; it makes haste to its oblivion. Where be the Chancellors of the Exchequer of yester year ? The poet, on the contrary, about whom in his life people speak shyly, has his name shouted from the housetop as soon as he is out of earshot. So great, indeed, is the gratitude of reading beings, that a very little poet, such as the author of *The Seasons*, is familiarly known by name to the English-speaking race nearly two centuries after his birth ; and now (1897) a new edition of his works has been issued with a memoir that does not spare a detail, and with notes—' critical appendices ' they are called—that indicate a laboured study of Thomson's text, on the part of so learned an editor as Mr D. C. Tovey.

Yet Thomson, all the time, is a poet only by courtesy—you could not find in all his formal numbers one spark of the divine fire. Pope may have helped Thomson with *The Seasons*, as Mr Tovey thinks Warton right in

JAMES THOMSON

saying; but between Pope and Thomson there is a vast dividing space of technical accomplishment. Between Thomson and Wordsworth or any other of the poetical poets, there is more than space, there is an impassable gulf. Yet Mr Tovey says ' we can trace his influence, we think, in Keats; we can trace it also in Coleridge. Again, between Wordsworth and Thomson we naturally seek affinities.' Coleridge no doubt, wrote many unreal and pretentious things about Nature—*The Hymn before Sunrise* we are bold to class among them—and these we can concede—a concession it is—to anybody to bracket with *The Seasons*. The essential Coleridge is the only Coleridge that the world of letters cares to keep; and there we must say to Thomson's editor, ' Hands off.' Mr Tovey thinks it worth while to suggest also a resemblance of ' essential thought ' between Keats' *Ode to a Grecian Urn* and Thomson's

> On the marble tomb
> The well-dissembled mourner stooping stands
> For ever silent and for ever sad.

The ' essence ' of the thing does not lie in the thought at all—the old and obvious thought of the permanent expression of emotion in sculpture. It is a matter of treatment; and Mr Tovey himself does not fail to distinguish the essential difference there. As for Wordsworth (who, by the way, preferred *The Castle of Indolence*

JAMES THOMSON

to *The Seasons*, a preference we share), the association of Thomson's name with his has become a commonplace, and, like most commonplaces, it stands to be revised. Thomson is the link, we are constantly assured, between Milton and Wordsworth, as an observer and an interpreter of Nature. A little feeling of heart-freshness in the Spring we may, by searching, find in him—not so much in *The Seasons* as in *A Hymn*, where the phrase, 'wide flush the fields,' and the line :

> And every sense and every heart is joy,

just seem to be a degree less distant and conventional than was usual with the eighteenth century Muse. But here, again, the thought is of ancient days; it is the presentment that is the essence; and three of the Spring lines in the *Intimations of Immortality* are worth many times more than all the six thousand or so lines of *The Seasons*, however indefinitely multiplied. The difference is, in truth, of kind and not of degree; and these comparisons between things which have no relativity make us feel like 'young Celadon and his Amelia,' when they 'looked unutterable things'—the only phrase by which Thomson is likely to be spontaneously remembered.

We do not forget that the Thomson-Wordsworth superstition had an illustrious origin—it began in Wordsworth's own saying

JAMES THOMSON

that 'from Milton to Thomson no poet had added to English literature a new image drawn from Nature.' That is one of the generous *obiter dicta* great poets have made from time to time for the bewilderment of the unwary. Dr Johnson, it is true, took Thomson seriously, or wrote as though he did; but we remember that when he read *The Seasons* aloud to his friend Shiels, and extorted the listener's praise, he added, 'Well, sir, I have omitted every other line.' He was angry, for all that, when Lyttelton, after the poet's death, abbreviated his poem on Liberty before publishing it—such mutilations, Dr Johnson said, tended 'to destroy the confidence of society and to confound the characters of authors!' Horace Walpole uttered his contempt for Thomson straight out; but Boswell was politic, as became him; and his own personal judgement is, no doubt, shrewdly pitted against Johnson's more favourable opinion in the phrase: 'His *Seasons* are indeed full of elegant and pious sentiments; but a rank soil, nay, a dunghill, will produce beautiful flowers.'

For and against Thomson, in seasons and out, the vain tale of opinions would take too long in the telling. But Cowper it was who said that Thomson's 'lasting fame' proved him a 'true poet.' He would be a yet truer poet to-day, on that reasoning, for his 'fame' is still lasting. His *Rule, Britannia* has a place in anthologies even now; he is the bard in popular possession

JAMES THOMSON

of the name he bears (a name that Praed hated), although stories are told of confusion in circulating libraries and book shops between the poet of *The Seasons* and the poet of *The City of Dreadful Night*—that later James Thomson who, conscious of the identity of his name with his predecessor's, added stanzas to the *Castle of Indolence*. The secret of this sustained name—we distinguish name from fame—is easily guessed. The common mention of Milton and Wordsworth in Thomson's company supports his superfluous immortality. Poet or no poet, he is mixed up with poets, and is a part of poetical history.

And the added irony of this careful preservation of a name that stands for little or nothing is this—that whereas Thomson's naturalism was, in his own time, sufficiently marked to set his reputation going, we, with all the great poets of Nature between him and us, read him now, if we read him at all, for the very opposite quality—for artificiality. We tolerate him for his last-centuryness. We have a certain curiosity in observing an observation of Nature which was rewarded no more intimately than by a knowledge of the time-sequence of snowdrop, crocus, primrose, and 'violet darkly blue.' We like to hear him speak of young birds as 'the feathered youth'; of his women readers as 'the British fair'; of Sir Thomas More as having withstood 'the brutal tyrant's useful rage.' Such phrases speak to us from another

JAMES THOMSON
world than ours, from a world which had taste that was not touched with emotion; from a world, in short, which lacked the one thing needful for poetical life—inspiration.

THOMAS DE QUINCEY

THE life of Thomas De Quincey is too well known to need much recounting. It is, indeed, the one thing that most people do know of him, even when they have not read his works. Born at Greenhays in the Manchester neighbourhood; brought up by a widowed mother with little in her of motherhood; shy, small, sensitive, dwelling in corners, with a passion for shunning notice, for books and the reveries stimulated by books; without the boy's love of games and external activities; the only break in his dreamy existence was the sometime companionship of a school-boy elder brother. That episode in his childhood he has told a little long-windedly, as is the De Quincey fashion; and with curious out-of-the-way humour, as is also the De Quincey fashion. He has told of the imaginary kingdoms ruled by his brother and himself; and how the brother, assuming suzerainty over De Quincey's realm, was continually issuing proclamations which burdened the younger child's heart. Once, for example, the elder brother, having become a convert to the Monboddo doctrine in regard to Primitive Man, announced that the inhabitants of De Quincey's kingdom were still in a state of tail; and ordained that they should sit down, by edict, a certain number of hours *per diem*, to work off their ancestral appendages. Also has Thomas told of the mill-youths with whom his brother waged constant battle, impressing the little boy as an auxiliary ; and how De Quincey, being captured by the adversary, was saved by the womankind of the hostile race, who did, furthermore, kiss him all round ; and how, thereupon, his brother issued a bulletin, or order of the day, censuring him in terrible language for submitting to the kisses of the enemy.

The *Confessions* contain the story of De Quincey's youth : his precocity as a Greek scholar, which led one master to remark of him : ' There is a boy who could harangue an Athenian mob better than you or I an English one ' ; his misery at and flight from school, his subsequent drifting to London, his privations in ' stony-hearted ' Oxford Street, which he paced at night with the outcast Ann ; and there laid the seeds of the digestive disorder which afterwards drove him to opium. His experiences as an opium-eater have become, through his *Confessions,* one of the best-known chapters in English literary history. The habit, shaken off once, returned on him, never again entirely to be mastered. But he did, after severest struggle, ultimately reduce it within a limited compass, which left free his power of work ; and, unlike Coleridge, passed the closing years of his life in reasonable comfort and freedom from anxiety. The contrast was deserved. For the shy little creature displayed in his contest with the obsessing demon of his life a patient

THOMAS DE QUINCEY

tenacity and purpose to which justice has hardly been done. With half as much 'grit,' Coleridge might have left us a less piteously wasted record. In the midst of this life-and-death struggle, De Quincey worked for his journalistic bread with an industry the results of which are represented in sixteen volumes of prose, while further gleanings have, in these late years, intermittently made their appearance. It is not a record which supports the charge of sluggishness or wasted life. Never, at any period, has it been easy for a man to support his family solely by articles for reviews and magazines. Yet De Quincey did it honourably; and if he was often in straits, it is doubtful whether this should not be set to the account of his financial incompetence.

His life brought him into contact with most of the great *littérateurs* of his time. 'Christopher North' was his only bosom friend; but in his youth he was an intimate of all the 'Lake' circle; and, finally, he who had known Wordsworth, Coleridge, Southey, Lamb, Landor, Hazlitt, and at least had glimpse of Shelley, lived to be acquainted with later men like Prof. Masson and others. Not all thought well of him: his talk, like his books, could fret as well as charm; and probably the charge of a certain spitefulness was earned. But, like feminine spite, it could be, and was, co-existent with a kind heart, a gentle and even childlike nature. His children loved him; and though he was a genius, an opium-eater, and married beneath him, he defied all rules by being happy in his marriage.

As a writer, De Quincey has been viewed with the complete partiality dear to the English mind, and hateful to his own. He was nothing if not distinguishing; the Englishman hates distinctions and qualifications. He loved to

> divide
> A hair 'twixt south and south-west side;

the Englishman yearns for his hair one and indivisible. The Englishman says, 'Black's black—*furieusement* black; and white's white—*furieusement* white.' De Quincey saw many blacks, many whites, multitudinous greys. Consequently to one he is a master of prose; to another — and that other Carlyle — 'wire-drawn.' To one he ranks with the Raleighs, the Brownes, the Jeremy Taylors; to another—and that other Mr Henley—he is 'Thomas de Sawdust.' And, as usual, both have a measure of rightness. Too often is De Quincey wire-drawn, diffuse, ostentatious in many words of distinctions which might more summarily be put; tantalizing, exasperating. Also, if you will suffer him with patience, he is never obvious; a challenger of routine views, a perspicuous, if minute and wordy, logician, subtle in balanced appraisal. He was the first to practise that mode of criticism we call 'appreciation'—be it a

THOMAS DE QUINCEY

merit or not. Often his rhetorical *bravuras* (as he himself called them) are of too insistent, too clamorously artificial, a virtuosity. Also, in a valuable remainder, they are wonderful in vaporous and cloud-lifted imagination, magnificently orchestrated in structure of sentence, superb in range and quality of diction. In a more classified review, he never criticizes without casting some novel light, and often sums up the characteristics of his subject in memorably fresh and inclusive sentences. His sketch biographies, marred by characteristic discursiveness, at their best (as in the Bentley or the Shakespeare) are difficult to supersede, eating to the vitals of what they touch. His historical papers are unsystematic, skimming the subject like a sea-mew, and dipping every now and again to bring to the surface some fresh view on this or that point.

To re-tell the old has no interest for him; it is the point of controversy, the angle at which he catches a new light, that interests him. But his noble views on insulated aspects of history have sometimes been quietly adopted by succeeding writers. Thus his view of the relations between Cæsar and Pompey, and the attitude of Cicero towards both, is substantially that taken in Dean Merivale's *History of the Romans*. On his prose fantasies we have already touched. In a certain shadowy vastness of vision we say deliberately that they have more of the spirit of Milton than anything else in the language—though, of course, they have no intention of competing with Milton. They are by themselves. The best of the *Confessions*; that vision of the starry universe which he greatly improved from Richter; parts (only parts) of *The Mail-Coach* (which is strained as a whole); portions of the *Suspiria*; above all, *The Three Ladies of Sorrow*—these are marvellous examples of a thing which no other writer, unless it be Ruskin, has succeeded in persuading us to be legitimate. Its admirers will always be few; we have no doubt they will always be enthusiastic.

His humour should have a word to itself. The famous *Murder as One of the Fine Arts* is the only specimen which we need pause upon. Much of that paper is humour out of date; a little childish and obvious. But of the residue let it be said that it was the first example of the topsy-turvydom which we associate with the name of Gilbert. The passage which describes how murder leads at last to procrastination and incivility—' Many a man has dated his ruin from some murder which he thought little of at the time '—might have come out at a Savoy opera. In this, as in other things, De Quincey was an innovator, and, like other innovators, has been eclipsed by his successors. Yet, with all shortcomings, the paper is likely to leave a more durable residuum than much humour which is now of the highest fashion. It is not certain that the slang on which a vast

THOMAS DE QUINCEY

deal of new humour is pivoted will any more amuse posterity than the slang on which De Quincey too often and unluckily relied.

A little, wrinkly, high-foreheaded, dress-as-you-please man; a meandering, inhumanly intellectual man, shy as a hermit-crab, and as given to shifting his lodgings; much-enduring, inconceivable of way, sweet-hearted, fine-natured, small-spited, uncanny as a sprite begotten of libraries; something of a bore to many, by reason of talking like a book in coat and breeches—undeniably clever and wonderful talk none the less; master of a great, unequal, seductive, and irritating style; author of sixteen delightful and intolerable volumes, part of which can never die, and much of which can never live: that is De Quincey.

nectar in place of Madeira. 'We are better clothed, better fed, better civilized';—so would have run the proclamation of Zeus-Macaulay. 'We no longer quarrel like children, drink like tavern-companions, and cut antiquated witticisms at the delicate jest of a limping cup-bearer black from the forge. The thunderbolts of Whitworth are of more skilled manufacture than the thunderbolts of Hephæstus. Poseidon still rules the waves, but he rules them with a better-made trident. He has his carriage from Bond Street, his horses would not disgrace the Row; he is a well-dressed gentleman, instead of a naked barbarian. Aphrodite has not lost the primacy of beauty, because her fashions are more those of Paris, and less those of Central Africa. The good old times were the bad old times: the very kitchens of Olympus bear witness that there has been such a thing as progress, the very toilet-table of Hera testifies to the march of enlightenment.'

He was content to take the goods the gods had provided him; satisfied with himself, his position, and his day. The day returned the compliment, as it always does, by being satisfied with him. 'Thou art a blessed fellow,' it said with Prince Hal, ' to think as every man thinks; never a man's thought in the nation keeps the roadway better than thine.' He was made for great success rather than great achievement. In all he did he was popular—honourably and deservedly popular; in all he did he was content

MACAULAY

to pluck something short of the topmost laurels. He was a successful politician, yet never reached the positions attained by men far more stupid; his speeches, immeasurably superior to the parliamentary eloquence of the present day, filled the House, yet he has left no great name as an orator; he was a great talker in an age of great talkers, yet the tradition of his talk has not impressed itself on literary history as did the traditional talk of Coleridge, Lamb, De Quincey, or Sydney Smith. He wrote history brilliantly, and no serious historian accepts his history as serious history. He wrote essays which profoundly influenced literary style—yea, even to the style of the newspaper-leader; yet it is not altogether certain whether they will maintain their place among the classical classics of English prose. His genius was so like prodigious talent that it is possible to doubt whether it was not prodigious talent very like genius. He was 'cocksure of everything,' in Melbourne's famous epigram, but posterity is by no means cocksure of him.

The most permanent part of his literary baggage is undoubtedly the Essays. It is easy to say what they are not, which Mr George Meredith has declared to be the national mode of criticism; a mode of criticism not without its uses when the universality of a man's fame has made fault-finding an unpopular task, but decidedly the cheapest and lowest part of a go, but proportion it always keeps; the thing is undeniably a miniature whole. Then, if the stimulant devices are too restlessly stimulant; if they are sometimes cheap; if balance, antithesis, point, artful abruptness, are carried to an extent which gives a savour of the accomplished literary showman calling attention to his wares: yet they are undeniably effective, touched in with a deft and rapid hand; the reader is lifted along unflaggingly.

And it is literature; if he have nothing new to say, old things are newly said, with surpassing cunning in the presentment. The flow of instances with which an extraordinary memory enables him to support his points may be excessive, may be inexact at times (as the argument by parallel and analogy rarely fails to be, except in the most scrupulous hands), but it lends surprising life and picturesqueness to what with most men would have been dry discussion. For his much-vaunted lucidity we have less praise. He is lucid by taking the obvious road in everything, which is the easy road; and his arrangement is often the reverse of clear from the logical standpoint. But if he is no starter of original views, if he keeps to the surface of things, he must not be denied the merit of presenting that surface with a painter-like animation. Here is his power; it is on this that his fame must rest. As a critic he is naught; as a biographer or historian he is naught so far as exactitude of treatment,

MACAULAY

novelty, or philosophy of view is concerned. But he can revivify a period, a person, or a society, with such brilliancy and conciseness as no other Englishman has done.

In one respect alone have we any disposition to quarrel with the routine view of him. We are disposed to put in a good word for his ballads. Mr Henley has truly remarked that *The Last Buccaneer* curiously anticipates some points in the methods of Mr Kipling. And we do, indeed, think that here Macaulay knew exactly what he wanted, and did it. The sayings and doings of the personages in these ballads are obvious and garish, it is said. But the ballad is essentially a product of a time in which people were dreadfully prone to do obvious things, and in no way concerned to be subtle. Fire, directness, energy of handling—these are the main necessities of the martial ballad, rather than any poetic subtlety; and all these were at Macaulay's command. ' Remember thy swashing blow ' is the Shakespearean advice which might be given to the writer of the ballad warlike. And Macaulay always remembers his swashing blow. He has none of the deep poetic quality which informs the best work of Mr Kipling. But he does not aim at it. He keeps within a limit and a kind ; and in that kind does very excellent pieces of work ; quite honest, healthy work, which may well be allowed to stand, even though a stronger than he be come upon him.

MACAULAY

In spite of modern æsthetic reaction, Macaulay, we think, will surely stand. If not an authentic god, he is at least a demigod, the most brilliant of Philistines, elevated to the Pantheon of literature by virtue of a quite supra-Philistine power. Macaulay is the Sauric deity of English letters, the artist of the obvious —but an artist none the less.

EMERSON

THERE was a child for whom the capital good and end of life was to see wheels go round. Before a carriage in the street he would stop, plunged in ecstatic contemplation, and—like a Buddhist devotee with his mystic formula—ejaculate at intervals in adoring rapture, ' Wheel-go-wound! wheel-go-wound!' In the works of watches, in tops, in the spinning froth of his tea-cup, in everything whirlable, this unconscious vortical philosopher discerned and worshipped ' wheel-go-rounds.' With that tyrannous mandate, ' Want to see wheel-go-wound,' he insisted on paying his devotions to every such manifestation of orbital motion.

Which things are a parable. That child, it strikes us, should find his ripened ideal in Emerson's writing, which, as one critic has already remarked, revolves round itself, rather than progresses. The remark was made depreciatingly: but we prefer to regard this trait in Emerson as a characteristic, rather than a limitation. This vortical movement of his understanding impresses itself strongly on one's mind after reading a succession of his essays— or lectures, as many of them originally were. Perhaps, indeed, the necessities of a lecturer, and the mental habit induced by much lecturing, may partly be responsible for it. An audience with difficulty follows an ascending sequence of thought, especially on abstruse subjects; where the snapping of a single link, a momentary lapse of attention, may render all which follows unintelligible; and, at the best, it is uneasy to pick up again the dropped clue. But if the lecture circle round a single idea, such slips of fatigued attention are not fatal: what you have failed to grasp from one aspect, is presently offered and seized from another. The advantages of such a method for such a purpose are obvious. It is, at any rate, Emerson's method to a very large extent. Some one idea is suggested at the outset, and the rest of the essay is mainly a marvellous amplification of it. In some of these essays he is like a great eagle, sailing in noble and ample gyres, with deliberate beat of the strong wing, round the eyrie where his thought is nested.

The essay on Plato is a notable example. He starts with the declaration of Plato's universality:

> These sentences contain the culture of nations; these are the corner-stones of schools; these are the fountain-head of literatures. A discipline it is in logic, arithmetic, taste, symmetry, poetry, language, rhetoric, ontology, morals or practical wisdom. There was never such range of speculation. Out of Plato come all things that are still written or debated among men of thought. . . . Plato is philosophy, and philosophy, Plato.

His genius allies the universal with the particular, so that it becomes all-continent. So Emerson begins, and round this declaration the whole essay revolves. This Allness of Plato, this combination of universality with particularity, —he takes this idea in his two hands, and turns it about on every side, surveys it from every aspect. Having trampled it out with his feet (one would say), he tosses it on his horns, till the air is alive with the winnowing of it. He conjures with it, till the Protean modifications and transmutations and reappearances of it dazzle the attention and amaze the mind. He touches on Socrates, and Socrates forthwith becomes a reincarnation of the same idea, in his homely practicality and dæmonic wisdom— again the universal and the particular. We will not say but that we sometimes tire of these brilliant metamorphoses, these transmigrations of a single conception through innumerable forms. Sometimes we could cry 'Enough!' and wish the repose of a more vertebrate method. But one thing he has effectually secured—we shall remember with emphasis that Plato was universal, and the synthesis at once of limit and immensity.

The 'wheel-go-round' quality of his mind appears even in the detail of his style; as (in Swedenborg's image) each fragment of a crystal repeats the structure of the whole:

A man who could see two sides of a thing was born. The wonderful synthesis so familiar in nature; the upper and the under side of the medal of Jove; the union of impossibilities, which reappears in every object; its real and its ideal power,—was now also transferred entire to the consciousness of a man.

EMERSON

That is a simple and casual, but characteristic, example. Statements are not left single, but are iterated and reiterated in form on form. You have thus within the great volutions of the essay at large innumerable little revolutions,—wheels within wheels like the motions of the starry heavens; nay, the individual sentence revolves on its own axis, one might say. The mere opulence of his imagery is a temptation to this.

No prose-writer of his time had such resources of imagery essentially poetic in nature as Emerson—not even Ruskin. His prose is more fecund in imagery, and happier in imagery, than his poetry,—one of the proofs (we think) that he was not primarily a poet, undeniable though some of his poetry is. He had freer and ampler scope and use of all his powers in prose, even of those powers in their nature specifically poetic. It is a thing curious, but far from unexampled. With such figurative range, such easy and inexhaustible plasticity of expression, so nimble a perception, this iterative style was all but inevitable. That opulent mouth could not pause at a single utterance. His understanding played about a thought like lightning about a vane. It suggested numberless analogies, an endless sequence of associated ideas, countless aspects, shifting facets of expression; and it were much if he should not set down a poor three or four of them. We, hard-pushed for our one pauper phrase, may call it excess in him: to Emerson, doubtless, it was austerity.

EMERSON

Moreover, when we examine closely those larger revolutions of thought on which we first dwelt, it becomes visible—even in such an essay as that 'Plato' which we took as the very type and extreme example of his peculiar tendency—that Emerson has his own mode of progression. The gyres are widening gyres, each sweep of the unflagging wing is in an ampler circuit. Each return of the idea reveals it in a deeper and fuller aspect; with each mental cycle we look down upon the first conception in an expanded prospect. It is the progression of a circle in stricken water. So, from the first casting of the idea into the mind, its agitations broaden repercussively outward; repeated, but ever spreading in repetition. And thus the thought of this lofty and solitary mind is cyclic, not like a wheel, but like the thought of mankind at large; where ideas are always returning on themselves, yet their round is steadily 'widened with the process of the suns.'

It was an almost inevitable condition of his unique power that Emerson's mind should have a certain isolation and narrowness, a revolving round its own fixed and personal axis, corresponding with the tendency already analysed. Yet in another view it often surprises by a breadth of interest no one could have predicted in this withdrawn philosopher, this brooder over Plato and the Brahmins. He has a shrewd, clear outlook upon practical life, all the sounder for his serene detachment from it. For example, the English nation was never passed through so understanding and complete an analysis as by this casual visitor of our shores. It took nothing less than this American Platonist to note at once with such sympathy and such aloof dispassionateness all the strength and weakness of the Saxon-Norman-Celtic-Danish breed. He perceives, let us say, the intense, victorious, admirable, exasperating common sense of the Englishman, with its backing of impenetrable self-belief; neither hating nor overpowered by it. Hear the enjoying *verve* of his brilliant summary :

> The young men have a rude health which runs into peccant humors. They drink brandy like water, cannot expend their quantities of waste strength on riding, hunting, swimming, and fencing, and run into absurd frolics with the gravity of the Eumenides. They stoutly carry into every nook and corner of the earth their turbulent sense : leaving no lie uncontradicted; no pretension unexamined. They chew haschisch ; cut themselves with poisoned creases ; swing their hammock in the boughs of the Bohan Upas ; taste every poison ; buy every secret ; at Naples they put St Januarius's blood in an alembic; they saw a hole into the head of the 'winking Virgin,' to know why she winks; measure with an English footrule every cell of the Inquisition, every Turkish caaba, every Holy of Holies ; translate and send to Bentley the arcanum bribed and bullied from shuddering Brahmins ; and measure their strength by the terror they cause.

EMERSON

It could only have been written by a man who united with the profound common sense of eminent genius the profound uncommon sense of eminent genius. The one gave him sympathy; the other enabled him to possess his soul before a spectacle which compels most foreigners either to worship or execration. So also he can write on wealth with a sanity of perception at once homely and philosophic, which is worth the reading either of a man of ledgers or a man of libraries, a poet or a pedlar. Uncle Sam had 'hitched his wagon to a star'; but he kept a vigorous sap of the Uncle Sam who hitches his wagon to a prairie-hoss—and knows how to swop it.

DANTE

THE enormous Roman Empire, blown upon by the winds of barbarism, split like a rending sail into East and West. Reunited for a space by Constantine, it tore again under his successors; and thenceforth 'East was East, and West was West.' The East shrank to the limp and meagre Byzantine Empire; the West smouldered away in Gothic fire, till Rome was tacitly abandoned to the Popes. Charlemagne took up the Western succession, and dreamed himself the father of a new Cæsarean line, Overlords of Italy and the West. But the worms had not finished their imperial banquet in the sepulchre of Aix-la-Chapelle, when his own dominion fell asunder to East and West, parting into Germany and France. Germany itself was dashed to fragments by the Sclavs, till loosely recompacted by a Saxon chief. His son Otho entered Italy, like Charlemagne, to help the Pope; and obtained Charlemagne's reward — the succession to the Roman Emperors of the West.

Thus the title of the German Emperors had to do much less with Germany than with a 'Holy Roman Empire' which was really as dead as Julius Cæsar. But the Papacy had planted a thorn in its own side; for thenceforth the German Emperors were obsessed by the ambition to make their Italian title a sovereign

DANTE

fact; whence constant strife between Emperor and Pope, in which Italians took opposite sides.

This, which is so little to us, was everything to Dante. For though his father had been a Guelf, he was a fierce Ghibelline, or partisan of the Emperor. To us, in the perspective of history, this Imperial claim seems the shadowiest anachronism. We wonder that sane Emperors could waste blood and treasure on it, with their own Germany turbulent and ununited behind them: as if Alfred had set out to conquer France before he had the petty kings of England under his heel. But four centuries of recognition had made the title real to the Italians, and all tradition was behind it. Moreover, it came to embody the perpetual struggle of State against Church: and it was in this practical light that it appealed to Dante. But in Florence the victorious Guelfs themselves split into 'Blacks' and 'Whites,' or *Neri* and *Bianchi;* and the Ghibellines (including Dante) curiously joined the *Bianchi*, the popular party.

Into this distracted city Durante, or Dante, Alighieri was born. Who dreams that the supreme Italian poet and the supreme English poet bore almost an identical surname? Yet so it is. Alighiero (the name of Dante's grandfather) is a German name, and probably was derived from Aldiger, which means 'Rulespear.' A better city for the growth of poet or

DANTE

artist there could scarce be than Florence It was more like a Greek than a modern city, and of all cities most like Athens in her prime. The same 'fierce democracy' clung with the same intense local patriotism to a fatherland nested within the city walls. The same fullness of trade nurtured it to importance. The same circumscribed life turned its energies inward, and created from a municipality the image of a State in miniature. Beyond the walls its territory was less than that of Athens. Its pent-up vitality seethed in the same relentless factions, though the final result was different. And this inward-driven vitality broke forth, like a volcano, in the same surprising and abundant shower of diversified genius. Narrow limits are good for genius. Dante and Michael Angelo are proof enough.

All the narrowed intensity and greatness of Florence seem to be in Dante, and must have been fostered by its training. He grew up in a little grey city, full of pictorial sight and sound, which was creating itself into art. He saw on market days, through its narrow streets overbrowed by the projecting upper stories of the houses, the mules pass laden with oil and wine from the country, carts piled with corn and drawn by great white oxen, across their foreheads the beam which yoked them to the cart. The oxen shone in the sun which cut the large shadows. In the small squares whence were seen the numberless towers of Florence, sharp

DANTE

against the intense blue, the red and green and white-gowned citizens paused to chat of politics. He grew up a politician, for politics were a second business to every Florentine. Were you for Pope or for Emperor? Were you a White and for the people, or a Black and for the nobles? You might see Corso Donati, the able and reckless leader of the Blacks, the Castlereagh of Florence, riding through the streets on his black horse, with a troop of friends and kinsmen. The people, despite themselves, cheer the handsome and stately dare-devil whom they hate: the White leaders, our rising Dante among them, pass with bent brows, to which he returns a disdainful glance; and it is well if no broil arise. For Corso presently was Dante's bitter enemy; and our friend Guido Cavalcanti is rasher of temper than we. Dante as a youth had seen the houses of the Galigai go to the ground because one of the family had killed a Florentine—in France!

Poetry, too, early engaged him. He was hand in glove with the Guido Cavalcanti already mentioned; and Cavalcanti had succeeded Guido Guinicelli as the second of mark to write Italian poetry in the 'New Style.' What had been written before, in Sicily for instance, was imitation of Provençal song. Dante himself had studied, perhaps written, Provençal verse, which was a second tongue to literary Italians. It had perished before the wrath of the Church which it assailed: the new style kept clear of the overt attack which had proved disastrous. Perhaps through his connexion with men like Cavalcanti he became the friend of Giotto the painter and most of the artistic and intellectual ' set ' of Florence. This Dante whom Giotto painted is other than the Dante we know. Student, politician, poet, self-centred, doubtless strong of will and passions, but a softer, lighter, more sensitive, perhaps gayer Dante; a brilliant youth, to whom all things were possible. He and his friends picked sixty Florentine ladies whom they judged fairest, and referred to them by numbers in their poems. Not much melancholy here ! Yet Dante, like Milton, it is likely, ' joked wi' deeficulty,' as some verses of his hint, no better than Milton's on Hobson the carrier. At the same time he was having his baptism of war at Campaldino, and felt not a little frightened, as he ingenuously says. The flower of this time was that beautiful and mysterious poem, the *Vita Nuova*, on which no two critics agree. There *was* a Beatrice, doubtless; but already she is so overlaid with allegory that not a fact about her can be deemed certain—save that she was *not* Beatrice Portinari. That is the tantalizing truth.

After what he calls the death of Beatrice, our Dante went considerably astray. We may take that from outside witness; though even here his own language is so largely allegorical that we can say little more. Perhaps it was in reaction from this that he made his fatal entry into leading politics. At any rate, it was no mere political wrong which soured and hardened him. Fiery inner experience and dire spiritual struggle had gone over him and set the trenches on his brow, before Florence cast him without her walls. Now, too, he began the grim study which made him one of the most all-knowing minds of the age. Then he came to power in a ' White ' government, to be overset by a ' Black ' revolution, was thrown forth from his city, and began that ' wandering of his feet perpetually ' which has made him, more truly than Byron, ' the Pilgrim of Eternity.'

Thenceforth he looked to a German invasion for his restoration; and a personal motive deepened the intensity of his stern Ghibelline politics. The ' bitter bread ' of clientage sharpened the iron lines about his mouth. All his learning, all his misery, all that Florence and his Florentine blood and the world had taught him, went to the making of his great poem. It is most narrow, most universal; it is the middle ages, it is Dante; it is Florence, it is the world. It is so civic, that the damned and the saints amid their tortures and beatitudes turn excited politicians; and not merely politicians, but Italian politicians; and not merely Italian politicians, but Florentine politicians; and not merely Florentine politicians but Ghibelline politicians; and not merely Ghibelline, but Dantean politicians. An act of

DANTE

treachery to Florence is enough for damnation. The heavens look forward and exult, to the coming of the German into Italy. We must realize that for Dante the Emperor meant the salvation of Italy, the Church, and himself, to understand these things.

Yet the vastness of his understanding and conception makes his poem overwhelmingly impressive to Teutons who look on mediæval religion as a myth. That poem is so august, so shot with lights of peace and tenderness, that it is accepted as the gospel of mediæval Christendom. Withal it has a severity stern even to truculence, which is of Dante pure and simple —another spirit from that ' Hymn to the Sun ' of the gentle Francis of Assisi. And all this because he is Dante—that strange unity of which we know so much, and so little.

THE 'NIBELUNGEN LIED'

SAVE by a heaven-born poet, who should perform on the Teuton epic the miracle which Edward FitzGerald performed on Omar Khayyám, the *Nibelungen Lied* could only be represented for Englishmen in prose—such Biblical prose as that into which Mr Andrew Lang and his coadjutors rendered Homer. This thing has been done. A woman, Miss Margaret Armour, is the successful translator, and I congratulate her on her achievement. She has, say *cognoscenti* in German, taken serious and indefensible liberties of omission and commission with the difficult and sometimes diffuse text of the original. Moreover, she is apt to be too stiffly and crowdedly archaic—overdoing her admirable model, Mr Lang. Yet, get only a little used to this, and her version will grow on you as a thing of spirit and picturesqueness. It is hardly gear for woman to meddle with, this hirsute old German epic; yet this woman has made of it better work than most men could do—an English narrative which holds you and strikes sparks along your blood. I, like thousands more, cannot read the crabbed Mediæval German; but in this translation I have exulted over genius, authentic genius, brought home to me in my mother tongue.

There is no space here to analyse the tale: an epic Homeric in primitive directness of

THE 'NIBELUNGEN LIED'

narrative, but brooded over by the fierce spirit of the murky North. Homeric are the repetitions of set epithet; Homeric is the simple pathos; more than Homeric the joy of battle; Homeric the overlaying of an earlier story with the manners of a later budding civilization. But there is no Homeric imagery; the narrative is utterly direct, and, when the poet strikes an image, he iterates it with *naïf* pride in his discovery. 'A fire-red wind blew from the swords'; 'They struck hot-flowing streams from the helmets'—this image is made to do duty with child-like perseverance in many forms. With simple delight he dwells on details of attire, rich yet primitive, costlily barbaric. The men's robes are of silk, gold-inwrought, and lined with —what think you?—fish-skins! Sable and ermine and silk adorn the damsels, bracelets are over their sleeves: but no pale aristocracy this of Burgundy. 'Certes, they had been grieved if their red cheeks had not outshone their vesture.' Very quiet and plain are the poet's grieving pictures, a lesson to the modern novelist, with his luxury of woe. They make no figure as elegant extracts; but in its place every simple line tells. Kriemhild is borne from her slaughtered lover's coffin in a swoon, 'as her fair body would have perished for sorrow.' No more; and one asks no more. But it is in battle that this truly great Unknown finds himself, and sayeth 'Ha! ha!' among the trumpets.

THE 'NIBELUNGEN LIED'

Unique in all literature is the culmination of this epic of Death. Kriemhild, the loving woman turned to an Erinnys by implacable wrong, has invited all her kindred of Burgundy to the court of her second husband, Etzel the Hun. With them comes dark Hagen, the murderer of her first husband, Siegfried the hero unforgotten. On him she has vowed revenge; and her trap draws round the doomed Burgundians. The squires of Gunthur, the Burgundian King, she has lodged apart: with them abides Dankwart, the brother of Hagen. In the hall of Etzel's castle Gunther and his nobles sit in armour, feasting with the Hunnish King and Queen: the little son of Etzel and Kriemhild, Ortlieb, is summoned in, and wanders round among the stranger guests. Fatal sits Kriemhild, watching her netted prey, expecting the signal which shall turn the feast to death. It comes; in other manner, and to other issue than she dreams. Arms clang on the stairs: the door flies wide, a mailed and bloody figure clanks in terrible. It is Dankwart. The Huns have set upon King Gunther's squires and slain them to a man; he has fought his way through the hostile bands, alone. At those tidings, grim Hagen springs erect, and mocks with fierce irony:

'I marvel much what the Hunnish knights whisper in each other's ears. I ween they could well spare him that standeth at the door, and hath brought this court-news to the Burgun-

THE 'NIBELUNGEN LIED'

dians. I have long heard Kriemhild say that she could not bear her heart's dole. Now drink we to Love, and taste the King's wine. The young prince of the Huns shall be the first.'

To the overture of that dusky mockery the Burgundians rise. 'With that, Hagen slew the child Ortlieb, that the blood gushed down on his hand from his sword, and the head flew up into the Queen's lap.' Up the hall and down the hall pace the terrible strangers, slaying as they go: Etzel and Kriemhild sit motionless, gazing on the horror. At last they fly: the doors are barred, and the Burgundians pass exterminating over all within.

It is but the beginning. All the country round flocks to Etzel's summons. Troop after troop of Huns win into the dreadful hall; but from the dreadful hall no Hun comes back. 'There was silence. Over all, the blood of the dead men trickled through the crannies into the gutters below.' In the midst of a magnificently imagined *crescendo* of horror and heroism, death closes in, adamantine, on the destined Burgundian band. I am almost tempted to say that it is the grandest situation in all epic. And of the dramatic force with which it is related there can be no question.

HEALTH AND HOLINESS

*A STUDY OF THE RELATIONS BE-
TWEEN BROTHER ASS, THE BODY, &
HIS RIDER, THE SOUL*

THIS is an age when everywhere the rights of the weaker against the stronger are being examined and asserted. Is it coincidence merely, that the protest of the body against the tyranny of the spirit is also audible and even hearkened? Within the Church itself, which has ever fostered the claims of the oppressed against the oppressor, a mild and rational appeal has made itself heard. For the body is the spouse of the spirit, and the democratic element in the complex state of man. In the very courts of the spirit the claims—might we say the rights?—of the body are being tolerantly judged.

It was not so once. The body had no rights against her husband, the spirit. One might say, she had no marital rights: she was a squaw, a hewer of wood and drawer of water for her heaven-born mate. Did she rebel, she was to be starved into submission. Was she slack in obedience, she was to be punished by the infliction of further tasks. Did she groan that things were beyond her strength, she was goaded into doing them, while the tyrannous spirit bitterly exclaimed on her slovenly performance. To overdrive a donkey was bar-

HEALTH AND HOLINESS

barous : to over-drive one's own lawful body a meritorious act. A poet I know has put, after his own fashion, the case between body and spirit :*

    Said sprite o' me to body o' me :
        ' A malison on thee, trustless creature,
    That prat'st thyself mine effigy
        To them which view thy much misfeature.
    My hest thou no ways slav'st aright,
        Though slave-service be all thy nature :
    An evil thrall I have of thee,
    Thou adder coiled about delight ! '

    Said body o' me to sprite o' me :
        ' Since bricks were wroughten without straw,
    Was never task-master like thee !
        Who art more evil of thy law
    Than Egypt's sooty Mizraim—
        That beetle of an ancient dung :
    Naught recks it thee though I in limb
        Wax meagre—so thy songs be sung.'

    Thus each by other is mis-said,
        And answereth with like despite ;
    The spirit bruises body's head ;
        The body fangs the heel of sprite ;
    And either hath the other's wrong.
    And ye may see, that of this stour
    My heavy life doth fall her flower.

But the hallowed plea for slave-driving the body was not poetry, of which this writer's fleshly spouse so piteously complains ; it was

[*The verses are Francis Thompson's own.]

virtue. And the crowning feature of the happy and approved relation between body and spirit was this : that the luckless body could not escape by obedience and eschewing rebellion : she was then visited with stripes and hunger lest she *should* rebel. The body, in fact, was a proclaimed enemy ; and as an enemy it was treated. If it began to feel but a little comfortable, high time had come to set about making it uncomfortable, or—like Oliver—it would be asking for more.

Modern science and advanced physiology must needs be felt even in the science of spirituality. Men begin to suspect that much has been blamed to the body which should justly be laid on the mismanagement of its master. It is felt that the body has rights ; nay, that the neglect of those rights may cause it to take guiltless vengeance on the soul. We may sin against the body in other ways than are catalogued in Liguori ; and impoverished blood— who knows ?—may mean impoverished morals. The ancients long ago held that love was a derangement of the hepatic functions. ' *Torrit jecur, urit jecur,*' says Horace with damnable iteration ; and Horace ought to know. And now, not many years ago, a distinguished Jesuit director of souls, in his letters to his penitents, has hinted over and over again that spiritual disease may harbour in a like vicinage.

Within the limits of his own meaning this spiritual director was wisely right. He was aware

HEALTH AND HOLINESS

that men of sedentary habits and unshakably introspective temperament may endure spiritual torments for which a fortnight's walking-tour is more sovereign than the Exercises of St Ignatius. And how many such men are there now? Perhaps for this very reason the delicate connexion between mind and body is recognized as it never was before. In truth, Health, as he suggested, may be no mean part of Holiness; and not by mere superficial analogy has imagery drawn from the athlete been perpetually applied to the Saint. That I do not speak without warrant let passages from his published 'Letters'* show:

'As for the evil thoughts, I have so uniformly remarked in your case that they are dependent upon your state of health, that I say without hesitation, begin a course of Vichy and Carlsbad.' .... 'Better far to eat meat on Good Friday than to live in war with every one about us. I fear much you do not take enough food and rest. You stand in need of both, and it is not wise to starve yourself into misery. Jealousy and all similar passions become intensified when the body is weak.' .... 'Your account of your spiritual condition is not very brilliant; still you must not lose courage. . . . Much of your present suffering comes, I fear, from past recklessness in the matter of health.'

We might quote indefinitely; but it is enough to remind the reader how much and

* Letters of George Porter, S.J., Archbishop of Bombay.

HEALTH AND HOLINESS

how wisely has the modern director adapted himself to the modern Man. Nay, the very conditions of modern sanctity may be said to have changed, so changed are we. There was a time—strange as it may seem, there was a time upon the earth when man flew in the face of the east wind. He did not like the east wind—his proverbs remain to tell us so; but this was merely because it gave him catarrh, or rheumatism, or inflamed throat, and such gross outward maladies. It did not dip his soul in the gloom of earthquake and eclipse; his hair, and skin, and heart were not made desiccate together. A spiritual code which grew into being for this Man whose moral nature remained unruffled by the east wind, may surely be said to have leaked its validity before it reached *us*. He was a being of another creation. He ate, and feared not; he drank, and in all Shakespeare there is no allusion to *delirium tremens;* his schoolmaster flogged him large-heartedly, and he was almost more tickled by the joke than by the cane; he wore a rapier at his side, and stabbed or was stabbed by his brother-man in pure good fellowship and sociable high spirits. For him the whole apparatus of virtue was constructed, a robust system fitted to a robust time. Strong, forthright minds were suited by strong, forthright direction, redounding vitality by severities of repression; the hot wine of life needed allay. But to our generation uncompromising fasts and severities

HEALTH AND HOLINESS

of conduct are found to be piteously alien; not because, as rash censors say, we are too luxurious, but because we are too nervous, intricate, devitalized. We find our austerities ready-made. The east wind has replaced the discipline, dyspepsia the hair-shirt. Either may inflict a more sensitive agony than a lusty anchorite suffered from lashing himself to blood. It grows a vain thing for us to mortify the appetite,—would we had the appetite to mortify!—macerate an evanescing flesh, bring down a body all too untimely spent and fore-wearied, a body which our liberal-lived sires have transmitted to us quite effectually brought down. The pride of life is no more; to live is itself an ascetic exercise; we require spurs to being, not a snaffle to rein back the ardour of being. Man is his own mortification. Hamlet has increased and multiplied, and his seed fill the land. Would any Elsinore director have advised austerities for the Prince, or judged to the letter his self-accusings?—and to this complexion has many a one come. The very laughers ask their night-lamps

Is all laughed in vain?

Merely to front existence, for some, is a surrender of self, a choice of ineludibly rigorous abnegation.

It was not so with our fortunate (or, at least, earth-happier) ancestors. For them, doubtless, the old idea worked roughly well. They lashed

HEALTH AND HOLINESS

themselves with chains; they went about in the most frightful forms of hair-shirt, which grew stiffened with their blood; and yet were unrestingly energetic. For us it would mean valetudinarian impotence; which, without heroic macerations, is but too apt to overtake us. They turned anchorites in the English country, the English fens, among the English fogs and raw blasts; they exposed themselves defenceless to all the horror of an English summer; and they were not converted into embodied cramp and arthritis. This implies a constitution we can but dimly conjecture, to which austerity, so to speak, was a wholesome antidote. Their bodies were hot colts, which really needed training and breaking—and very strong breaking, too. They had often, questionless, to be ridden with a cruel curb. When we look at Italy of the Renascence, at England of the sixteenth century, we are amazed. There were giants-in those days. Those were the days of *virtu*—when the ideal of men was vital force, to do everything with their whole strength. And they did it. In good and in evil they redounded. *Pecca fortiter*, said Luther; and they sinned strongly. Ezzelin fascinating men with the horror of his tyranny, Aretin blazoning his lusts and infamies, Sforza ravening his way to a throne, Cæsar Borgia conquering Italy with a poisoned sword, would have sneered at the scented sins of the present day. The seething energies of our sixteenth century,—fighting, hating, stabbing,

HEALTH AND HOLINESS

plotting, throwing out poetry in splendid reckless floods and cataracts,—seem to emanate from beings of another order than ourselves. And these men who are thrown to the forefront of history imply a fierce undercurrent of general vitality. The mediæval men fight amidst the torrid lands of the East jerkined and breeched with iron which it makes us ache to look upon; our men in khaki fall out by hundreds during peace-manœuvres on an English down. They cheapened pain, those forefathers of ours; they endured and apportioned the most monstrous tortures with equal carelessness, reckless of their own suffering or that of others. Read the tortures inflicted on the rebels against Henry IV; and how 'good old Sir Thomas Erpingham' rode round one of them, taunting him in the awful crisis of his agony. Yet Sir Thomas died at Agincourt in the odour of knightly honour, and doubtless was as far from remembering that thoughtless little incivility as any one was from remembering it against him. We cannot conceive the exuberant vitality and nervous insensibility of these men. Some image of the latter quality we may get by turning to the ascetics of the East, who still swing themselves by the heels over a smoky fire, and practise other public forms of self-torture, with (apparently) small nervous exhaustion. Here and there among ourselves, of course, such conditions still exist to witness what was once usual. Such bodies, we may well

HEALTH AND HOLINESS

believe, needed the awe of hunger and stripes, and, without rigorous rebuke from the spirit, were always lying in wait for its heel.

But not only have conditions changed: there is another influence, unrecognized, yet subtly potent in affecting an altered attitude towards the externals of asceticism. The interaction between body and spirit is understood, or at least apprehended (for comprehended it cannot be), as never it was before. St Paul, indeed, that profoundly original and intuitive mind, long since saw and first proclaimed it, in its broad theological aspect. ' I do not that good which I will; but the evil which I hate, that I do. . . . The good which I will, I do not; but the evil which I will not, that I do. . . . I find then a law, that when I will to do good, evil is present with me. For I am delighted with the law of God, according to the inward man: but I see another law in my members, fighting against the law of my mind, and captivating me in the law of sin that is in my members. Unhappy man that I am, who shall deliver me from the body of this death ? '

That was the primal cry of the discovery, which has never been more pregnantly and poignantly expressed. Upon it arose a complex theological system; but outside that system the realization of this mysterious truth went no further. One might almost say that its intimacy was removed and deadened by the circumvallation of theological truisms. But the

HEALTH AND HOLINESS

progress of physiological research has brought it home to the flesh of man. Science, not for the sole time or the last, has become the witness and handmaid of theology. Scripture swore that the sins of the fathers should be visited on the children to the third and fourth generation; Science has borne testimony to that asseveration with the terrible teaching of heredity. Of the internecine grapple between body and spirit, Science, quick to question the spirit, has in her own despite witnessed much. With the fable of *Dr Jekyll and Mr Hyde* Stevenson has simply incarnated St Paul's thesis in unforgettable romance.

But upon this quickened and vital sense of the immemorial grapple has come also a sense of its unsuspected complexity. We can no longer set body against spirit and let them come to grips after the light-hearted fashion of our ancestors. We realize that their intertwinings are of infinite delicacy, endless multiplicity: no stroke upon the one but is innumerably reverberated by the other. We cannot merely ignore the body: it will not be ignored, and has unguardable avenues of retaliation. This is no rough-and-tumble fight, with no quarter for the vanquished. We behold ourselves swayed by ghostly passions; the past usurps us; the dead replay their tragedy on our fleshly stage. To the body itself we owe a certain inevitable obedience, as the father owes a measure of obeisance to the child, and the ruler is governed by the

HEALTH AND HOLINESS

ruled. The imperial spirit must order his going by his fleshly shackles; he must hear it said, 'Thou shalt stretch forth thy hands, and another shall bind thee, and lead thee whither thou wouldst not.' And wisdom will often submit to the tyrannous impotence of the inferior. For though weak compliance be fatal, arrogant rigidity is like to be only less so. The stumbling of the feeble subject shall bring down the strong ruler; a brain-fever change a straight-walking youth into a flagitious and unprincipled wastrel. But recently we had the medically-reported case of a model lad who after an illness proved a liar and a pilferer. It were unsafe, truly, to reason from extremes; but extremes bring into light forces and tendencies which in their wonted action go unsuspected.

Even in the heroic ages, of men and religion, did these things play no part unrecognized? Was the devil always the devil? Whether the devil might on occasion be the stomach (as the Archbishop hints) may be a perilous question; though some will make small scruple that the stomach may be the devil. That the demon could have been purged from Saul by medicinal draughts were a supposition too much in the manner of the Higher Criticism; though to Macbeth's interrogation: " Canst thou not minister to a mind diseased ? " the modern M.D. of Edinburgh would answer: ' Sire, certainly!' He can often purge from

HEALTH AND HOLINESS

the mind a rooted trouble; nor do we in such cases throw physic to the dogs. But as men lay their sins on the devil who indeed save him the labour of tempting them, so he may be accused for that which comes only from the mishandling of their own bodies. The author of mischief can leave much mischief to be worked for him, and needs but to wait on men's mistakes. Even in the ascetic way, shall one aver such error could not have intruded? It is dangerous treading here; yet with reverence I adventure: since the mistake of personal speculation is after all merely a mistake, and no one will impute to it authority.

Grace does not cast out nature; but the way of grace is founded on nature. Sanctity is genius in religion; the Saint lives for and in religion, as the man of genius lives for and in his peculiar attainment. Nay, it might be said that sanctity is the supreme form of genius, and the Saints the only true men of genius; with the great difference that sanctity is dependent on no special privilege—or curse—of temperament. Both are the outcome of a man's inner and individual love, and are characterized by an eminent fervour, which is the note of love in action. Bearing these things in mind, it should not surprise us to find occasional parallelisms between the psychology of the Saints and the psychology of men of genius,—parallelisms which study might perhaps extend, and which are specially observable

HEALTH AND HOLINESS

where the genius is of the poetic or artistic kind, in the broad sense of the word 'artistic.' Both Saint and Poet undergo a preparation for their work; and in both a notable feature of this preparation is a period of preliminary retirement. Even the Poets most in and of the world experience it in some form; though in their case it may be an inward process only, leaving no trace on their outward life. It is part of the mysterious law which directs all fruitful increase. The lily, about to seed, withdraws from the general gaze, and lapses into the claustral bosom of the water. Spiritual incubation obeys the same unheard command; whether it be Coleridge in his cottage at Nether Stowey, or Ignatius in his cave at Manresa. In Poet, as in Saint, this retirement is a process of pain and struggle. For it is nothing else than a gradual conformation to artistic law. He absorbs the law into himself; or rather he is himself absorbed into the law, moulded to it, until he become sensitively respondent to its faintest motion, as the spiritualized body to the soul. Thenceforth he needs no guidance from formal rule, having a more delicate rule within him. He is a law to himself, or indeed he is the law. In like manner does the Saint receive into himself and become one with divine law, whereafter he no longer needs to follow where the flocks have trodden, to keep the beaten track of rule; his will has undergone the heavenly magnetization by

HEALTH AND HOLINESS

which it points always and unalterably towards God.

In both Saint and Poet this process is followed by a rapid and bountiful development of power: in both there are throes, as it were the throes of birth. Light and darkness succeed each other like the successive waves of sun and gloom on a hillside under a brightly windy sky; but the gloom is prolonged, the light swift and intermittent. The despairing chasms of agony into which the Saints are plunged have their analogy in these paroxysms of loss and grief related by Chateaubriand, Berlioz, and others. How far these things are conditioned by the body in the case of the Poet is obscure. If the uniform nature, in them all, of these emotional crises points to a psychic origin, it is none the less difficult to avoid the suspicion, the probable suspicion, that physical reaction is an accessory cause. In the case of the Saint, shall we hold the body always guiltless? Did those passionate austerities of the Manresa cavern (for one typical instance) leave the body hale and sane? Had we to reckon solely with the natural order, the answer would not be doubtful; and, since sanctity has never asserted itself an antidote against the consequences of indiscreet actions, I know not why one should shrink from drawing the likely conclusion and adventuring the likely hypothesis. That celestial unwisdom of fast, vigil, and corporal chastening must, it is like, have exposed Ignatius to the

HEALTH AND HOLINESS

reactions of the weakened body. Fast is the diet of angels, said St Athanasius; and Milton echoed him:

> Spare Fast, that oft with gods doth diet.

But when mortals surfeit on that food, and superadd stripes and night-watchings, the forespent body is prone to strange revenges. In some measure, is it not possible such may have mingled with the experiences and temptations of Ignatius? The reality of these ghostly conflicts there is not need to doubt; I do not doubt. But with them who shall say what may have been the intermixture of subjective symptoms fumes of the devitalized flesh? When, the agony past, the battle won, the wedlock with divine law achieved, Ignatius emerged from the cave to carry his hard-won spiritual arms against the world, he saw coiled round a wayside cross a green serpent. Was this indeed an apparition, to be esteemed beside the heavenly monitions of the cavern, or rather such stuff as Macbeth's air-drawn dagger, the issue of an overwrought brain? I recall a poet,* passing through that process of seclusion and interior gestation already considered. In his case the psychological manifestations were undoubtedly associated with disorder of the body. In solitude he underwent profound sadness and suffered brief exultations of power: the wild miseries

[* The poet was Francis Thompson himself.]

HEALTH AND HOLINESS

of a Berlioz gave place to accesses of half-pained delight. On a day when the skirts of a prolonged darkness were drawing off from him, he walked the garden, inhaling the keenly languorous relief of mental and bodily convalescence; the nerves sensitized by suffering. Pausing in reverie before an arum, he suddenly was aware of a minute white-stoled child sitting on the lily. For a second he viewed her with surprised delight, but no wonder; then, returning to consciousness, he recognized the hallucination almost in the instant of her vanishing. The apparition had no connexion with his reverie; and though not perhaps so strongly visual as to deceive an alert mind, suggests the possibility of such deception. Furthermore, one notes that the green serpent of St Ignatius, unlike the divine monitions in the cave, unlike the visions in general of the saints, was apparently purposeless: it had no function of warning, counsel, temptation, or trial. Yet repetitions of the experience in the Saint's after life make it rash, despite all this, to decide what is not capable of decision, and to say that it may have been a trick of fine-worn nerves.

There is at any rate a possibility that, even in the higher ascetic life, the means used to remove the stumbling-block of the body may get up in it a fresh stumbling-block, to a certain degree; that, even here, Brother Ass may take his stubborn retaliation; and this is a possibility of which our ancestors had no dream. St

HEALTH AND HOLINESS

Ignatius himself came to think that he had done penance not wisely but too well at Manresa ; nevertheless it was only the after-effects at which he glanced, the impairing of his physical utility in later years. With modern lack of constitution the possibility is increased. No spread of knowledge can efface asceticism ; but we may, perhaps, wear our asceticism with a difference.

The devil is out of most of our bodies before our youth is long past ; in many it scarce exists. The modern body hinders perfection after the way of the weakling ; it scandalizes by its feebleness and sloth ; it exceeds by luxury and the softer forms of vice, not by hot insurgence ; it abounds in vanity, frivolity, and all the petty sins of the weakling which vitiate the spirit ; it pushes to pessimism, which is the wail of the weakling turning back from the press ; to agnosticism, which is sometimes a form of mental sloth—' It is too much trouble to have a creed.' It no longer lays forcible hands on the spirit, but clogs and hangs back from it. And in some sort there was more hope with the old body than with this new one. When the energies of the old body were once yoked to the chariot-pole of God, they went fast. But what shall be made of a body whose energies lie down in the road ? When to these things is added the crowning vice and familiar accompaniment of weakness—selfishness, it is clear indeed that we require an asceticism ; but not

HEALTH AND HOLINESS

so clear that the asceticism we require is the old asceticism. Can this inertia of the modern body be met by breaking still further the beast already over-feeble for its load ? It is not possible. In those old valiant days, when the physical frame waxed fat and kicked, the most ardent saints ended in the confession of a certain remorse for their tyrannous usage of the accursed flesh. St Ignatius, we have said, came to think he had needlessly crippled his body—after all, a necessary servant—by the unweighed severity of Manresa. Even the merciless Assisian—merciless towards himself, as tender towards all others—confessed on the deathbed of his slave-driven body : ' I have been too hard on Brother Ass.'

Yes, Brother Ass, poor Brother Ass, had been inhumanly ridden ; and but for his stubborn constitution would have gone nigh to hamper the sanctity he could not prevent. In these days he is a weak beast, and may not stand a tithe of the burdens a Francis of Assisi piled upon him with scarce more than a responsive groan. Chastening he needs : he will not sustain overmuch chastisement. Rules have been mitigated, in some of the severer Orders, to meet modern exigencies : but no mitigation can effectually alter their unsuitability to this modern Britain. They are not only obsolete : the whole incidence of them was devised for a sunny clime, a clime of olives, wine, and macaroni. Fasts fall plump and frequent in the

HEALTH AND HOLINESS

winter season, when in the North they mean unmeditated stress upon the young constitution; while the summer, when fast could be borne, goes almost free of fast. So you have Orders where scarce the rosiest novice passes his profession without an impaired, if not a shattered, constitution. Not so much the amount, but the incidence, of austerity needs revision. Not solely in the kingdoms of this world, but in the kingdom also of God, the administration may become infected by the red-tape microbe.

But this is to invade the domain of monastic asceticism, which is beyond my province. Quite enough is the weltering problem of secular religion. How shall asceticism address itself to this etiolated body of death? For all that I have said regards only the externals of asceticism. Asceticism in its essence is always and inevitably the same. The weak, dastardly, and selfish body of to-day needs an asceticism—never more. The task before religion is to persuade and constrain the body to take up its load. It demands great tenderness and great firmness, as with a child. The child is led by love, and swayed by authority. It must feel the love behind the inflexible will; the will always firm behind the love. And to-day, as never before, one must *love* the body, must be gently patient with it:

> Daintied o'er with dear devices,
> Which He loveth, for He grew.

HEALTH AND HOLINESS

The whole scheme of history displays the body as 'Creation's and Creator's crowning good.' The aim of all sanctity is the redemption of the body. The consummation of celestial felicity is reunion with the body. All is for the body; and holiness, asceticism itself, rest (next to love of God) on love of the body. As love, in modern Christianity, is increasingly come to be substituted for the motive-power of fear; may it not be that love of the body should increasingly replace hatred of the body as the motive even of asceticism? We need (as it were) to show a dismayed and trembling body, shrinking from the enormity of the world, that all, even rigour and suppression, is done in care for it. The incumbency of daily duty, the constant frets of the world and social intercourse, the intermittent friction of that ruined health which is to most of us the legacy from our hard-living ancestors, the steady mortification of our constitutional sloths and vanities—may not these things make in themselves a handsome asceticism, less heroic, but not less effectual than the showy austerities of our forefathers? A wise director, indeed, said, 'No.' Such external and unsought mortifications came to be borne as an habitual matter—grudged but accepted, like the gout or some pretty persistent ailment. The observation may be shrewdly right; but I confess I doubt it. The accumulated burthen of these things seems to me to exact a weary and daily—nay,

HEALTH AND HOLINESS

hourly fresh intention. If, however, voluntary inflictions be necessary to subdue this all-too-subdued body, they should not be far to seek without heroic macerations which very surely our stumbling Brother Ass cannot support.

The co-operation of the body must be enlisted in the struggle against the body. It is the lusts of the healthy body which are formidable; but to war with them the body (paradoxically) must be kept in health; the soldier must be fed, though not pampered. Without health, no energy; without energies, no struggle. Seldom does the *fainéant* become the Saint; the vigorous sinner often. *Pecca fortiter* (despite Luther) is no maxim of spirituality; but he that sins strongly has the stuff of sanctity, rather than the languid sinner. The energies need turning Godward; but the energies are most necessary. Prayer is the very sword of the Saints; but prayer grows tarnished save the brain be healthful, nor can the brain be long healthful in an unhealthy body. So you have that sage Archbishop already quoted advising against long morning devotions for weaker vessels: 'The brain requires some time after the night's rest, and some food, to regain its normal power,' says he. And again: 'You are suffering the consequences of the wilfulness as regards health in years long past; these consequences cannot be prevented now. The most you can do, the most you can hope for, is to lessen them as much as possible.' Or yet again: 'The most you can do is to be patient, to avoid swearing and grumbling; to say some prayers mechanically, or to look at your crucifix.' These things are not said to Saints : but alas ! sanctity has small beginnings ; there are no short cuts, no ' royal roads ' (as à Kempis says) to God. One must start even like these unheroic souls ; and on those most weary small beginnings all the after-issues rest. Not so much to restrain, but to foster the energies of our *dilettanti* and foreweary bodies, and throw them on the ghostly Enemy ; that is the task before us. For that, is this Fabian strategy all which remains to us ?

To foster the energies of the body, yes ; and to foster also the energies of the will : that is the crying need of our uncourageous day. There is no more deadly prevalent heresy than the mechanical theory which says : ' You are what you are, and you cannot be otherwise.' Linked with it is the false and sloven charity which pleads ' We are all precious scoundrels in some fashion ; so let us love one another ! '—the fraternity of criminals, the brotherly love of convicts. That only can come out of a man which was in a man ; but the excessive can be pruned, the latent be educed ; and this is the function of the will. The will is the lynch-pin of the faculties. Nor, more than the others, is it a stationary power, as modern materialism assumes it to be. The weak will can be strengthened, the strong will made stronger. The will grows by its own exercise, as the thews and

HEALTH AND HOLINESS

sinews grow: *vires acquirit eundo:* it increases like a snowball, by its own motion. I believe that the weakest man has will enough for his appointed exigencies, if he but develop it as he would develop a feeble body. To that special end, moreover, are addressed the sacramental means of the Church. But it is also terribly true that the will, like the bodily thews, can be atrophied by indolent disuse; and at the present time numbers of men and women are suffering from just this malady. ' I cannot ' waits upon ' I tried not.' The active and stimulative, not the merely surgical asceticism, which should strike at this central evil of modernity, is indeed a thing to seek. Demanding so much sparing, so much spurring; so much gentleness, so much unswervingness; never so much to be considered, and never exacting more anxious consideration; this poor fool of a present body is indeed a hard matter for the spiritual physician to handle, yet not beyond his power. The Church is ever changing to front a changing world; *et plus ça change, plus c'est la même chose.* She brings forth out of her treasuries new things and old—even as does that world to which she ministers, which moves in circles, though in widening circles. She is so divinely adjusted to it, that nothing can it truly need but she shall automatically respond: the mere craving of the world's infant lips suffices to draw from her maternal and ever-yielded bosom the milk.

So she is now proving, with that insensible

HEALTH AND HOLINESS

gradualness in change, as of Nature's self, which is her secret. When very persecution has recognized the profound change in men, and vindictiveness forgoes the infliction of tortures which justice once held paternal amenities of correction, it would be strange if so tender a mother as the Church had maintained the rigidities of a discipline evolved for a race at once ruder and hardier than ourselves. The continual commutations of fasting and other physical penances, in the present day, sufficiently attest her policy. Of that more intimately discriminating relentingness which must rest with the private director, those letters of Archbishop Porter, more than once quoted, furnish a singularly commendable and sagacious example. The degree to which the current of a life is ruffled by the wind of circumstance, coloured by its own contained infirmities and affected by the nature of its source, has only in these latter days begun to be realized in all its profound extent. An age which sees the apotheosis of the personal mode in literature, an age in which self-revelations excite not impatience, but a tenacious interest far from wholly ignoble or merely curious, an age which has shifted its preoccupation from the type to the individual, naturally apprehends more subtly these complexities of the individual life. And the result is perhaps (even in that Church always the very heart, and that priesthood always the very members, of charity) a charity a thought nearer to the charity of the

HEALTH AND HOLINESS

Eternal. For it is a charity based on a more sensitive delicacy of justice ; and He is archetypal Charity because He is archetypal Justice.

And if the maternal cares of the Church be thus increased by the frailty of the modern body, she is not without maternal recompense. We have thus far regarded that profound change, so widely evident, as though it were an unmixed evil. But in all change, well looked into, the germinal good out-vails the apparent ill. A regard thus one-sided misses the most potent ally of the Church and ultimate stickler for ascetic religion—Nature. Nature, which some say abhors asceticism, in her larger and subtler processes steadily befriends—nay, enforces it. A favourite employment of men is the venting of these shallow libels on Nature. They have called her foe to chastity—her, who ruthlessly penalizes its violation. No less, looking largely back over human history, I discern in her a pertinacious purpose to exalt the spirit by the dematerialization (if I may use the phrase) of the body. Slow and insensible, that purpose at length bursts into light, so to speak, for our present eyes. For all those signs and symptoms, upon which I have insisted even to weariness—however ill from the mere material standpoint, what do they mean but the gradual decline of the human animal, the gradually ascending supremacy of the spirit on the stubborn ruins of the bodily fortress ; that we have, by an advance evident from its very pain,

HEALTH AND HOLINESS
Moved upward, working out the beast ?
In one large word (is it over-bold ?) Nature is doing for the Church what each individual saint, passionately anticipative, had formerly to do for himself. She is macerating the body.

Look but back on the past. Realize the riotous animality of primitive man. Witness the amazing progenitive catalogue of Jewish king after Jewish king, the lengthening bede-roll of his wives : then reflect that these men still thirsted, with more than the thirst of a second Charles or a Louis Bien-Aimé, after illicit waters. Or recall, if you will, the two thousand wives of Zinghiz Khan. Remember, from a hundred evidences, that all the passions of these men were on a like turbulent scale ; and estimate the distance to the British paterfamilias, a law-abiding creature in every way, who (according to the Shah's epigram) prefers fifty years with one wife to a hundred years with fifty wives. A poor and sordid comparison enough, you may think, but it measures a distance, the better because no one imputes it to him for a merit ; and a distance you have not thought to measure.

There is another measure far nobler, deeper, less obvious. Its two *termini* are Dante and St Paul. The teaching of St Paul with regard to marriage represents the eternal mind of Christianity : out of it have unfolded all the lilied blossom of Christian wedlock and (by consequence) Christian love. Yet the spirit, the tone, of St Paul concerning marriage (with reverence

HEALTH AND HOLINESS

be it said) in our modern perspective seems but a little way from that of the heathenesse around him. Doubtless there was a world between them, to the sense of his day; but in the perspective of nineteen hundred years the gulf becomes a crevice. To what silver spirals would climb that spirit which he rooted fast in dogma St Paul could not foresee; and even yet has it put forth its apex-bud? For the Christian love-poets it was left to incarnate the spirit of waxing Christianity in regard to that love which was the effluence of the Pauline counsels. Thus it is that the passage from the first great Christian teacher to Dante is the passage to 'an ampler ether, a diviner air' in the relations of man and woman. And that transition is the measure of a vast insensible spiritualism bathing the very roots of human society.

Along uncounted lines you may follow up, with attentive meditation, this steady working of history towards the higher man, this secret treaty between Nature and her asserted antagonist, asceticism. Constantly obscured, or seemingly contradicted, in historic detail, in particular periods, it becomes arrestingly patent in a large and spatial view. The existing valetudinarianism of our overspent bodies is, I would suggest, a mere stage in the wider beneficent process. But are the iniquitous potencies of the body to be checked by the destruction of all potency?—a question to be asked. It would be a poor world if the ultimate issue were a

HEALTH AND HOLINESS

mere stagnant virtue, in which morality should luxuriate like duckweed; if (after the saying of a departed Bishop) we were to put off the old man merely in order that we might put on the old woman. But against that prospect, against a remedy which might justifiably be accounted worse than the disease, comes in another force—the force of sanctity itself. For *holiness energizes*. The commonest of common taunts is that of 'idle monks,' 'lazy saints,' and the like. But most contrary to that superficial taunt, a holy man was never yet an idle man. The process of sanctity, like the Egyptian embalmers, destroys only to preserve the lustiness of the body, and a saintly could never be an effete world.

Let us, again, look back to the basis of Nature. In our times Science has partially brought into daylight the obscure physiology of the will: we know that the will of one man may heal or quicken the body of another. We call it therapeutic hypnotism; and the long name confers scientific orthodoxy on what was a pestilent heresy. Nor only this: we know, also, the possibility of self-hypnotization; we know that a man's own will can heal or quicken a man's own self. Are not these the days of 'Christian Science,' and many another over-seeding of this truth? Solely as a natural matter, by its profound effect on the personality, by its quickening of the will, sanctity (then) would produce a quickening of the body. But that is only the basis, the physical basis of the process. The body (I might say) is

HEALTH AND HOLINESS

immersed in the soul, as a wick is dipped in oil; and its flame of active energy is increased or diminished by the strength or weakness of the fecundizing soul. But this oil, this soul, is enriched a hundredfold by the infusion of the Holy Spirit; the human will is intensified by union with the Divine Will; and for the flame of human love or active energy is substituted the intenser flame of Divine Love or Divine Energy. Rather, it is not a substitution; but the higher is added to the lower, the lesser augmented by and contained within the greater. The effective energies of the fleshly wick, the body, are correspondingly and immensely augmented. If self-hypnotization have quickening power, how life-giving must be that force when the human is reinforced by the Divine Will, the human soul gathered into the Soul of all being! In such fashion is it that sanctity the destroyer becomes sanctity the preserver; and through the passes of an ascetic death leads even the body, on which its hand has lain so heavy, into a resurrection of power.

This truth is written large over the records of saintliness. The energy of the saints has left everywhere its dents upon the world. When these men, reviled for impotence, have turned their half-disdainful hand to tasks approved by the multitude, they have borne away the palm from the world in its own prized exercises. Take, if you will, poetry. In the facile forefront of lyric sublimity stand the Hebrew prophets: not

HEALTH AND HOLINESS

only unapproached, but the exemplars to which the greatest endeavour after approach. The highest praise of Milton, Dante, supreme names of Christian secular song, is to have captured spacious echoes of these giants' solitary song. In so far, then, and from one of their aspects, these great poets are derivative; and could not so have written without their sacred models. Yet the Hebrew prophets wrote without design of adding to the world's poetry, without purpose of poetic fame, intent only on their message (unblessed word, yet ' an excellent good word till it was ill-sorted ') : they thought only of the kingdom of God, and ' all these things were added unto them'! Or consider, in another field of human endeavour, St Augustine. Throughout his brilliant youth he was simply a rhetorician of his day ; a dazzling rhetorician, a noted rhetorician, but he produced nothing of permanence, and might have passed from the ken of posterity as completely as the many noted rhetoricians who were his contemporaries. He rose to literary majesty and an authentic immortality only when he rose to sanctity. Yet those works which still defy time were the by-product of an active episcopal life, a life of affairs which would have soaked in the energies of most men. With like incidentalness Francis of Assisi sang his Hymn to the Sun, that other Francis—of Sales—wrote his delightful French prose, John of the Cross poured out those mystical poems which are among the

HEALTH AND HOLINESS

treasurable things of Spanish literature, and unforgotten prose works besides; all in the leisure hours of lives which had no leisure hours, lives which to most men would have been death.

For holiness not merely energizes, not merely quickens; one might almost say it prolongs life. By its Divine reinforcement of the will and the energies, it wrings from the body the uttermost drop of service; so that, if it can postpone dissolution, it averts age, it secures vital vigour to the last. It prolongs that life of the faculties, without which age is the foreshadow of the coming eclipse. These men, in whom is the indwelling of the Author of life, scarce know the meaning of decrepitude: they are constantly familiar with the suffering, but not the palsy, of mortality. Regard Manning, an unfaltering power, a pauseless energy, till the grave gripped him; yet a 'bag of bones.' That phrase, the reproach of emaciation, is the gibe flung at the saints; but these 'bags of bones' have a vitality which sleek worldlings might envy. St Francis of Assisi is a flame of active love to the end, despite his confessed ill-usage of 'Brother Ass,' despite emaciation, despite ceaseless labour, despite the daily hæmorrhage from his Stigmata. In all these men you witness the same striking spectacle; in all these men, nay, and in all these women. Sex and fragility matter not: these flames burn till the candle is consumed utterly. 'We are always young,' said the Egyptian priests to the Greek emissaries;

HEALTH AND HOLINESS

and the Saints might repeat the boast, did they not disdain boasting. It was on the instinctive knowledge of this, on the generous confidence they might trust the Creator with His creation, that the Saints based the stern handling of the body which some of them afterwards allowed to have been excessive. For though the oil can immensely energize and prolong the life of the wick, it is on that corporeal wick, after all, that the flame of active energy depends. The fire is conditioned by the fleshly fuel. No energy can replace the substance of energy; and while some impoverishment is a necessity of ascetic preparation, waste is a costly waste. For, even as a beast of burthen, this sore-spent body is a Golden Ass.

But with all tender and wise allowance (and in these pages I have not been slack of allowance) it remains as it was said : 'He that loseth his life for Me shall find it.' The remedy for modern lassitude of body, for modern weakness of will, is Holiness. There alone is the energizing principle from which the modern world persists in divorcing itself. If ' this body of death ' be, in ways of hitherto undreamed subtlety, a clog upon the spirit, it is no less true that the spirit can lift up the body. In the knowledge of the body's endless interplay with the spirit, of the subtle inter-relations between this father and daughter, this husband and wife, this pair whose bond is at once filial and marital, we have grown paralysingly learned in late days. But our

HEALTH AND HOLINESS

knowledge is paralysing because it is one-sided. Of the body's reactions and command upon the spirit we know far indeed from all, yet fearfully much. Of the potency, magisterial, benevolent, even tyrannous, which goes forth from the spirit upon the body we have but young knowledge. Nevertheless it is in rapid act of blossoming. Hypnotism, faith-healing, radium—all these, of such seeming multiple divergence, are really concentrating their rays upon a common centre. When that centre is at length divined, we shall have scientific witness, demonstrated certification, to the commerce between body and spirit, the regality of will over matter. To the blind tyranny of flesh upon spirit will then visibly be opposed the serene and sapient awe of spirit upon flesh. Then will lie open the truth which now we can merely point to by plausibilities and fortify by instance : that Sanctity is medicinal, Holiness a healer, from Virtue goes out virtue, in the love of God is more than solely ethical sanity. For the feebleness of a world seeking some maternal hand to which it may cling a wise asceticism is remedial.

Health, I have well-nigh said, is Holiness. What if Holiness be Health ? Two sides of one truth. In their co-ordination and embrace resides the rounded answer. It is that embrace of body and spirit, Seen and Unseen, to which mortality, sagging but pertinacious, unalterably tends.

NOTES
SHELLEY

AFTER he had read this *Shelley* Essay in *The Dublin Review* (July 1908), Mr George Wyndham wrote to the editor of that periodical, Mr Wilfrid Ward, the following letter, afterwards printed as the Introduction to the separate re-publication :

I HAVE read Francis Thompson's *Shelley* more than once to myself, and once aloud. For the moment I will say that it is the most important contribution to pure Letters written in English during the last twenty years. In saying that, I compare this Essay in criticism with Poetry, as well as with other critical Essays.

Speaking from memory, Swinburne's last effective volume, *Astrophel* with *The Nympholept* in it, came out in '87 or '88 ; Browning's *Asolando* in '87. Tennyson's *Œnone* is also, I think, at the verge of my twenty years. But, even so, these were pale autumn blossoms of more radiant springs. It may be, when posterity judges, that Thompson's own poems alone will overthrow this opinion.

In any case there is a strain in a comparison between criticism and poetry ; prose and verse. It is more natural to seek comparison with other essays devoted to the appreciation of poetry. I have a very great regard for Matthew Arnold's *Essays in Criticism*, partly reasoned, partly sentimental. But they were earlier. They did not reach such heights. They do not handle subjects, as a rule, so pertinent to Poetry. When they do, in the *Wordsworth* and *Byron* (Second Series), they are outclassed by this Essay. The *Heine* Essay deals with Religion rather than Poetry. The only recent English Essay on Poetry—and, therefore, life temporal and eternal—which challenges comparison, as I read Thompson's *Shelley*, is Myers's *Virgil*, and specially the First Part.

I think those two are the best English Essays on Poetry, of our day. Myers gains by virtue of Virgil's wider appeal

NOTES

to mortal men in all ages. Thompson gains by virtue of the fact that he is himself a poet, writing on the poet who, in English, appeals specially to poets. His subject is narrower, but his style is incomparable in the very qualities at which Myers aimed; of rhythm and profuse illustration. Both, perhaps, exceeded in these qualities. But Thompson, the poet, is the better man at varying and castigating his prose style. He is rich and melodic, where Myers is, at moments, sweet and ornate. Both are sentimental; and each speaks out of his own sorrow. Myers sorrowed after confirmation of Immortality. Thompson sorrowed out of sheer misery. When Myers writes of Virgil's ' intimations ' of Immortality, he is thinking of his own sorrow. When Thompson writes of Mangan's sheer misery, he is thinking of his own Slough of Despond. Both mean to be personally reticent. But Thompson succeeds. Unless I knew Thompson's story, I could not read between the lines of his wailing over Mangan. But anyone who reads Myers sees the blots of *his* tears. Again, Myers is conscious of Virgil as a precursor on the track of unrevealed immortality. Thompson seems—is, I believe—unconscious of any comparison between himself and Shelley, as angels ascending the iridescent ladders of sunlit imagination. He follows the ' Sun-treader ' with his eye, unaware that his feet are automatically scaling the Empyrean.

That his article is addressed to Catholics in no way deflects its aim. It begins with an *apologia* for writing on Shelley. It ends with an *apologia* for Shelley. These are but the grey goose-feathers that speed it to the universal heart of man. There it is pinned and quivers.

The older I get, the more do I affect the two extremes of literature. Let me have either pure Poetry, or else the statements of actors and sufferers. Thompson's article, though an Essay in prose criticism, is pure Poetry, and also, unconsciously, a human document of intense suffering. But I won't pity him. He scaled the heavens because he had to sing, and so dropped in a niche above the portals of the temple of Fame. And little enough would he care for that!

NOTES

Why should he ? Myers doubted. But Thompson knew that souls, not only of poets but of saints, ' beacon from the abode where the eternal are.' He is a meteor exhaled from the miasma of mire ; and all meteors, earth-born and Heaven-fallen, help the Heavens to declare the Glory of GOD. *Cæli enarrant*. But the grammar of their speech is the large utterance of such men made ' splendid with swords.'

GEORGE WYNDHAM.

Saighton Grange, Chester,
September 16, 1908.

A leading article, entitled ' Poet to Poet,' appearing in *The Observer* (August 1908), said :

NO literary event for years has been so amazing an instance of buried jewels brought to light as the posthumous article by the late Francis Thompson.* *The Dublin Review* has leaped into a second edition with a memorable masterpiece of English prose. Brilliant, joyous, poignant are these pages of interpretation, as sensitive and magical as the mind of one poet ever lent to the genius of another. Yet when we turn from the subject to think of the author, the thing is as mournful as splendid. As for Francis Thompson, whose existence was as fantastic in the true sense as De Quincey's, and far more sorrowful, it is as though fate, even after death, pursued him with paradoxes. In this part of his fame he has no share, and his finest piece of prose—and much of his prose, though unknown to the world, was notable—sets London ringing in a way that reminds us of music never played until found among the papers of a dead composer. There are doubtless many who still ask ' Who was Francis Thompson ? ' There are probably many more who, mistaking knowledge of a poet for familiarity with his name, would do well to ask ' Who was Shelley ? ' The Essay answers

* This essay, offered to *The Dublin Review* when first written in 1889, and then refused, had appeared in its pages nineteen years later, after the death of its author.

NOTES

both questions equally. As in all the highest work of that kind, its author divines the secrets of another nature by the certainty that his own was akin to it; and sympathy, inspiring true vision, reveals the seer as well as the seen. That the Essay should appear at last, instinct with the first freshness of life—that the expression of the inward glory of a man's youth should become his own rich epitaph—this is perhaps worth all the years of oblivion out of which a masterpiece has been redeemed.

Shortly after he wrote this *Shelley* paper, Francis Thompson set down some ' Stray Thoughts on Shelley,' owning at least a ' correlated greatness ' in association with the longer composition. Speaking again of the close relation between the poet and the poetry—that ' sincere effluence of life ' which Thompson's own verse ever was—he protests against a writer who had said that Shelley, though himself a wretch, could write as an angel:

Let me put it nakedly : that if Heliogabalus had possessed Shelley's brain, he might have lived the life of Heliogabalus, and yet have written the poetry of Shelley. To those who believe this, there is nothing to say. I will only remark, in passing, that I take it to be the most Tartarian lie which ever spurted on paper from the pen of a good man. For the writer *was* a good man, and had no idea that he was offering a poniard at the heart of truth.

Again, Francis Thompson says :

The difference between the true poet in his poetry and in his letters or personal intercourse, is just the difference between two states of the one man ; between the metal live from the forge and the metal chill. But, chill or glowing, the metal is equally itself. If difference there be, it is the metal in glow that is the truer to itself. For, cold, it may be overlaid with dirt, obscured with dust ; but afire, all these are scorched away.

NOTES

The last of these 'Stray Thoughts' carries Shelley with it into the far possibilities of an environment other than that which was his own:

The coupling of the names of two English poets [Keats and Shelley] who have possessed in largest measure that frail might of sensibility suggests another problem which I should like to put forward, though I cannot answer. What may be the effect of scenic and climatic surroundings on the character and development of genius such as theirs? Had he drunk from the cup of Italy before, not after, the cup of death, how would it have wrought on the passionate sensitiveness of Keats? Would his poetry have changed in kind or power? Cooped in an English city, what would have betided the dewy sensitiveness of Shelley? Could he have created *The Revolt of Islam* had he not risen warm from the lap of the poets' land? Could he have waxed inebriate with the heady choruses of *Prometheus Unbound*,

Like tipsy Joy, that reels with tossing head,

if for the Baths of Caracalla with their 'flowering ruins,' the Italian spring and 'the new life with which it drenches the spirits even to intoxication,' had been substituted the blear streets of London, the Avernian birds, the anæmic herbage of our parks, the snivel of our catarrhal May, and the worthless I O U which a sharping English spring annually presents to its confiding creditors? Climate and surroundings must needs influence vital energy; and upon the storage of this fuel, which the imaginative worker burns at a fiercer heat than other workers, depends a poet's sustained power. With waning health, the beauty of Keats's poetry distinctly waned. Nor can it be, but that beings of such susceptibility as these two should transmute their colour, like the Ceylonese lizard, with the shifting colour of their shifted station. I have fancied, at times, a degree of analogy between the wandering sheep Shelley and the Beloved Disciple. Both are usually represented with a certain feminine beauty. Both made the constant burden of their teaching, 'My

NOTES

little children, love one another.' Both have similarities in their cast of genius. The Son of Man walks amidst the golden candlesticks almost as the profane poet would have seen Him walk :
 ' His head and His hairs were white like wool, as white as snow ; and His eyes were as a flame of fire ; and His feet like unto fine brass, as if they burned in a furnace ; and His voice as the sound of many waters.'
Receive from Shelley, out of many kindred phantasies, this :

> White
> Its countenance, like the whiteness of bright snow. . . .
> Its hair is white, the brightness of white light
> Scatter'd in string.

And, finally, with somewhat the same large elemental vision they take each their stand ; leaning athwart the rampires of creation to watch the bursting of over-seeded worlds, and the mown stars falling behind Time, the scytheman, in broad swaths along the Milky Way. Now, it is shown that the inspired revelations of the inspired Evangelist are tinged with imagery by the scenery of Patmos. If, instead of looking from Patmos into the eyes of Nature, he had been girt within the walls of a Roman dungeon, might not his eagle have mewed a feather ? We should have had great Apocalyptic prophecy ; should we have had the great Apocalyptic poem ? For the poetical greatness of a Biblical book has no necessary commensuration with its religious importance; Job is greater than Isaiah. Might not even St John have sung less highly, though not less truly, from out the glooms of the Tullianum ? Perhaps so it is ; and, perhaps, one*who hymned the angel Israfel spoke wider truth than he knew :

> The ecstasies above
> With thy burning measures suit—
> Thy grief, thy joy, thy hate, thy love,
> With the fervour of thy lute—
> Well may the stars be mute !
> * E. A. Poe.

NOTES

Yes, Heaven is thine; but this
   Is a world of sweets and sours;
   Our flowers are merely—flowers,
And the shadow of thy perfect bliss
   Is the sunshine of ours.

   If I could dwell
   Where Israfel
Hath dwelt, and he where I,
He might not sing so wildly well
   A mortal melody,
While a bolder note than this might swell
   From my lyre within the sky.

NOTES

HEALTH AND HOLINESS

When first published, this Essay had the following Preface by George Tyrrell.

'IT is dangerous treading here,' says the author (p. 260), 'yet with reverence I adventure.' For whether as a defence, or as a criticism, of the ascetical tradition of Christianity, what he says will perhaps raise objections on this side or on that. Else it were not worth saying. Let it first be clearly noted that he is not dealing with the austerities of sanctity so far as they are inspired by the purely religious and mystical motives of atonement and expiation. His theme is Asceticism, which is to the 'psychic' man, to the passions and desires, what athletics are to the 'physical' man, to the limbs and muscles. It is an instrument or method for the perfecting of our whole nature by the due subjection of the lower to the service of the higher; for the harmonious subordination of the 'psychic' to the 'pneumatic' or spiritual. It is therefore 'for building-up and not for destruction.' In the Saints, the ascetical tendency is frequently complicated with the sacrificial and self-destructive tendency. This latter is a problem apart, a problem for mystics rather than for moralists. But if at times the mystic may transcend, yet he may never transgress the clear dictates of moral reason; and so he too may meditate with profit on these pages. The crippling of Brother Ass is eventually as fatal to the mystical as to the moral life, both of which require the free use of unimpaired faculties.

Midway between an exaggerated pessimistic spiritualism on the one side, and the naïve animalism (against which it is the equally naïve reaction) on the other, stands the Great Physician of soul and body alike, 'with healing on his wings,' the Giver of the meat which perisheth no less than of the meat which endureth. Christian asceticism has ever been in principle and in aim a synthesis, a tempering of contraries.

NOTES

But if, as an imperishable principle of conduct, asceticism comes more directly under the jurisdiction of divine tradition, yet its application changes with ever changing conditions of life and society, and still more with our growing understanding of the functions of soul and body, and of the precise degree and nature of their interdependence. To adhere rigidly and blindly not merely to the ascetical principles of the Past, but to their old-world applications, were to ignore the bewildering changes that have since swept over the face of society, and to deny all value to the light which has been given us from the Giver of all light through the progress of Physiology and Psychology. An asceticism whose zeal is untempered by such knowledge may easily defeat itself by inducing those very same nervous and mental disorders which proverbially dog the heels of indulgence, and whose root in both cases is to be found in the violation of the due balance of sense and spirit. On the other hand, the laws of perfect hygiene, the culture of the *corpus sanum*, not for its own sake, but as the pliant, durable instrument of the soul, are found more and more to demand such a degree of persevering self-restraint and self-resistance as constitutes an ascesis, a mortification, no less severe than that enjoined by the most rigorous masters of the spiritual life.

In these pages the thoughts of many hearts are revealed in speech that is within the faculty of few, but within the understanding of all. They are an expression of fallible opinion, not of infallible dogma. Mistakes there may be, but, as the author says, ' The mistake of personal speculation is after all merely a mistake, and no one will impute it to authority.'

G. TYRRELL.

Richmond, Yorks.